The State and the Tributary Mode of Production

The State and the Tributary Mode of Production

JOHN HALDON

VERSO
London · New York

First Published by Verso 1993

Verso
UK: 6 Meard Street, London W1V 3HR
USA: 29 West 35th Street, New York, NY 10001–2291

Verso is the imprint of New Left Books

ISBN 0 86091 496 8
ISBN 0 86091 661 8 (pbk)

British Library Cataloguing in Publication Data
A catalogue record for this book is available from the British Library

Library of Congress Cataloging-in-Publication Data
A catalogue record for this book is available from the Library of Congress

Set in Monotype Baskerville by Ewan Smith
48 Shacklewell Lane, London
Printed and bound in Great Britain by Biddles Ltd,
Guildford and King's Lynn

Contents

Foreword

This book began as an attempt to clarify for myself certain questions about the Marxist concept of feudalism and about the nature of pre-industrial state forms which had attracted my attention as a historical materialist historian of medieval societies, and which traditional historical research had largely ignored. It was encouraged by the appearance of Michael Mann's *The Sources of Social Power: A History of Power from the Beginnings to AD 1760* (Cambridge 1986), at once both a challenge to some traditional Marxist social-economic and historical analysis, and a confirmation of the validity of a realist and materialist epistemology. There is much to disagree with in Mann's first volume (of three) both in respect of empirical material and, more importantly, in respect of his own theory of socio-political causation and historical change. But in trying to come to grips with one or two aspects of the work, certain key questions presented themselves as particularly deserving of further attention: the notion of state autonomy, for example, the constitution and dynamics of 'social power', and, especially, Mann's hard-hitting but, I think, ultimately flawed critique of the historical materialist conception of the 'economic' and its fundamental role in relations of production and, therefore, relations of power. This book is, in consequence, an attempt to answer one or two of the criticisms that 'state theorists' have made about Marxist analyses. But it is not an attempt to revive dogmatism or reductionism. There is in western countries, and has been for some twenty-five years (although many critics will not see it), an ongoing attempt to construct a historical materialism which is both internally consistent and yet not exclusivist, which both recognizes and builds upon the fundamental contributions of thinkers such as Marx and Engels, yet recognizes also the contradictions, fallacies, inconsistencies and gaps in their construct. That this is difficult is clear enough, as the various competing 'Marxisms' in the world today testify. But this is not simply an academic exercise, one 'school' of thought versus another, one group of vested (intellectual, career-furthering) interests opposed to another. There are good reasons for the effort, both in respect of the politics of socialism and the struggle for human dignity and individual freedoms across the world, which goes hand in hand with efforts to understand relationships of power and exploitation, how they are generated and maintained, and the elaboration of general theories which will cast light on these elements of human society; as well as in respect of intellectual satisfaction and explanatory value. I hope some of this will become clear in what follows.

But there is another context within which the book can be understood. Given the enormous changes in the political structures of eastern Europe and the former Soviet Union in recent years, and the consequent social and economic upheavals, many western commentators – academics and intellectuals (not always the same), journalists, political pundits of all hues – have loudly pronounced the end of communism/Marxism. For Marxists outside the former 'communist' bloc, such pronouncements are both problematic and premature. In the first place, the conflation of Marxism with 'communism', as the latter is popularly understood in respect of the politics of these formerly 'communist' states, without further comment or nuance, badly misconstrues both the intellectual and the political evolution of 'western' Marxism since the 1950s (if not already before, although Stalinism constitutes chronologically the great divide). Not only has this tradition, in its various national contexts, continued to evolve because it has always been an oppositional and critical force, but the close parallels between communist parties and a particular version of Marxism began to break up already in the 1940s and 1950s, with the result that mutual criticism (not always free from internecine squabbles) and criticism from other intellectual and political traditions has produced today, in spite of fluctuations in political-intellectual fashion and the various national politics of education, what is really a major flowering of Marxist social, economic and political criticism and analysis. Never free from internal conflicts and disagreements, always in the position of a minority and usually oppositional force, western Marxism has retained (or developed) a dynamism and variety which has never been matched in the so-called communist states. Pluralism, rather than monolithic hegemony, has rescued what was (but is generally forgotten in hostile political polemic) in origins a western European tradition of social criticism, a tradition which, in spite of the dominance of New Right thinking at times, continues to prosper because it offers the possibility of a systematic critique and a viable alternative. The end of eastern bloc communist state systems, therefore, really has very little to do – except in respect of ideology and political identities in the West – with the continued existence of historical materialist or Marxist debate, analysis and comment.

On the other hand, it does directly affect notions of communism, particularly in the formerly communist countries, where the term is synonymous with Stalinist police-state repression and inhuman treatment of individuals, simplistic command-economy planning (although the historical context for the evolution of this 'system' must not be forgotten), and intellectual/ideological repression on a massive scale. In such countries, even those who consider themselves still socialists, and who were always critical of the state-imposed ideological straitjacket of the preceding years, can thus no longer use either term in any positive sense. And it is western crowing over the collapse of this system, echoing eastern bloc relief (for the most part) at its demise, which has encouraged the assumption of the end of Marxist thinking as a political and intellectual system. According to some commentators, it is simply too old-fashioned to outlive the twentieth century. The more sheep-like and naive or ignorant in the academic community, indeed, profess puzzlement at its continued existence in western educational and political and social institutions. The least familiarity with contemporary European and North American Marxist thought, or with that of political, social and historical thinkers in a number of non-western countries, such as the Indian sub-continent, for example, would quickly demonstrate that none of these assumptions or assertions is accurate. The present book is, I hope, at the very least a demonstration of the liveliness and complexity of the debates with which Marxists and non-Marxists are both engaged.

As usual, many friends and colleagues have contributed, in different ways, to the writing of this volume. In particular, I want to thank Chris Wickham, Halil Berktay and Greg McLennan, whose interest in, and discussion or criticism of, my ideas, from often different perspectives, has proved invaluable. I also owe a debt of thanks to the members of the Birmingham historical materialism group, especially Rodney Hilton, for the stimulating discussions and debates over the last ten years which have proved to be such a rich source of encouragement, and which have certainly generated more questions than they have answered.

Needless to say, none of these is in any way responsible for the shortcomings of this book. For by its very nature, there are probably more of these than I would wish. The attempt to understand a wide range of historical phenomena from a comparative perspective should need no apology, but it is inevitably fraught with dangers and with problems: ensuring an adequate and balanced account of the relevant secondary literature for various areas of specialism is itself a major task; representing that material in a broader discussion, without thereby doing an injustice to the work of other scholars or to the interpretational possibilities permitted by the material upon which those secondary analyses are based, presents further dangers. This is particularly true in this book of the Indian sub-continent and its complex history (and modern historiography), the area with which I am least familiar. While I cannot expect that specialists in all the fields addressed here will necessarily accept all the conclusions offered in this book, I hope they will accept the spirit in which the effort to understand the problems of their own specialism has been made. Needless to say, the failings of this undertaking are my responsibility alone.

Birmingham, March 1993

1

Introduction

The state is a central concept in historical materialist, that is, Marxist, thinking, since it has traditionally been regarded as the institution, or set of institutions, which above all others functions to maintain and reproduce class domination and exploitation. Marx's view of the state as the instrument of a ruling class (so described in respect of its control of the means of production) was never a simple economism, however – the state was never conceived of as a merely derivative and superstructural reflection of dominant social and economic classes, although this view certainly represented the opinion of many Marxists in the period of domination of Stalinist political theory, and is still invoked to caricature Marxist discussion by many non-Marxist writers. Marx criticized Hegel's conception of the state (that it represented the general interest of society, embracing all parties, yet able to overcome the schism between 'civil society' and the state on the one hand, between private persons and citizen on the other) for its inversion of what he argued were the actual relationships which pertained. He proposed instead that the state defends not the general interest, but rather the interests of property. But he also argued that this was no simple functionalism, and that the relations of production which determined the nature of property and its possession were crucial.

Marx and Engels argued two key propositions: (1) that the state was the state of the most powerful (that is, economically dominant) class 'which, through the medium of the state, becomes also the politically dominant class, and thus acquires new means of holding down and exploiting the oppressed class',[1] and (2) that the state, once established as an institutional complex, can be taken to have 'interests' and purposes independent of those of any socio-economic class.[2] While such formulations do not preclude, from a theoretical standpoint, a deeper structural analysis of state power and power-relationships within given state formations, neither do they answer the specific question of how the state, as an institution separate from the dominant class, actually functions both as an independent set of structures with its own 'interests', and also as a defender of the interests of the dominant class. Nevertheless, the state is often still implicitly taken as determined by, and therefore subordinate to, forces *external* to itself; in other words, as a mere agent or tool of other social and economic forces. Such a position both implies that the state is somehow separate from the rest of society, yet also ignores the possibility, and the historical fact, of states on occasion acting for themselves, a possibility clearly enunciated by Marx.

It is this position, however, or variants thereof, which has been criticized, justifiably, by recent 'state theorists' (see chapters 2 and 3) for the reduction of the state to its supposed underlying economic and class functions. They have also gone on to assume no fundamental difference between this position, and one which argues for the 'relative autonomy' of states and state elites, an approach which dominates Marx's own ideas, as well as contemporary Marxist thinking on the state. I will argue in this book that it is perfectly possible to construct a historical materialist approach to the state which can explain both facets of state functions, one to which this difference is fundamental.

Some criticisms made of Marxist or historical materialist approaches to the state can be questioned simply on the grounds that they tend to highlight the inadequacies (in their view) of the work of particular Marxists, and then to generalize from such failings to the level of a general theoretical failure. For the most part, historical materialist theory is usually accused of being inevitably either class reductionist and/or economistic and hence unable adequately to theorize the complexities of social power relations and constitutive social praxis. Let me make it clear at this point that such criticisms are not entirely invalid: but they address for the most part individual historians or sociologists, not the general framework and heuristic potential of a historical materialist approach. In contrast, I see no problem, within the terms of theoretical premises sketched out by Marx, and employing some of the heuristic models (such as mode of production), in approaching any of these questions.

A second point needs also to be made, and that is, quite simply, that in the process of generalizing such critical arguments from the level of individual analytical/interpretative practice, whether justified or not, the historically and culturally-embedded nature of much historical and sociological work on the state and on the relationships between state structures and 'society' at large (especially for those working within a Marxist paradigm) is regularly forgotten. Yet all work in the social sciences is very heavily so embedded or contextualized, and reflects, therefore, the issues of the day felt to be most important at the time of their writing. The fact that certain historians did not ask certain questions, or pose certain problems in a particular light, and the fact that a particular theory or set of theories about the nature of human society prioritized certain issues relevant to a particular generation, does not necessarily mean that the theory as a whole cannot cope with a different set of questions (one which is today felt to be more important or interesting), nor that it is therefore to be abandoned. While this is true of all general theories of society and economy, it is particularly the case with a historical materialist perspective since, I would argue, the latter embraces both a 'grand theory' as well as the possibility of 'nesting' a multiplicity of meso- and micro-structural analytical approaches within the overall paradigm. The case is argued convincingly by McLennan, who emphasizes also the holism as well as the potential to generate explanatory models at the micro-level of social action, and in which the non-exclusiveness of a historical materialist mode of analysis plays an important role.[3]

The crucial factor is the nature of the social relations of production within which states evolve. The fact that states often appear to act autonomously, in terms of specific ideological and organizational imperatives, which do not directly reflect any specific class interests, does not mean that states do not also function to provide a framework (enshrined in law, for example) which at least provides a stable context for the reproduction of prevailing relations of production – class relations. In the following I shall argue, against the strong 'state theorist' position, that, while states can and do evolve an autonomy of political action dependent upon their own structural and organizational demands, and the ideological perceptions of their personnel, such demands (and the structural possibilities open to them) are always constrained and determined by the dominant relations of production within a social formation. While the state institutions are, therefore, not a simple reflection of economic relationships, the latter constrain the possibilities state forms can take, and set certain limits to their autonomy. Much of this, of course, depends upon how we understand the notion of 'the economic', and what 'relations of production' can be taken to involve in respect of the relationship of people to productive means and to surpluses, and of the social practices through which those relationships were expressed and reproduced. More importantly, it depends upon our grasp of the different forms of structural constraint typical of each mode of production and the ways in which, and institutional forms through which, such constraints actually function in real social formations. I will look at these problems in chapters 2 and 4, although it will remain a recurring theme throughout the book. But it is important to stress at the outset that there is nothing fundamentally new in this position – part of my purpose in this book is to re-affirm what I believe to be a valid approach to the state, politics and the question of the relationship between the state and 'the economic', because those who have objected to this approach have done so largely – or so it would appear – on the basis of a sometimes deliberately one-sided caricature of historical materialist analyses.

The 'pre-capitalist' state, with which I am concerned, is a large subject, even for a book. On the other hand, and perhaps obviously, it is important and, in many respects, has been a rather neglected area, both in respect of Marxist historiography, as well as in terms of state theory in general, until relatively recently. And in view of the vast range of historically-attested state formations of a pre-modern or pre-industrial (pre-capitalist) type, I have had of necessity to select a very limited number of examples, in order to illustrate the points I wish to make, and to address certain key questions common to the analysis of all such states. In practice, however, and in spite of the chronological range of the state formations dealt with (up to the eighteenth century, in effect), I shall be dealing with what are generally regarded as pre-industrial and pre-capitalist states, and will leave aside, for the most part, consideration of 'ancient' empires and political systems. But this will, in the end, make little difference to the main questions I want to ask, and to attempt to answer, in this book. What universals can one detect (or should one look for) in the structure and evolution of states so widely separated in both time and place as the barbarian successor kingdoms in the early medieval West, on the one hand, and the Ottoman empire, on the other, or between the later Roman state and that of China in the Sung period? Do such common denominators, if we can locate them, imply the existence of specific structural constraints and patterns fundamental to all states? Or is this really a reflection of the fundamental economic relationships in which they are engendered and embedded? What role do social-economic classes play in state formation and how far do states function to represent the interests of a ruling class? Are certain types of state formation really unique – such as is sometimes implied, for example, about western medieval states and societies and the transition to capitalism – or is this merely evidence of a failure to distinguish the forms of expression in a specific culture from the structures they represent? All these point to important areas of possible enquiry. I will address only some of them in this book.

In some ways the title of this book begs a number of important definitional questions. There are several reasons why a general discussion of pre-modern states is overdue. In the first place, the very notion of the state itself lacks definition: we are accustomed to thinking in terms of states (modern state formations) as more or less national units representing specific cultural and ideological, and sometimes social and economic, characteristics or tendencies. In fact, of course, this a peculiarly slanted way of looking at things. Recent Balkan history alone shows that such assumptions may be both ill-founded and certainly misleading. And while it is obvious that this is not usually the case with pre-modern states, it is worth emphasizing the point, since such unjustified assumptions are often implicit in the analysis of medieval societies.

Furthermore, it is worth stating at the outset that even where political boundaries were fairly clearly defined, they did not always mark the limits of either a social formation (a set of social relations, and hence of material practices, and the cultural forms through which they were expressed) or a 'symbolic universe' (sets of cultural assumptions, perceptions, beliefs and so on, and the accompanying social reproductive practices which they both explain and are in turn reproduced by). There are always overlapping fields of influence at a variety of levels between neighbouring societies – whether in respect of the basic structure of the family and household, patterns of kinship and lineage attribution, economic relationships, religious and political ideologies, and even legal systems. States may overlap or intersect in all of these features; and even though legal structures usually depend upon a specific set of institutions embedded in a state, and serving both as representative of the political structure and the power-relationships of that state and its territories, and as legitimating ideology, there are historical examples where the same set of legal and juridical principles are adopted by several states sharing a common inheritance. The obvious example for a European commentator is the Roman legal inheritance of both eastern and western Christian states (with certain exceptions) in the early medieval period. But even where a formally recognized or assumed difference exists, common practices expressed through different forms may actually cut across them. Thus – to name a further example – the political-religious boundaries between the Islamic and Christian worlds of the Near and Middle East from the seventh century AD existed, and had material effects, at a public and formal diplomatic/political level, directly influencing military organizations and activity, for example. Yet, common to both sides of the divide were patterns of urban-rural structures, local exchange relationships, village and, to a degree, household organization, many of which survived for centuries, many of which were modified quite rapidly by the dynamic effects of the political and religious changes in the area.[4]

In the second place, once we have set about defining a state, we encounter all sorts of problems concerning the nature of power-relations within state apparatuses, and between them and the society at large over which they stand – but in which they are rooted. How independent of society could state functionaries, individually or as a group, actually be? How limited in their fields of action were state apparatuses by the social and economic relationships dominant in a given society? How dependent was the state, as a set of institutions, upon a dominant social and economic elite or class? What role in this set of relationships did locally-legitimate non-central political authorities, such as tribal groups, play, particularly in the case of nomadic or semi-nomadic populations (whose mobility gave them a greater freedom of movement in respect of the state's officials and apparatus)? And how significant in the process of state formation and consolidation are class relations as such, given the variety of forms, and therefore of economic relationships, which may be present?

Third, since we are actually dealing with the state in pre-industrial formations, it should be said that, in respect of their qualitative differences, ancient and medieval states alike share a wide range of features which makes any distinction based on purely material structural divergences or developments redundant. Only when we begin to consider the fundamental *modal* differences which may exist between them (in respect of their relationship to the mode of appropriation and distribution of surplus), the role of ideology (for example, with regard to modern perceptions and the construction of a 'Middle Ages', or in terms of the role of fundamental determining features such as the world religions, Christianity and Islam) and qualitative shifts in the technologies of transport and communications, can we begin to discern real variation. And although it is the specific societies and cultures of the period stretching from the later Roman empire to the sixteenth century which interest me in this book, the conclusions to be drawn apply much more widely. The fundamental economic relationships of exploitation, surplus appropriation and distribution – those that determine how we establish the dominance of a particular mode of production – and the connection between these and their forms of expression in structures of political power and social praxis will be the focal point.

There is one final reason, closely connected with these points. For there is a danger in comparative historical work of this sort of forgetting both the synchronic element in social evolution, and the cumulative and qualitative nature of such evolution – or process – over the longer term. I have selected the examples found in this book, therefore, on the basis of certain elements which are comparable, in respect of technological achievement, ideological development (in particular the dynamic religious systems of Islam, Hinduism and Christianity), and political and economic organizations and structure. This does not mean that the state formations in question did not also exist in sometimes very different contexts – the Byzantine and Frankish polities were subject to qualitatively very different sets of influence and pressure from those of the late medieval and early modern Ottoman and Mughal states, for example, which evolved in a period of ever-widening commercial, economic and political horizons and contacts. And to omit these key constitutive elements of a state formation, as some comparative analyses have done, is to invalidate the whole point of the comparison. On the other hand, the modal similarities in respect of access to and control over the means of production and distribution of surplus, and in consequence the sorts of political structures that were possible, make the comparative analysis of such very different state systems particularly revealing.

The factors we require in order to define a particular historical political structure or coincidence of structures as a state are many and varied: a class or group of persons able to mediate the relationship between the ruler/ruling group and the producing population, both economically (extracting resources and redistributing them according to the prescription of the centre) as well as ideologically; a degree of institutional reproduction of key administrative functions within the state, potentially (at least) independent of rulers' whims and changes in personnel (although not necessarily entirely free from them); and a political-ideological system (which in the optimum case will be hegemonic, but will at least provide the ruling elements of society with a legitimation for their rule). All the states I will look at which were successful either possessed these qualities or developed them, and it seems to me that states do not survive for long, or indeed properly come into being, without them. But there are many other constitutive aspects, and I will examine these in chapter 4 in particular.

These features of medieval states are evident and typical also of ancient states. Thus to a degree I shall be examining the fundamental structural aspects of pre-industrial (and pre-capitalist) social formations and the states they supported. While substantial quantitative differences in the potential of states to reproduce themselves and to absorb neighbours or to influence more distant societies appear already with the Roman empire and its military organization, qualitative differences begin to develop only in the later medieval period, as European, and South and East Asian states and culture evolve the economic relationships and technological innovations which made possible the great expansion of international sea-borne and overland commercial and industrial interests. And by this time – as the 'nation state' and absolutist monarchies develop in tandem in different parts of Europe and in the Ottoman empire – we have already reached the stage of early capitalist relations of production which were to transform radically the potential of states to secure their existence.

In this book I will describe some aspects of the evolution of several tributary, that is to say 'feudal', state formations (terms which I will discuss at length below) and suggest that, under certain conditions, state apparatuses working within specific ideological contexts actively react upon and determine the evolutionary track of the societies they dominate. This brings us to a second element (to which social scientists have pointed): the nature of the distribution of the different cultural discourses which bind the elements of a social formation and its state structures together – or not. Some refer to such patterns as structures of social power, others as discourses of hegemony, and so on. What concerns us is: what do they represent in terms of social praxis? How do they function? And what are their effects?

Two points need to be made. The first is that power relations function both explicitly and implicitly. Explicitly, they are expressed as commands issued and obeyed, as institutionalized routes through which resources can be put to use, as particular social hierarchies and status differences. Implicitly, they function as features of belief and routine social reproductive practice. They are represented in the day-to-day assumptions about the nature and purpose of one's existence. Relations of power are inscribed in ideology. In other words, power (which we can define in its social setting as the control over a variety of types of resource – money, people, knowledge, depending upon the context – motivated by a specific aim or set of aims) can be effective both through direct command-relations and through indirect or diffuse channels embodied in, for example, a particular politico-religious culture.[5]

The case of the Byzantine state, discussed (along with others) in chapters 3 and 4, provides good examples of both: on the one hand, the fundamental values of the state as expressed through its political ideology were refined out of a universally accepted soteriological world view – orthodox Christianity – in which political and religious pluralism were virtually non-existent (although this does not exclude a considerable degree of heterogeneity at the 'folk' level of practice and belief). On the other hand, the particular means by which specific emperors could implement their policies depended on direct command or instruction, and the effectiveness and loyalty of the state bureaucracy and the civil and military establishments. The less power the state or the emperor had over individuals (in respect of determining, or appearing to be able to determine, the career and life-chances of individuals within imperial service, for example), the less they had over the state apparatus and the empire's territory and resources as a whole. Thus, as the magnate clans of the ninth and tenth centuries evolved into an increasingly self-aware aristocratic elite with power independent of the state, so the state's power was contingently reduced. As we shall see, it is the fluctuations in power relations between the state and its organizational demands and imperatives, on the one hand, and the economically more-or-less independent dominant elite, on the other, that provides the key to the political/cultural conflicts in the history of Byzantine society from the seventh century on. In this respect, the constraining effects of a particular mode of production must be taken into account.

The states I shall deal with in what follows are all tributary, or 'feudal' states, in the historical materialist sense of the term, that is to say, they were all founded upon the same mode of surplus appropriation in combination with the same basic mode of bringing the producing population and the means of production in land together. I will discuss and define in greater detail the tributary/feudal mode of production in chapter 3; and in chapter 4 I shall look at the ways in which tributary or 'feudal' relations of production function in a particular way, differently from those of capitalist societies, to set certain limitations on the autonomy of state elites or rulers. But in this book I shall use the term 'tributary' mode as a synonym for the 'feudal' mode of traditional or classical Marxist discussion, partly to avoid semantic squabbles with non-Marxists over the value of the term 'feudal' itself. Partly, however, I shall use it both because I believe it better represents the intention of Marx's original analysis of 'feudal' production relations when contrasted with those of other modes of production, and because it moves away from the nineteenth-century vocabulary which Marx was necessarily constrained to employ in setting out his ideas about different historical epochs and economic systems and their distinguishing features.

At the heart of discussions about state formations are questions concerning the role of social classes, and the relevance of the economic relationships in society to the evolution and reproduction of states themselves.

These questions have been raised in several important contributions recently which deal with the comparative study of historical societies, in particular the nature of power and power-relations and the question of the autonomy of states in respect of the societies over which they stand.[6] The main direction of such debates has been to assert that contrary to certain traditional (and, it is claimed, inadequate) approaches to state formations, whether modern or premodern, state apparatuses can and do function independently of society, because they are determined in their actions by various forms of power-relationship – political and military power, for example, or ideological power, and by the 'organizational imperatives', to quote one commentator, of the state apparatuses themselves. They are held to possess an independent dynamic power of their own, and the discussion around them has often related directly to problems of a historical social-psychological nature: how are identities of class, gender and group constructed, under what conditions do they function in a particular direction, and why, and how are they determined by the system of roles and power-relations within which they operate? In other words, these debates have raised in a very acute form questions about the degree to which human beings are constituted by the social relations they inhabit, on the one hand, and how much they are constitutive of those relations, on the other.[7]

In particular, they have challenged traditional approaches in several ways and historical materialist, or Marxist, analyses of the state have borne the brunt of these criticisms. The latter are accused of both economic reductionism and determinism: that is, of reducing all the important features in a society or state formation to the basic economic relationships in that society; and of analysing the historical data strictly on the assumption that the economic 'base' of a social formation is the determining factor in fixing the character and possibilities for the 'superstructure', which nominally includes ideologies, social institutions and so on.[8] As already mentioned above, this often misrepresents the validity of the general paradigm offered by a historical materialist approach; but while it is not always a particularly accurate characterization of much modern Marxist history-writing, it does nevertheless reflect some major problems in Marxist approaches to the relationship between states and their societies, and between individuals and the social institutions they maintain and reproduce in their everyday lives.

I will come back to some of these problems, and suggest some answers to the questions they pose, in the course of this book. In the process, I shall look at some of the main features of certain medieval state formations, as we know them from the historical record, to see if we can draw any generalizations about the constraints upon their institutional forms, the composition and personnel of those institutions, and their relationship with the societies over which they were set, as well as with neighbouring states or cultures.

There is one more point that is perhaps worth making in this connection. Traditional, non-Marxist historiography (which does not imply all non-Marxist historiography) inevitably remains suspicious of undertakings such as this. Attempts to draw conclusions about a historical culture which are thought not to be based on, and more significantly *in* the empirical data for a given society are often regarded as flawed, and rejected because they do not appear to concern themselves with the subjective perceptions of the culture in question (that is, they tend not to give priority to the political and ideological perceptions of that culture). They are seen as not being concerned with what medieval writers, for example, wrote in respect of their own subjective descriptions of political community, and as failing to demonstrate that there is any connection or match between the theoretical categories of state formation, which derive from a twentieth-century analytical vocabulary, and the historical political configurations under examination. Such criticisms are generally summed up in the accusation that one is seeking to impose modern political or socio-economic categories ('class' is often cited, 'class struggle' even more frequently) on the past.

But while presenting itself as the only proper approach for a genuine historical analysis – being constrained by the empirical data available – this point of view misses the intention of such comparative analyses. Of course, theory without empirical data is meaningless – a point I stress (and which Marx also stressed very heavily) in chapter 2. The crucial point, however, is that we are simply not interested merely to analyse medieval state structures from the point of view of the subjective perceptions, or ideologies, of the societies or cultures in question. This would produce simply a medieval description in modern language which, when applied to other societies, would in turn produce an unending list of 'unique' types, which could be compared only on the basis of an *ad hoc* and quite superficial descriptive basis. It would be, to paraphrase Marx, merely a collection of juxtaposed phenomenal forms (or perceptions of forms) which would have little analytic value, and which represents a naive historicism.[9]

I do not suggest that description and analysis of primary sources is an unimportant enterprise: quite the reverse, since they are fundamental to research, and without them neither the building up of a picture of how medieval societies (or particular elements in them) viewed themselves, nor of how they explained their world, as it was perceived and defined, in the context of their own culture, for themselves, is possible. They provide insights into motivations and modes of causal explanation, too. And by looking at the relationship between the ideas and values expressed both explicitly and implicitly in medieval sources, and the social practices in the context of which such values are generated, we can also obtain valuable insights into the attitudes which may have informed both group and individual action, which can then in turn be related to wider structures of causation.

But descriptive comparison by itself remains just that, a more-or-less entirely descriptive exercise. Byzantine, Ottoman and Frankish views of, and explanations for, their society as they perceived or understood it hardly approximate to a structural analysis of the actually pertaining relationships which causally account for the forms and developmental trajectory of their different social and political institutions. Description alone explains neither how social formations work, nor how change occurs – although the effects of these processes can be observed. In short, it cannot reveal by itself the structural and causal relationships referred to already. And history is, if anything, about explaining change, not merely describing the fact that it happens.

A further point needs to be made. The 'modern political categories' so roundly condemned by those who espouse this purely descriptive comparative approach are employed not as descriptions of really-existing societies, nor are they meant to be fitted onto medieval societies in order to categorize them within the framework of modern, actually-existing political structures. It is precisely such *ad hoc* methods, which so often do produce unreflected, badly thought through and anachronistic models or versions of the past, that rigorous theorizing is intended to avoid. The categories employed are heuristic devices – generalized abstractions from observed phenomena – intended to provide a guide to the elucidation of relationships, and therefore causal connections, which have generated specific trajectories of historical change. It follows that they cannot be 'compared' with anything, still less with medieval ideas about the world as it may then have been perceived.

The present book does not aspire to present a particularly or uniquely Marxist or historical materialist 'theory of the state'. Still less is it intended to rival any of the recent comparative historical-sociological treatises such as those discussed in chapter 2. On the contrary, I want merely to suggest some doubts about the causal eclecticism of some recent theorists of social evolution in this respect, and to make some suggestions with regard to the role of 'the economic' and how it is to be understood by both Marxist and non-Marxist historians and social scientists, in respect of pre-capitalist states and economic relations. I hope that at the least it will be read as a worthwhile contribution to the ongoing debate over the establishment of a more broadly founded, yet still materialist and realist approach to understanding the human past.

2

State Theory and the Tributary State: Some Comparative Perspectives

1. The Debate

Interest in the state and its formation, from the earliest times to the modern era, has been stimulated in the English-speaking world particularly by a number of recent comparative historical and sociological works of synthesis which have taken up the question of the underlying causal relationships leading to the wide range of political structures and forms of the distribution of power within human society. Two of these in particular present major challenges to both traditional Weberian as well as Marxist approaches to these problems, although themselves deriving much of their impetus from within these traditions. The books in question are Michael Mann's *The Sources of Social Power*, and W.G.Runciman's *A Treatise on Social Theory* (in particular volume two, which offers a range of specific analyses).[1] They present a challenge because both are clearly based on what are essentially materialist epistemological premises (although they cannot be considered in any way to be *historical* materialist), and because both usefully propose new ways of conceiving of and then analysing social relations (whether in the economic, political-ideological or social-structural sense). Specifically, both form part of a developing tradition of analysis in which the key motif is the relationship between human agency and social structure. They challenge the tendency to ignore individual subjectivities in their structure-constituting role, which they argue is inherent to Marxist discussion and theories of agency and causation; and they attempt to rehabilitate in various guises what might be seen as a methodological individualism, a perspective which immediately poses problems and a challenge to a historical materialist history or sociology. Most importantly of all, they represent one aspect of a growing trend towards macro-historical sociology, the analysis of long-term historical and societal evolution through the interrogation of micro-historical analyses.

Crucial to Mann's work, for example, is the notion of social power, which – to summarize a complex and well-argued case rather crudely – can be seen as fundamental to the actual configuration of different networks of social relations and to the state formations which develop out of them. Equally important is his conceptualization of the state as constituting itself as an autonomous actor in the evolution of social-economic and power relations.[2] Expressed somewhat differently, and with a different emphasis upon what is held to be analytically prior, neither of these assumptions would be, in itself, inimical to a Marxist analysis. But they are presented as a substantial critique of what they take to be the assumptions of historical materialism.

Runciman's book, in contrast, is both more broadly comparativistic and less concerned with a long-term historical evolution. Where Mann is concerned to explain, in effect, the reasons and processes behind the dominance of the West on the world-historical scene, Runciman is interested in the micro-structural elements which make change in social relations possible and which lead to the development or blocking of certain modes of the distribution of power. In particular, he is concerned to reconcile a hermeneutic approach to social theory, on the one hand, with a theory of social structure, on the other (or, to put it in his own words, to build a bridge between 'phenomenological hermeneutics' and 'positivist empiricism').[3] Both books, however, and several others which have appeared in the last few years,[4] have provided a great deal of food for thought for those concerned with trying to understand the reasons why states develop and evolve and the ways in which they do, and how, why and if they do or do not transform the social relations within which they were embedded and upon which they were based. Both are founded on particular sets of assumptions about the nature of the relationship between human agency and social structure, and about the ways in which social power is expressed under specific historical conditions. Both explicitly reject a Marxist approach to social evolution as too economistic and class reductionist.

In view of this continuing and important debate, therefore, and of the fact that there is a long and important Marxist tradition of interest in state formation which has produced several alternative ways of looking at states and their relationships with social formations,[5] I want in this chapter to introduce one particular problem:

what is the relationship between state structures, their personnel (state elites) and the relations of production in pre-capitalist social formations? In other words, how 'autonomous' can such states become, and under what conditions? But since this question immediately raises the problem of the role of the economic in determining or not the ways in which this relationship functions and evolves, I will look also at this problem, and again in the specific context of pre-capitalist state formations.

For Marxist historians this has become particularly important. A great deal of criticism, both explicit and implicit, has been directed at Marxist writings on the state, and the related question of class and economic relations. A symptomatic example is the book edited by J.A. Hall, *States in History*, which appeared in 1986,[6] and in which the majority of the contributors evince either a clear suspicion of or, in some cases, hostility to a historical materialist approach. In spite of this, several of the contributions present stimulating and useful criticisms of what they present or perceive as Marxist analyses. Given the failings of some traditional Marxist writing, both empirical and theoretical, in respect of the state and its relation to the economy, this attitude is hardly surprising, the more so since, in response to non-Marxist challenges with regard to the apparent autonomy of historically-researched political and ideological practices from their supposed economic 'base', Marxists have not always mounted a particularly clear or effective counter-offensive. Where a coherent argument has been deployed, this has been based, reasonably enough as we shall see, around the notion of 'relative autonomy', an approach first enunciated by Engels. In discussions among structuralist Marxists, for example, a distinction has been drawn between dominance and determination. Thus Poulantzas, following Althusser (who derived much of the vocabulary of his alternative, structuralist schema from much earlier Marxist thinkers such as Plekhanov), argued that, while the economy (the relations of production and reproduction of a social formation) is always determinant 'in the last instance', it does not necessarily play the dominant role: this may be expressed by certain 'superstructural' levels – ideology, for example – although the possibilities for this dominance are inscribed within the structure of the economic sphere. Hence elements which, according to the classical model, belong to the superstructure can possess a 'relative autonomy'.

This structuralist Marxist approach still remains open to criticism from those who assert that it allows no space for the autonomous effects of the political – as well as from those critics who find the Marxist theory of class and class struggle unacceptable. And quite apart from this, of course, there have been strong criticisms of this particular version or formulation of the notion of determination 'in the last instance' from within Marxism, most especially in respect of the radical 'de-subjectification' of human social practice and history inscribed in the Althusserian model, itself a reflection of the powerful structuralist and anti-humanist element which informed its evolution.[7] Partly, it was the attempt to avoid altogether the traditional base-superstructure metaphor, while at the same time adhering to a spatial model of social relations based on the notion of 'levels' and 'instances' of which human individuals were merely the bearers, and within which they were constituted and inscribed, which underlay much of what was wrong with the Althusserian project. For these various instances are invoked as separate entities, divorced from the human practice which they actually represent, with the result that it becomes difficult to understand how the economy, as one independent instance or level, can determine, ultimately or not, any of the other independently-constituted instances. The implication was that the role of the individual and ultimately the possibility of resistance to a particular set of social practices and conditions of existence were denied.

As I will suggest, following Godelier, there is an alternative, focused around the functional position of social practices within the totality of the social relations of production, which can both learn from the structuralist critique and avoid its pitfalls. And one purpose of this chapter will be to suggest that much non-Marxist criticism of historical materialist theories of the structuring and determining role of 'the economic', as well as the accompanying accusations of reductionism of one sort or another, reflect both a lumping together of a wide range of differing, and not always compatible, interpretative approaches, as well as a fundamental misunderstanding of how class and class struggle, agency and structure are to be invoked in historical explanation.

In fact Marxist historians are by no means alone in being guilty of such 'reductionist' tendencies in respect of the political. The Annales school itself (if 'school' is the right word for such a diverse set of tendencies and research programmes), as embodied in, for example, the work of Braudel and the notion of the *longue durée*, can certainly be shown to represent in some ways a reductionist approach to politics, in which structures – natural, climatic, geo-political 'givens' and so forth – overwhelm the human, individual moments of social evolution and change. In fact, it is apparent that the majority of these challenges to Marxism in particular represent one of two basic attitudes: either they are a genuine response to the success of historical materialist interpretations in both establishing research agendas and defining problems as well as suggesting practicable hypotheses for their resolution, and so represent serious critical engagement with historical materialist interpretations; or they reflect a certain political-ideological hostility to what is simplistically claimed as the failings of 'traditional' Marxism which is (at least to a degree, and even if unconsciously so) partly a reflection of the political-ideological situation of the 1980s and the years immediately before and after in Europe and the United States. And it needs to be said that various erstwhile representatives of historical materialist approaches have been among some of the most prominent partisans of this attitude, an attitude which, while condemning Marxist principles of analysis for their supposed reductionism, generally have failed to demonstrate the validity of their criticisms through rigorous argumentation, relying rather upon what Norman Geras has referred to as a series of forms of obloquy.

A second set of criticisms related to the same question revolves around the problem of Marx's society-orientated humanism. The philosophical anthropology which underlies much of his writings and clearly informed his socialist ideals undoubtedly represented an evolutionary and moral vision in which human history would culminate in the 'withering away' of states and the re-assertion of the essentially good and non-conflictual qualities of humankind. But if we accept this avowedly very general perspective, are we thereby condemned also to accept the idea that the state must in consequence possess merely a subordinate and effectively non-causal value (for example), acting simply as an appendage (albeit a necessary one) to class society?

The answer, of course, is no: the state Marx envisaged as withering away was the state of class oppression, not the organized administrative means of distributing social wealth and resources. As will be emphasized below, states represent organized means to particular ends, of which class domination has, historically, been one of the most apparent effects. But it is only one among several complexly interrelated functional attributes of state forms; and indeed, if we wish to avoid a teleological or functionalist logic, it might be more useful to assert that, among the effects of the existence of state structures is the domination of society by a socio-economic elite or ruling class. But this, too, can take us too far in the direction of a structuralist denial of the element of intentionality involved in all social praxis (whether or not we think the intentions which are postulated can be either identified or were fulfilled). I will refer to this issue again, briefly, in what follows.

The question has been asked in many contexts, of course, both in respect of Marxist approaches to the state and state formations in general as well as of Marxist attempts to explain historical processes in which war plays a major role. Ernest Gellner has tried to argue that the central premise of Marx's approach seems to be that the root source of conflict, evil and maladjustment in society is class exploitation, and that consequently political coercion has no independent ontological foundations: it is merely a reflection of class struggle within the institutionalized structures of the state. Again, this point of view wilfully ignores the space left by Marx for a multiplicity of inter-related causal factors within the context of a particular, dominant factor – in this case, economic contradictions as expressed through class struggle. But this is by no means to exclude the role of the individual, of the emotional and personal elements which go to constitute human social praxis, which Marx clearly did take into account at a general level, even if he was not prepared, or not willing, to undertake the sort of socio-psychological analysis and studies of ideology required.[8] A second purpose of this chapter is to suggest that these readings are, perhaps, possible readings – if crude and partial – of the writings of both Marx himself and many later historical materialists; but that anyway historical materialism, as a coherent intellectual and political project, is bound neither by a biblical and exegetical loyalty to Marx's writings nor to the cultural-ideological discourses within which Marx the individual lived.

2. Historical Materialism and Historical Explanation

Before addressing the issue of the state itself, therefore, it is necessary to make a partial response to some of these fundamental criticisms, beginning with the whole question of the philosophical underpinnings of the Marxist project. And here, I would make two essential points.

In the first place, it seems to me that Marxists have traditionally been seen as constrained by the ideological demands of the various historical conjunctures through which they have fought their political struggles, whether at a predominantly intellectual level or not, to place excessive emphasis, explicitly and implicitly, on their 'Marxological' inheritance, too little on the structure of a historical materialism.[9] It is generally recognized that Marx's writings on history embody three major strands, whose original development and elaboration were mutually contingent, and the existence of each of which demands the others as its precondition. These three strands have been characterized as, first of all, the general philosophy of history, entailing both the notion of progress and of evolution, a moral vision which owes much to Hegel and which entails a process of human self-realization through conflict and the resolution of contradictions in the structure of the process of production and distribution of wealth; a 'philosophical anthropology', or notion of what it means to speak about 'human nature' is fundamental to this, as several commentators have noted. The key in this is the idea of production, but in the context of intentionality, self-consciousness and the capacity to self-reflect or abstract. Language plays, likewise, a basic role in this array of phylogenetically human capacities. A process of socially-embedded self-realization through productive activity is what differentiates human beings from other animals, which at the same time makes it possible to conceive of the structures produced by social praxis as both limiting and facilitating change in patterns of human social and cultural life.

Second, there is a general theory of historical causation and change depending upon arguments for the primacy of productive forces. Developed, later modified, and then rejected by Cohen, taken up again by others,[10] this approach has been criticized from within Marxism for its supposed determinism, on the one hand, and the fact that 'productive forces' seem to vary in respect of their definition from historian to historian. As McLennan has pointed out, the questions raised by productive forces arguments can only be resolved at the most abstract and formalistic level. The teleology supposedly implicit in their deployment as fundamental causes of change and evolution ('progress') makes them both unsustainable as formal categories and inadequate to the demands of any detailed analysis of actual historical processes and the data which these have generated. Nevertheless, and in respect of arguments which take the productive forces into account in respect of the general social evolution of human society, and hence with regard to the first of the three elements referred to already, recent discussions have credited them with some value. In particular, the notion has recently, and plausibly, been argued that over the course of human history there is discernible a 'weak impulse' towards the constant (but repeatedly interrupted and often dormant) tendency of the forces of production in human society to develop and expand their potential across time; and that this can be understood as promoting a degree of direction and movement in history. Such a position may at first appear teleological. In fact, it represents no necessary outcome in terms of specific social formations and their evolution, nor does it demand any pre-determined hierarchy or sequence of social development. As I will suggest below, such an assumption underlies the work of Mann, for example, in his efforts to grasp the dynamic behind the evolution and rise to predominance of particular historical political formations. I will return to this issue below and in chapter 3 in connection with the notion of a historical 'prime mover'.[11]

Thirdly, there exists the analytical strand, concerning the concepts of modes of production, their historical sequence, and the relationship between actual social formations in all their complexity and the set of heuristic concepts through which they can be approached. Recent arguments have tended to concentrate on these last two strands, and it is at this level in particular that problems of relative determination or causal autonomy have had to be confronted in terms of theoretically-informed empirical research.

I will not go into these complex discussions here. But it is only recently, I think, that Marxists have begun critically to examine, perhaps the better to appreciate, Marx's own specific views in order to construct a contemporary, epistemologically realist and historical materialist account of social change, founded upon the principles of analysis set out in works such as *Capital*, amongst many. Marx and Engels laid out a vast range of materials informed by a number of key principles of analysis, principles which run through all their later writings and from which – in spite of occasional contradictions – the broad outlines of a coherent materialist theory of history can be drawn. But they never formalized their ideas, and the debates which have fired the proponents of one view or another have been fuelled by this gap. I would argue that, while Marx and Engels were certainly the original stimuli behind the development of a materialist conception of history as it is understood today, it is one which need no longer be affected by the Hegelian influences which, it has been argued, underlie much of Marx's own thinking.[12] Such a theory must be able to respond flexibly both to the demands of detailed, on-the-ground empirical research, as well as to those of a higher order metatheory of human social development and the causal principles underlying change and transformation. As Marx and Engels themselves insisted, the key elements for a heuristically useful conceptualization of human society need to be extracted from the detailed study of actual historical cases, not derived *ex nihilo* on the basis of implicit or un-thought-through teleological assumptions.

I can do no better here than to paraphrase the discussion of McLennan,[13] who has argued that a realistic epistemology provides the framework within which a number of different historiographical and sociological tendencies can be accommodated, and in which their residual antagonisms can be overcome, not by reducing them to the same common denominator, but rather by conceding their different functional intentions and coverage. For McLennan, realism embodies a conception of history as a structured process, complex but unitary. It posits also – and importantly for our purposes – a correspondence theory of truth in history.[14] Thus the idea that rival research programmes are necessarily incommensurate is rejected. It goes against epistemological pluralism, but permits pluralism of historiographical debate; and it insists upon the complex and interrelated structure of causal processes. But historical materialism, which is a realism, and which can, I would argue, take adequate account of other competing realist interpretative positions (feminist theory, the Annales tradition, state-formation theory), is nominally superior to them because its general model of long-term and short-term structural change claims to be able to handle both synchronic and diachronic elements; its theory of modes of production represents a holistic way of conceptualizing the relations of cause and function across the long term, and of establishing a fruitful way of determining general tendencies. And, as I shall argue, its fundamental categories themselves constitute the premise for alternative trans-historical explanation based on, for example, the analysis of power and power relations. As Ellen Meiksins Wood has noted, Marx left – apart from the general principles of a (realist) materialist approach to the study of society – two important starting-points:

> a point of entry into historical processes ... a means of discovering a logic of process in history, by means of his general principles concerning the centrality of productive activity in human social organization, the proposition that the 'innermost secret' of the social structure is the specific form in which 'surplus labour is pumped out of the direct producers' ... . And he provided a monumentally detailed and fruitful specific application of these general principles to the analysis of capitalism.[15]

Note that a logic of process is neither a logic of progress nor a logic of inevitability.

But a second point needs to be made. A reappraisal of Marx's concepts does not entail abandoning either the theoretical principles of his analysis, or a socialist project to realize the emancipatory conditions under which exploitation and oppression will disappear, or the need to take economic relationships as determinant of both the structure and the possibilities for change, transformation or extinction of social formations, and hence as explanatory of the actual course of human history, or of particular historical developments and specific progressive 'leaps forward'.

In the first place, all historical analysis is informed by theory determined by cultural context and antecedents and hence imbued also with a general philosophy of human development (even if a negative, or indeterminate and anti-teleological one). It seems to me no bad thing to espouse a somewhat more positive approach to the problems of the world, even if a more agnostic reading of future possibilities and trajectories is advisable than has sometimes been the case in socialist politics. But apart from this, human history as a whole has, in both a quantitative and a qualitative sense, been the history of the expansion of resource-use and of the creation of wealth, even if it has also been the history of increasingly complex divisions of labour, and modes of surplus appropriation and distribution, of exploitation and oppression, at both a local and an international level. It has also been the history, on occasion, of conscious efforts to improve society for the good of all, even if we also feel that these attempts have, on balance, been less than successful in many respects (partly because, perhaps, many of the micro-structural facets of precisely such aspects of human and social relationships of power have received no or only very little attention from those involved in such events). And it is the study of history which can (or should be able to) explain why and how this process occurs in some areas but not in others, and in particular ways, and what the effects might be upon those regions where it is not primary – this is surely the burden of both Cohen's efforts to theorize the causal effects of the forces of production in the movement of human history and of Elster's 'torch-relay' metaphor of social development. It is also the reason why Marxists quite rightly continue to regard the forces of production as a key element, in combination with the relations of production, for understanding the transition from one mode of production to another.[16]

Because it is built upon the determining effects of economic relationships, as I will argue, Marxism, or historical materialism, cannot break its ties with the socialist project and become one option among many competing historiographical or sociological discourses, since the possibilities for what is currently referred to as a 'socialist' future (I write the word thus because, without giving up any of the notions that currently go to make up our ideas of what a post-capitalist society will have to involve, the use of words or terms such as socialism and, certainly, communism will without doubt be subject to revision or re-thinking in the future, given the ideological connotations of such terms in both 'western' society and in recently transformed 'eastern bloc' states) depend very much on questions of wealth production and distribution in the primary sense (for I will argue that, although political control and geopolitical competition may determine the distribution of wealth, these elements are themselves determined in the first place by access to control and distribution of the means of production).

In the second place, the connection between historical process and economic relationships sets a broad agenda, but must not necessarily indicate either the methodologies employed or indeed the purpose (and therefore function) of specific historical or sociological analyses. It leaves plenty of room for the increased incidence of comparative and awkward questioning which has been the form taken by one of the major challenges to historical materialism (from comparative sociology and anthropology); and it is not undermined by a decrease in the 'guiding' role of any general and programmatic theory which follows. Such a connection certainly does not prevent a detailed micro-analysis of specific moments in the history of specific social formations; nor does it condemn us blindly to accept categories or causal relationships without first examining them for their explanatory power and analytic adequacy. This was a point made very clearly by, for example, Plekhanov in the 1890s, when writing about the role of individuals in historical interpretation and causality, a context in which he also warned against precisely the sort of reductionism of which Marxists are supposedly guilty. But it has been argued just as forcefully more recently.[17]

Marxism is at its most exposed, however, in precisely this area of the connection between the general, macro-theoretical model of social-economic evolution and the micro-level of specific social formations, their internal articulation and structuration, and the ideological/motivational 'interests' they embody. Much of the blame may be placed, perhaps, on the fact that interest has tended to concentrate around the problems of general theory and metatheory, rather than on specific empirical research. Is a model which operates at such a high level of abstraction as that of mode of production actually able to explain the specific features of the societies it is applied to? Or are its general categories so all-embracing as to be useless? My own view is that this is a question which is best resolved by demonstration. But we might begin by noting that historical materialist premises provide a heuristic framework through which the particular forms of macro-level structures can be located at the micro-level and articulated with the trajectories of development in a given social formation. The definition of a mode of production (which I will discuss below and in greater detail in chapter 3) is reached through theoretical abstraction from historical data collated by examining all those social formations corresponding approximately to the same stage in the development of the productive forces. As such, it represents a concept of how certain sets of economic relations work and, in consequence, roughly how we might expect them to develop under certain sets of circumstances and in certain conditions. It is thus intended to help the historian look for and locate the causal relationships underlying the political and cultural evolution of a given social formation or group of social formations. It does not predict the form structures take, but it does provide an analytical and functional model for their limiting, enabling or dynamic results. Only through detailed empirical analysis can this be obtained, however, and only through such work can the multiplicity of social, economic and political agencies be causally related within a properly holistic analysis. And it is perhaps in this respect that both Marxists and their critics have on occasion asked or expected too much of their framework. Of course, we do not expect to be able to relate societal changes and the forms through which the social relations of production are expressed in each different culture, to reflect directly the demands of 'economic' factors. It was indeed the fundamentally mistaken nature of criticism based on this misapprehension which thinkers like Plekhanov took time to answer and to expose. And except in the broadest sense, the political economy of any given set of relations of production will be masked by forms of cultural praxis and role-formation specific to each specific cultural area. It is just this 'unmasking' that constitutes a crucial area of Marxist research. Marx's *Capital* is the classic statement of the method in its specific and applied form. And Marxists who have in the past tried too hard to tie the microstructural level too rigidly to the macrostructural context within which it is to be understood, as though the former were merely a reflection of the latter, have rightly formed the target for both Marxist as well as non-Marxist criticism.

From one point of view, therefore, historical materialism, while firmly embedded within the philosophical terrain of a realist materialist epistemology, is less a philosophy itself than it is an empirical theory. It rests not on abstract dogmas derived philosophically, but, as has been argued, on premises that can be verified by empirical analysis. The debate over whether such premises are so derived, or represent merely a set of a priori statements, goes on; but it is only its ability to provide a viable research programme that will vindicate its claims.

In the last analysis, therefore, my own preference for a theory of history and social change which awards priority to the determinant effects of the economic is founded on what I would argue is its heuristic superiority: in spite of the teleologies and reductionisms of some versions of Marxist historical interpretation, in spite of its omissions and gaps, the principles of Marx's historical materialism still seem to me to present the best opportunity for providing a holistic account of historical change without losing any of the dialectical complexity of history as 'power relations' or the complexities of human psychology and the field of motivation, intention and identity which has been so important in recent theoretical debates – the work of Elster, and especially that of John Roemer (epitomized as 'rational choice Marxism'), which has done a great deal recently to re-orientate post-Althusserian Marxist theory and to re-assess the effects of the 'structuralist moment', whatever we may think of its ultimate coherence as a radical alternative to what it describes as 'traditional' Marxist analyses, highlights this point quite clearly.[18] Crucially, a Marxist approach claims to be able to account for power-relations, state formations and forms of conflict and oppression, within the framework of the forces and relations of production – that these have not always been on the main agenda or are thought to have been only inadequately theorized does not in itself, as some have implied, invalidate the Marxist project. Every research programme has its priorities, which reflect contemporary political and/or scientific concerns, and historical materialist analysis, in whatever field, is not alone in this. It does set up a range of challenges, however, which Marxists are beginning to take up. This is especially true within what Anderson has dubbed the 'Anglo-Marxist' tradition.[19]

The above represents a rather weak formulation of the relationship between Marxism and socialism, of course, and it may be that in attempting to escape or avoid a determinism, I have proposed an overly pluralist approach by default. If this is so, I do not consider it an insurmountable objection. The socialist project is bound, in its very nature, to emphasize the economics of human social organization as fundamental, whatever the nature and structure of the individual choices and selection of practices that are made. Historical materialism, which takes the material conditions of the existence and reproduction of human cultures (a category which must be understood to include social praxis itself if it is to have any validity) as determinant, must continue to provide the conceptual apparatus for a socialist politics. The task is to demonstrate why this conceptual apparatus need be neither economically determinist, nor functionalist, nor unilinear in its mode of explanation. Dialectical explanation does not entail eclectic pluralism, any more than economic determination entails the loss of the political, emotional or psychological as crucial causal stimuli.

What I do not wish to do in this context is to try to rescue traditional propositions and beliefs of Marxist social theory which may seem already to have met justifiable rejection, merely by asserting their superiority or validity, or to claim that they have been improperly applied or understood by critics (although this has certainly occurred in many instances). I think this would be both time-wasting as well as intellectually and politically pointless. But it does seem to me to be the case that many criticisms levelled at Marxism depend on the specific version and interpretation of a particular tradition of Marxist history-writing, from which generalized points of disagreement can then be elaborated. And in point of fact, Marxist historical-sociological analysis is in general much more sophisticated and much more open-minded than the cruder dismissals would have us believe.

This book does not pretend to set out a detailed theoretical statement of the philosophical and sociological underpinnings of historical materialism, however. But since any analysis and discussion of states necessarily involves certain views about the nature of power, the relationship between social structures and human action and that between sets of practices and relationships in both their economic and non-economic aspects, I will state very briefly some of the basic assumptions guiding my understanding of these different elements, and define some of the basic categories of analysis which will be employed.

To begin with, I will assume the term 'structure' to refer to the socially-determinate results of past human actions repeated on a regular basis sufficient to determine certain behavioural forms and social practices. In this sense the social relations of production, which involve certain repeated patterns of human activity having the effect of reproducing the human agents involved together with the social environment they inhabit, are structures. As such, they both limit and facilitate human activity: limit in the sense that they provide a social framework which determines the possibilities open to individuals and groups in respect of their perceptions of the world they inhabit and the roles or positions they occupy – roles which are themselves both constitutive of human individuals and their praxis and constituted by that practice. But structures also provide capacities and possibilities to human beings to pursue aims within the framework they establish and hence, ultimately, to transcend the structures themselves through evolving or adopting practices which challenge the very structures which endow them with those capacities.[20]

In this sense, and here I follow the arguments made by Callinicos, structures determine also the access people have to resources, and hence the 'causal powers' agents have by virtue of the social practices associated with the reproduction of these structures. To quote Callinicos and Wright, they determine the structural capacities open to human beings in their social context.[21]

Secondly, and implicit in this definition of structure, adequate understanding of human action must take human beings as possessing intentions, beliefs and desires in their activity, hence reconciling both the constitutive and constituted aspects of human personality and self-perception. This serves, importantly, to emphasize that ideology, as the expression of human perceptions of the world and their effectiveness in it, can also be a material force, and can provide an account of the world, based in one set of structural relationships, which can promote practices which transcend or transform those relationships. The mechanisms by which this occurs can be revealed most clearly, I suggest, by socio-linguistic analysis, in particular in a theory of the organizing of experience through narrative reconstruction, and which I have discussed elsewhere.[22] Of course, in asserting the relevance of intentions as a fundamental element in human consciousness and practice, I am not thereby assuming either that intentions can ever be identified or located, or – more importantly – that the intentions ascribed to actions by the actors, or by other commentators, are necessarily true. Indeed, Marx's comment at the beginning of his *The Eighteenth Brumaire of Louis Bonaparte* is a useful reminder of this: 'Men make their own history, but they do not make it just as they please; they do not make it under circumstances chosen by themselves, but under circumstances directly encountered, given and transmitted from the past'.[23]

Callinicos has argued in this sense that historical materialism is a theory of structural capacities. It will be worth quoting a section of his conclusion in this context *in extenso*:

> Marx indeed quite explicitly identifies the development of the productive forces in bourgeois society with 'the absolute working-out (of humanity's) creative potentialities, with no presuppositions other than the previous historic development, which makes this totality of development, i.e. the development of all human powers as such the end in itself'. The productive forces are thus best understood as the productive *powers* of humanity, reflecting a particular, technically determined form of labour-process. But the relations of production also involve particular kinds of powers. This is clearest in G.A. Cohen's analysis of production-relations as the powers agents have over labour-power and the means of production ... . Agents' structural capacities are thus determined by their relative access to productive resources, to labour-power and means of production.[24]

While it may be that Marxism does not provide a fully-grown social theory, it certainly provides most of the elements for such a theory, a map or plan as to the shape such a theory might take. What it emphatically is not is a dogmatic set of propositions which must be taken as a whole and which cannot evolve, although some of its severest critics have actually taken its dogmatic character for granted. But if we assume a certain flexibility, then we are justified in asking to what extent it can be re-interpreted without altering its fundamental character and consequently its value as a means of understanding human society and activity.

These are important points, because many recent attacks on aspects of Marxist theory – especially in respect of state formations, for example, or the question of power-relations – have been unwilling to see the different functional intentions and coverage of the work they have in their sights, or have launched their critique from a level of analysis which is incommensurate with that of the work under review, attributing a dogmatism and reductionism to Marxist analysis as its inevitable accompaniment. They have regularly failed, or refused, to get to grips with serious discussions among Marxist philosophers and social scientists, discussions that represent both an extremely sophisticated reconsideration and reassessment of the fundamental principles of historical materialist analysis, as well as a re-affirmation of the value of Marx's key insights. A good example is provided by the book on states referred to already.

Hall's objection that Marxism cannot handle the causes of wars without resulting in an economic reductionism, for example, reflects both a generalization from one particular version of Marxist/Leninist thinking, on the one hand, and a reductionist notion of how the 'economic' is to be understood, on the other. There is no reason why, from a historical materialist perspective, imperialism should not have been 'in fact the result of geopolitical rivalry rather than of economic necessity'.[25] But whether this rivalry is based upon an open commitment to control over disputed resources, or an ideological conflict which is itself founded in antagonistic commitments to different ways of organizing society and the distribution of resources, it is the latter which are at issue. The struggle over resource control and exploitation, and consequently the struggle over the particular forms of production relations in the societies in question, surely play a key role.

The various interests in question are represented for the actors concerned in a variety of ideological terms – national pride, military tradition, communism vs. capitalism and so on – yet this does not alter the fact that state elites do not go to war for ideas alone. Would anyone seriously argue that the USA committed itself to a war in Vietnam, or the USSR to a war in Afghanistan, as a result of ideological imperatives alone, which had no roots in the organization and structure of the societies which produced them? Unless we are to hypostatize ideologies and deny them any foundation in the structure of social praxis and state formation, such an argument would be manifestly absurd. And if we were to reject the idea that there was any potential direct or indirect economic gain from Indo-China for the USA (although everywhere is a market, potentially, and constantly expanding markets are essential to the demands of capitalist production) we still have to explain the context within which 'ideological imperatives' are generated. And it is surely beyond doubt that that context is one of political and therefore economic competition between state systems. And within states, there exists competition between politico-economic factions and vested interests, whose position may itself be best maintained by either promoting or opposing investment in military technologies or war itself. Both sides, whether we are speaking of states or political factions, present arguments in an ideological form, but the reality is, in the end, control of resources and the preservation, strengthening and extension of one or another set of political-economic relationships. Where states do appear to go to war for ideological reasons alone (such as treaty obligations, for example), we can be sure that something lies behind those ideas: it may not be a one-to-one link, or reflection, of any clear set of interests. But it would be a foolish historian or social analyst indeed who accepted what the sources appear to say at face value. Ideas are formed in a context, and such ideas represent interests in respect of power. And power is about means to ends, that is to say, about the control of resources, both human and material, in order to achieve or attain a specific goal or set of goals: usually, the maintenance, reproduction and (where there is, physically and ideologically, a perceived possibility) extension of a given set of institutions – systems of power relations themselves and, therefore – and unavoidably – relations of production. Even where power is sought for its own sake (where, for example, the motivating force behind a particular political conflict is at least in phenomenal terms the expression of a given psychology or programme), the effects of that conflict and its resolution must take the form of the maintenance or disruption of specific sets of practices, which are themselves constitutive of the relations of production and reproduction of the social formation.

Of course, no-one would seriously wish to link the causes of the First World War to direct economic necessity, although this is what Hall claims Marxist theory is bound to do. But that war is 'the characteristic product of a multipolar state system' is hardly an adequate refutation of the determining role of those states' vested or perceived economic interests, on the one hand (external factor), and the relations of power within those states in respect of the dominant relations of production as expressed through the contingent local political ideologies, on the other (internal factor).

Similarly, Hall's objection that Marx's theory of class is flawed because the various national working classes failed to unite in a transnational anti-capitalist movement is itself odd. The collapse of proletarian internationalism is an interesting and important example of the defeat of one political credo by another emotionally and politically much more powerful and deep-rooted one, whatever the contradictions it may have demonstrated. The fact that economic relationships can be overdetermined by ideologies for very considerable periods of time is no argument that the former may not be transnational. The differential relationship of the English, French and German working class to the means of production is systemically the same, although the political and institutional forms through which this relationship was expressed varied. And capitalists the world over tend to respond in much the same ways when confronted by perceived threats to their livelihoods. Just as French capitalists chose to invest in imperial Russia, where greater profits were to be had than in their own country or its colonies, so English investment capital has traditionally flowed away from the United Kingdom to areas where labour is cheap, the work-force easily controlled, the rate of exploitation higher and investment returns quicker.[26] The fact that economic classes in the world capitalist system are determined also in respect of political activity and ideologies by national and intranational identities does not alter their common economic condition. Neither does it exclude the possibility that, sometime in the future, a transnational class politics will come into existence. To a degree, this already holds for international capital and corporate investors. The results of 1992 and the debate over the European social charter has already highlighted some possibilities in this respect.

But Hall's comments nevertheless embody very real and serious criticisms of some actual Marxist historical and sociological writings, and it remains to demonstrate how a coherent theory of the state, for example, framed within a materialist paradigm, can answer them. I will return to the question of the economic frequently in the following sections.

3. A Marxist Approach to the State

In order to elaborate these arguments, I want to pursue the question raised in my introduction concerning a historical materialist approach to the state, state elites, the relative or absolute autonomy of state structures and practices, and the role of the economic in Marxist historical interpretation.

To begin with: what is a state? This is, in itself, something of a problem, since there is no formal consensus (not surprisingly) on what defines a state generally in use among all historians and sociologists. A wide range of definitions has been employed reflecting the particular intellectual and political backgrounds of those who have worked on the problem. In what follows, I will adopt as a descriptive starting-point the general definition which has been evolved by recent commentators, notably Skalník and Claessen, Krader and, most recently, Mann.[27] That is, that the state represents a set of institutions and personnel, concentrated spatially at a single point, and exerting authority over a territorially distinct area. As Mann notes,[28] this description combines both institutional and functional elements, pertaining to the appearance of the state's apparatuses as well as to their functions and effects. But in addition, I would qualify the definition by adding that the central point at which state power is nominally located may be mobile; that authority is in principle normative and binding, and relies ultimately on coercion; and that the effectiveness of such authority will depend upon a series of contextual factors: geographical extent of the state, institutional forms through which power is actually exercised (for example, through a centralized and supervised central bureaucracy or through a dispersed provincial ruling elite). And while, with Radcliffe-Brown, we can agree that the state is the product of social and economic relations and must, therefore, not be reified or personified in the process of analysis, it is important to stress that the state does have an identity as a field of action, as a role-constituting site of power and practices which can be independent, under certain preconditions, of the economic and political interests of whose who dominate it. As a general point, this consideration has been expressed frequently in both Marxist and non-Marxist history and sociology in recent years. But as the criticisms of Marxist analyses outlined above should have made clear, it has not always been put into practice in the actual examination and interpretation of states.

It needs also to be stressed that state formations differ qualitatively in the degree of their 'stateness'. Some of these differences will be highlighted in chapter 4; but there are also considerable variations between the way in which the institutional structures, patterns of administration, forms of surplus extraction and so on operate in, say, the fully-developed Byzantine state of the tenth–twelfth centuries, and the nascent Ottoman 'state' of the later fourteenth and fifteenth centuries in which the interests of a particular dynasty and its clients, in the context of an ideology of territorial expansion based on and legitimated by the concept of Holy War, predominated. The stage of evolution of states must, therefore, be borne in mind when making comparisons, as also in respect of examining the ways in which power relations were forged and reproduced in such very different structural contexts.[29]

Finally, it is worth stressing that, in a purely functional way, all states (and indeed all similar, institutionalized structures) have an autonomy of practice, insofar as they represent a nexus of specialized roles and practices divorced from the routines of day-to-day social and cultural reproduction. Their personnel occupy and act out institutionalized and behaviour-determining roles specific to the ideological and the functional demands of their allocated tasks. To a degree, these roles contribute to the 'organizational imperatives' and to the apparently 'self-constituting' nature of the state apparatuses, as well as to the degree of their independence from the basic structural constraints of the social formation in which they exist. Some of the possible historical variations in the way such relationships and institutions have actually evolved will be examined in the following chapters.

Marxist theory is not bound to see the state merely as a tool of the ruling class, however. Certainly, Marxists have tended to see the state as a set of institutions which underwrite the maintenance and reproduction of exploitative class relations – in my view quite correctly. But this does not mean that that is their only effect. Nor does it mean that this is a simplistic or reductionist view; or that we must adopt a functionalist or teleological argument and maintain that states come into being in order to achieve this end. It is, however, undeniably one of the results of their existence. And, given the 'strong' interpretation of human agency referred to above, it must not be forgotten – indeed, it needs to be emphasized – that individuals or groups (leading elements of dominant clans or tribes, for example, as in the Ottoman case discussed in chapter 4 below) may well demonstrably and intentionally set out to create 'state' structures – military and fiscal organizational practices in particular, supported by appropriately legitimating ideological discourses – in order to maintain and reinforce their own authority and political dominance.

The functionalism of reductionist Marxism (especially of the 1930s to 1950s) has been highlighted by Giddens. But some critics of a historical materialist approach still find it easier to attack this prey, long-since deceased, than to engage with more recent Marxist work. Thus Marxist approaches to the state, which in recent years have tried to relate social relations of production as a whole to the state structures within which they exist but with which they have a dialectically constitutive relationship, have been dismissed by Mann, for example, as follows:

> most general theories of the state have been false because they have been reductionist. They have reduced the state to the pre-existing structures of civil society. This is obviously true of the Marxist, the liberal and the functionalist traditions of state theory, each of which has seen the state predominantly as a place, an arena, in which the struggle of classes, interest groups and individuals are expressed and institutionalized.[30]

Such a broad generalization seems to me unjustified. For both Marx and Engels attributed to the state a great deal of autonomy – the problem has lain partly in the appropriation of limited elements of their work and its application to specific problems by later writers working within a particular political-intellectual moment. And it has also, of course, lain in the particular priorities of Marxist political analysts of the state who, like everyone else, work within specific conjunctural constraints and demands. On the other hand, it is certainly true that Marxism has traditionally paid only limited attention to the social psychology of individual or group power-seeking, personal self-interest and culturally-situated greed – not surprisingly, since its emphasis has been on the broader relations between groups. This hardly means, however, that it cannot handle such phenomena.[31] What recent critiques have achieved is to point out the gaps and the consequent inadequacy of empirical work based on general theories which do ignore these elements, and to make it imperative for Marxists to take account of the socially-constitutive nature of these aspects of human agency.

In fact, in dealing with various aspects of state history – notably of the nineteenth-century French state, for example – Marx was very conscious of the interests and purposes which a state machinery might develop, independent of the interests of the dominant class as a whole. But he also insisted that the institutions of a state were formed by human practice and realized through the activity of human agents who also existed in relationships other than those entirely determined by the state.[32] And while neither Marx nor Engels wrote in detail on pre-capitalist states (contributing thereby to the inevitable inconsistencies and contradictions of later elaborations on this theme), they were always aware of the potential autonomy of state structures (albeit expressed in what has been seen as a class-reductionist formulation): 'periods occur in which the warring classes balance each other so nearly that the state power ... acquires ... a certain degree of independence from both'.[33]

Whether or not we accept explanatory devices such as relative autonomy, on the one hand, or the notion that there exists a 'partnership' between the dominant economic class and the state elite, on the other,[34] it does seem that, while a Marxist approach to the state which retains all the flexibility demanded by recent critiques of traditional historical materialism is perfectly possible, it still has to be adequately theorized. The influence of Gramsci, naturally, has been considerable in this respect – for example, the notion that the domination of the ruling class is elicited by consent as well as coercion, and that the state plays a key role in the process of legitimating a given social order and establishing a hegemonic cultural-political framework. This has been developed in the context of mainly modern, twentieth-century states; but it has important implications for an understanding of the crucial relationships between ideology and the political-economic relations within a social formation, on the one hand, and the role and actions of state elites on the other.[35]

That the state has the potential to exercise authority and coercive force on behalf of interests which may respond more to the imperatives of a specific political ideology than to those of the interests of the dominant social and economic class is, therefore, not to be denied. Yet at the same time, this autonomy must by definition be circumscribed since, as I will argue below, the state is also embedded in the social formation from which it draws its personnel and its legitimate further existence. Marx was quite clear on this, as a well-known passage from volume three of *Capital* – which also sets out the basic principles of a historical materialist understanding of the relationship between the economic and the other aspects of social praxis – makes plain. It is perhaps worth quoting in full:

> The specific economic form, in which unpaid surplus-labour is pumped out of direct producers, determines the relationship of rulers and ruled, as it grows directly out of production itself and, in turn, reacts upon it as a determining element. Upon this, however, is founded the entire formation of the economic community which grows up out of the production relations themselves, thereby simultaneously its specific political form. It is always the direct relationship of the owners of the conditions of production to the direct producers – a relation always naturally corresponding to a definite stage in the development of the methods of labour and thereby its social productivity – which reveals the innermost secret, the hidden basis of the entire social structure, and with it the political form of the relations of sovereignty and dependence, in short, the corresponding specific form of the state.[36]

The question, therefore, of 'autonomy from what?' imposes itself at this point.

As we have seen, the traditional approach attributed to Marxism has been the argument that, because states develop out of the growth of private property, a social division of labour and the growth of antagonistic class relations between rulers and ruled, dominant and subordinate groups, they must necessarily function in the interests of the ruling class, through the medium of whose particular class interests they develop. Put in such a functionalist and reductionist way, this is clearly too simplistic, although not entirely wrong either. However, this is not the only or necessary reading of either Marx or Engels on the state, nor of the potential of a historical materialist reading generally. On the contrary, neither Marx nor Engels had any doubt that states were to be understood within the framework of the existence of contradictory relations of production and social-economic classes, that is to say, they were to be viewed both as a *de facto* instrument of class oppression and an area for class struggle, on the one hand; and as an institutional nexus of power relations on the other which generates its own practices independent of the specificities of that class struggle. But – and this is important for a historical materialist approach – this independence is always relative: however much a bureaucracy or state elite, which has been freed or partially freed from its social, economic and cultural roots through state service, might identify itself with, or re-interpret in its own institutional interests, the perceived interests and functions of the state in respect of the prevailing political ideological forms, and consequent political activities and policies, two key factors continue to operate. In the first place, a dominant social class is always able to exploit the existence of the state to maintain or enhance its position (where it can); and the state (or rather its leaders and power-elite) can only survive if it retains the allegiance of this class (however antagonistic the latter might be in political terms to the specific policies or individual rulers of that state). In the second place, it must be axiomatic that the state, as a set of institutional structures and practices, is itself always inscribed within exploitative relations of production and must of necessity constitute an arena which facilitates the promotion of the interests of the dominant class, or at the very least, does not intervene in a way which is contrary to the maintenance of those interests. This point has been made very clearly for modern, capitalist state forms by Miliband, and it does not mean either, as Mann has suggested, that this is its *only* function or effect. But it will become equally clear for pre-capitalist states in the course of the discussion in the rest of this book. The fact that state leaderships or elites, or indeed the producers whose surplus the state appropriates in part as tax, may not perceive this effect (or 'function') of the existence of state apparatuses is neither here nor there. And in fact, when the hierarchical and fundamentally exploitative nature of these relationships is perceived, it is always represented ideologically as a necessary and inevitable reflection of the (culturally-determined) order of things.[37]

We can thus re-assert, albeit in a more nuanced form, Engels's original and much criticized formulation: since states develop in the context of class antagonisms, they rarely fail to provide conditions favourable to the interests of the socio-economically dominant class, which, through the state's institutional arrangements, functions also as the politically dominant class, and is thereby able to ensure the reproduction of the prevailing relations of exploitation and subordination. But this in no way denies the possibility that state elites might themselves constitute the dominant class, or act in the short term in ways which may run counter to the interests of a dominant class. Neither does it exclude the possibility that such elites may over the longer term act in ways which are 'class neutral', where a balance exists between the vested interests of both state elites and dominant classes. In any or all of these cases, the state is still part of a set of relations of production in which exploitative economic relationships determine the possibilities of action open to the individuals and groups in question. On the other hand, and as we shall see, the dominant class and its supporters generally are able to negate hostile actions – either by seizing the state itself, or by forcing a modification of state policies by non-co-operation, open rebellion, or in the capitalist context, by the withdrawal of capital and other forms of economic and fiscal sabotage. And finally, it must be remembered that such relative autonomy of state apparatuses or policies and practices must always be understood within the context of specific ideological discourses: the rationales invoked by different factions and interests, and which may promote one course of action as opposed to another, are the key elements for an understanding of why, and under what conditions, state elites, or factions within them, exploit the relative autonomy of the apparatuses which they themselves constitute.

A Marxist approach to the state, then, is based upon the assumption of social stratification in the economic sense, that is to say, the existence of economic classes which bear differential relationships to the means of production and which are, therefore, antagonistic – whether or not this antagonism is expressed in political action, for example, or remains immanent; the existence of an economically dominant class with whose interests in both economic (that is, class) and political/ideological terms (factions, interest groups and so forth, determined by conjunctural political-ideological orientations) the state elite may or may not be in contradiction; the potential relative autonomy of the state under the direction of a ruler and dependent or less dependent state elite (or a faction thereof); the limitation of this relative autonomy in respect of the relations of production within which all members of the society and the apparatuses and institutions they constitute are inscribed, a limitation which operates both structurally and temporally. Such an approach must also take account of the structuring role of ideology and the symbolic universe within which the culture in question is constituted, and hence also the power of symbolic systems and beliefs to overdetermine economic relationships, that is to say, to transcend the structures within which human agents normally function. In particular, it must take into account and be able to account for the fact that the existence of antagonistic classes in pre-capitalist social formations does not mean that the latter were not also divided institutionally and ideologically along other lines: the estates of medieval Europe, for example, or the tripartite political division of the eastern Christian world by theologians and others into producers, defenders and spiritual protectors. Such divisions are also relations between groups, however, and can function also as forms of the relations of production, as we shall see below; and on both theoretical and empirical grounds I would argue that economic (class) relations have always determined the parameters within which such other relationships develop and function.[38]

Such an approach must also have an evolutionary aspect as well as a descriptive one – synchrony must be complemented by diachrony. Structures are never fixed and stable over time, since institutions, whatever their nature, are always effectively structures of social reproduction, that is to say, there is a process inherent in their very existence. History must be incorporated into any structural analysis, not left out as an added ingredient to be mixed in at the appropriate moment to account for that otherwise awkward phenomenon, change.

A theory of the state must also imply an integrated theory of state formation, and although I will be discussing state origins to a degree in what follows, I do not want to carry my argument further at this point. For it seems to me that recent work on state theory by both Marxists and non-Marxists has contributed a great deal to the generation of such a theory, the results of which I have tried to take into account in my own discussion.

In particular, the typology of states and social formations (for both are represented) evolved by Runciman[39] founded on both Weber and Marx is, if not entirely compatible with a historical materialist approach, a source of much relevant discussion. As I have argued above, it addresses a different level of analysis, a different degree of specificity, from that normally elaborated from within historical materialist programmes, and is at the same time founded on a rather different theory of agency and structure. In other words, it has different functional intentions and consequently a different degree of coverage of certain problems. This does not mean that it cannot be valuable in considering the way states and state power work.

Runciman distinguishes four crucial stages, tracks of evolution which may or may not lead from one to another, but in which the degree of social stratification, social division of labour and development of contradictory relations of production play a fundamental role. These are articulated together to form modes of the distribution of power, in which the forms of economic, ideological and coercive power, distributed among differently-located roles, give each social structure its particular form and content.[40]

First, there are social formations with either 'dissipated power' or 'shared power' – hunter-gatherer groups, for example, or in social-anthropological terms, small societies characterized by segmentary lineage organization (that is, where 'stratification' exists as a vertical line between kin-groups and attributed functions within the society, rather than horizontally between groups with different economic power), among other pre-class systems. Second, there are semi-states, usually temporary extensions of the power of a single chieftain as a result of warfare or internal conflict. Third, and involving a greater elaboration of both coercion and more explicitly political ideology, there are proto-states which develop, to quote Runciman, 'from the existence of specialized political roles which fall short of an effective monopoly of the means of coercion to the existence of potentially permanent institutions of government properly so-called'.[41] Runciman goes on to elaborate some fourteen types of state according to what he terms their 'distribution of power'; and I will return to the question of how we should define states and their effects in greater depth in chapter 4. But before we go any further, it will be appropriate to take up one fundamental point already briefly mentioned – the role of 'the economic' as the key determining element in Marxist analysis of human societies.

4. The Economic and the Nature of Determination

As will by now have become clear, critics of Marxist approaches to the state have founded their disagreement upon the question of whether or not states represent, or function on behalf of, the economically dominant class in a given social formation, and whether or not this embodies an unavoidably functionalist approach. This is, in its turn, a reaction to the emphasis placed by Marxists on the economic structure of social formations and the role of class struggle. It is necessary at this point, in consequence, to clarify the ways in which this aspect of social structure is understood and employed in analysis.

An examination of the debate both within Marxist history-writing and among its critics reveals a great flexibility in the application of terminology. On the one hand, critics of Marxist approaches have regularly and almost programmatically misconstrued the direction of some Marxist work, and on the basis of a sometimes sloppy use of notions such as 'economic base' among Marxists themselves have been able to brand much Marxist writing as economistic on the grounds that primacy in both the structure and function of social and ideological institutions has been attributed to economic relations, without due consideration for other elements: politics, ideology, institutional stasis, warfare, and so on. On the other hand, and while much of this criticism has actually come from Marxists themselves, there has been a great deal of Marxist writing which was guilty of an over-deterministic and economistic interpretation of social relations and institutions, so that such attacks have sometimes been well-founded. Particularly problematic has been the tendency of economic reductionism to ignore the epistemologically fundamental dialectical nature of social praxis, and hence produce a form of functionalist logic which ascribes causes rather than generates them from the social context.

Marx was, as is well-known, primarily interested in the actual workings of capitalist relations of production. His comments and analyses of pre-capitalist social formations, and even more so of pre-capitalist modes of production, were sketchy to say the least. But a basic framework for the analysis of such historical societies can be developed from his and Engels's work on the subject and within a contemporary historical materialist framework.

What do we mean, therefore, by 'economic base', 'the economic', 'economic relations' and so forth? First, and crucially, these terms do not refer to a partial or discreet institution or set of material conditions. What is meant is the sum total of production relations or, in other words, the class relations of society as a whole. The famous passage from the *Introduction to A Contribution to the Critique of Political Economy* in which this is made clear is reinforced in many places in

Marx's work. In volume 3 of *Capital*, for example, Marx notes, as we have seen, that

> It is always the direct relationship of the owners of the conditions of production to the direct producers – a relation always naturally corresponding to a definite stage in the development of the methods of labour and thereby its social productivity – which reveals the innermost secret, the hidden basis of the entire social structure, and with it the political forms of the relations of sovereignty and dependence, in short, the corresponding specific form of the state.[42]

For Marx, therefore, the 'base' or 'basis' represented the fundamental sets of economic relationships which typified each mode of production in the sense of an abstract, idealized system. It meant, for example, that for the 'ancient' mode, feudalism (our tributary mode), or capitalism, all societies which functioned on the basis of the same pattern of structured relationships could be reasonably described as belonging to the ancient, feudal or capitalist mode. This could only be determined by empirical research. But the point of the exercise, as we have already seen, was precisely to enable the historian to look behind the 'phenomenal forms', the infinite range of culturally-determined social praxis (the 'superstructure') through which these fundamental relationships were expressed; and hence to locate the causal relationships which explained the direction, speed and degree of socio-economic change.

This was intended neither to obscure the fact that all social practices can be described, in respect of their effects, as multi-functional or multi-dimensional, nor to suggest that social practices and institutions did not in turn affect the ways in which these underlying economic relationships were expressed and hence could develop. Indeed, Marx's whole point about the relations of production fettering the forces of production (to which I will return in chapter 2) assumes this possibility.

In the second place, it is important to remember that the spatial image of economic base and superstructure was intended as a metaphor, not an attempt to describe any ontologically real hierarchy of social practice. But its metaphorical aspect can be, and has often been, misconstrued. Both Marx and Engels were clearly aware of this danger. Marx was keen to emphasize the relationship between the two as historical and contingent, corresponding to, that is, compatible with, the institutional, organizational and ideological framework of the society, to which he also attributed an effectivity. As Marx says himself, the fact that it is the relationship between the owners of the means of production and direct producers which 'reveals ... the hidden basis of the entire social structure', does not

> prevent the same economic basis – the same from the standpoint of its main conditions – due to innumerable different economic circumstances, natural environment, racial relations, external historical influences, etc., from showing infinite variations and gradations in appearance, which can be ascertained only by analysis of the empirically given circumstances.[43]

This is emphasized by his answer to the criticism that the economic determination of social institutions is a specifically capitalist phenomenon and cannot apply to, say, medieval society, where ideology and politics (religion) play the key role. Marx noted that 'the middle ages could not live on Catholicism, nor the ancient world on politics': but these are the forms through which economic relations were in part expressed, rationalized and lived out.[44] Engels himself used the notion of 'ultimate determination' by the economy as a way of pointing to these social relations of production as providing the framework within which other aspects of social life are inscribed, but where at the same time a dialectical process exists, through which 'secondary structures' can also determine the form and development of economic relations within the parameters set by the latter.[45]

The point about all this, of course, is that Marx and Engels were constrained, on the one hand, by a model – the base/superstructure model – which was designed specifically to highlight the inadequacies of classical political economic ideas about how societies work from an economic perspective, and, on the other, by traditional ideas about the nature of the state, ideology and so on. Unhappy formulations, such as 'secondary structures', inevitably give a false idea about what is intended to modern thinkers. When it came to the point, both realized the inadequacies of this particular heuristic for a wider-ranging analysis, and tried to escape from its apparent determinism by the sorts of comments referred to above. 'We have all neglected [this aspect] more than it deserves. It is the old story: form is always neglected at first for content.'[46] And it is understandable that this spatial model of base and superstructure, which, while being more than just a metaphor, was never intended to provide more than a general guide to the way in which economic and social relationships could be thought, has been frequently both misused and misunderstood.[47] It tends to give the impression that systems of belief, institutional structures, cultural traditions and so on are merely secondary, thus promoting a functionalist and deterministic account of social change rather than an explanatorily motivated dynamic analysis of a complex of interrelated elements.

In order to avoid this, and yet retain and justify the notion of the totality of social relations of production (the economic) as being fundamental to the ways in which any given social formation can function – as being determinant in the sense that they frame the possibilities of institutional and cultural forms, set limits to the exploitation of social power, yet facilitate the possibility for human practice to transcend those structures – two related points need to be made.

In the first place, and as Godelier has argued,[48] those dimensions of the social structure which appear to dominate very many non-capitalist societies, but which are equally, in appearance, non-economic dimensions, regulate nevertheless the reproduction of specific sets of social relations. As examples, the dominance of religion in many social formations (in medieval Europe, for example), or of kinship structures in Australian aboriginal societies, or yet again of politics and religion in the classical Greek world, have all been used as rods with which to beat Marxist approaches for their ostensible economic reductionism. But as Marx had already noted, and as Godelier re-affirmed, these supposedly entirely non-economic 'superstructural' dimensions fulfilled also the *function* of relations of production; for all societies consist of structures which function to maintain and reproduce the sets of social relations of production of which they are composed. Dominant non-economic structures function also with this effect. This formulation is not in the least to reduce all reality to economics, nor the various dimensions of social structure to whatever aspect happens to be dominant. Structures are always multifunctional or, better, multi-effectual; but they remain both autonomous institutionally and structurally integral to the reproduction of the social relations of production. Descent, marriage and inheritance are regulated in all societies by kinship (whether or not this is represented through a particular set of religious and ideological institutions); and in all societies the relationship between human beings and the supernatural is regulated and explicated by religion of a greater or lesser degree of theoretical sophistication. Yet not all societies are dominated by either kinship or religious systems; and the explicit function of these regulatory systems alone, where they represent the dominant mode of public and private discourse, cannot in itself explain this pre-eminence: another function must also be in play. And this function must be that of a social relation (or set of relations) of production. By the same token, Marx clearly envisaged the forces of production themselves as a relation of production, since they entail both the means of production and the ways in which production is carried on (see the passage already cited from volume 3 of *Capital*, in which the forces of production are described as the 'methods of labour and thereby its social productivity'). These are clearly 'economic' relationships, yet in the great majority of traditional societies this process – the labour process – is assured and reproduced precisely through sets of practices and social-institutional arrangements which have no such transparently 'economic' appearance: kinship arrangements, family structures and a gendered division of labour, caste and lineage attributions, age-sets, or legal statuses, all representing particular forms of political organization, all functioning as a particular set of social relations of production. In other words, the fundamental point to bear in mind is not what social relations appear to be – politics, kinship, religion – but what their role is; or, if this is too teleological a formulation, what their effect is in the totality of social relationships. It is the historian's task to locate the nature of the dominance of a particular dimension, and to find out how it has evolved also as the representative form of the relations of production. But this is not to fall into a functionalist mode of argument. 'Function' and 'necessity' can be used in both a weak and a strong sense. The contingent effects of social reproductive practices amount, amongst other emergent consequences and practices, to the maintenance of particular structures, chiefly relations of production. In this sense, we may speak of the function of a particular combination of practices insofar as their combination has certain effects. And it is precisely because the intentions of human agents are constrained within the cultural possibilities opened to them by the totality of practices in their society that their unintentional effects causally contribute to the reproduction of those culturally limiting or delimiting sets of relationships and practices. Where major transformations or shifts in relationships occur, we can expect also to find breakdowns in the effectiveness of cultural constraints on the relevant practices; and the site of such ruptures is likely also to be the site of contradictory relations of production.

In the second place, human beings in social contexts occupy a multiplicity of roles – as Roy Bhaskar has emphasized – and the institutions which such roles constitute are also multifunctional and multi-effectual, insofar as they bear a dialectical relationship with other institutions, roles and individuals. This is a point stressed also in the work of Mann and Runciman as well as of much post-structuralist writing, albeit with very different emphases and intentions. The 'economic' is therefore to be understood in its wider sense, the 'production and reproduction of everyday life', a point made by Engels himself in his attempt to stem the development of more reductionist applications of Marxist theory.[49]

Now crucially, it is human practice that actually constitutes both economic and other activities in the totality of social life. Economic relations are thus also multi-faceted – practices which have an economic aspect in one context or field of action have also, and inescapably, cultural and social aspects. Equally, social practice in general is normally commensurate with social reproductive practice, and hence with the reproduction and maintenance of a particular set of production relations – economic relations. Without the fact of surplus production, which permits social formations to change, there can be no quantitative movements in the accumulation and expression of power, and no qualitative shifts in economic relations. In this respect it seems to me both logical and necessary to see economic relations as determining and delimiting the possibilities for change, advance or regression in human societies. One could argue from the standpoint of the cultural and symbolic effects/function of social relationships in respect of the way societies appear to work. However, the explanatory priority Marxists attribute to the economic aspect of social relations (that is, to their effects as social relations of production) exists precisely because it is productive activity and human labour, the labour process and the technical level of the means of production, combined in a series of particular ways and giving rise to particular types of social and economic relationships (the mode of production) which determine the possibilities open to each specific social formation.

As I have noted already, this position is not congenial to either Runciman or to Mann, who adduce three or four mutually interdependent but non-reducible dimensions of social power. Runciman, for example, argues that to suggest that one dimension is determinant of all the others in any way, except when merely the effect of a specific historical conjuncture, is both untestable and represents an a priori pre-emption of analysis. But the difficulty with this is that it defines the level at which analysis is to take place – that at which economic, ideological and coercive power interact to effect changes in, or the direction of, practices – also on an aprioristic basis. For as I will suggest, both Mann's and Runciman's microanalytical frameworks are actually aimed at (and, in their own terms, effective at) a level of analysis which itself deals with consequences or relationships, and must first be situated within a primary framework or dynamic structure.

It could similarly be pointed out that the three basic modes of the distribution of power elaborated by Runciman tend to function as descriptive and evaluative categories, but are not explanatory of causal relationships. As Runciman himself admits, the valuable notion of 'the competitive selection of practices' which he elaborates in his opening argument is valid at a descriptive level – but it can only answer the question: how does this selection come about in terms of an essentially functional response? Certain practices were competitively selected (that is, they survived better in their context) because they had the effects, in a specific historical and cultural situation, of meeting the specific demands of social structural reproduction – which is not to suggest that they were therefore necessarily the more 'efficient' from an outside standpoint: cultural and ideological 'needs' are vital in this respect. He shows very well how this schema works also for paths of social evolution which turned out to be either dead ends, or to lead to major transformations. Yet this seems to be much the same, in its results and some of its assumptions, as the formulation of Godelier. For it appears to me, contrary to what Runciman claims, that all his examples rest upon what are, in the last analysis, essentially economic criteria: threats to, shifts in, and realignments of the social relations of production, albeit expressed through different cultural-ideological means and represented by different institutional responses in different societies.

The difference between Runciman and Mann, on the one hand (and I pass over the considerable differences between them), and the historical materialist position which I am arguing here, on the other, thus lies in the types of social praxis one identifies as autonomous, and the degree of structural and causal primacy one wishes to attribute to them, as well as in a rather different theory of human agency, mentioned in an earlier section of this chapter. In addition, some of the differences stem from the context within which one wishes to employ these types of social praxis in the posing of specific questions. Obviously, the framework within which questions are posed and the nature of the answers one seeks has a basic functional relevance for the types of questions which can be asked. A Marxist approach takes social relations of production – along with forces of production – as primary because, as Mann also suggests, using different criteria, human history taken as a whole demonstrates a qualitative evolution in both wealth and power, and because this has been based upon the gradual but increasingly intensive production, exploitation and distribution of economic resources, even if this occurs in a partial, sporadic and uneven way (the 'weak impulse' and 'torch-relay' metaphors of Elster and others are apposite here). But this, of course, tells us little or nothing about the location, probability, rapidity, extent or frequency of such developmental change.[50] It is in this context precisely that class struggle between groups with different and contradictory relations to the means of production becomes important (whether or not it remains a potential or expressed quantity, mediated through political-ideological institutions or through violence); and it is for this reason that Marx was quite correct when he asserted that human history has been the history of class struggle (a concept which I will define more exactly in the next section).

A more agnostic approach to the problem of determination, as adopted by both Mann and Runciman in their different ways, prefers a plurality of interrelated causal elements which determine and overdetermine one another according to context – time, place, structure. This pluralism itself constitutes a rejection of a key element of Marxist social and historical theory. But the taxonomy of analysis employed (as opposed to the degree of causal autonomy attributed to specific elements within it) is not necessarily without value to a historical materialist framework: the dialectical relationships between institutions, roles and practices are taken for granted in Marxist analysis. The task for Marxists, it seems to me (and as Godelier in particular has emphasized), is to demonstrate how and why apparently non-economic relationships can be effective as relations of production.

Finally, Runciman in particular directs his level of analysis and explanation at the specific and conjunctural interstices of the societies he examines. But this represents a level which has already moved away from, and taken for granted, the fundamental delimiting/facilitating (or enabling) structure of economic relationships, a point I have raised already. It deals with phenomenal forms, as they have evolved in each culture-specific and tradition-bound case. His three dimensions of social power are therefore already inscribed within their determinant (economic) frame of reference and possibility. His analysis revolves around the micro- and meso-structural elements of social practice, and seeks to elucidate the multifactorial and emergent characteristics of their interaction. But this is, in itself, no challenge to a heuristic approach which sees economic terms of reference as ultimately determinant, since it is perfectly clear – and again, as any practising Marxist historian would emphasize – that at this level the 'economic' plays only very rarely a direct or visible role in the movement of social forces, the social-psychological 'interests' (that is, perceptions) and intentional activities of social actors, or the structuring of state policies and the forms which the social relations of production actually assume in the process of their reproduction. In this sense, of course, and as Miliband has also noted, the work of Skocpol, Mann and Runciman is as much a challenge to Marxists to actually apply their theories on the ground through detailed empirical work as it is to the premises of a historical materialist conception as such.

The argument has been made pointedly by Norman Geras. In replying to the assertions of Mouzelis (that all versions of Marxism embody a reductionist tendency, subtly 'downgrading' the political, even when it is attributed with a relative autonomy, to the level of agency and conjuncture, without granting it the weight required for its different forms or institutional structures to be theorized in their own right), Geras remarks that what this actually represents is the noticeable underdevelopment of the political within Marxist thinking. And in fact (and as Hall, for example, has also noted), this 'underdevelopment' is by no means confined just to Marxist research. In practice, however, Marxists have rejected notions of absolute autonomy of the political because, in the historical materialist perspective, the competing influences, limits and pressures imposed by the economic aspect of such relationships (i.e. structures of exploitation and class) carry more causal weight. But relative autonomy is no less real, as Geras insists, because it is relative: 'the judgement they [Marxists] make here, concerning the explanatory primacy of relations of production and class' is not 'an a priori truth: it is an empirical hypothesis, albeit of long historical range'.[51] And it is worth adding that while the economic is determinant, it is no more autonomous than any other relation or level or field within a social formation. How could it be, if it is taken as a set of relations with practical effects rather than of social institutions? Relations of production no more float free than political, ideological, coercive or any other structures of a social formation, since relations of production are precisely social relations of a social formation taken in their economic aspect. This is precisely what is represented by the combination of different modes of production in a particular social formation, and gives different social formations dominated by the same basic mode of production (or combination of such) their uniqueness and distinctive *modus operandi*. This is what makes different developments and forms of organization possible within the same basic system of economic relations – as understood from the political economy point of view. And it is these other, 'non-economic' aspects of social relations of production which can overdetermine and react back upon their economic effects to bring on crises and even overcome them by opening the way to transformations at all levels, even though the solutions to such crises are also and in turn constrained by the totality of the social relations of production: that is, by the limits set up by the multiple combination of elements which make up the 'economic structure' of society in Marx's formulation. This is precisely what historians and historical sociologists are concerned with. But it does not mean that the economic is only one element in a group of equivalent values – a point I will emphasize in the following chapters.

What we have to do with, therefore, are the numerous differential values or effects of social praxis in respect of the reproduction of daily life. Each individual member of a social formation occupies a range of different positions on the grid of social praxis. In other words, each combination of social practices or roles has a different effect. Such positions all possess two qualities: they contribute causally to the maintenance and reproduction of a number of sets of relationships with other members of the society; and they furnish the actor/bearer with a set of perceptions of self and, therefore, of the world. Different cultural formations will highlight or prioritize different roles or positions according to their symbolic universe and the political ideologies which are refined out of that symbolic universe. But it is the modern analyst who has to decide which combinations of social relations causally contribute towards the breakdown or transformation of certain social and cultural reproductive practices, and how new practices (and where possible, why particular practices only) evolve. It seems to me that it is ruptures within the pattern of social reproductive practice – within the social relations of production and distribution of surpluses – rather than in the extension or contraction of power relations or shifts in patterns of belief (which are themselves constrained by, but may determine the phenomenal form of, the relations of production, the degree of surplus appropriation and the nature of its distribution, as I will argue) which are determinant.

This is not to deny that human praxis is both dialectical and constitutive of, as well as being patterned or constituted by, the pre-existing structures of practice into which each member of a society is born. On the contrary, this multifactorial and dialectical model of human social relations is crucial to a properly materialist understanding of society. In the subjective experience of daily life most activities are granted an equivalent value in the social whole of existence. Only when specific questions or problems arise are some given a specific, and explanatorily functional, significance. Thus it is with historical and sociological explanation. In order to arrive at an understanding not just of the fact of change, but of its trajectory, we need to locate a dynamic or motor, we need to highlight for functional reasons of explanation and clarification specific relationships, which can then be related back to the actual causal sequences and structures which affect the social formations in question. The historian, in attempting to determine the factors underlying change, however limited in scope, will be drawn back to those elements which constrain, limit, promote or dissolve economic, political, legal and cultural forms and practices. Those factors are, I would argue, always to be found in the functional realm of the economic.

5. States and Social Formations: Modes of Power Distribution vs. Mode of Production

Runciman defines his typology of state formations on the basis of their different modes of the distribution of power. In all, he elaborates some fourteen different modes, covering the simplest social formations through to modern industrial societies. Five categories are listed which are relevant to us, all representing, for Runciman, developed forms of a fundamentally patrimonial set of power relationships. These are: those in which there is a fundamental distinction between citizens and non-citizens; between warriors and subjects; between a bureaucracy serving a ruler, and the body of citizens or subjects; the feudal type, where power is decentralized and in the hands of a magnate class; and the bourgeois type, where the dominant group is actually located in the 'middle', between the mass of citizens or subjects and an absolute ruler.[52]

This typology both cuts obliquely across political-ideological as well as economic relationships; and addresses an already evolved set of social practices. It will readily be seen that all the definitions represent political organizational structural forms, rather than directly economic ones. As a general typology, it also cuts across the Marxist framework of modes of production (ideal types of social relations of production) and social formations (actual historical examples of those ideal types, generally in combination). Runciman's schema is also one of ideal types, as he admits; although there is an interesting tension here, so that he feels compelled to give special treatment to 'hybrids' (such as ancient Babylonia and Anglo-Saxon England in the tenth–eleventh centuries).[53]

But this tension actually reveals a major problem. For Runciman elaborates his schema in terms of actual historical societies, extrapolating the five major modes of power distribution that concern us from them. Assuming we were to accept this choice of types, he is still clearly unhappy about societies that cannot be made to fit the models neatly. Now, a set of ideal types is meant to describe not just an appropriate set of variants on actually existing systems, but a set of coherent structures and relationships which are conceptually necessary to the construction of a causal explanation of such systems, on the basis of certain common denominators. There are always examples which do not fit any schema precisely. Indeed, given the infinite degree of variation between actual social formations, most societies demonstrate inconsistencies or awkward elements. There seems little point in trying to explain all hybrids as such, and thus placing them outside the schema, since the result is to nullify the theoretical value of having such a schema in the first place. The same problem arose with Balibar's notorious 'transitional' mode of production. Either we take the conceptual framework as adequate, and within the bounds of which all variables can be explained; or we abandon it, and treat each historical example as an *ad hoc* variant on the theme 'distribution of social power'. For the former, of course, we need to generate a conceptual framework which is both sophisticated and flexible enough to do this convincingly. In practice, Runciman uses his schema purely as a useful sorting-code: on the basis of certain descriptive traits in respect of the distribution of power and political organization, societies of a particular technological and socio-economic type can be grouped in five modes. Those that do not fit the pattern are dealt with as 'hybrids'. And this does not seem to me to provide us with any sort of model generative of causal explanation.

The ideal types thus tend to be concretely exemplified in actual historical terms, contrasting, therefore, with the concept of mode of production, which represents a specific theoretical space within which, heuristically, various social formations can be thought.

The concepts 'mode of production' and 'social formation' have been to a large extent taken for granted in the foregoing, but they deserve further discussion at this point. For there has been a good deal of debate, among both Marxists and non-Marxists, on this subject. I will deal with the questions this debate has raised in chapters 3 and 4, but I should like to deal with a few fundamental points here, if only to justify my continued use of the terms.

To begin with, mode of production tends to be employed in one of at least three ways which are, in the last analysis, mutually exclusive, and certainly confusing. In the first case, the term is applied to historically verifiable instances of the structure of the labour process, which are then generalized and universalized to provide a series of 'types' of productive organization: the domestic mode, the peasant mode, the nomadic mode and so on. As has been cogently pointed out by Frank Perlin, however, this parcellization of instances or types of labour organization provides in the end only a description, divorced from the original social-economic conditions in which it arose and applied arbitrarily to any social formation which exhibits signs of this particular set of relationships. This method has been described elsewhere as the 'fetishising of "organizational forms", a focus upon finite institutions and production units at the expense of the wider sets of generative relationships of which they form part'. And as we have already seen, the techniques of production and the nature of the labour-process are only one element in the set of relations which make up a mode of production in Marx's sense.[54] Such a procedure has no analytic or heuristic value at all in respect of the search for causal relationships. It does not help us to see either how the relations of production, appropriation and distribution of social wealth are achieved, nor how the production, accumulation, distribution and redistribution of surplus wealth is integrated into a process of social reproduction of the society in question as a totality. Neither does it help to motivate political power relations except as a *deus ex machina*, thus failing to attain one of the fundamental purposes of materialist analysis.

A second approach involves the confusion of the concept mode of production, and the ideal-typical economic relationships each mode describes, with actual historical social formations, and the corollary, the identity of a mode of production on the basis of institutional forms familiar from a given historical example generally accepted as belonging to the mode in question. The best example, of course, is provided by the debate over feudalism, in which, according to this view, societies can only be 'feudal' if their institutional arrangements approximate to those of western Europe at the appropriate time; but there are other examples. Likewise, modes of production proliferate as descriptive terms applied to specific types of social formation which, according to the organization of the dominant labour process, do not appear to fit into any of the 'classical' modes. Thus we read of the African mode, for example, or indeed of the Asiatic mode which, while never intended by Marx to be employed in this way, tends to be used negatively of all those social formations which cannot be fitted into one of the other established modes.[55]

Finally, there remains a third variant which more accurately reflects the intentions of Marx in elaborating the concept and applying it to the development of different types of human societies. Here, mode of production is theorized, although of course on the basis of known historical examples, as a set of ideal-typical economic relationships (and bearing in mind what has been said earlier about the definition of 'the economic' in pre- or non-capitalist societies). It does not represent any specific society, but rather one set of possible social relations of production from a limited number of such sets.[56] It is important to emphasize the *limited* here: across the vast terrain of human social-economic evolution, it is possible to reduce the almost infinite variety of forms of socio-economic organization (that is, culturally-determined institutional arrangements) to a relatively small number of ideal-typical sets of economic relationships. Distilled out into their most basic features, there are at most five historical modes of producing, appropriating and distributing wealth and of combining labour-power with the means of production; and each of these has as its corollary certain ecological and organizational conditions necessary to its reproduction.[57] If a mode of production, which represents, therefore, a model of a set of socio-economic relations, has been adequately theorized (that is to say, if the relations between its constituent elements are coherent) it should serve as a heuristic device intended to suggest what questions should be asked of the evidence about a particular set of social and economic relationships, and how one can set about understanding the disparate and disjointed historical data as representative of a dynamic social totality.

It was Marx's great achievement to have presented just such an analysis for capitalist relations of production as a general type, based on his painstaking researches on nineteenth-century British and European economies, and his elucidation of a series of 'laws' which govern the enormous complexity of capitalist production and exchange relations. Fundamental to the efficacy of his analysis and its social scientific value was the simple fact that he was able to demonstrate that, however different the various forms of capitalist economy actually were, they all operated on the same fundamental principles. 'Capitalism' was thus, for Marx, an ideal-type, a heuristic model of social-economic relations – a mode of production – while at the same time 'capitalist' was a descriptive term adequately applied to a wide range of actually existing social formations in which the set of production relations and forces of production described by that term were dominant.

In the process of analysing capitalist relations of production, Marx inevitably had to think about social-economic relationships which were clearly of a non-capitalist nature, and it was in this way that his partial and often relatively uninformed (by modern standards) conceptualizations of the 'primitive communist', 'slave', 'ancient' and 'feudal' modes came into being. Of course, Marx never devoted as much attention to theorizing these modes as thoroughly as he did capitalism, which has opened the door to a great deal of discussion on just these issues. But he grounded his ideas on feudal relations in his studies of the late ancient and medieval history of western and central Europe. He took as his descriptive term for the fundamental features of the set of economic relationships he found the word 'feudal' because it was the dominant term current among historians at the time to describe the medieval societies they dealt with. It described in particular a set of juridical and institutional relationships which had come into existence over the period from the sixth/seventh to the ninth/tenth centuries, based upon a particular organization of labour-power and surplus appropriation (dependent peasant tenants of varying degrees of social subordination paying rent in kind, services or cash to their landlords) within the structure of a particular system of political power relations (the feudal 'pyramid' of subinfeudation and vassalage rooted in mutual military obligation). Marx's initial search was for that generalized system of surplus appropriation and distribution which preceded capitalism in England in particular, and out of which capitalist relations grew. Given the historical and geographical specificity of early capitalism, he was bound to look at the same region for its predecessor. But, just as capitalist relationships can be (and have been) universalized, it seemed to Marx that whatever he found as immediately pre-capitalist must also represent (a) a fundamentally different way of organizing the production of wealth and the appropriation of surplus and, therefore, (b) a 'mode of production' which might similarly be universalized, regardless of the particular institutional characteristics differentiating western European pre-capitalist social formations from those in other parts of the world. It was on this basis that he also set out both to locate other fundamental 'modes of production' upon which the societies and cultures of the past had been based, and to determine the key differentiating elements which distinguished one mode of production from another.

Theoretical justification for a heuristic such as mode of production is not difficult. If it is possible to isolate the fundamental defining characteristics of a capitalist mode of production, it should be possible to do the same for pre- or non-capitalist modes. Where it is successful (and I would argue that it is possible to define a coherent set of relationships necessary to the feudal, slave, ancient and primitive communist or 'lineage' modes, although more discussion needs to be devoted to this) historians have at their disposal an invaluable heuristic device which is both rooted in empirical data and yet makes naive dependence upon it – and the empiricistic/positivistic methodologies which are the consequence of this – unnecessary. It frees historians to employ historical evidence dynamically, to seek to establish on the basis of fruitful hypothesizing bound by the logic of the model – the mode of production – the causal relationships which are the stuff of the historical process, rather than limiting them to the purely descriptive, or to *ad hoc* conjecture. It is also a device which necessarily imposes upon historians a totalizing, holistic approach to social evolution and the process of transformation, a rejection of any compartmentalizing of historical evolution and the search for compatibility in the order of evidence adduced and in the theoretical basis for the explanation of change in each different social formation.

For Marx, therefore, and for contemporary Marxist historians, mode of production refers quite straightforwardly to an ideal-type of a set of economic relationships, consisting of a specific combination of forces and relations of production. 'Forces of production' are taken to refer both to means of production and to the technical levels or methods of production (including the labour-process, which assumes collective labour, that is to say, co-operation); 'relations of production' refers to the way in which the means of production (land, tools, livestock, etc.) are effectively controlled, and by whom; and the ways in which the direct producers are associated with those means of production and with their own labour-power.[58] To a degree, the two sets of criteria overlap; but it is the specific manner in which direct producers and means of production are combined which, in Marx's words, 'distinguishes the different economic epochs of the structure of society from one another', that is, to say, which differentiates one mode of production from another.[59] The fundamental elements necessary to differentiate one mode from another are already clear from Marx's analysis of capitalism, although his discussion of non-capitalist modes is sketchy and incomplete. But the mode of appropriation of surplus, the ways in which the direct producers are combined with the means of production, and the mode of surplus distribution are all crucial. Less explicit in Marx's analysis, but a point I will stress in the following chapters, is the fact that different modes of production place different constraints upon the possibilities for change, on the one hand, and upon the structures of political power, on the other, which are particularly important for an understanding of the internal dynamic of a given historical social formation.

There is a particular difficulty with 'feudalism', a difficulty which has plagued the work of those Marxists in particular who have tried to employ it to analyse various non- or pre-capitalist formations. For it has proved to be extremely difficult to achieve the necessary intellectual distancing from medieval western European history. Too many Marxists have continued to conflate ideal-type with real social formation, so that the latter are constantly defined or not defined as 'feudal' on the basis of whether or not their institutional and social appearance can be directly compared or contrasted with those of medieval Europe. In other words, many historians have applied the term in the first two ways described above, primarily because, it seems to me, there has been neither clarity nor consensus on what should be the fundamental defining elements of a mode, and of the feudal mode in particular – in spite of Marx's fairly clear remarks on this issue. As we have seen, this is itself partly a result of the failure to differentiate between institutional and juridical structures (what Marx sometimes called the superstructure) and the underlying relationships which make their reproduction and their form possible.[60] But this is not to imply either that the problem is easily solved, as we shall see in chapter 3 in the discussion of the tributary mode, and as the foregoing discussion on the nature of 'the economic' has suggested.

And there remains the question of the nature of the tension between the forces of production and the relations of production, the problem of the 'fettering' of the forces by the relations of production which Marx conceived as a prime mover in the process of transformation of production relations and hence of historical change *tout court*. Rather than deal with this entirely at an abstract level (although there exists a number of exemplary treatments of the problem) I will reserve discussion until a later chapter, in which empirical data can be employed to support a specific line of argument.

The term 'social formation' suffers equally from a certain ambiguity in usage. On the one hand, it refers to types of society in general dominated by specific modes of production, such as 'feudal' or 'capitalist' social formation; on the other, it is used to refer to specific historical societies, for example, the Byzantine or late Roman or colonial Indian social formations. I have tended to apply it in the second sense, although I have also generally defined it more exactly by adding further descriptive epithets of both time and place. Although some Marxists have argued that 'social formation' is more analytically useful than 'society' because it has a more open-ended significance and because it implies in the word 'formation' a complex of constituent elements, I do not think that the traditional term 'society' is necessarily inferior – both describe sets of relations of production together with the cultural and institutional contexts necessary to their material and ideological reproduction, and it seems to me that as long as this is borne in mind, there is little to choose between them. Marx mostly used 'society', although the term social formation appears on occasion as an equivalent.[61] In particular, both terms should imply not only complexity of structure – the dialectical nature of human social praxis is clearly central here – but also fluidity and short-term evolution and transformation. The concept of mode of production is at once analytic, because it generates and motivates dynamic social-economic relationships, and also descriptive, because as a concept there inheres in it no actual historical movement. Social formation/society imply human praxis and therefore the dialectics of process, change, transformation and so on. It is only through applying the concepts embodied in mode of production to actual, historically attested social formations that their actual evolutionary trajectory and the causal relationships which this reflects can be grasped. We cannot have one without the other.

In this respect, I think Perlin is wrong to suggest that the concept of mode of production, because of its very success as a macrological concept, cannot grasp the minutiae of social change. He has argued that what he terms the 'macrological' nature of the concept mode of production is itself a hindrance to a deeper understanding of the fluid complexity of short-term historical movement. Reasonably enough, he cites the example of western Europe between the eleventh and fifteenth centuries, a period during which, in spite of the predominantly 'feudal' nature of social relations, a great number of changes took place which substantially altered the appearance of society and modified the ways in which the fundamental relationships functioned.[62] Perlin represents this problem in terms of the traditional dichotomy between the essential (that is, mode of production as representative of the continuous, law-like, 'deep-structured' nature of social evolution) and the contingent (disjointed, event-laden, historical). The problematic has been expressed differently by Braudel's different *durées*. The problem is neatly illustrated in the 'stages' theory of historical development: long stages of stability are connected or punctuated by short periods of 'transition' (the word itself is highly inflected in this context), in which there is an explicit assumption that there are two orders of social process: that which effects no change in the mode of production, and hence in the society under examination; and that which possesses qualities able to transcend or overcome the resistance of a particular mode to fundamental change. In this approach, of course, historians are obliged either to find 'external' influences which upset the internal equilibrium of the system, or to posit some sort of inevitabilist dynamic which achieves the same result – the problem of the 'prime mover', with which I will deal in greater detail in chapter 3.

As far as it goes, I have no objection to this argument. And Perlin has gone on to argue for a more open-ended and dynamic conceptualization of the social process, using the concept of mode of production, yet in a way which refuses to separate causal relationships into lesser and greater degrees. But I do not think that mode of production, in the sense preferred here (as well as by Perlin himself), necessarily generates these failings itself. On the contrary, in conjunction with the notion of social formation or society, it seems to me to possess all the flexibility and dynamism necessary for a sophisticated and nuanced analysis of any societal structure and its evolution. The limitations accurately delineated by Perlin reflect rather the intellectual failings (and the political and cultural contexts) of those who have used the concept in this way.

For it is surely the case that the notion of mode of production is not by itself intended to function at the micro-level of empirical detail: it represents ideal-typical relationships only, and change and process remain, as it were, immanent but unfulfilled. But while it is only through the examination of specific societies that the micro-social relationships and processes can be observed, they cannot in turn be understood as a dynamic and dialectical whole without the concept of mode of production. The two go hand-in-hand.

Of course, it is true that notions such as society or social formation set artificial limits to any analysis, so that the uncritical generation of conceptual and empirical 'boundaries', creating thereby artificial entities as objects of investigation, is always a danger. In particular, and as noted already, there is a danger of seeing certain phenomena as somehow external to whichever 'system' is being treated, so that the descriptively useful but analytically artificial limits established for it take on an inclusive–exclusive character accordingly. Not only does this lead to the creation of an artificially extended range of discreet societies, each with its own economy; causal relationships thus become particularly problematic since a hierarchy of exogenous and endogenous factors must then be constructed in order to relate entities which were never separate in the first place. Perlin cites the case of the role and structural importance of commerce and urban life in medieval England, which were considered by some historians not to be an integral part of the feudal system, yet represent the source of the contradictions which led to its breakdown and the transition to capitalism.

I do not see that these dangers are inherent and inevitable in the concepts themselves, nor that they are averted merely by insisting on a radically open-ended approach. It seems to me that, if we work with the definitions suggested here, we do a great deal to emphasize what I would term the 'structured contingency' of the historical process. Just as importantly, the careful definition and identification within a given historical social formation of those relationships and practices which represent the key elements in a mode of production should be enough to prevent the sort of atemporal rigidity to which Perlin objects. This is especially the case if it is remembered that a mode of production is not an ontologically real system of relations, but a conceptualization of an ideal type. Only if we reify mode of production and conflate it with social formation or society is this a serious danger. The use of mode of production, as a rigorously defined concept, together with the notion of social formation, as the empirical realization of social relations of production and social reproduction, is quite adequate to the task of analysing the process of both long-term and short-term historical change.

There are thus substantial differences between Runciman's pluralist model of the networks of social power and a Marxist approach; the former represents its various modes of the distribution of power chiefly from the point of view of political structures. Both ancient and feudal societies are thus described from the perspective of the dominant forms of political organization, for example, which is seen as the sum of a range of practices and roles, and in turn the expression of the distribution of power. As a descriptive and evaluative procedure this is useful; and since the three modes of production, coercion and persuasion are granted equivalent causal values, shifts within and between them in respect of the practices from which they are constituted are enough to motivate an adequate explanation of the origins and results of change.[63] Social practice is not ignored – on the contrary, it receives a great deal of prominence.

It should be recalled, however, that Runciman's use of the concept 'mode of production' is actually very close to that application of the term described by Perlin and others as 'labour-process' or 'productive organization' fetishism, as discussed already. In this sense, it bears very little relation to the holistic heuristic concept of Marxist analysis. As second-level descriptive categories, however, Runciman's modes are actually very useful. Thus individuals are enabled only by the flexibility of practices (which they embody) to adapt to changes in environment, and hence to mutate or recombine practice in order to retain the economic, ideological or coercive power attached to their roles. There is nothing un-Marxist about such an approach, as Callinicos has recently made very clear.[64] But for Runciman, history appears to be essentially the sum of a series of ever-widening and mutually intersecting 'pools' of ideological, economic and coercive power, in which competition for power is the underlying motive and dynamic.

At this point, definitions of power are crucial. In the discussion to which I have referred so far, power is generally understood as social power, as a generalized means to specific ends. Power is thus control over a variety of types of resource (wealth, people, knowledge), these resources then depending upon the areas of social life in which such ends are to be attained. Power can thus be exercised at a variety of levels – from the most personal (the exercise of power by one individual over another based on resources such as knowledge or the possibility of physical coercion) to the most public (political-military power exercised through authority over armies, police forces, food supplies and so on). But in all these contexts, the exercise of power tends towards an end (even if, in the example of personal physical coercion, bullying, that end is psychological gratification).

From a Marxist viewpoint, power is the political and psychological expression of economic dominance (since resources are, in the end, an essentially economic category), although this element may not necessarily be obvious to the modern commentator nor clearly be conceptualized as such by those who wield it. For as we have seen, social relations of production, and hence control over key areas thereof, are generally represented in an ideological form which has no obvious single economic point of reference. Power is a product of the combination and articulation of human psychology, cultural forms and economic context. And while, as I have said, it is exercised in a relative autonomy from other structures in respect of its immediate effects, it does not spring out of nothing. Power, coercion and ideology are forms or expressions of praxis. They are modes through which particular sets of relationships can be maintained and reproduced. Power may indeed be central to social theory. But the struggle for, attainment and exercise of power is about resources, and must by definition be understood within the limits and possibilities set by the existing forces and relations of production.[65]

The general validity of a Marxist theory of modes of production determined, in the first instance, by the fundamental differences between contradictory systems of political economy can now be reaffirmed. Within this set of categories there is, of course, plenty of room for a second-level taxonomy of political and power structures, such as that elaborated on the basis of practices and roles by Runciman. It is thus possible partly to agree with him when he states:

> study of societies is the study of people in roles, and the study of people in roles the study of the institutional allocation of power; and since power is of three irreducible but interdependent kinds, societies can be modelled as catchment areas of three-dimensional space in which roles are vectors whose relative location is determined by the rules of the institutions made up of them

but in which power (in its 'three irreducible forms') is understood as both a real product of social praxis and a function of social reproduction.

The value of the historical materialist approach lies in its economic specificity. Broadly-defined modes of production enable the historian to suggest for different social formations positions on a grid of social relations of production, in respect of both the general dynamic of the social formation, and the ways in which economic relations are expressed institutionally through different sets of roles and practices – that is, structures. It also places limits on the types of state formations, for example, which may develop under the conditions of specific relations of production, and provides thereby a second causal explanatory framework for understanding how change occurs and why. In chapters 3, 4 and 5, I will examine particular medieval state formations within the terms of reference of the tributary (feudal) mode of production – defined in respect of the fundamental economic relationships which differentiate it from other modes, rather than through a description of its institutional forms.

6. The Feudal or the Tributary Mode?

The concept of the feudal mode of production has, of course, like those of all the modes mentioned by Marx at different points in his writings, been the subject of heated debates within historical materialism, and of criticism from without.[66] The criticism from non-Marxists has generally taken the form of disagreement over the supposed economic reductionism of the concept or, from the historians in particular, its lack of historical specificity and institutional continuity across cultures. While I do not wish to embark upon a full-scale discussion of all the debates necessary to resolve these questions here, a few salient points are in order before we can move on. The first point has in any case already been addressed. The second point, regarding the lack of historical specificity of the concept, can be answered in two ways. In the first instance, it might be pointed out that a mode of production, as a theoretical model of an ideal-type of sets of relations of production, is not meant to have any historical specificity (except insofar as we generally assume that the 'feudal' or tributary mode, or the slave mode, are generally most useful when discussing pre-industrial or non-industrial social formations). It is intended as a heuristic device against which particular types of historical social formations can be compared, and through which guidance for further questioning of the primary data can be obtained. It helps to suggest interpretative possibilities, to establish the limits of what is a possible or reasonable explanation of the causal relationships which pertained in a given social-economic structure. In the second instance, it can be argued that its lack of specificity in respect of institutional continuities depends on how one understands 'institutional'. If we expect to find the same forms of institutional organization in all those societies said to represent a feudal/tributary mode of production, we will be disappointed. If, on the other hand, we are looking for similar patterns of social relations of production (between producers and non-producers, or with regard to the modes of surplus appropriation and distribution, and so forth), then a mode of production is quite specific – it describes the ideal form of these fundamental economic relationships, and is in consequence a very valuable instrument for narrowing down the field of possible interpretations of the empirical data.

But the main debate has been about the degree to which the tributary (or 'feudal') mode can be extended to cover a much wider range of social formations than those whose phenomenal forms and institutional arrangements resemble or approximate to those of the two most widely-recognized 'feudal' societies *par excellence*, medieval western Europe from the ninth century, and medieval Japan from the eleventh century. In this context, it needs to be remembered that the history of the concept 'feudalism' has in large part been the history of European historians attempting to understand the essence of European culture. With this in mind, it is surely time that historians made the leap from a descriptive methodology whose roots lie in eighteenth-century humanist empiricism, to a broader and more analytical approach. A re-working of concepts such as feudalism, in which Europe no longer figures as the empirical focus and the measure of other social and cultural systems, but in which sets of social and economic relationships have a value for the analysis of other societies and histories, has been one of the obvious results of the expansion of European historical awareness to non-European social formations. It has also been one of the most valuable contributions to practical research as well as theory made by Marxists. I have argued for a broad application of the concept of feudalism, for example,[67] since it is within the general framework of sets of relations of production organized along tributary or 'feudal' lines that the appropriate pre-capitalist formations can be discussed, rather than with a plethora of cross-cutting sub-categories (potentially one of the results of the method invoked by both Mann and Runciman).

As we will see, 'feudalism' (I will continue to employ the traditional term for the moment) can be understood as the basic and universal pre-capitalist mode of production in class societies. It coexists with other modes, of course, but the set of economic relationships which marks it out has tended historically to be dominant. And it is worth recalling two important points. First, Marx never evolved a single, coherent theory of feudalism. On the contrary (and according to the purpose of his particular argument) he varied between a descriptive and empirical Eurocentric approach, in which the specific characteristics of European feudal social formations dominate, and a much broader theoretical exposition of feudal relations of production. Second, he arrived at his modes via theoretical abstraction from empirical data ('historical facts') collected from each historical social formation as a whole, and assembled in a hierarchy of types according to the level of productive forces in each example, in order to be able to make such broad generalizations.

As far as concerns feudalism, the chief characteristics consist in the following key, differentiating propositions: (1) that the extraction of rent, in the political economy sense of feudal rent, under whatever institutional or organizational guise it appears (whether tax, rent or tribute) is fundamental; (2) that the extraction of feudal rent as the general form of exploitation of pre-capitalist autarkic peasantries does not depend on those peasantries being tenants of a landlord in a legalistic sense, but that non-economic coercion is the basis for appropriation of surplus by a ruling class or its agents; and (3) that the relationship between rulers and ruled is exploitative and contradictory in respect of control over the means of production.

Now, as has recently been forcefully pointed out, this fundamental class structure 'corresponds to and is determined by that level of productive forces which roughly speaking emerged with the Neolithic revolution, and comprises field cultivation based on organic energy plus hand implements, capable of sustained surplus production as well as reproduction of the peasant family'.[68] In its historical specificities, the feudal mode is represented in social formations where these conditions and production relations dominate. But at the same time, each society develops its own particular institutional practices and ideological forms through which those relations are lived, founded on pre-given cultural traditions; and the states which arise, or are imposed upon, parts or all of such cultural formations will be correspondingly different in their forms and in their ideological and legitimating practices.

It is important to recognize, however, that the word 'feudal' continues to be employed by Marxist historians and social scientists in this sense because it is a historically-determined, inherited and convenient label. Reluctance to accept its wider application by some historical materialist thinkers and by most non-Marxists is clearly bound up with a (mostly) Eurocentric historiographical semantics, which hankers after a historically-specific correspondence between a technical term and the categories to which it is applied. 'Feudalism' is still a term which invokes particular historical societies. And alternatives have proved difficult to agree upon or find acceptance.

As I have already suggested, there is a viable alternative, embodied in the 'tribute-paying' mode outlined by Samir Amin, although it has to be redefined somewhat. Wickham has already pointed to this possibility and, without wishing to enter a major new debate at this point, it will be worthwhile making a few comments on this. According to Wickham, Amin's 'tributary' mode (or 'tribute-paying mode') was intended to replace the defunct 'Asiatic' mode. In fact, Amin argues that the feudal mode itself represents merely a developed form of this mode, so that the tributary mode can be seen as 'the most widespread form' of pre-capitalist class society, and that which, as a rule, always succeeds the primitive communal mode. It is the tribute-paying mode which 'when it assumes an advanced form, almost always tends to become feudal – that is, the ruling class ousts the community from *dominium eminens* of the soil'. The feudal mode, for Amin, appears as a 'borderline' or 'peripheral' case of the tributary mode, marked out by the specific nature of the degradation of the community in respect of its control over the land, and consequently its means of subsistence and reproduction.

In fact, this is a somewhat artificial distinction, since based upon a legalistic differentiation between peasant and landlord control over the means of production. In both of his modes, tributary and feudal, the essential process of surplus appropriation is the same, as is the economic relationship (however defined juridically) between producers and means of production. Once more, in Amin's words:

> The tribute-paying mode of production is marked by the separation of society into two main classes: the peasantry, organized in communities, and the ruling class, which monopolizes the functions of the given society's political organization and exacts a tribute (not in commodity form) from the rural communities.

And further:

> Characteristic of this [i.e. tribute-paying] mode is the contradiction between the continued existence of the community and the negation of the community by the state; and also, as a result of this, the confusion of the higher class that appropriates the surplus with the class that is dominant politically. This circumstance makes it impossible to reduce production relations to legal property relations, and compels us to see

production relations in their full, original significance as social relations arising from the organization of production.

This description in no way contradicts the standard, traditional historical materialist definition of feudal relations of production at the basic level of mode of surplus appropriation and mode of combination of direct producers with means of production. What varies between Amin's tributary and feudal modes is simply the degree of control exercised by the ruling class, or the state or state class over the community. So that, while this certainly affects the rate of exploitation, it does not affect the actual nature of the mode of surplus appropriation.

Elster has argued that the distinction between 'feudal' and 'tributary' modes needs to be retained, since while the two modes may be indistinguishable from the point of view of the producers (that is, surplus labour – in the form of tax or rent – extracted from a smallholding peasantry) the nature of those who have effective control over the means of production (resting ultimately on coercion, and regardless of legal arrangements and so on) varies (that is, the state as opposed to a ruling class of landlords), so that this must be taken into consideration in any discussion of the promotion or fettering of the forces by the relations of production. As we will see in the next chapter, Wickham supports this insofar as he believes that tax and rent constitute two different modes of surplus extraction. But I will show that this is not the case: the fundamental difference between these two forms of the same mode of surplus extraction lies in fact in a political relation of surplus appropriation and distribution.[69]

I would suggest, in consequence, that one way to avoid the semantic confusion (between non-Marxists and Marxists, in the first instance, but also between Marxists themselves) which has been at the root of so many discussions would be to adopt the terms 'tributary mode' and 'tributary production relations' and so on to replace the terminology of a feudal mode. By adopting such terms and applying them henceforth to those relationships of production and surplus appropriation hitherto described under the rubric 'feudal', we would be free to limit this latter term to specifically political and juridical forms, which is to say, those which prevailed in European societies from the ninth or tenth century up to the sixteenth, broadly speaking. The term 'feudal' would now describe the political and institutional constitution of a specific social formation (or of specific social formations), based upon tributary relations of production, but distinguished by particular juridical relationships, rather than an abstract model of a particular set of political economy relationships, a mode of production, as hitherto.

It may well be, of course, that Marxists will not be happy to abandon a conceptual category such as feudalism as a mode of production so readily. But that is a separate debate, and I will not go further into the question at this point. For the purposes of my arguments in this book, I will gloss the traditional terminology with the term 'tributary' or 'tribute-paying', in respect of mode of production and mode of surplus appropriation; but not in respect of those institutional forms typical of medieval European society from the ninth to the sixteenth century. In this respect, it will generally be clear from the context whether or not the term 'feudal' is employed in this political and constitutional sense.

It is in terms of the tributary/feudal mode, therefore, that I will begin my discussion of the medieval state formations referred to at the beginning of this chapter. My intention is to demonstrate two main points: (1) that whatever the degree of autonomy a state structure and the elite personnel which staff it may appear to show, however extended their institutionalized power may be, both in ideological terms and in real terms, its historical development and its potential for transformation are determined by economic relations, by the social relations of production which breathe life into it, and which represent the specific modal determinants and constraints (through the infinity of possible culture-specific institutional forms) operating upon it; (2) states can only act autonomously from the ruling class of their social formation for a limited period and under certain ideological-political conditions. When they oppose the interests of a ruling class in such a way as to endanger the potential for that class to reproduce itself and maintain its accustomed position (as it perceives it), a political and structural crisis may follow; where they are successful in promoting an independent line which is antagonistic to the interests of a dominant social class, the result is usually the collapse or fragmentation of the state. Even where the state is able to constitute an effective ruling class itself, the maintenance and reproduction of such an elite has usually been determined by the possibilities inscribed within the relations of production and, more specifically (as I will argue in chapter 4), the relations of surplus distribution.

It is through the institutional forms which express these relations of production that such an examination must take place, since it is the historical forms specific to each social-cultural formation which the historical data represent. In this book, I have chosen to look at pre-capitalist states and societies dominated by feudal, that is to say, tributary relations of production, and for two reasons: first, this provides the possibility of examining quite different manifestations of a single basic mode of surplus appropriation; secondly, it provides the common ground on which to examine the internal dynamic and structure of states in very different temporal, political-geographical and cultural environments. The point is to avoid a simple comparativism, and to demonstrate the underlying structural unity of the constraints (in their various contextually-determined forms) imposed by feudal relations of production upon state formations.

But first, I will begin with a more detailed discussion of the tributary/feudal mode itself, the heuristic category from the point of view of which these states are to be examined.

3

The Tributary Mode: the Dominant Mode of Production in Pre-Capitalist Class Societies

1. The Tributary Mode in South-East Europe and Anatolia – the Byzantine Model

As I have noted, the debate among historians and social scientists over the adequacy or not of concepts such as 'feudalism' has been a prominent feature of historiographical discussion for many years. For both Marxists and their critics, the debate has focused in particular on the question of how such concepts are to be employed, and what exactly their content is supposed to be. For historical materialist discussion especially the ways in which theoretical categories such as mode of production can be invoked to understand complex historical societies has been a central issue. In what follows, and bearing in mind recent contributions on the problems confronting Marxists in their use and understanding of the concept mode of production, and more specifically, whether or not pre-capitalist modes of production can be considered as having a universal applicability and heuristic value, I will look at the relevance of this debate for an understanding of both the problems of transition in past social formations, as well as its own role in contemporary historical (and political) analysis. I shall concentrate on a specific theoretical problem, that is, how the concept of the tributary mode of production is to be understood; and on a specific historical question, namely, to what extent can the social formation of the Byzantine empire, which dominated Asia Minor and the Balkans from the seventh to the thirteenth century, be described as dominated by tributary production relations and, concomitantly, what sort of state formation does it represent? And it is worth emphasizing here that I have chosen to examine the Byzantine state, along with the other state formations discussed in this book, for the most part precisely because it has traditionally been denied that they were representative of, or dominated by, 'feudal', which is to say tributary, production relations at all, at least until relatively late in their history (and as a result, more often than not, of 'external' influences or pressures). Yet, as I will try to demonstrate, it is through the tributary mode and the relations of production, appropriation and distribution of surplus which typify it, that the political forms and evolution of these states can be most clearly understood. For, as I noted in chapter 2, it is precisely in determining the character of a mode of production that an account is given of the specific combination of the forces and relations of production which it involves.

From the point of view of the first question noted above, there have been a number of attempts to define more rigorously the concepts of various modes of production through which the social, economic and political structures of ancient and medieval societies can best be understood.[1] This debate has linked in with discussion both inside and outside Marxism on the nature of ancient and medieval state formations and on the structure of pre-capitalist societies viewed from the social anthropological perspective.[2] From the historical perspective, attention has centred on the question of the nature of the transition between ancient and medieval socio-economic and political structures, notably – and with an obviously Eurocentric bias – that from the ancient or post-classical world of the late Roman state (and the various cultures throughout the Mediterranean region which it subsumed) to the medieval and 'feudal' world of Europe after the fifth and sixth centuries.[3] On the question of the validity of this equally Eurocentric periodization, in particular in respect of the notion of a qualitative difference between forms and structures of 'ancient' as opposed to 'medieval' societies, I shall have more to say at the end of this chapter. But it is within the context of these debates that I shall concentrate on the particular historical problem of the nature of the East Roman, or Byzantine, social formation.

Importantly for this discussion, Byzantium has come to represent for many, at least from the European perspective, the classic example of a social formation which failed conspicuously to develop 'full' feudal relations of production in the medieval period. This attitude is in part to be ascribed to the nature of the definition of feudalism employed, which relates quite specifically to the political structures and institutional forms of western European society in the High Middle Ages. Most western Byzantinists (the vast majority of them not being Marxists), for example, refuse to concede that Byzantine society was ever feudal; or that, if it was, then only at the very end of its long history, from the twelfth and thirteenth centuries on, and only as a result of western, that is to say, external, influence. In contrast, and using a political-economic definition of the concept, Soviet and East European historians have traditionally split into two opposing parties or camps: those who see 'feudal' relations already in the later Roman period (from the fifth century, but most clearly from the seventh); and those who find evidence for such relations only after the tenth and eleventh centuries. More recently, there has been some move towards accepting elements of the 'western' critique, and to push the development of 'full' feudal relations forward into the thirteenth century and after. As we shall see, the premises upon which such reasoning is based are open to criticism.[4]

For the western historian of the Byzantine world, therefore, feudalism is defined chiefly in terms not of the economic relationships which underlie the phenomenal forms of the political structures of surplus distribution and power, but of the types of political/legal structures themselves – structures of vassalage, enfeoffment, and so on, together with the supporting elements of dependent tenant or serf peasantries, and the fragmentation of judicial and political authority and powers. In other words, and logically enough, Byzantium cannot be considered feudal because its institutional and superstructural appearance never approximated to the appearance of western European feudalism in the tenth century and after. Non-Marxist western Byzantinists who do favour a feudal stage are usually constrained to place its inception in the eleventh century, with the appearance of the *pronoia* system, whereby the state granted the revenue from certain taxes or dues in particular regions or districts, and for limited periods, to individuals in return for (predominantly) military service.[5] But once again, the crucial determining factor for a feudal order is the secondary institution of *pronoia*, one variation of the many forms of the redistribution of surplus wealth by the state (initially), rather than any relation of production.

While these two approaches – the 'legal/institutional' approach of the non-Marxist tradition and the political-economic approach of historical materialism – are not necessarily mutually exclusive, at least in respect of the fact that they were intended functionally to address different sets of questions (although they certainly represent distinct analytical and descriptive strategies), each party to the debate has tended (often for manifestly political-ideological reasons) to ignore the functional value and analytical point of the definition employed by the other. The result is that the discussion has, on the whole, been one in which deliberate obfuscation, misunderstanding and a plethora of alternative and usually mutually exclusive definitions and usages have littered the pages of historical journals. More importantly, and further complicating the issues, Marxists of varying theoretical colours have often, and unwittingly, attempted to describe and discuss 'feudal' societies by combining both economic (Marxist) and institutional (non-Marxist) criteria, in a way which is generally both confusing and analytically of little value to any discussion which attempts to do more than merely describe medieval and early modern societies in isolation.

Soviet and East European historiography up to the mid 1980s, nominally at least Marxist in its theoretical underpinnings, concentrated largely on the question of when Byzantine social relations became feudalized, for example, and this has inevitably involved problematizing the ways in which the state and its institutions intervened at different levels of the social and economic formation. The two positions, which are evident from the late 1950s to the present, can be represented most readily in the work of two scholars, Shtaermann and Syuzyumov. In spite of their differences, both implicitly include in their definition of feudal relations of production also institutional and political organizational forms, which render their discussion extremely problematic from the point of view of feudal (that is, tributary) social relations as representing a mode of production.

Shtaermann presents in many ways a Soviet precursor of Anderson's thesis, which it pre-dates by many years: namely, that 'feudalism' in the West is the result of a synthesis of the Roman slave mode of production with the barbarian tribalism or primitive communalism of the Germanic invaders. In contrast, the Balkans and Anatolia moved directly from the slave mode to the feudal mode, without external stimulus, as the developing relations of landlord–tenant subordination were subsumed within the state's fiscal apparatus, so that the taxes raised by the state can in effect be seen as a centralized form of feudal rent.[6]

Syuzyumov, in contrast, argued that this position denied the concept of revolutionary change altogether, erecting in its place a notion of mechanical synthesis. At the same time he argued that it broadened the concept of the feudal mode to include virtually all forms of dependency and rent-extraction, and rendered it as a result too general to be of any analytical value. Syuzyumov's view was that synthesis of a sort did occur in the West, but only at a much later date; while in the East the strength of the institutions of the ancient state, its ability to extract taxes, and the destruction of the large landholding elite from the seventh century on, delayed the development of feudal relations of production until, in the tenth century, a new class of landed magnates had arisen to challenge the state's interests in respect of the surpluses generated by the agricultural population of the empire. But their rise was itself promoted by the 'war economy' of the imperial state, which succumbed to feudalism chiefly because of the debilitating effects of constant warfare and the requirements of defence.[7] In other words, Syuzyumov considers Byzantine society to have represented a stable combination of forces and relations of production, a combination destabilized by external forces.[8]

From a historical materialist perspective, this seems a barely defensible view, at least in the stark form in which it is expressed by Syuzyumov, if only because the absence of any analysis (or suggestion) of internal contradiction and class conflict, however defined, deprives the description of any dynamic element. In contrast, indeed, another Soviet scholar, Alexander Kazhdan, has argued that it was precisely the internal contradictions of Byzantine society which explain its particular characteristics, a result of the impasse which he sees between developing 'feudal' relations and the economic and ideological structures of the ancient centralized state.[9] Kazhdan has also argued that, while neither 'feudal' nor ancient relations of production were able to assert themselves fully until after the eleventh century (when 'feudalism' finally becomes dominant), the taxes extracted by the ancient state did constitute already a form of 'centralized feudal rent'.[10] As we shall see in the discussion below, however, since tax represents a mode of surplus extraction, the particular form of which is the hallmark of a particular mode of production, there arises a certain contradiction within his argument. I will return to this below.

There is no point here in reviewing the vast Soviet and East European literature of the years before 1988–9 concerned with these issues. But it is worth noting that – with the exception of the more recent work of Khvostova referred to already – the majority of Soviet scholars came to agree that the seventh century marked the end of the ancient world and the accompanying slave mode of production; that there followed a long period of pre- or proto-'feudal' development (as outlined by Kazhdan, for example), succeeded from the eleventh or twelfth century by the full development of 'feudal' relations of production. Within this schema, the debate then concentrated in the 1970s and 1980s on the question of whether or not tax is the equivalent of 'centralized feudal rent'; on the quantitative relationship between independent peasant cultivators and dependent tenants (whether of the Church, state or private landlords); and on the process of erosion of independent peasant holdings and peasant communities subject directly to the fisc, in favour of the expansion of large estates and the gradual 'enserfment' of this formerly free peasantry.[11] All seemed agreed on the crucial role of the state in the development of Byzantine 'feudalism', especially its role in patronizing and promoting what became by the tenth and eleventh century the aristocracy, and its ability to hold back the expansion of aristocratic landholding in the provinces – less deliberately, than through the inertia of the state's institutional apparatuses of fiscal and military administration.[12] Many of these arguments would not be rejected by a majority of western and non-Marxist historians and, indeed, the final position is again not too distant from that espoused by Anderson in his own survey.[13]

For western Marxists, too, the Byzantine state presents a number of problems. And part of the reason for these lies in exactly the problematic outlined in the recent discussion of the transition from the ancient to the 'feudal' mode of production in the West, namely, that of clearly conceptualizing how the feudal mode of production – what I wish to call now the tributary mode – is to be understood in respect of the actual data at the disposal of the historian. Is tax to be assimilated to a centralized form of feudal, that is to say tributary, rent? Was it the institutional inertia of the state apparatuses which neutralized for so long the development of tributary relations of production? What role does ideology play in this picture? – a feature often deliberately avoided or denied any relevance in discussion over the ways in which a particular mode of production is articulated within historical social formations.

2. Tax, Rent and the Tributary Mode

These questions represent several different levels of argument: how is the tributary mode to be conceptualized and invoked in historical discussion? And, in the second place, how is the historical evidence relating to the specific history of our chosen example, the late Roman and Byzantine world, to be understood in the light of any conclusions drawn in answer to the first question? I want, therefore, in the first instance to confront what seems to me to be the crux of the matter – what are the differences, if any, between 'rent' and 'tax' as modes of surplus appropriation; and to what extent can either or both be subsumed under the heading '(centralized) tributary/feudal rent'?

It has been argued[14] that the notion of a tributary mode of production as proposed by Amin,[15] which the latter intended to replace the concept of the Asiatic mode of production (now generally considered in western Marxism to be obsolescent, since rooted in both ambiguities in the writings of Marx in particular, and in misapprehensions and inadequate empirical data on the part of many later 'Marxists'[16]), and to function as a concept within which localized sub-types, such as the ancient mode of production, could be accommodated, provides a useful alternative construct which historians and economic historians might employ to avoid the often sterile discussions about the general application of the notion of 'feudalism'. Feudalism, in Amin's account, is seen as both a peripheral and developed version of the tributary mode. On an alternative interpretation of Amin's thesis, however, the crucial common element which can be used to identify social formations belonging to this mode is identified as tax, a 'public' or 'state' method of surplus appropriation which differentiated it from the feudal mode, distinguished by feudal rent, that is to say, by (coercive) rent-taking, the extraction of surpluses from the direct producers based on extra-economic and 'private' power. At first glance, this distinction between tax and rent, as two different modes of surplus appropriation, seems convincing, and certainly fits the historical data descriptively with regard to the political transition in Europe from ancient to feudal society – rent being the hallmark of feudalism, tax of the ancient (Roman) state.

But this understanding of the differences between tax and rent has been criticized, and the value of a 'traditional', broadly-based definition of the concept of the feudal (tributary) mode re-asserted. Halil Berktay has argued instead that tax and rent are merely two variants of the same mode of surplus appropriation, 'feudal' rent (that is, the general form of surplus appropriation consistent with non-capitalist agricultural exploitation in a class society in which the producers are directly combined with the means of production and, thereby, of their own means of reproduction); so that, as a result, the feudal or tributary mode can be seen as the dominant mode throughout much of the pre-capitalist world. This view finds support in traditional Marxist thinking, as is well known, including the writings of Marx and Engels themselves (although, as is equally well known, neither ever developed an explicit theory either of modes of production or of the process of transition from one mode to another within specific social formations). As Marx said,

> It is furthermore evident that in all forms in which the *direct labourer* remains the 'possessor' of the means of production and labour conditions necessary for the production of his own means of subsistence, the property relationship must simultaneously appear as a direct relationship of lordship and servitude, so that the direct producer is not free; a lack of freedom which may be reduced from serfdom with enforced labour *to a mere tributary relationship*.[17] (my emphases)

It seems to me that, if we are to retain the concept of mode of surplus appropriation as a fundamental element which serves to differentiate one mode of production from another, then this is a crucial point. For both sides of the couplet tax/rent are, in fact, expressions of the political-juridical forms that surplus appropriation takes, not distinctions between different modes. Both tax and rent are forms of surplus appropriation based upon the existence of a peasant producing class occupying and exploiting its holdings – whether these peasants are dependent tenants leasing their lands merely as exploiters, not as legal owners, whether they are free proprietors grouped in independent village communities, or a mixture of varying degrees of the two (as in the later Roman and Byzantine world from the third century on), is therefore not important within the context of the fundamental mode of surplus appropriation here described. Nor are the origins of their economic and juridical condition: what matters for our point is the processes through which surpluses are actually extracted by the state or by a private landlord.[18]

Now it is clear that the extraction both of rent, on the one hand, and of tax, on the other, is achieved by means other than economic pressure (in contrast to capitalist exploitation). As Marx put it in respect of feudal rent, its foundation was the 'forcible domination of one section of society over another', secured by both actual or potential violence, that is, by physical force and by ideology.[19] This represents something fundamentally different from slavery or the slave mode of production, where human beings are treated as chattels, as (potential) commodities, being both separated absolutely, as the property of their owners, from their own means of reproduction, as well as being assimilated as 'vocal instruments' to the means of production themselves.[20] It is likewise very different from capitalist production, where labourers have complete possession only of their labour-power, being forced (by economic pressure) to sell this as a commodity to the owners of the means of production. And it is, lastly, also very different from anything that we might identify as typical of the ancient mode, in its various forms, characterized in the ancient Greek world, for example, by 'state' control over the producers' means of production only insofar as the state depended in the first instance on its ability, as the community of citizens, to distribute and control the means of production – land – by right of citizenship and membership of the body politic. Tax in this context still represents ultimately that part of the surplus contributed by members of the community of citizens, on the basis of internal clan and tribal reciprocity, later on a formalized and contractual basis, towards the maintenance and reinforcement of the political, legal and military structures which secured their continued possession of their own means of production and reproduction. The lineage/kinship origins of this mode of appropriation of surplus are clear enough to distinguish it from anything that we might wish to call feudal/tributary; although it must be added that it has, in concrete historical terms, generally evolved in the direction of either or both of feudal/tributary and slave-dominated production relations as the division of labour developed and as the state/city came to represent increasingly the interests of a dominant class of citizens rather than those of the whole community in opposition to subordinated/outsider groups.[21]

I would argue, therefore, that there is no modal opposition between tax and rent, which are aspects of the same essential relationship: between, on the one side, a power able to enforce the extraction of surplus by virtue of custom, legal relationships, contractual arrangements backed by sanctions or simple bullying enshrined in traditional rights and dues; and on the other side, peasant producers of a wide range of different legal statuses, possessing, if not owning, their own means of subsistence and reproduction.

Indeed, Marx makes explicit reference to the fact that his concept of feudal rent (tribute or tributary rent in our terms) is a general concept of political economy, the general form of a type of surplus extraction: labour rent, rent in kind, money rent and tax are all forms of the expression of unpaid surplus labour in pre-capitalist economic class formations. Rent in this sense contrasts directly, for example, with surplus value in capitalism, as the general form taken by exploitation and the extraction of surplus wealth. It is clear that where rent on peasant freeholdings is not paid, then tax is its political economy equivalent. Marx sometimes differentiated between serfs or tenants of a private landlord, on the one hand, and those for whom the state functions in effect as landlord, on the other; but this represents no real contradiction between the mode of appropriation of rent and tax: terms such as 'lack of freedom', 'bondage', 'landlord', for example, have different nuances according to the context in which they appear in Marx's writings:

> should the direct producers not be confronted by a private landowner, but rather ... under direct subordination to a state which stands over them as their landlord and simultaneously as sovereign, then rent and taxes coincide, or rather, there exists no tax which differs from this form of ground-rent

The point has been emphasized by several commentators: what is crucial is the effective control exercised by the economically dominant class, whether or not this involved actual ownership enshrined in legal terms.[22]

Of course, the actual conditions in which coercion occurs, and which makes possible its continuation, are fundamental to the ways in which the claims to the appropriation of wealth are enforced and validated. But these can take a multiplicity of different forms and, while they are fundamental to the process of the reproduction of the social relations of production in a specific historical context, are still not a part of the economic relations of appropriation. Tax exists in modern states, too, yet it is once again not a determining feature of the mode of surplus appropriation. In capitalism, tax is imposed upon, and is secondary to, the actual process of surplus appropriation, representing the chief mode of surplus redistribution available to states. In pre-capitalist, class-based social formations, not dominated by slavery and vestiges of kinship and lineage modes of surplus production, tax and rent are the only forms that the appropriation of surplus can take. And this means two things: first, that states, and dominant social-economic classes which have an existence independent, or partly independent, of the state and its institutions, both appropriate surplus at the same, primary level; and second (and consequently) they directly affect both the rate of exploitation and that of surplus production in exactly the same way, by virtue of this coercively-backed direct expropriation of the producing class.[23]

Now, it might be objected that viewing tax and rent as essentially two different forms of the same general category is to ignore what is often assumed to be a crucial and distinctive element of feudal production relations: the role of the landlord, through rent-taking, as a direct agent in the process of production. In ignoring or overlooking this aspect, are we not bound also to ignore the different capacities of the non-producers in each case (the state in the case of tax, private landlords in that of rent), and thereby the ways in which the productive forces are or are not fettered?[24]

This point of view rests, I believe, on a misinterpretation of Marx's discussion of pre-capitalist forms of rent, on the one hand, and on the other an ignorance of the actual forms taken by the appropriation of surplus in western European and other feudal social formations, as well as of the nature of the degree to which both landlords and states could or did intervene in the production process. Let us take these points in order. As we have seen, Marx defined pre-capitalist rent as the general form in pre-capitalist class society through which surplus-labour was 'pumped out of the producers'. Whether this takes the form of rent in labour services, rent in kind, or rent in money makes no essential difference to this;[25] although Marx does note that the two last forms may give the direct producers 'more room for action to gain time for surplus-labour whose product shall belong to himself', hence permitting a greater degree of social differentiation within the peasant community; equally, in the case of rent in kind, the proportion of the produce demanded by those in effective control of the means of production can be so great as to inhibit the expansion of production and 'seriously imperil reproduction of the conditions of labour, the means of production themselves'.[26] For Marx, money-rent,

> as a transmuted form of rent in kind, and in antithesis to it, is, nevertheless, the final form, and simultaneously the form of dissolution of the type of ground-rent which we have heretofore considered, namely ground-rent as the normal form of surplus-value and of the unpaid surplus-labour to be performed for the owner of the conditions of production.

He notes that it leads, in its further development, and 'aside from all intermediate forms, i.e. the small peasant tenant farmer', either to the transformation of land into peasants' freehold or to capitalist relations, 'rent paid by the capitalist tenant farmer'.[27]

What has attracted attention in this analysis is Marx's stress on the role played by the 'owner[s] of the conditions of production'. The degree to which peasant production is directly affected by the rate of surplus appropriation, that is, the amount of labour-time involved in producing the rent in labour-services, kind or cash, obviously plays a role here, and Marx clearly thought that this affected both the economic situation of the direct producers and their ability to reproduce themselves or to expand (quantitatively as well as qualitatively) production. The degree and rate of surplus appropriation can thus fetter or further the forces of production.[28] Marx is in no doubt that these relationships apply both where rent in one of these forms is extracted by a private landlord and where the state extracts tax, as we have seen already. Given what we know about the extraction of these forms of surplus wealth in pre-capitalist class societies, I see no reason to challenge that conclusion. The question therefore arises, to what extent is there a real difference between the control exercised by private landlords or individual controllers of the means of production, and states? If there is a substantive difference, are we not then obliged to conclude that the different potential of landlords taking rent, on the one hand, and states extracting tax, on the other, represent fundamentally different sets of relations of production; and that, in consequence, there is a real modal difference between the two?

The relevant passage is worth quoting at length, since it makes the closeness of the effects of state and landlord control apparent, and yet raises an important problem central to the issue at stake here.

> Should the direct producers not be confronted by a private landowner, but rather, as in Asia, under direct subordination to a state which stands over them as their landlord and simultaneously as sovereign, then rent and taxes coincide, or rather, there exists no tax which differs from this form of ground-rent. Under such circumstances, there need exist no stronger political or economic pressure than that common to all subjection to that state. The state is then the supreme lord. Sovereignty here consists in the ownership of land concentrated on a national scale. But, on the other hand, no private ownership of land exists, although there is both private and common possession and use of land.[29]

It is the last sentence which has, I believe, misled many commentators, and which reflects also Marx's misapprehensions about possession and ownership in many pre-capitalist formations. To begin with, it must be emphasized that Marx normally uses the term 'ownership' in the sense of 'having effective control over', a point generally accepted, as made clear above. In the second place, as will become very clear from the analyses offered in chapters 4 and 5 below, states in Asia may at times (although by no means always) have claimed a theoretical 'ownership' of all land, and they may even, at times (although again, as we shall see, for fairly limited periods), have been able more-or-less effectively to control the distribution of the surpluses appropriated therefrom. But in general, the land was under the effective control of a ruling class of one sort or another, usually at least partially integrated into the state's apparatuses of rule, which in practice treated the land and the direct producers no differently from the ways in which western European feudal landlords who had full legal possession treated their own lands and tenants. Marx's notion that 'no private ownership of land existed' where the state claimed absolute ownership rights must be interpreted very carefully, therefore, especially in the light of the rider which he adds (perhaps expressing his own doubts as to the exactitude of his terms): 'although there is both private and common possession and use of land'. I suggest that this passage by itself in fact provides no grounds for seeing tax and rent as somehow mutually exclusive. These points are re-inforced when we turn to the actual historical evidence for the processes through which landlords and state agents actually extracted surplus and were or were not involved in the production-process.

In the first place, it is quite clear that, while Marx was certainly correct to point to the ways in which the effects of the extraction of rent in labour-services or in kind might, under certain conditions, adversely affect the production process, labour-services of this type were in the medieval European period relatively restricted. As Wickham has made very clear (and on the basis of his own wide-ranging empirical work) they presuppose in practice no landlordly control over the labour-process different in type than that required to extract rent in kind and to determine what types or produce should be rendered at which times of the year.

> In fact, landlords did not often regard their demesnes as the places *par excellence* where they could closely direct the work-process of subjected labourers; peasants performed their labour-services according to the same locally-determined procedures that they used in cultivating their own land.[30]

In the second place, tax in most ancient and medieval states was extracted in a mixed form – a combination of tax in kind and in cash, but also involving sometimes considerable amounts of state 'labour services' (such as bridge and road maintenance, for example, or the billeting and feeding of soldiers and state officials), was common throughout Asia and, where states which taxed existed, in Europe as well. So the difference in the forms of surplus appropriation can be said to differ hardly at all as between either tax or rent.[31] Is there, then, a substantial and generalizable difference in the degree of intervention in the process of production exercised by state agents, on the one hand, and private landlords, on the other, sufficient to warrant a modal distinction here?

The brief answer is, simply, no: states, through their agents, whether those agents are closely supervised and effectively centrally-controlled, or whether they constitute a semi-independent and autonomous provincial elite, also intervene in the process of production just as do private landlords. Of course, the conditions under which this intervention occurs, the stimuli to such intervention, and its effects on the forces of production, vary according to both conjunctural and structural variations between areas and periods. State inauguration and maintenance of irrigation projects; state demands for and specification of particular types of produce – cereals, legumes, minerals – in respect of the maintenance of the military and other requirements of the centre; state demands for particular forms of tax – agricultural produce or livestock, or labour, or cash; state agents' direct involvement, in some state formations, in the local processes of production – all suggest the degree of intervention states can (but do not necessarily) exercise, forms of intervention which certainly have an impact on production, the extent to which peasant producers can build up surpluses and, therefore, on the forces of production in general. The incidence of taxation, that is, the amount and frequency of demands for tax, which is to say, the rate of exploitation of the producers, is especially crucial. All the states treated in this book illustrate all these aspects, at different times and in different modalities.

In no case do I believe any difference can be established between the activities of states in this respect, and those of landlords. Of course, and as Wickham has again made very clear, states can also neglect their tax-payers or so over-tax them that considerable damage is done, both to the state's own resource base and to peasant-productive capacity. In contrast, there are many positive examples of landlords' intervention in the production-process: investment in mills, irrigation programmes, livestock and seed, the production of cash-crops, and so on. But equally, and depending on particular conditions (such as the demand for cash rents, increased labour-services, a growth in long-distance commerce, the presence or absence of local markets and so on), landlords can over-exploit their tenants, equally damaging their ability to reproduce both themselves and the means of production, and no less serious than state over-taxation. The point is clear in the history of the western European peasantry during the fourteenth century in particular, but there are many other examples.[32]

What this means, in effect, is that there is little to choose, at the level of historical generalization, between the effects of states and of landlords on peasant production. The forms of intervention vary quantitatively, to a degree; but states and their agents could also be just as involved in the process of production and extraction of surplus as landlords (indeed, in Mughal India, for example, tax-farmers also involved themselves in these relationships). Once again, I see no grounds for differentiating on this basis between rent and tax as reflecting two different modes of surplus appropriation.

The problem may lie partly in mistaken assumptions about the nature of state taxation, in the first place, and the degree of real central authority actually exercised by states in the second. As we shall see, in two cases at least (the Ottoman and Mughal empires) where the state is supposed to have exercised a real and effective central supervisory control over its provincial representatives – at all levels – this was actually drastically compromised by all sorts of other factors, with the result that, while appointed by the centre and while fully integrated into state service, provincial state elites also operate as local landlords, with all that this implies for local processes of surplus production and appropriation.

We can look at the same problem from another standpoint. If tax and rent represent different modes, then we should also expect to find two contrasting ways of combining the direct producers with the means of production (see *Capital*, Volume 2, p. 34 and Volume 3, pp. 791–2, quoted above) and in consequence two different types of surplus appropriation. The result will be, following Marx's formulations, two different economic class structures. But as I have shown already, this is not the case. Wickham, for example, in arguing that the structural opposition between the state, extracting tax, and landlords, extracting rent, is of a modal character, notes that states also 'characteristically tax landlords too'. That states tax landlords is certainly true (although he then adds, quite correctly, but rather weakening his case, that in taxing landlords the state is actually taking 'a percentage from the surplus the landlord has extracted'). But the effect of arguing that the state and a landlord class represent two different modes of surplus appropriation is to argue that the state and the ruling class are entirely independent socio-economic categories, two different classes.[33] A further consequence of this would be that all social formations in which a state and a landlord class exist would have to be characterized as always representing combined feudal-tributary modes in perpetual contradiction. Now Marxists would not normally wish to argue for the existence of two, separate 'ruling classes', for, given their similar structural position in respect of the direct producers, this is what the logic of Wickham's argument demands they must both be. And empirically, we should have to show that state centres with their (more or less effective) tax-raising apparatuses represent a different mode of surplus appropriation from the provincial agents to whom they invariably come to delegate their tax-extracting functions. In all the examples of social formations with centralized, tax-raising states and a landlord class examined in this study, this cannot be done – indeed, quite the reverse is the case.

For what we are confronted with empirically are two elements, two factions of a single ruling class; as we will see in the remaining sections of this and in the following chapters, these two elements may function as a unity; but they may equally function as two elements in contradiction not because of their economic position vis-à-vis the direct producers, but rather in respect of the degree of their control over the means of distribution. Tax and rent, in consequence, represent not a modal distinction, but a differential relationship to the means of distribution of surplus wealth. This is a relationship internal to a mode, not between two different modes. As such, it is a political relationship, and represents no fundamental difference in either the mode of surplus appropriation or the ways in which producers are combined with the means of production.[34]

We may conclude, therefore, that the difference in the degree to which landlords, on the one hand, and states, on the other, are directly involved in the control of the labour-process, and in consequence, the degree to which each of them affects the forces of production in general, is internal to the mode of surplus appropriation and to the social relations of production of social formations dominated by the tributary mode. Of course, there are considerable variations in the form the relations between states and landlords have actually taken; and it would be foolish to deny that the European feudal variant represents one of the most clear-cut examples of antagonisms between states and landlords, on the one hand, and of the relationship between landlords' interests and the forces of production, on the other. But this must be placed in the historical context of expanding demands for surplus on the part of a feudal ruling class, the growth of towns, and the growth in power of European states over the period from the eleventh to the fifteenth centuries. And the most useful model of economic relationships within which these developments can be understood is that represented by the tributary mode of production. Feudalism is, as I suggested in chapter 2, one specific historical variant on that pattern.[35] As Marx reminds us:

> It is always the direct relationship of the owners of the conditions of production to the direct producers ... which reveals the ... hidden basis of the entire social structure, and with it the political form of the relation of sovereignty and dependence, in short, the corresponding specific form of the state. This does not prevent the same economic basis – the same from the standpoint of its main conditions – due to innumerable different empirical circumstances ... from showing infinite variations and gradations in appearance, which can be ascertained only by analysis of the empirically given circumstances.[36]

Thus the institutional and juridical forms by which each social formation gives expression to the fundamental structure of production relations are crucial to an understanding of the particular history of that social formation. The nature of the relations of exploitation between producers, landlords and the state, in terms of the relative significance of tax to rent, of free but bonded tenants to unfree tenants or slaves, of communal village solidarities, both fiscally, in respect of the mode of assessment and collection of tax, and socially/juridically, in respect of the state's or the landlords' legal authority over tenants, for example, is likewise central to any understanding of the evolution of class conflict, the relationships underpinning rural production, rural–urban relations, and so forth. These forms represent the historically- and culturally-determined ways in which a social formation expresses fundamental relations of production, that is to say, through which the dominant mode of production (and elements of other modes which may also be present) actually functions. They also represent the necessary (but historically specific) conditions for the reproduction and maintenance of these production relations. And it is through an analysis of these institutions that the historian identifies the forms taken by the contradictions and antagonisms implicit in the social formation, therefore, and the ways in which they work themselves out in each specific social formation. I will attempt to illustrate this empirically, in respect of the evolution of the social relations of production within Byzantine society below.

We must beware, however, of the descriptivist trap of assuming that different political forms and institutions of surplus appropriation, as between two or more societies, signify differences also in the basic political economy of those societies, in other words, that they represent different modes of production, precisely the implicit assumption made by many Soviet Byzantinists and a number of western Marxists, and an obvious feature of the discussion above on the relationship between tax and rent. While it *may* be the case, a careful analysis of the underlying relationships those forms actually express is first necessary. I would argue that in many examples, including those singled out for analysis in the present book, differences are due to the specific genesis and particular, context-bound cultural/historical (organizational, ideological, political or military) fortunes and evolutionary trajectories of state formation and class conflict determined by the structural constraints and capacities of the tributary mode of production, and cannot be said to reflect modal differences as such.

The functional economic equivalence of forms of tax and forms of rent in pre-capitalist social formations has been pointed out by many historians; and it seems to me that the reluctance of many others to accept this as fundamental to a vast range of historically-attested social formations is based less on the lack of a logical appreciation of its value than a tendency and a desire to incorporate elements which are in essence superstructural and conjunctural into what should remain a basically descriptive and heuristic model of economic relationships: a mode of production is not a concrete social reality.

3. Mode of Production, Social Formation and the Nature of the Tributary Mode

Within tributary production relations, therefore, we must be prepared to differentiate empirically between a wide range of disparate sub-types, actual social formations with very different historical trajectories of development, different superstructural characteristics, different modes of self-expression.[37]

Three results follow all of these considerations, taken together. The first is that most ancient societies which had moved out of the stage of kinship-based or 'primitive communal' exploitation (whether 'urban'-centred or not) and begun to develop a class structure founded upon the differential relationships of various social-economic groups to the means of production and distribution, can be understood, at least partially, through the concept of the tributary/feudal mode of production, even in those cases where the dominant social and political class derived their wealth and social power from the large-scale exploitation of slave labour. Here I would agree with de Ste Croix that the dominance of a mode of production depends upon the role it plays in providing the ruling class of a given social formation with its wealth and political power, and not whether there were, for example, more slaves than free tenants or serfs. But it is equally clear that classical Greek and Hellenistic society represented a structural combination of both slave and tributary/feudal modes of surplus appropriation. In absolute terms it would seem that tributary relations dominated the greater part of Greek and Roman society in, say, the second century BC. In relative terms, slavery produced the greatest surplus, most rapidly, and concentrated in the hands of the ruling class.

Second, tributary relations of production always necessarily exist in, or generate, state or state-like political-economic formations, however limited or localized these may be. The transformation of kin- and lineage-based modes of surplus appropriation, with only a limited degree of internal economic, but still kin-based, differentiation, into those based clearly on class exploitation, invariably involves the loosening of kinship ties and dissolution of the associated forms of social praxis, although the extent of this 'loosening' process depends upon historically local factors such as the degree to which kinship and lineage structures serve also as production relations, for example. The concomitant extension of networks of coercive political and economic power across a much wider social and geographical space than kinship ties can adequately handle, at least in the long term, leads to the development of state-like structures. This does not have to mean that localized or regional bonds of kinship and lineage do not continue to play a key role in the regulation of the relations of production and distribution, indeed, and from the economic perspective (as outlined in chapter 2, section 4) to function as social relations of production; only that such ties no longer dominate the mode of surplus appropriation and distribution. For the increasing complexity of the division of labour, and the domination of the producing population by a social and economic elite, promote at the same time the rapid evolution of institutional means of maintaining and reproducing their class domination (whatever the culturally-determined form these relationships may actually take).

This is not to argue that state forms are necessary to class exploitation – on the contrary, it is clear that relations of exploitation can be maintained through lineage structures too, as a number of anthropologists have tried to show. Nor is it to ignore the fact that the process of state formation, where it is an endogenous development and not imposed by conquest/assimilation, is often very gradual; nor, yet again, that in the process of transformation to tributary production relations there may not likewise be a relatively long-drawn-out period of symbiosis and struggle for pre-eminence between two antagonistic and contradictory sets of production relations, represented by institutional forms which may, in part (but depending upon their functional significance), be assimilable to whichever mode of surplus appropriation finally dominates. I would argue that this applies certainly to the later Roman state, and as we shall see in chapter 5, it applies in a particularly clear way to the history of Indian social formations and the states which they supported.

Third, the slave mode of production, which is now generally recognized to have had a relatively limited chronological and geographical dominance in the ancient world in those periods when it did develop, can be seen on the whole as a much more volatile and contingency-bound mode of surplus appropriation. This has not yet, it seems to me, had the recognition it deserves; so that Soviet historians, for example, continued until the 1980s to describe the ancient world in the West almost exclusively in terms of the slave mode, a position which often seems to be forced and the result of considerable over-generalization. Slavery may well have dominated relations of production at times in the late Roman republican period and the early Principate (chiefly based in Italy) and in Greece in the fifth and fourth centuries BC (in certain city-states),[38] in the sense that it was through the labour of slaves, whether organized on an intensive plantation basis or not, that the ruling classes of these social formations received their wealth, as we have said.[39]

But the contradictions within this type of slave exploitation are such that it seems always to have given way to more reliable and less unstable (if also less profitable, in the short term) forms of exploitation. And contrary to the views of Shtaermann and many others, the late Roman state was certainly not representative of such a slave-dominated conjuncture.[40]

Equally, it becomes impossible to talk of the 'ancient mode in its class form', as does Wickham in his article on the transition to feudalism, and as I have done myself using a slightly different terminology.[41] For the ancient mode as described by Marx, and as elaborated by Hindess and Hirst, for example, is no more than an urban variant on the theme of primitive communal exploitation, in which clan- and kinship-relations determine access to land or to other forms of wealth and to the exploitation of resources.[42] Marx had in mind the early city-states of the Mediterranean world as the developed and urbanocentric form of this still basically agrarian community, whose state represented the incorporation of the citizen body as a group of landowners with collective rights in public lands. The exploitation of citizens by other citizens and by the state takes place in the first instance through the collective appropriation of surpluses for common ends – warfare, for example. But as slavery comes increasingly into the picture along with other forms of social and economic subordination and stratification among the community's members, so the division of labour becomes more complex, and the appearance of class antagonisms marks a new stage, indeed a transformative one, in the development of the relations of production. As objective antagonisms between social groups with regard to their different relationships to the means of production evolve, so the state becomes the legislative and executive arm of the ruling class of citizens, which can exploit it thereafter to maintain and promote their own class interests and the extraction of surplus.[43]

But as soon as a society has attained this stage, of course, it can properly be said to have transformed its relations of production, and more especially, the mode of appropriation of surplus. No longer does the community, whatever kinship and lineage structures it still exhibits, control the means of production as a community (of clans or families, for example, within which other forms of non-economic subordination existed) with equal, or at least equivalent, rights in their exploitation and distribution. Instead, one group can now exert control over both the rate of exploitation (that is, the amount of surplus actually demanded) and the mode of surplus appropriation. By invoking the various instruments of non-economic coercion (the law, customary practice, military force, and so on) one group, a class in the economic sense, exploits the labour of other groups. Whether this is referred to under terms which may be rendered as one or another form of tax or rent or tribute makes no difference.[44] The 'ancient mode in its class form', therefore, is not a mode of production at all, but an example of a specific historical social formation in which both the slave mode and the tributary mode were represented, and according to the local context and other conditions, in which now one, now the other – but finally the tributary mode – came to dominate. This is the story, therefore, of a specific social formation, one historical variant on the combination of modes, and has nothing to do with the development of a specific mode of production.

So far, I have been speaking about only one aspect of the equation 'mode of production', albeit the single most important distinguishing feature of each different mode – together with the ways in which the direct producers are combined with the means of production, these were the two key features which differentiated modes of production for Marx. And in respect of the ancient mode as it is usually understood, the development of classes, that is to say, a shift in the relations of production from non-class-based to class-based exploitation, must also be commensurate with a shift in the fundamental mode of production. One mode cannot encompass both forms.

As has often been pointed out, an apparently strong objection to the use of the term feudalism (that is, our tributary mode) to define the mode of production dominant in such a vast range of actual social formations which this line of reasoning must imply (ranging from those of classical antiquity to those of medieval and early modern Asia) is that it is so broad as to deprive it of any analytical value. But the real difficulty with this argument is that its proponents have without exception tried to elaborate alternatives by bringing into the picture a range of elements which are, in fact, conjunctural and determined by actual historical specificities: a particular type of state fiscal administration, specific (legalistic) forms of landlord–tenant relationship, culture-bound definitions of 'free' and 'unfree', of the 'parcellization of sovereignty', 'private' versus 'public' power, and so on. This is true of both Syuzyumov and of Kazhdan, for example, for the latter, who is aware of the convergence of tax and rent as forms of the same essential mode of surplus appropriation, is unwilling to concede 'real' feudalism in Byzantium until the eleventh century or so – that is, until the dominance of a class of magnates was assured and the beginnings of a western-style institutional feudalism had appeared.[45] The same, of course, applies to Perry Anderson's account of the difference between the feudal West and the Byzantine and non-feudal East, as it does to Wickham in his differentiation between tax and rent – these are not differences between modes of surplus appropriation, they are differences in the forms one particular mode, the tributary mode, takes in specific historical formations. Similarly, the Soviet scholar Litavrin concedes feudalism in Byzantium only from the eleventh century and after; but it is an institutional feudalism whose phenomenal forms can be compared with those of the medieval West, which he sees.[46] And, of course, it goes without saying that, if the feudal mode of production (that is to say, the tributary mode) is our concern, as opposed to a western-style feudal social formation (one variant of the tributary mode among many), then western, non-Marxist Byzantinists are also wrong to deny a Byzantine 'feudalism'. The application in this context of 'tributary' instead of 'feudal' is intended partly to overcome this particular problem, and to remove at the same time the inclination or the temptation to bring medieval western European institutional forms into the picture. They are not relevant to any definition of a mode of production, whether we call it 'feudal' or something else, except insofar as it was out of them that Marx abstracted the fundamental relations of production of his feudal mode.

Anderson's critique of what he refers to as 'the promiscuous extension of the rubric of feudalism beyond Europe' is particularly sharp, and is worth looking at more closely. He makes a series of key critical points, which for ease of reference I will quote at length:

> For if, in effect, the feudal mode of production can be defined independently of the various juridical and political superstructures which accompany it, such that its presence can be registered throughout the globe whenever primitive and tribal social formations were superseded, the problem then arises: how is the unique dynamism of the European theatre of international feudalism to be explained? No historian has yet claimed that industrial capitalism developed spontaneously anywhere else except in Europe and its American extension, which then, precisely, conquered the rest of the world by virtue of this economic primacy ... If there was a common economic foundation of feudalism across the whole land mass from the Atlantic to the Pacific, divided merely by juridical and constitutional forms, and yet only one zone produced the industrial revolution ..., the determinant of its transcendent success must be sought in the political and legal superstructures that alone distinguished it. Laws and States, dismissed as secondary ... re-emerge with a vengeance .... In other words, once the whole structure of sovereignty and legality is *dissociated* from the economy of a universal feudalism, its shadow paradoxically governs the world: for it becomes the only principle capable of explaining the differential development of the whole mode of production.[47]

He goes on to note that, since all modes of production in class societies before capitalism extract surplus through non-economic coercion, it is therefore impossible to identify them on the basis of economic relationships as such. They cannot be defined except by virtue of their superstructural differences, so that:

> The precise forms of juridical dependence, property and sovereignty that characterize a pre-capitalist social formation, far from being merely accessory or contingent epiphenomena, compose on the contrary the central indices of the determinate mode of production dominant within it. A scrupulous and exact taxonomy of these legal and political configurations is thus a pre-condition of establishing any comprehensive typology of pre-capitalist modes of production.[48]

These comments, which Anderson illustrates with a host of further examples, noting in the process that Marx too was dubious about the generalization of the description 'feudalism', represent a powerful argument that must be addressed seriously. But it contains also a number of crucial flaws, which can be grouped under two headings: questions of general theoretical relevance, and questions relevant to the nature of feudalism as a mode of production.

First of all, the nature of the concept of a mode of production. According to Marx (and as generally accepted by Marxist historians), a mode of production is a combination of forces and relations of production, a combination which is expressed through the social relations of production. The totality of the social relations of production represents what Marx generally referred to as the economic base of a given society (a definition to which I will return later). These relations of production constitute in effect the mode of appropriation of surplus and thereby the social division of labour, since it is the relations of production which generate a particular distribution of the means of production. And the crucial distinguishing element, which makes one mode of production different from another, lies precisely in 'the mode in which ... surplus labour is in each case extracted from the actual producer, the labourer', together with the specific manner in which labourers are united with the means of production.[49] In other words, modes of production are to be determined and distinguished through these two features, rather than in terms of the superstructural effects or conditions of that mode.

As can be inferred from the passages referred to above, Anderson presents a very different model, in which pre-capitalist modes are differentiated not by their modes of surplus appropriation, but rather by the variations in the forms of their superstructures. Not only this, but the particular form taken by the extra-economic means of surplus extraction appears itself to be constitutive of the mode of surplus appropriation and, therefore, the mode of production: 'The "superstructures" of kinship, religion, laws or the state necessarily enter into the constitutive structure of the mode of production.' The justification for this apparent inversion of a historical materialist position is based on the fact that 'capitalism is the first mode of production in history in which the means whereby the surplus is pumped out of the direct producer is "purely" economic in form', and that 'in capitalist social formations, the first in history to separate the economy as a formally self-contained order', the superstructure provides 'by contrast its "external" precondition'.[50]

But there is, in the first place, an obvious weakness in an argument that rejects mode of surplus appropriation as a means of modal differentiation. Of course, if this criterion alone were applied, then it would be true that, since all pre-capitalist modes of production extract surplus through non-economic coercion, this offers no obvious way of differentiating them. But this ignores absolutely the fundamental second element in Marx's equation, namely the way in which labourers are combined with the means of production. It is these two elements together which differentiate one mode from another.

In the second place, Anderson's argument for the analytical and heuristic priority of superstructures is surely to misconstrue the nature of 'the economic'. It implies that, whereas capitalism has an economic level or structure which is not to be connected with the forms of social praxis through which it is realized and reproduced, non-capitalist modes have no distinct relations of production, since everything is part of the superstructure. And this in its turn implies that the necessary conditions of existence of a mode of production are the same thing as the mode of production itself. If pre-capitalist modes of production can only be specified through the different superstructural forms they take, the result is precisely that which the heuristic concept of mode of production is designed to avoid: there can be as many modes of production as there are different forms of social praxis and legal-political structures through which they are realized. Mode of production merges into social formation. This also ignores that fact that, as I have argued in chapter 2, 'superstructural' elements function (also) as relations of production, they are the forms through which the relations of production are expressed.

At the same time, Marx's theoretical insistence that the mode of appropriation of surplus should not be confused with the phenomenal form or superstructural conditions of this mode is lost sight of: it is the political economy form of appropriation (through rent, for example) which constitutes the relations of production, not the types of extra-economic coercion which maintain it. And since it is the case that the crucial distinction between the relations of production and the social and institutional forms through which they are realized is ignored, the possibility that there will be discrepancies or variations between production relations and their political conditions of existence is similarly ignored. The result is, in effect, the abandonment of the concept mode of production for all but capitalist economies, and the analysis of non-capitalist societies on the basis of purely descriptive differentiating categories. The consequences of this for understanding the development and evolution of such societies have been pointed out by others: chiefly, the dependence upon a theory of genesis or origins to explain different evolutionary tracks, and the privileging of state forms as the chief criterion within that model.[51]

This brings us then to a second set of questions, concerning the nature and form of tributary or 'feudal' relations of production. Anderson challenges the adequacy of the broad definition of the feudal mode on the grounds that it is simply too all-embracing a category to have any value. For, if all differences between various pre-capitalist social formations are merely superstructural, as Anderson's denial of the relevance of the mode of surplus appropriation as a distinguishing feature leads him to conclude, and yet they all experience different or relatively different evolutionary trajectories, then only those superstructural variations can explain these divergences – which would be an unacceptable idealism. Yet it is precisely this that his method leads him to: claiming, on the one hand, that the superstructures are the relations of production, he then, on the other, elaborates differences between social formations of a pre-capitalist type on the basis of their various superstructures, but in terms of the way these superstructural forms were originally generated. In other words, the different end results of various historical evolutionary trajectories are explained not in terms of the different ways in which various expressions of given modes of production were realized in the day-to-day material praxis of different cultures, but in respect of the origins of each of these social formations. In Anderson's specific project, this is part of his attempt to determine the reasons for the supposedly unique origins of capitalist development in the West – a project which is immediately rendered pointless if, as one critic has noted, the question is changed to establishing the reasons for the priority of capitalism's development in western Europe at a given moment.

What concerns us here, however, is the denial of the notion of 'feudal', that is, tributary relations of production – as determined by the political economy of its mode of surplus appropriation – as a universal phenomenon. To a degree, the limitations of Anderson's critique are made clear in the comparison he makes between Japanese and European forms of feudalism. The comparison is legitimated by the similarities of organizational forms (fief-system, vassalage, benefice, immunities) which are generally accepted by scholars as demonstrating that Japanese society between the twelfth and nineteenth centuries was feudal in the same way that European society had been. The reasons for the failure of capitalism to develop here is ascribed to the specific and unique nature of the late antique/ Dark Age origins of western feudalism. But this ignores two crucial points: first, there is no way of knowing that Japanese feudalism would not have eventually engendered capitalist production relations; second, while not ignoring the possibility, inscribed in Marx's own remarks on the actual form concrete social formations take (that social formations usually consist of elements from different modes, with one dominant), the results of this combination are assumed to be random, so that only the moment of origin can explain its specific nature. Indeed, Anderson concedes that 'there was ... no inherent drive within the feudal mode of production which inevitably compelled it to develop into the capitalist mode of production. The concrete record of comparative history suggests no easy evolutionism.' But then, instead of looking at the specific processual conditions, both structural and conjunctural, which made western European capitalism both possible and prior, we are left only with the supposed context of genesis, to be compared with other moments, all determined largely arbitrarily (when does a process of social and economic genesis begin and end?), upon which to speculate. The whole procedure is rendered the more dubious in view of the fact that the causal value of the features highlighted for examination can only be guessed at, and certainly not compared directly with 'similar' features from other, different social formations on anything other than an intuitive basis.

It is thus made impossible to analyse the structural limitations imposed on various different historical societies by the forms of articulation and therefore reproduction of modes of production. Yet it is this, rather than the search for origins, which explains the differences between social formations dominated by the same mode of production. And it is just through determining the nature of the structural limitations and the conditions of existence of such combinations that the actual phenomenal forms of the mode of surplus appropriation and the underlying dynamic of a given social formation can be explained. This, it seems to me, is the value of the broad definition of the tributary/feudal mode, for it is in precisely this that its heuristic value lies.

This procedure is not the same as defining modes of production themselves in terms of the juridical or institutional appearances through which their modes of surplus appropriation are expressed in the historical record, a point which should now be clear. But it is, in contrast, to assert the importance of analysing these forms in each social formation in order to discover how each dominant mode of production actually operates. 'A scrupulous and exact taxonomy of these legal and political configurations is thus a pre-condition of establishing any comprehensive typology' not of pre-capitalist modes of production, as Anderson would have it, but, on the contrary, of social formations dominated by the same mode of production – in this case, tributary/feudal production relations – and the conditions of their existence and reproduction in different historical circumstances.[52]

An important point in this connection is that a mode of production cannot of itself give rise to a different mode of production, a point which, as mentioned already, Anderson would also accept. But it can generate at times the conditions which may lead to its break-up or transformation. The latter is a possibility determined by the actual institutional forms of expression of the underlying economic relationships, which are subject to change or disruption at the level of class struggle and the political relations of power distribution. It is essential to bear in mind that these institutional forms are, after all, the combination of sets of social practices, which local conditions have evolved to express fundamental relations of production and surplus appropriation. As Godelier has stressed, and as I argued above, therefore, these institutions are the forms of expression of relations of production, they function as production relations.

Equally importantly, and as already emphasized, modes of production do not exist in any real form – they represent merely the theoretical exposition of specific sets of economic relations. In actual social formations, they are always present in combination with other modes; and it is the way in which these modes are articulated together that gives each social formation its particular configuration. The crucial point about this, however, is that we must recognize that modes of production do not develop. On the contrary, it is social formations that change, so that we must look at the shape, and the local and international context, of each social formation (or group of social formations) to see how transformative shifts in the dominance of particular sets of social relations of production are actually brought about. Mode of production provides a broad agenda, so to speak, delineating the essential nature of contradictions within production relations and the basic economic possibilities, as we have seen. But it is at the level of social formation that change actually occurs, that these contradictions work themselves out, and it is therefore at this level that the explanation for change must be sought.

Insofar as the roles and institutions of a society are the unique, particular, and locally-evolved expressions of basic sets of relations of production, therefore, Anderson's idea that we must look to the superstructure of a social formation to see what is specific to its development, and why, is not so far off the mark, and this is what, I believe, his original argument was intended to achieve. But he fails to make the functional connection between the economic base and the superstructure apparent, emphasizing rather the autonomy of the superstructure, and thence implying that the superstructure is in effect the mode of production. In contrast, I would emphasize precisely the role played by the superstructure as the institutional mode of expression of these economic relationships. And, as I have already said, these concrete, historically-attested institutional or superstructural expressions of a mode of production are not themselves to be misrecognized as a mode of production, which is a theoretical, heuristic construct.

None of this is to suggest that Anderson's attempt to clarify the framework for establishing the reasons for the particular shape of western European feudalism and the transition to capitalism has not been extremely important and provoked important debates, as the numerous critical and positive responses to his two books on the subject make clear. What I have tried to suggest in the above is that the incorporation of institutional forms and phenomena into the definition of a mode of production immediately confounds two levels of analysis – abstract and concrete – as well as promoting the proliferation of an ever wider range of modes of production, or sub-modes, instead of encouraging the analysis of the specific forms which the combination of different modes of production in concrete circumstances actually takes.[53] When this happens, any difference between a Marxist and a non-Marxist enquiry vanishes.

It seems to me that objections to a wider application of the concept of the feudal mode of production are groundless if we recall that the whole point of correctly elaborating the concept of a specific mode of production is to facilitate a better understanding of the wide range of historical social formations in which it occurred, that is to say, by enabling the right questions to be asked about their internal articulation, ideological and institutional structures, and so on; and not simply in order to erect an internally consistent but entirely abstract model. This is not Anderson's sin, of course, but it is a danger of which Marx was very aware:

> events strikingly analogous but taking place in different historical surroundings led to totally different results. By studying each of these forms of evolution separately and then comparing them one can easily find the clue to this phenomenon, but one will never arrive there by using as one's master key a general philosophico-historical theory, the supreme virtue of which consists in being supra-historical.[54]

More recently, the Indian historian Ashok Rudra has mounted a vigorous critique of any use of the concept mode of production at all, and particularly of the broad application of the feudal, that is to say, the tributary mode, as argued here. Like Anderson, he contends that, if the feudal mode is so generalized, it loses precisely in specificity and analytical value. Contingently, he also argues that some of the best Marxist historical work is that which was written without the aid of 'mode of production' in any substantive way, but in which movement in history is analysed 'in terms of interaction between the forces of production, and the relations of production, and not just that but also interaction between these two with the super-structure'.[55]

While I am sympathetic again to the intentions behind this position, there seem to be two difficulties here. Of course, analysis should be in terms of the interaction between the two elements referred to. But the statement leaves once again out of account the fact that in pre-capitalist social formations supposedly superstructural elements may function also as relations of production, they are the mode of expression and realization in social praxis of these relations. So that in using a broad category 'feudal mode of production' or 'feudal relations of production', in its political economy sense, the infinite variety of forms of relations of production and their societal multifunctionality is already taken into the equation.

But more importantly, the point of using the concept in such a universalizing way is that it constitutes a heuristic means of locating certain key elements, a guide to a research programme. That the concept does not then appear regularly explicated is, perhaps, regrettable in the work Rudra has in mind, but it clearly informs the research priorities of the historians in question. It is perhaps the fault of Marxist historians that modes of production have often been treated as self-contained, descriptive categories applied to historical societies in an overly precise and rigid way. But in spite of the fact that in defining modes of production through the means of surplus appropriation we are left with only a rather small number of such modes, this does not seem to me to be a serious objection.

For, in the first place, however different their actual historical appearance, and however different the medium through which surplus is extracted (rent in kind, cash, labour services, etc.) societies dominated by a particular mode of surplus appropriation do have certain fundamental features in common, and are constrained in respect of their further development by these features (especially in regard of the distribution and consumption of such surpluses, a point which I will discuss at greater length in chapter 4). And, in the second place, if we are to deny, say, the tributary/feudal mode of production a potential universal application, that is, the possibility or probability that tributary/feudal production relations have developed at one time or another in many (most?) parts of the world, and that they subsume certain general laws of development, then we must logically deny this to capitalist production relations too – which is clearly absurd. Either we use the concept of a mode of production as a general analytical category, or we abandon it altogether. It is not consistent to apply it to capitalism alone since it would then lose entirely any comparative analytical value it possesses. Nor is there any question of attributing to feudalism the power to universalize itself, either, which is the point at issue with capitalist production and exchange relations. Rather, it is a question of asserting that production relations which can be described as tributary from the point of view of their political economy have existed in many parts of the world at different times in human history, and that they have tended to predominate in historically-attested state formations. This is explicitly not the same as asserting that the tributary or feudal mode is a 'world system' in the same way that capitalism has become.

The point is that capitalist relations of production already dominate the world's economies (although they may not constitute the only set of production relations within a given social formation). What is different, given the variation in technological levels of achievement and expansion of the productive forces, is the nature of that universality. Capitalism is powerful enough to make disparate social and economic traditions conform to its demands, and to integrate disparate systems regardless of the particular stage of development which they may have attained, at least at the level of world market exchange. In this sense it is accurately described by Marxists as the first 'world system', for this dominance results from the specific mechanisms of capitalist production, more particularly from the generalized nature of commodity production based on wage labour. Feudalism, as one mode of organization of pre-capitalist class society, has never achieved or possessed the technological or the economic power to attain this. And it is also true to say, in addition, that the universal laws of capitalist production are, in themselves, no more capable of dynamically transforming capitalist relations of production into something else, full of objective class antagonisms and contradictions in respect of forces and relations of production though they clearly are, than are feudal production relations. Within both feudalism and capitalism, or any other mode of production, it is the specific contexts generated by specific conjunctures or configurations in time and place – in other words, particular moments at which structural disparities between forces and relations of production are realized in terms of social praxis – which lead to modal transformations. These are predictable only in the most general possible sense, delimited by the conditions of existence of given sets of relations of production and by the historically specific forms of their internal contradictions. Transformation is not, therefore, an inevitable consequence of process in time; but it is always a possibility, under specific sets of conditions. And it is important to recall one of the points of Mann's analysis: that the evolution over time of increasingly wide-ranging patterns of cultural and technological influence and power makes even ancient societies of the Neolithic revolution parts of a highly regionalized but nevertheless 'international' system at the very least.

Modal transformations within systems of production relations, certainly before capitalism, have generally occurred locally and in a piecemeal fashion, as internal contradictions (antagonistic relations of production in the context of tensions between forces and relations of production) become conjuncturally open to qualitatively different solutions, resulting from either or both 'external' influences (but bearing in mind the overlapping or intersecting nature of social-economic structures, which do not always respect political or cultural divisions), or the increased availability of surplus wealth generated by changes in, say, agricultural techniques or animal husbandry.

It is important to bear in mind at this point what exactly is meant by 'external' features or 'internal' dynamic. The former are often invoked in debate with reference to particular social formations as though such social formations were to be understood as rigorously segregated from neighbouring societies.. But modes of production are more often than not common to several neighbouring social formations, which may share a wide range of key structural elements in common, even if cultural and political modes of expression of those elements varies. Factors external to a particular social formation, therefore, are not necessarily external to the mode of production. By the same token, the dynamic of a mode of production is common to all the social formations in which it is dominant, and must not be seen as a limited option open only to that social formation which is the historian's object of scrutiny.

This point of view nevertheless seems to underlie the opposition of several historians to a universal application of the concept of the feudal mode of production. To quote Harbans Mukhia, 'focusing on these general features [of the economic structure of societies] and treating them as the hallmark of feudalism reduces feudalism to a catch-all category; such a category can hardly serve as a rigorous definition capable of distinguishing one medieval society from another'.[56]

This is precisely to confuse these two different levels of analysis: modes of production, as Marxists would generally accept, are not to be equated with social formations. Yet Mukhia goes on to elaborate the argument that the broad or 'universal' definition of feudalism (which he takes to be the same as asserting that feudalism was, therefore, a 'world system') has little or no specificity through which societies dominated by the same basic set of relations of production and distribution can be distinguished one from another. But surely, neither does the concept of the capitalist mode of production. This is equally broad – yet do we differentiate modern capitalist societies such as England, Germany, Japan and the United States from each other on this basis? Of course not – it is precisely on the grounds of regional, cultural and institutional differentiation and the varying modes of political organization that such a distinction can be made, not on any modal comparison – they are, after all, without exception capitalist societies, and the definition 'capitalist' can at best serve to distinguish them from non-capitalist social formations or provide a basic model of the dominant system of production relations within them.

But to quote (and paraphrase) Mukhia, 'what then remains of

the concept of feudalism' (or capitalism) 'as a social structure [sic] capable of illuminating all, or most, of the medieval (or modern) world's variant regional and sub-regional economies?' The answer, of course, is: not much. For 'capitalism' and 'feudalism' are not 'social structures', as I have tried to make plain, they are, on the contrary, ideal sets of social relations of production, precisely 'modes of production' which serve as heuristic categories for the elucidation of the actual workings of historically-attested social formations. They must not be conflated with the real societies themselves.

To return to the point originally under consideration, however: whereas relations of production are never static, they can be very stable, and over considerable periods of time; centrally, they do generate the preconditions for their own transformation. But the possibilities for such transformations are immanent – it is particular, only very broadly predictable, conjunctural developments which affect particular sets of production relations at particular times and in particular ways (developments which express the fundamental contradictions of the mode of production in question), which may or may not stimulate a qualitative transformation. It is precisely the historian's task to (a) clarify these fundamental relationships and their contradictions, in order to (b) ascertain why it is only at specific moments or under certain sets of conditions that qualitative transformations at either the micro or macro level are generated.

What I have been dealing with, as hinted already, is the question of the 'dynamic' or 'prime mover' of a mode of production. Rudra regards the search for such a basic mechanism as a waste of time – claiming that it must necessarily lead to an essentially mechanistic or 'clockwork' model of the nature of the relations of production, since – unlike with capitalism – historians have not yet located or defined such a 'prime mover' for 'feudalism'.

In fact, while dismissing it more or less out of hand, Rudra refers to Hilton's definition: that, in respect of feudal relations of production, the 'prime mover' consists in the class struggle between lords and serfs. Leaving aside the variations between different sets of historically-attested versions of feudal production relations, this formula does not seem to me to be so lightly dismissed. Hilton was guilty, if anything, of understating the case. For while class struggle exists in all class societies, it is the particular nature of the relationships of expropriation of surpluses, and the contradictions which these involve, which lend to tributary societies their particular form and trajectory. If Rudra, or anyone else, is looking for a single dynamic law or set of laws which will account for the transformation of feudal relations into proto-capitalist or capitalist relations, then he will be disappointed. Even the laws of capitalist production explain not how it is transformed into something else, but how it is reproduced and how its periodic crises arise (and can or cannot be resolved).

Similarly, the dominant feature of tributary/feudal production relations is the struggle over surpluses produced in the process of the social and physical reproduction of rural peasantries. This struggle takes on an infinite range of forms in actual historical societies, but its existence (and the fact of contradictory and antagonistic relations of production) is central to the ways in which dominant elites are configured in these various societies, and more importantly for our concerns in this book, to the possibilities of state formation and state embedding.

Indeed, the example of medieval Indian rural society (which I shall argue in chapter 5 was dominated by tributary production relations) provides us with a classic case, for here we find internally- and externally-differentiated peasant lineages exploiting land within the framework of a wide range of communal and produce-sharing structures, facing the constant efforts of local power elites, whether in the form of individuals or of dominant lineage groups, to extract a portion of the surplus for themselves. Whether this takes the form of hereditary produce-sharing by local notables and powerful men (such as the *zamindars*, for example), or of the maximization of fiscal demands by local representatives of state apparatuses (*mansabdars* and others), or of the demand for the rendering of traditional prestations or 'rights' by corporate organizations such as temples, is not important for the fundamental structure of the mode of surplus appropriation. Nor is the ideological form that this process takes. As I will suggest in chapter 5, such intermediaries, contrary to much that has been traditionally claimed for both Mughal and pre-Mughal Indian states, have been shown to be, or can plausibly be assumed to have been, present throughout medieval Indian history.

Whether those with rights to share in the produce attempted to maximize their appropriations or not depended upon the historical conjuncture, the strength of the traditional kinship and lineage ties between producers and expropriators (and they were not always entirely distinct), and other features. But we must remember that when appropriation was not maximized, the producers were themselves able (among several options, again determined by local conditions, both cultural and economic) to exploit the surpluses remaining to them, in terms of increased consumption (with potential demographic consequences), gift-exchange, commercial sale and social investment, and so on – all of which had non-predictable repercussions on the ways in which the social relations of production worked. Commercialization and monetization of economic relations, the nature and function of urban centres, these and many other aspects of social formations dominated by tributary relations of production are thus drawn into the picture, as Hilton has suggested for western Europe.

Class struggle, of course, must not necessarily be expressed in actual political-economic conflicts involving physical violence. 'Class struggle' is a term which represents both an immanent structural condition (objective antagonisms in respect of control over means of production and distribution of surplus wealth) and an actual set of historically-occurring events. Class struggle is an organic element within any set of contradictory relations of production, and the actual forms it takes (through legal and judicial procedures, for example, as well as various sorts of direct action against those perceived as oppressors or exploiters, or their agents, together with the various ideological vehicles which may be conscripted into its service, such as schismatic or heretical movements) vary enormously in the historical record. Which is not to claim, of course, that all conflicts are necessarily determined by class relations, nor that ideological movements or tendencies necessarily represent such expressions of class relations. It is to agree wholeheartedly with de Ste Croix when he argues that 'Class ... is the collective social expression of the fact of exploitation', which is to say 'the appropriation of part of the product of the labour of others', and that those who constitute a given class 'may or may not be wholly or partly conscious of their own identity and common interests as a class, and they may or may not feel antagonism towards members of other classes'.[57]

It seems to me, therefore, that the underlying dynamic element which regulates tributary relations of production is the struggle for surplus between producing and exploiting classes, a struggle concentrated around the institutional forms which express the basic mode of surplus appropriation. This is, in fact, a fairly precise location, although it embodies no predictive laws. But it does focus attention on the mode of surplus appropriation and the ways in which the producers are combined with the means of production, both in conceptual terms and in respect of empirically verifiable historical examples. And again, and as Marx notes, the specific historical form this struggle takes can only be elucidated through research in the history of the society in question.

What becomes, therefore, of the notion that there are laws of motion of modes of production which can not only reveal their internal contradictions, but also give rise to the next mode of production? Insofar as he rejects the possibility of locating exact laws which do the latter, I am in broad agreement with Rudra when he says that this is a chimera: 'the sooner [such a law] is recognized as unattainable, the better'. Even the periodic crises in capitalist production relations at both the national and international levels, crises which reflect its inbuilt contradictions, cannot by themselves give rise to a different mode of production (although in respect of capitalism Rudra appears to believe that they can). What they can do, however, is generate from time to time conditions under which capitalist production relations could conceivably break down – it is a question of the conjunctural circumstances and other cumulative developments as to whether such transformations would be possible. In particular, this is so if we take into account the potential of the forces of production to develop. In recent discussions, Marx's original and classic formulation in respect of the role played by the forces of production in the process of the transformation of the relations of production has been both re-defined but also re-affirmed in its essential point.[58] In effect, Marx argued that the contradictions inherent in the situation brought about by the fettering of the productive forces by the social relations of production would lead to a period of revolutionary transformation of the latter, and hence the establishment of the dominance of a new mode of production. The idea is fundamental to Marx's notions of social-economic change, and has received accordingly a great deal of attention. It is possible to read an inevitabilist and deterministic account of historical change into it, for example, to the extent that some Marxists have wanted to severely limit the role of the forces of production as a determining element in the historical process.[59] Recent discussions, however, have tended to emphasize a less teleological or functionalist model interpretation of the role of the forces of production in Marx's writings, so that Callinicos, for example, following a similar line of argument to that of Wright and Levine, has argued that *if* the forces develop, *then* they will come into conflict with the relations of production.[60] The form that any 'fettering' can take will be determined by the mode of production in question (in respect of the structural limitations and possibilities it permits); while the crisis which follows from such a conflict will be 'organic' (a term Callinicos borrows from Gramsci). Those socio-economic interests which perceive themselves as threatened by the potential shifts in the relations of production will hence feel compelled to address the issue directly and take action to inhibit such shifts and the transformation in social and political structures they entail. The ruling class may well succeed in instituting political and economic measures sufficient to stabilize the situation to their own advantage, of course; but it is precisely this that gives the political and economic struggle between contradictory class interests a particular centrality in respect of the outcome. At the same time, the 'organic' crisis may represent a long-term state of affairs, in turn promoting a situation in which first one, then another, antagonistic set of production relations is dominant. In historical terms, this may take several forms. It may give rise to a situation in which new relations of production come to dominate in one social formation but not its neighbours, so that external competition for resources as a result of the internal shifts in the political relations of distribution of surplus wealth creates the conditions for conflict and war. The divergent interests of the nascent nation-states in Europe from the seventeenth century in particular until the triumph of industrial capitalism in the middle of the nineteenth century provides a good example. Similarly, the tension between the slave mode, which dominated Italy in the first century BC and AD, for example, and the tributary mode which was characteristic of production relations throughout the rest of the empire, and which eventually came to dominate, provides another example. In such contexts the way is open for a third factor, namely the state, to impose a degree of equilibrium between the conflicting interests, of which it is both a product and yet from which, given the appropriate circumstances, it can remain relatively autonomous. Importantly, Callinicos stresses that the interests, perceptions, and identities of both individuals and groups play a fundamental role in the 'actualization' of any transformations that do occur.

The relationship between the productive forces and the social relations of production, in the context of the structural capacities of the human agents whose praxis constitutes those social relationships, is thus one of explanatory significance for historical materialism. It means, in effect, that the conditions which might promote crisis for a given mode can be specified in broad terms, just as the structural possibilities within which the social relations of production can respond to such contradictions can be broadly sketched in. But this involves no substantive predictive capacity: it is merely to assert that, where certain sets of conditions are met, then certain types of transformation may follow, dependent upon the outcome of the struggle for control of the means of production between antagonistic classes. The actual form such changes take and the configuration of the social relations of production which evolve out of them must depend upon empirical analysis for further elucidation.

These considerations apply to all modes of production. So that much of the debate in search of a 'prime mover' for the transition from feudalism to capitalism in western Europe, where it has sought this on a purely internalized basis, and as an unavoidable result of certain laws which inevitably lead to transformation, has been searching for what Rudra correctly refers to as a chimera. What most of the historians involved in the debate have done, of course, is to note the ways in which, at a given moment, and under certain specific conditions pertaining to western Europe at a particular time, the tributary relations of production characteristic of this region were sufficiently (quantitatively and qualitatively) loosened as to permit the expansion and consolidation, within a social formation still dominated by feudal relations of production, of production relations substantially different from, and indeed antagonistic to, those which had hitherto dominated.[61]

This must be understood in the context of both 'national' and 'international' pools of influence. This is where those who have stressed the concentric, overlapping and reciprocally (but unevenly) influencing relationships which pertain across the boundaries of social formations have correctly drawn attention to the question of centre–periphery influence. Mann expresses it in terms of 'social power'. I would prefer to retain the formulation of 'social formation' which, in contrast to 'society', is intended rather to render the notion of reciprocity and openness of social structural features.[62]

As I have argued elsewhere, it is the potential for shifts and transformations which general laws elucidate for each specific mode of production. But I would want to argue against any teleology or inevitabilism. This may well not be in keeping with what some have considered Marx to have said; but, as I also argued in chapter 2, that is beside the point. The point is, to try to elaborate a historical materialist mode of analysis which is both internally consistent and usable as a heuristic and explanatory system; which avoids both 'internalist' models of causality and static models of production relations, yet which, through its general categories, offers a set of conceptual guidelines and heuristic formulae which assist the historian in analysing causal relationships and the conjunctural stimuli to change.

4. The Byzantine Paradigm

Given these considerations, it is possible to regard late Roman and Byzantine society as having been dominated by tributary relations of production. That is to say, surplus was appropriated through a variety of forms of tax and rent, which are 'the sole prevailing and normal forms of surplus value, or surplus labour'[63] in the tributary mode. This does not mean that they were the sole existing forms of surplus appropriation in this particular social formation. Slavery continued to exist, but even as early as the fourth century, in the East, seems to have played only a very limited role in production and, more importantly, in the production of the wealth of the dominant class. There is plenty of imperial legislation to suggest that from this time on agricultural slaves were being rapidly turned into the equivalent of *coloni adscripticii* or serfs, given their own holdings or portions on estates, allowed to take partners and have children, and so on. The legal definition of a slave as an unfree person continued in use, of course, and reduction to slave status remained a punishment throughout the Byzantine period. But as agricultural slaves came to approximate more and more to various degrees of tied but free tenant, the economic reality of slavery disappears: rent and tax, not the intensive, plantation-based exploitation of chattel-slaves, seem to be the main form of surplus appropriation from the later third century and afterwards.[64] Domestic and small-scale industrial slavery continued to exist, too, but this hardly affects the dominant mode of surplus appropriation. And even when large numbers of prisoners were taken in war and 'enslaved', they were often then given state or other land to cultivate, and expressly freed for a specific period from state taxation in order to allow them to bring their plots into production – hardly the typical treatment of slaves in the classical sense of the term.[65] In spite of some exaggeration, therefore, slaves do not appear to have played a significant role in overall production, and in particular in the production of surplus wealth, in the late Roman and Byzantine world after the fourth century.[66]

The various institutional forms which surplus appropriation could take were many. Private landlords normally collected rent in cash or kind, according to the nature of the contract or lease and according to the economic conditions of the time or area (availability of market exchange was clearly essential). The state exacted surpluses in both cash and kind (for the regular taxes on land, for example), as well as through a variety of labour-services: maintenance of the postal stations and horses, for example, or the production of iron-ore, woven cloths, and so on, which would be calculated according to centrally-determined tables of equivalence. Equally, local communities were on occasion required to help with the building of roads and bridges or fortifications, and to billet and feed soldiers and their officers, imperial officials and messengers, and so on. By the ninth century, and probably from the seventh century, the state demanded the production of weapons and various items of military equipment from the appropriate craftsmen among the provincial populations, imposed as additional corvées; extraordinary levies in food or grain were common; while military service itself, while not meriting exemption from the chief land- and hearth-taxes, did bring freedom from extraordinary levies and similar impositions.[67] But the crucial point about all these forms of surplus appropriation is that they were obtained without exception through non-economic coercion – whether 'customary' obligations and the force of law, as in most cases, backed up ultimately by imperial military might, or by simple threat and bullying, by state officials, Churchmen or private landlords. This was an agrarian society of peasants and rural artisans, and they were the only realistic source of surplus wealth production.

What sort of state does this social formation support, therefore, and more especially, what enabled the state to survive the very dramatic changes in its conditions of existence which took place over the period from the fifth to the seventh century, culminating in what can reasonably be seen as a genuine crisis which the Islamic conquests promoted?

In fact, it is clear that the state not only survived, but survived with a centralized fiscal and military apparatus which had clearly been able to evolve successfully new ways of dealing with the problems it encountered. But there are two phases in this 'survival', and, indeed, two 'survivals', which should be differentiated: in the first place, the continued existence of the eastern Roman empire after the final fragmentation of the western half into a number of Germanic successor kingdoms; and second, the continued existence of a state, although no longer the late Roman state (I would argue), after the seventh century, after Slavs and other peoples had overrun much of the

Balkans, and after the rapid expansion of Islam had swept away Roman power in the Middle East and North Africa.

The first of these survivals has attracted, on the whole, more attention than the second, at least until recently; for there has been an unfortunate, if understandable, tendency to treat the evolution and history of the East Roman and Byzantine states after the fifth century as an undifferentiated curve on the graph of historical change by both general commentators and specialists.[68] Since the basic reasons for the continued existence of the eastern half of the empire after the middle of the fifth century have been elaborated by a number of historians, I need do no more than summarize results which, while they may be differently nuanced by Marxists as opposed to non-Marxists, nevertheless do represent the current consensus.

In the first place, the power of the eastern senatorial elite[69] was to a large extent moderated by a greater density of cities and by the continued existence throughout the eastern regions of a middling class of landowners. There was, furthermore, always a greater number of more or less autonomous peasant communities, subject fiscally directly to the state; while the landowning elite in the East never came to dominate either the central imperial establishment or the civil bureaucracy in the way that the western senatorial establishment did.[70] The dominance of the military by outsiders was never as great in the East as it was in the West, and this was itself also the consequence of two interrelated aspects of late Roman culture in that area: first, the greater ideological and political cohesiveness of the Constantinopolitan bureaucratic establishment, the greater dependence of the office-holding senatorial elite on the imperial palace and the emperor for its social and economic position, and its more self-conscious cultural elitism and exclusiveness.[71] The East was able to deal with specific problems on its own terms in a way that appears to have been impossible in the West – the successful handling of the 'German problem' in the early fifth century, for example, has been explicitly related to this aspect of East Roman political and economic (as well as cultural) resilience.[72] Second, and as has frequently been pointed out, senatorial economic interests and cultural identity in the West did not correspond as closely as they did in the East with those of the state, especially in the fifth century when the central power was under the more or less permanent influence of military commanders of 'barbarian' origin, and when the cultural and political identity and vested interests of the provincial elites with Rome was seriously called into question. Tax evasion on a massive scale and the extension of relations of landlord–tenant subordination and patronage (*patrocinium*) ensured that the western half of the empire, with its smaller resource base, its less developed urban economic structures and its greater class tensions (there were no uprisings in the east to match those of the various groups of *Bacaudae* in Gaul and Spain in the fifth century, although this does not mean that rural discontent was entirely absent), presented a much less cohesive set of structures and a much more fundamental series of antagonisms between state structures and the interests of the central authority and dominant factions, on the one hand, and the rest of society, especially the provincial elites, on the other.[73]

In spite of the problems faced by the eastern half of the empire in the middle and later fifth century, therefore, its greater political and social cohesiveness, the greater flexibility and pluralism of its structures, enabled it to survive both external attacks as well as the disruption of economic and trading patterns in the Mediterranean – the establishment of the Vandal kingdom in North Africa based at Carthage, which by the late 450s had expanded far beyond its original treaty-borders and, with its developing naval potential, presented a possible substantial threat to both the central and eastern Mediterranean basins. Even the factional conflicts and civil wars of the reigns of Leo I (457–74), Zeno (474–91) and Anastasius I (491–518), which certainly divided the population and destabilized the imperial government, did not adversely affect the essential structures of the state apparatuses.[74] Indeed, during the reign of Anastasius I a major reform of the bronze coinage was undertaken which was to provide the basic framework for the monetary system of the empire until the twelfth century, and which promoted and facilitated the further monetization of the systems of taxation and revenue-collection, as well as market-exchange activity throughout the empire: it should be recalled that the traditional coinage, through inflation and through the inability of the state to maintain a reliable rate of exchange between bronze and gold, had fallen into considerable disarray during the fifth century.[75]

This solid, urban-centred social and cultural formation not only survived the demise of the western empire, it was able during the sixth century, especially during the reign of Justinian I (527–65), to take the offensive and to recover large regions which had been lost to invaders or settlers: the Vandal kingdom of North Africa was destroyed and re-incorporated into the empire in a brief campaign in 533–4; parts of south-east Spain were seized from the Visigoths in 550, although these were all lost again during the first half of the seventh century; and in a long-drawn-out war, the Ostrogothic kingdom of Italy was destroyed between 535 and 555 (although some Ostrogothic districts held out until 562).

The cost of this expansionist politics was very great. Minor reforms of the fiscal apparatus meant greater exactions from the producing population of the empire; Italy itself was devastated, its rural and urban economies shattered; the army was neither adequately resourced nor its ranks filled on the one hand; yet neither could the revenues of the state support a greater demand from this quarter, on the other. The enormous cost of warfare in ancient states is strikingly summed up by the anonymous compiler of a sixth-century treatise on strategy, who notes that the greater part of the state's income is expended each year on the army.[76] And within ten years of the final reconquest of Italy, the invasion of the Lombards (from 568) had destroyed what little peace the peninsula had enjoyed. Henceforth it becomes increasingly marginal to imperial interests – although its ideological significance remains considerable for years.

In addition to the exhaustion of resources resulting from these vast campaigns of reconquest (and the constant drain of fighting also with the Persian Sassanid state in the East), various forms of bubonic plague were endemic from the 540s, and certainly took their toll. The graphic account of the contemporary historian Procopius – while based on the account of Thucydides of the plague in Athens in the fifth century BC, and while now shown to be considerably exaggerated in many respects – suggests nevertheless the psychological effect it had.[77] From the 570s, the infiltration of groups of Slav immigrants across the Danube and into the Balkans, penetrating even into the Peloponnese by the 590s, the constant wars with the Persians, and with the Turkic Avars in the Balkans, all represented a massive expenditure in resources, cash and manpower. During the reign of Justin II (565–78) the state's fiscal exactions became ever more burdensome, so that his successor, Tiberius II Constantine (578–82) had to remit all taxes for a year in order to give the peasant producers time to recover (although there was also a powerful element of imperial largesse and ideological manipulation involved in this very popular act).[78]

Yet in spite of these problems, and the recommencing of the war with the Persians in 602–3 (lasting up until the final victory of the East Romans under Heraclius in 626–7), the East Roman state in the early 630s still embraced North Africa, Egypt, all of what is today

Syria, much of western Iraq and Jordan, along with the Lebanon and Palestine, Anatolia, much of the Balkans, Sicily, Sardinia and still considerable areas of Italy. In practice, however, much of the Balkans was out of effective central control, dominated by Slav or indigenous tribal, clan and urban regional principalities. Again, the cohesiveness of the central state apparatuses and the still considerable resources at their disposal lies behind this success. But the old imperial system could only tolerate so much pressure. And when in the 630s the Arabs emerged from the Arabian peninsula under the banner of Islam and the holy war, imperial resistance was little more than token. Low morale, insufficient resources, ideological divisions, insufficiently flexible defensive strategies all played a role. By 642 all of Egypt and the Middle eastern provinces had been lost, Arab forces had penetrated deep into Asia Minor and Libya, and imperial forces had been withdrawn into Asia Minor, across the provinces of which they were to be settled as the only available means of supporting them. Within a period of some twelve years, therefore, it has been calculated that the empire lost something over half its area and three-quarters of its resources – a drastic loss for the imperial state, which still had to maintain and equip a considerable army and an effective administrative bureaucracy if it was to survive at all.[79]

The effects of this catastrophe can hardly be calculated, and a detailed analysis would take up too much space here. But as a result of all these developments, which interwove with the evolution of East Roman social and economic structures and ideology over the same period, there arises a rather different social and cultural formation. The physical context – greatly reduced in size – the conditions of climate and geography, remain very much the same. But late Roman culture vanishes almost completely, together with a great deal of the cultural capital it carried with it. It must be stressed that many of the developments which led to this transformation were in train long before the seventh-century crisis; but that crisis brought things to a head and promoted structures and responses embodied in ideology and social practice which must otherwise have been rather different. New systems of thought develop, new approaches to visual representation. The emphases within literary culture, and indeed the bearers of that culture, change considerably, radical transformations of the fiscal and military administration occur. The relationships of power to land and to office within the ruling elite change. The old senatorial establishment, with much of the literary cultural baggage associated with it, disappears (or is transformed) during the seventh century to be replaced by a service elite of different and heterogeneous ethnic, social and cultural origins. And while there is little reason to doubt that this new, pseudo-meritocratic elite incorporated many elements of the older establishment, those aspects of traditional elite culture which did survive, or were 'rediscovered', came to play a very different role in the symbolic universe, in the ideological world, of the evolving culture. The disappearance of the cities as municipalities (although very many survived as small defended settlements or fortresses with little or no urban exchange activity) meant that there took place what can reasonably be described as a ruralization of the state. Wealthy provincials found access to positions of authority blocked off at the local level, both by local economic conditions as well as by the predominance of centrally-appointed provincial military and civil officialdom; henceforth they turned to Constantinople, the seat of empire, the one source of wealth, status and power, in which to invest their social capital and in order to become part of that system. Only the Church provided an alternative and equivalent career structure, and that too was centred in Constantinople, its administrative structures paralleling in many ways those of the state. Centralization of fiscal administration, which had anyway been slowly increasing in pace since the middle of the fifth century as the municipalities and their dominant elites found themselves less and less able (and consequently less willing) to carry out their fiscal obligations in respect of the state; together with 'rationalization' of various departments of civil and military administration, produced a very different administrative establishment. The emperor and the court became, more than ever before, the source of social advancement: while there were all sorts of minor routes to power which were not directly pulled into that nexus, nevertheless the imperial court constituted the dominant mode of entry. One of the most striking symptoms of this changed social and cultural environment is the acute nature of the ideological struggles over imperial authority in the religious and political-military sphere during the later seventh and eighth centuries.[80] One or two of these changes are worth particular attention.

To begin with the transformation in late Roman urban structures, it is now generally agreed on the basis of both literary and archaeological evidence that the urban centres of the late ancient world were almost entirely eclipsed during the course of the seventh century. The classical city, the *polis* or *civitas*, had come during the Roman period to occupy a central role both in the social and economic structure of Mediterranean society (and to a lesser extent of those northern European regions to which it was imported), as well as in the administrative machinery of the empire. Cities might be centres of market-exchange, of regional agricultural activity, occasionally of small-scale commodity production or, where ports were concerned, major foci of long-distance commerce. Some fulfilled all these roles, others remained merely administrative centres created by the state for its own fiscal administrative purposes. Crucially, all cities were also self-governing districts with, originally, their own lands, and were made responsible by the Roman state for the return of taxes. Where cities in the Hellenistic or Mediterranean sense did not exist, the Roman state created them, sometimes establishing entirely new foundations, sometimes amalgamating or changing the nature of pre-existing settlements and providing them with a corporate identity, institutional structure and legal personality of a *civitas*.[81] These cities were, on the whole, dependent on their immediate hinterlands for their (usually highly localized) market and industrial functions, where these existed at all, as well as for the foodstuffs from which the urban populace lived. They acted as local centres, but on the whole were parasitic on their *territoria*. And as the social and economic structure of the empire evolved away from the relationships and conditions which gave rise to and maintained these urban structures, so the cities became the first key institution of the classical world to feel the effects of these changes.

The forms which these changes took are complex, but mirror the effects of a growing conflict between state, cities and private landowners to extract surpluses from the producers; and the failure of the cities to weather the contradictions between their municipal independence, on the one hand, and, on the other, the demands of the state and the vested interests of the wealthier civic landowners. Although there is evidence well into the first half of the seventh century in the East that many *curiales*, or city councillors, did honour their obligations with respect to both state and city, it is clear already by the later fourth century that many did or could not. The *curiales* as landowners and leading citizens had been responsible both for the upkeep of their cities by voluntary subscription, and for the local assessment, collection and forwarding of the revenues demanded by the state. But as many were able to obtain senatorial status, which freed them from such duties, so the burden fell more and more upon the less wealthy and privileged, who were in consequence less able to extract all the revenues demanded (especially as tax evasion among the wealthy, through bribery as well as physical resistance, was endemic). In fact, the process was much more complex and nuanced, subject also to regional variations according to the traditional pattern of landholding and urbanization, for example, than I am able to describe here, but these were some of its most obvious features. As a result, and over the period from the later fourth to the later fifth century (in the West until the empire disappears as well as in the East), the state had to intervene ever more directly to ensure the extraction of its revenues, which it did both by appointing supervisors imposed upon the city administrators, as well as through the confiscation of city lands, the rents from which were now the guarantee that the state's fiscal income was at least to some extent assured, and eventually through the appointment of tax-farmers for each municipal district. The *curiales* seem still to have done the actual work of collecting, but the burden of fiscal accountability seems to have been removed during the reign of Anastasius (491–518).[82] While this certainly relieved the pressure, and possibly helped promote the brief renaissance in urban fortunes which appears to have taken place in some eastern cities in the sixth century, it did nothing to re-establish their traditional independence and fiscal responsibilities.

By the early years of the seventh century all the evidence suggests that cities as corporate bodies were simply less well-off than they had been before about the middle of the sixth century. But this does not mean that urban life declined in any absolute sense, or that cities no longer fulfilled their role as centres of exchange and production. Literary and archaeological sources suggest, for example, that they continued to function as local foci of exchange and small-scale commodity production as well as for the social activity of the landowners and the wealthy of their districts. It is possible that there was as much wealth circulating in urban environments as before, with the difference that the city as an institution had only very limited access to it. They had had their lands and the income from those lands taken from them. The local wealthy tended also, during the later sixth century in particular, to invest their wealth in religious building or related objects, and it is important to bear in mind an evolving pattern of investment as well as the possibilities of a decline in investment. In addition, the Church was from the fourth century a competitor with the city for the consumption of resources. And however much their citizens might donate, individually or collectively, this can hardly have compensated for this loss.[83] Indeed, such contributions became the main source of independent income for many cities. The archaeological data suggest a shrinkage of occupied areas of many cities, and even an increasing localization of exchange activity; but again, this does not have to mean a change in their role as local centres of such exchange.

It is worth examining one other facet of the state's role in all this. The first point to make is that the Roman state had quite deliberately during the third, fourth and fifth centuries followed a policy of 'rationalizing' patterns of distribution of cities. Many cities in over-densely occupied regions were deprived of the status and privileges of city, others which were of importance to the state in its fiscal-administrative structure were 'incorporated' and received city status for the first time. This had nothing to do with economic interests, but reflected rather the desire of the emperors to establish a network of centres adequate to the demands of the fiscal system. Considerable numbers of the 'cities' which were suppressed in this process had been little more than villages representing the autonomous or semi-autonomous communities of the pre-Roman states incorporated into the empire.[84] By endowing certain settlements with city status and, more especially, with local fiscal-administrative functions and responsibility, the state assured such cities of their continued existence and at the same time enhanced their local importance, whatever their original economic and social situation may have been. It is a logical concomitant that, when the elites in such communities were, for the reasons already referred to, no longer able adequately to fulfil this role for the state, and when the state began to supervise city fiscal affairs directly, employing the *curiales* merely as assessors and collectors of tax rather than guarantors, the continued existence of such cities would become a matter of indifference to the central government, at least in functional terms. Of course, the ideological and symbolic importance of cities and urban culture in the Roman world, expressed through imperial involvement in urban building and renewal in several cases, prevented this happening at this stage. In addition, cities particularly associated with Christianity – through a local saint's cult, for example – enhanced their chances of flourishing where they did not already possess a primary economic character.

A second point concerns the role of Constantinople. The establishment of a new imperial capital on the site of the ancient city of Byzantium had far-reaching consequences for the pattern of exchange and re-distribution of goods in the Aegean and east Mediterranean basin, a point well-attested by the distribution of ceramics.

The city's markets increasingly determined the pattern of ceramic production in the Aegean and beyond throughout the medieval period. In addition, the establishment of an imperial court and a senate, with all its social, economic and administrative consequences, had a similar effect upon the pattern of socio-cultural investment across the same macro-region. That is to say, that by the early seventh century, with a few exceptions, social interest for the investment of personal wealth and the accretion of prestige and status was increasingly focused on Constantinople as the best way of ensuring a niche within the imperial system. Of course, there are exceptions to this – Alexandria, for example. Nevertheless, the changing pattern of imperial administration and patronage must be considered yet another factor bearing on the ways in which late Roman elites invested their wealth, and hence on the amount of social investment in provincial cities.[85] The ceramic evidence demonstrates the exceptional position of Constantinople, and makes its pre-eminence as the key centre for the consumption and re-distribution of both luxury and non-luxury goods very clear.[86] But the provincial urban archaeological record reflects these developments also – an almost universal failure of cities to maintain their public buildings, water supply and roads in their 'classical' form and, in spite of the numerous (usually quite small) churches which were constructed during the sixth and into the early seventh century, what is generally taken to be a general impoverishment in the public life of the cities.[87]

The expansion of the state bureaucracy into provincial urban affairs, a direct result of the state's efforts to secure its control over resources, conflicted clearly with the corporate interests of the cities. As they lost ground to the central administration, so they lost the support of their local landowning elite. The civic pride formerly attached to their administrative functions continued a sort of twilight existence; but by the middle of the sixth century the state was the only institution which could afford to invest in civic buildings on a large scale – usually defensive or administrative structures reflecting the state's own priorities. The Church might also intervene, of course, especially in respect of the construction or maintenance of philanthropic institutions such as orphanages and so forth. But the clear results of these changes was that by the middle of the sixth century cities had effectively lost their autonomy and were no longer centres of administratively self-governing regions. Apart from the requirements of local civil and ecclesiastical administrators, they were by-passed by the state, replaced by the salaried bureaucracy of the

Constantinopolitan establishment.[88] It was the capital which now attracted the attention of the provincial elites.[89]

The survival of urban settlements during and after the Arab invasions (which, it must be stressed, lasted with varying degrees of intensity in Asia Minor from the 640s until the 750s on a more or less yearly basis) owed much to the fact that they might occupy defensible sites, as well as be centres of military or ecclesiastical administration. But the great majority played no commercial or market-exchange role of significance. Any economic role they may have played was peripheral to, and derived from, the economic and social life of the countryside, and reflected if anything the needs of state and Church. The invasions of the seventh century dealt what was simply the final blow to an already dying institution.[90]

A further major factor of significance is the situation of the producing population over the period in question, that is to say, from the sixth to the twelfth and thirteenth centuries, and I shall present this in some detail.

In the sixth century, the state (in the form of both private imperial lands and state – 'public' – domains) along with the Church and the senatorial elite formed the most powerful group of landowners or landholders in the empire. The state especially, but other landowners also, sub-let its lands to tenants, who received a rent from the actual cultivators themselves. Along with free emphyteutic tenants (see below), land was farmed for the most part by dependent peasants of one category or another, such as *coloni adscripticii* and *coloni liberi*, who, until the sixth century, certainly appear to have constituted the largest group. The latter were free persons restricted to their holdings for a period of up to thirty years, after which they were permitted to leave and move elsewhere if they wished; the former were bound to their holdings hereditarily and entered in the tax-assessment records (*adscripticii*) accordingly, under the name of their landlord. The term *colonus* originally meant a free peasant farmer, then a free tenant farmer, and eventually (from the middle of the third century approximately) a tenant of dependent status. By the middle of the fifth century the status of *colonus* had been made hereditary (a reflection of both demographic decline and labour shortages, and political considerations in respect of the relationship between the state and the landlord class), and by the sixth century the majority were regarded as unfree as far as their mobility was concerned, being classified as 'slaves of the land'. They could be released from their obligations only by their landlord, and only if certain conditions with regard to their plots were met.[91] In contrast to the *adscripticii*, however, the *coloni liberi* paid taxes directly to the state, and continued to be entered in the tax registers under their own names, rather than under a landlord's name. They were free to make wills and to inherit and dispose of property, although they were, as we have seen (from the time of the emperor Anastasius, 491–518) forbidden to leave their holdings for a specified period. In spite of this apparently superior juridical status, the *coloni liberi* were only slightly better off than the supposedly inferior *adscripticii*: it seems that the latter could also take out leases and act as legally independent and free persons. The fact that their *peculium* or personal property and the rights attaching thereto came under the authority of their landlords – generally taken to be a sign of their more-or-less servile status – has recently been shown to be a factor of their political-juridical position in respect of their landlords and the estates of which they were a part. For such estates owed revenue to the state and *munera* or civic liturgies to the local municipality in whose *territorium* they were located. Thus the distraint (or the possibility of distraint) by the landlord of the *peculium* of the tenants 'tied to the land' functioned in the same way as the distraint exercised by the municipality as a legal personality or corporation of the property of a member of the curial class (the local landlord class whose duties were closely bound up with the civic and revenue functions of the cities) who failed to fulfil such duties. It served in effect as a security on the returns from agricultural production, in which relationship the landlord functioned effectively as an agent of the city and thence, ultimately, of the state fisc. And it should be emphasized that, while the adscripted *colonus* had no freedom to leave his holding, neither had the landlord the freedom to move or expel him, or to increase the basic rent or tax imposition on his holding. Of course, landlords found all sorts of ways to exploit this relationship in practice. Nevertheless, the state attempted to regulate affairs to the benefit of both sides, but chiefly for the benefit of the state itself.[92]

Alongside these two major groups were free smallholders, often hardly different in respect of their economic situation from the *coloni*, with whom they might share a village and community. They were of slightly higher status legally, of course, since they owned their properties, and could alienate them at will. But since they were subject to both pressure from the fisc for tax, on the one hand, and from the more powerful landlords around them, on the other, their position was rarely secure. There is evidence for communities of such freeholders throughout the empire into the early seventh century, and indeed Justin II (565–78) expressly forbade officials of the imperial estates in the empire to lay claim to the surrounding villages and their lands, whether these were of freeholders, on civic lands, or on the estates of either senatorial landlords or the Church.

To what extent this pattern of landownership and land-exploitation survived into and beyond the seventh century is difficult to say. Of the groups of landowners who dominated in the sixth century and before, there is no doubt that the Church and the state continued to be major landlords within the territories remaining to the empire after the territorial losses of the middle and later seventh century. Bishops were important, for example, both in respect of the interests of the provincial congregations of the Church, and from the point of view of local civil administration and economic organization, since they represented the Church also as a major landlord, and belonged, therefore, to the class of provincial magnates in respect of surplus appropriation. It was often the bishop who was responsible for directing municipal action in respect of works of fortification and supplying a city in times of danger, for example, even extending their role to the administration of the public (state or municipal) granaries and the provisioning of locally-based troops.

By the same token, the continued existence of the senate in Constantinople, the power and authority it wielded on occasion during the seventh century, and its reinforcement through newcomers from the imperial bureaucracy and administrative apparatus, meant that large landed properties in all probability survived. The actual composition of the senate, and the degree of continuity from the sixth century in terms of families and specific estates, remains impossible to assess. It does seem, however, that the older senatorial magnate families gradually lost power to the rising service aristocracy of the Constantinopolitan establishment, although there is no reason to doubt that a large proportion of the old elite were assimilated to the new elite of the second half of the seventh century. Whatever the origins of the military and civil officials of the period, personal wealth could only be assured beyond one generation through the acquisition of land. Landed property remained an essential element in securing one's future and also in cementing one's position within the establishment. Marriage into older and established landed families, on the one hand, and the purchase of land – from other landowners, including both state and Church (in the form of perpetual but transferable leases), or from impoverished or threatened peasant communities – made the continued existence of large-scale landed property a necessary element in seventh- and eighth-century society. And there is enough evidence to show that large private estates existed – side by side with those of the state and the Church – in the later seventh and eighth centuries, although the degree of physical continuity remains unknown. The sources refer also to the large estates of the Church, and to villages of independent peasants, who own and farm their holdings, paying taxes directly to the state. But the extent of such communities was especially important for the state, since it was greatly to its advantage to have as large a proportion of the producing population directly under its fiscal authority as tax-payers, and thus maximize its share of the surplus appropriated.[93]

This is especially important in the context of the seventh and eighth centuries. As we have seen, those who worked the land can be divided into several categories according to their legal and their economic status. But the proportion of free tenants and freeholders seems to have become increasingly important during this period, a process begun already in the sixth century, as imperial legislation suggests. Of particular interest are tenants leasing lands on an emphyteutic basis, that is to say, those who leased land on the basis of a fixed rent, whose leases could be transferred and were often held in perpetuity and hereditarily. Just as significantly, the evidence of the use of certain technical terms for peasant or farmer in a variety of texts has been reasonably interpreted to mean that a gradual assimilation of all three categories of tenant smallholder (*coloni liberi*, free tenants and emphyteutic lessees) into a single body of tenants occurred during the seventh and eighth centuries, tenants who paid a rent to their landlord and tax to the state, bound to their holdings or not according to the nature of their tenancy (which meant that emphyteutic lessees could cede or sell their land – that is to say, their lease – to a third party, and were often regarded, at least in respect of non-Church lands, as the possessor and not simply the tenant, *locator*).[94] Further evidence from this period illustrates the continued existence of villages of predominantly free peasants. But it is clear that such communities now represented a more important element in the totality of the relations of production, especially with respect to the state and its revenue-collecting apparatus. The sources suggest that in both Byzantine society in general and in the eyes of the state (and the officials who exercised judicial powers in the provinces) the village community was, or was rapidly becoming, an economic and social element of much greater relative importance than had hitherto been the case, a fact which can be related directly to the decline in the administrative importance of the towns and municipal centres of the empire.

Such communities had existed throughout the late Roman world, and indeed the nucleated village settlement was the usual form of settlement outside the city, whatever the legal status of its inhabitants. The qualitative change in their role does not necessarily mean that there were more of them, although, as we shall see in a moment, this was probably the case. What the evidence does suggest is that the village, and its individual landholders, was in addition becoming a key element in the state's administration of revenue extraction and collection – a clear contrast to the later Roman period, when it had been the landlord and the city who had been the chief intermediaries. The evidence from the later period (after the eighth century), when the village as a fiscal and juridical entity clearly did play the central role, illustrates the results of this process. And the terminological changes referred to above, evidenced especially by the increasing use from the later fifth and through the sixth century of the same technical term for both village and fiscal community, show that the social, administrative and economic shifts which this development represents were already under way.[95]

The increased importance of such independent communities, if the sources have been adequately interpreted, may also imply that the number of such villages increased as well. Some of the reasons for this expansion have been argued at length by several scholars: the abandonment by landlords of their estates in threatened areas, and the consequent assertion by the agrarian producers of their independence; the state-organized immigration of large numbers of Slav settlers with their own community structures and organization; and the increasing independence of peasant smallholders with perpetual or long-term, heritable leases, paying low and fixed rents to landlords who may often have been permanently resident away from their properties. Of these, the first and last are generally seen as the most plausible, and two fundamental causes seem to have been operating.

In the first place, the change in emphasis in the mode of exploitation of large properties: the gradual weakening of the adscripted colonate in favour of long-term and often heritable leases on state, Church and private lands tended to reduce the need for estate owners to supervise either directly or indirectly the production process. As long as rents were collected, interference was unnecessary; while the producers were responsible under the terms of their lease anyway for the state's taxes. This reduced both the administrative costs and the fiscal obligations of landlords. It removed the need for bailiffs, except as rent-collectors. But it also weakened the landlords' direct control over their property, while re-inforcing the relationship between producers and state. The juridical differences in status of the various types of producer – *coloni*, leaseholders, smallholders and peasant proprietors – thus became less significant to the fiscal requirements of the state, less relevant to the production process itself, and less relevant to the landowners.

The long-term cumulative result seems to have been a considerable increase in the number of communities subject directly to the fisc, albeit made up of persons of very varied legal status. Most importantly, the great majority possessed freedom of movement and were, in effect, possessors even if not owners of their holdings, whatever their original condition. Of course, the peasants of the various sources of the period must not be taken to represent a uniform body of free proprietors. They represent subsistence farmers with freedom of movement, freedom to transfer their land or to transmit it to their heirs. All of these provisions were possible within the terms of the normal emphyteutic lease, as well as straightforward proprietorship.

In the second place, there occurred also a change in emphasis, similarly reflected in the sources, in state fiscal policy. The cities had been for some time unable to cope with the problems of taking fiscal responsibility for their *territoria*. State officials had taken over the supervision and administration of such tasks since the fifth and sixth centuries. By the same token, landlords – estate owners – no longer played an important role in this context either. The state had as a result to concentrate on the level at which wealth-production actually took place, in other words, the land and the communities who farmed it. The centres of production were the villages, and these came to replace the cities in the fiscal administrative structure of the early Byzantine state. In a more visible way than before, the village comes to occupy a central position in the society and administration of the empire from the later seventh century.

The expansion of independent smallholding appears to have been both a result of the changes in the relationship between agricultural producers and landlords, and to a degree also the result of the reorganization of the system of fiscal assessment by the state, in turn brought about by the dislocation of the warfare of the second half of the seventh century. At the same time, it has been suggested that the conditions promoted by war and constant insecurity cast a large number of the agricultural population of threatened areas adrift, as refugees – either from the tax-collector, the rent-collector and bailiff, or the Arabs. It stimulated an increase in demographic mobility. The relocation by the state of refugee populations in several different areas of the empire further complicated the picture.[96]

But while the changes which I have described so far did constitute a modification in the institutional expression, and the balance, of the relations of production, there was no change in either the mode of surplus appropriation or the relationship of peasants to their means of subsistence and reproduction. While labour-power was scarce, cultivable land often deserted, and the state able to impose a uniform policy on the rural population only with great difficulty – the latter an effect of the divergent interests of the older landowning element of the ruling class and the new, particularly the military, service aristocracy – the condition of the peasantry with regard to the assertion of its rights of tenure, and communal solidarity in respect of the fisc, improved. But clearly, a number of factors militated against the disappearance of large estates and social equilibrium in peasant communities.

Social differentiation within peasant communities, the impoverishment of some smallholders to the advantage of others and in particular the sub-division of holdings among heirs, leading to properties which might eventually become too small to be economically viable, these factors all facilitated the encroachment of the wealthier peasants on the lands of the poorer, and of the big estate-owner on the lands of peasant communities in general.[97] Together with poor harvests, seasonal or climatic fluctuations, natural disasters and similar perennially present elements, and in addition to the demands of the fisc, of the local provincial or military administration, such factors always left peasant farmers very vulnerable to changes in fortune and sudden household economic failure.[98] The abandonment of holdings and the attribution of the taxes due from these to the owners of neighbouring lands was clearly a normal occurrence for the compilers of the legal hand-books of the eighth and ninth centuries, and their evidence portrays a rural society with many internal gradations.

Peasants of *colonus* status, bound to their land by private contract, continued to farm the estates of powerful landlords, whether private, Church or state, spread over several provinces or districts. They shared villages with free tenants, emphyteutic lessees and so forth. In areas relatively free from hostile threat, the well-established bond between landlord and tenants, whatever the legislative intervention of the state may have done to relax or weaken the connection, remained. So that, while the conditions of the seventh century seem to have resulted in a number of important and substantive changes, not all areas within the empire will necessarily have been affected in the same way. While the overall effect of the economic and social dislocation of the second half of the seventh century and the opening years of the eighth century seems to have promoted an increase in peasant mobility and in the numbers of peasant freeholders directly subject to the fisc, already the disadvantages which accompanied a peasant subsistence economy, together with the rise of the new magnate elite of the provinces, were leading to a new phase of polarization between estate owners and peasant communities, on the one hand, and within such communities, on the other. The evidence of eighth- and ninth-century sources in respect of the tax-burdens of the rural population, especially of those which affected the poorer members of each community, make this clear. The long-term result was a general decline in the numbers of these independent communities, and the reduction of the vast mass of the peasantry to the status of tenants of one condition or another by the later eleventh century. Once again, however, it needs to be stressed that no marked shift in the mode of surplus appropriation can be detected. The crucial changes concerned the mode of distribution of surplus, a point to which I will return below.

The final factor of importance which is worth dwelling on is more difficult to elucidate, because of the nature of the limited evidence available, but can be sketched in with a reasonable degree of certainty by looking at the ways in which the state apparatus functions in the period up to the middle of the seventh century, and after the later part of the eighth century. I refer to the fate of the late Roman ruling class, and the relationship between the state and the evolving military-bureaucratic elite which begins to appear in the sources from the later seventh century, to which reference has already been made.

There is little doubt that this new elite owed its origins to the period of turmoil and re-organization of state structures which occurred in the seventh century. The need of the state to find persons competent to deal with both civil and military matters in the provinces in this period of crisis is a central consideration. The advantages an individual had over both local landlords and peasantry if he occupied a position of military or civil authority in the provinces were considerable – a monopoly of armed force, for example, the power to seize or confiscate food or other produce for the army, and so on. Persons appointed to such posts thus had every opportunity to further their own interests if they desired. But what is particularly important, and emerges from a number of careful prosopographical analyses of state officials at the time, is that the composition changes both of the senate in Constantinople and of the state's leading officials. The old senatorial elite, in the broadest sense, gradually gives way to persons of different origins. Although there had always been a place for 'newcomers', under imperial patronage, in the state establishment during the later Roman period, the greater proportion of non-Greek names, for example, of officials known from all types of source, is very striking from the 660s and after.[99] At the same time, the old system of senatorial dignities and titles (in three groups, the *clarissimi*, the *spectabiles* and the *illustres*) seems to drop out of use, only the leading category of the *illustres* group, referred to as *gloriosi* (*endoxos* or *endoxotatos* in Greek) retaining any significance. Together, these developments suggest both a considerable change in the cultural and social origins of key personnel in the imperial establishment at all levels; and the increasing irrelevance of titles which no longer corresponded to either social or political realities. This is made clear in the evident re-jigging of the whole system of titles and precedence during the seventh century, in which the importance of titles and posts dependent directly upon imperial palatine service increases to the disadvantage of older titles associated in one way or another with the senatorial order. Power was concentrated and focused more than ever before on the figure of the emperor and in the imperial palace, while the older, much more pluralistic system of rank, privilege, wealth and power disappears. And all these developments in turn suggest that, while many senatorial landowners probably did hold on to their properties during this period of massive economic disruption and sometimes severe political repression (confiscations of senatorial property and waves of executions are supposed to have occurred in the reigns of Phocas [602–10] and Justinian II [705–11] in his second reign) the old elite must have suffered very considerably as the economic effects of constant warfare came to be felt.[100]

The sum of all these changes, however, is not simply that the dominance of the older aristocracy was broken, or that the state administration was increasingly filled by newcomers. It is that the new pseudo-meritocratic service elite depended, at least in this period, entirely upon the emperor; and although the sources are few and often difficult to interpret, one feature above all stands out: the seventh century witnessed a massive re-concentration of power and economic control in the hands of the state. The shrinkage of the empire territorially, the centralization of fiscal administration, the effective disappearance of cities as intermediaries, socially and economically, between the provinces and Constantinople, the apparent increase in the numbers of peasant communities independent of private landlords, as well as the other features outlined already, were all part of this shift in emphasis. And it gave the imperial system a new lease of life which was to last until the eleventh century. But by then the service meritocracy of the later seventh century had become, by virtue of its close affiliation with the state and with imperial patronage, the provincial aristocracy of the middle and later empire. The inherent contradictions between the economic interests of an increasingly independent landowning magnate class dominating the machinery of the state, and the fiscal interests of the state itself and of the particular power elite or ruling class faction which directed it at any given moment – fought out over the surplus which could be wrung out of the producing population – became clear. Should that surplus go to the magnates, as rent, or to the state (and thence, indirectly, the power elite of the moment) as taxes and other impositions? Part of the resolution, from the eleventh century, given the dependence of the state upon this class for all its chief civil and military functionaries (although distinct class fractions existed, which used the state against their particular opponents), was for the state to concede revenue extraction to those upon whom it depended. The other part of the resolution was the seizure of the state by the representatives of a particular fraction of the ruling class, and the establishment of a more openly dynastic and aristocratic system of administration, dependent upon a precarious network of clan alliances and patronage supported by the leading magnate families. But it is important to note that the state even at this stage, when it had become politically much more obviously tied to the interests of the ruling class, never conceded assessment, and what eventually became *de facto* a hereditary concession was never conceded *de jure*.[101]

5. Institutional Forms and Real Relations

Here we can stop for a moment to examine more closely the key elements which, it is claimed by those who maintain that Byzantium represents a form of the ancient or slave modes, are indicative of developing 'feudal', that is, tributary, production relations in the Byzantine world, and without which, so the argument runs, no 'feudalism' in Byzantium can be said to have existed. Two aspects above all have been singled out: first, the granting, from the later eleventh century, of *pronoiai* to individuals, that is to say, the concession by the state of the right to receive the revenues from certain public (fiscal, or taxed) districts, or of certain imperial estates, and their tenants, along with part or all of the rents and taxes raised from them. Such grants were made for a variety of reasons to individuals by the emperors. They took the form of personal grants from the ruler, who represented the state in the institutional sense; and while there was also a more general meaning of the term *pronoia*, that which concerns us involves *pronoia* grants in return for military service. The second aspect is concerned with the increasing subordination of the peasantry to both private landlords and to holders of *pronoiai*, a development alluded to already.

The arguments adduced by Ostrogorsky, as well as by a number of Soviet scholars, maintain that these developments constitute the first signs of a process of feudalization. Up until the appearance of military grants of *pronoia* (that is, until the later eleventh century), it is argued that the central state had maintained its forces on the basis of salaries and tax-exemptions for certain categories of peasant, in order to keep up the recruitment of (a) mercenary or 'professional' units and (b) the regular, provincial but quasi-militia forces, or *themata* (*thema* being the technical word for an army and the district from which it was recruited). The predominantly free peasantry, while they became increasingly liable to the depredations and encroachments of the big landowners and magnates (especially in the tenth century),[102] as well as those who were also the tenants of large landlords, were all still subject to the fisc, that is to say, they were taxed directly (although some estate owners, particularly monastic or ecclesiastical, were exempted as a special privilege by certain emperors). With the introduction of the *pronoia* system, a process of alienation of the state's fiscal and juridical rights sets in, which leads ultimately to the privatization and parcellization of surplus appropriation by the ruling class at the state's expense.

Feudalism is thus, according to these arguments, identified with what are claimed to be specific institutional forms of surplus appropriation, which are similar to those also found in the classic feudal structures of the medieval West, and which mark a major change from the mode of surplus appropriation dominant in the previous period: the *pronoia* is seen as the (evolving) equivalent of the fief; the increasing subordination of a free or semi-free peasantry to the magnate class and the *pronoia*-holders is seen as leading to a serf-like rural population.[103]

Now there is no doubt that, at the descriptive level, these institutions are similar to those of the West in many respects. Neither is there any doubt that, while they were always revocable and limited in theory, many such grants were eventually given on a semi-permanent basis (for several generations, for example) and thus tended to become the private property of the grantee, particularly where grants of estates and peasants were concerned – the other type of grant, of fiscal revenues alone, was less likely to follow this path. On the other hand, such grants only seem to have become generalized from the middle of the twelfth century as a means of supporting soldiers, and many of them were very small – not major estates designed to support a knight and his retinue, but quite small revenues intended to maintain a soldier for a limited period. And it is worth noting that this generalization occurs well after the state had been seized by the Komnenos clan, one of the leading magnate families, and its allies, in 1081.

But the crucial question is this: are these institutional developments the sign of the appearance of tributary/feudal relations of production, that is, of relations of production different from those which prevailed before this time? And do they really represent a different mode of surplus appropriation? I do not think so, and for a number of reasons.

In the first place, the basic mode of surplus appropriation remains just as it had been: the direct producers, in possession of their holdings, continued to hand over surpluses on the basis of non-economic coercion. The only difference is that they now handed over that surplus – or a part of it – to the revenue collectors of those who had received grants of *pronoia*. Where only revenues had been granted, of course (and this was probably the majority of cases in the first instance), even this did not change. It was the state tax-collector who handed over the appropriate sum to the *pronoia*-holder. The relationship of the peasantry to the means of production – land – similarly remains unchanged, even though the peasantry came increasingly under the domination of estate owners and the number of free communities declined from the tenth century.[104] In economic terms, therefore, there is absolutely no change in either the mode of surplus appropriation or the relationship of the primary producers to the means of production and their means of subsistence. And since, as we have seen, these are the two key elements which distinguish one mode of production from another, no change in the latter can be said to have taken place.

What did change, of course, were the institutional forms in which surpluses were distributed: no longer through the state to the state apparatuses, but directly to elements of that apparatus, in this case, sections of the army, and, eventually, to private landlords. And this is where the confusion has arisen: what historians have wanted to see as a mode of surplus appropriation is, in fact, merely a form of surplus distribution, and this is determined very much at the superstructural level.

By the same token, what have been seen by other historians as different modes of surplus appropriation at an earlier period (private landlords with tenants existed side by side with independent peasant communities subject only to the fisc, or its equivalent, throughout the Roman and into the medieval – Byzantine – period) are, as I have argued, merely different institutional forms of one mode, namely, that of feudal rent or tribute. The earlier period, from the fifth, sixth or seventh century is, therefore, not a 'proto-feudal' period, in which two antagonistic modes of production – modes of surplus appropriation – struggle for dominance. On the contrary, the tributary/feudal mode clearly dominates. The struggle is between two institutional forms of surplus appropriation, forms which represent the vested economic and ideological interests of a class of magnates able to assert their independence of the state which produced them, on the one hand, and, on the other, the relative autonomy of the bureaucratic and centralized state apparatus, run by a particular fraction or coalition of fractions drawn from that magnate class, its clients, and other dependent social groups. The appearance from the ninth century and after, on a larger scale than hitherto, of private estates with tenants of varying degrees of subordination does not mean that the dominance and centrality of the state in the preceding period (seventh and eighth centuries) represents a non-tributary or feudal (that is, ancient or slave) mode of production. What it does mean is that the various strata of the bureaucratic pseudo-meritocracy which ran the state, which owed their position and existence to the state, and which received surplus wealth through the state apparatus, constituted during this period a tributary/feudal ruling class in the form of a state elite.

This seems to me especially important. The difference between and evolution of these forms represents one of the key structural contradictions within the late Roman and Byzantine social formation. To misrecognize it as a modal difference is to misunderstand the whole internal dynamic of the Byzantine social and economic formation. What the evidence in fact represents is the development from the late seventh century on of two dominant and antagonistic sets of interests within the ruling class: that which remained embedded within the state apparatus, and whose ideological interests were perceived to be commensurate with those of the state; and that which, while retaining (necessarily) powerful vested interests in the state structures, nevertheless developed economic bases strong enough to obtain a degree of independence of the state, which facilitated a challenge to the state for resources. This does not mean either that the former did not also possess or invest in landed property, nor that the demarcation between the two groups was not always very fluid and subject to a wide range of conjunctural pressures, factional alliances and individual personalities. It is particularly important to bear the latter in mind, for these sets of interests were represented and embodied precisely in individual social practice and the narratives through which this was realized. Competition for power and influence within the context of a patrimonial political structure, dominated by the formal hierarchies and system of honours and status of the imperial state, was an important factor. Thus, while landed wealth played without a doubt a crucial role in the consolidation of magnate independence, families and individuals invested also very heavily in the imperial system itself: posts and sinecures, state 'pensions', often amounting to considerable yearly incomes in gold and precious cloths, as well as thesaurized coin, jewellery, plate and so on. All members of the dominant social class, as well as their clients, invested in this way. While many families thus consolidated their position economically over a number of generations through the acquisition of lands, equally large numbers seem to have possessed relatively little landed wealth, and were in consequence much more directly dependent upon the state or, more specifically, the particular ruler and palatine faction of the moment. Such persons may be described, in fact, as clients of the state itself, and formed thus an important group of interests at the capital and in the palace. And it must be stressed that even the more independent magnates – both individuals and clans – depended for titles, honours and, to a certain extent (depending upon distance from the capital, relationships with local society and similar factors), social status and respect on this bureaucratic, imperial system.

Within the complex set of social, economic and political relationships which this social elite represented, with all the variations and shades I have referred to, there can nevertheless be discerned two modes of surplus distribution, one based directly on the appropriation of surplus through land ownership or control, the other on the redistribution of social wealth through the medium of the imperial system. These different modes generated social identities and economic-political interests which, having co-existed from the seventh century, finally came into open conflict in the later tenth and eleventh centuries.[105]

Within Byzantine social relations of production there existed a struggle not between different modes of surplus appropriation, therefore, but rather over the mode of distribution of that surplus within and between different elements of the ruling class. It is a particular stage of that struggle which is expressed in the development of the military *pronoia*. And the latter is itself evidence of a compromise solution to the question of manpower and resources faced by a centralized state which had already begun to lose control over its resource-base to an independent landed elite. Grants of *pronoia*, once they had become usual (and the evidence for this is only really clear from the thirteenth century), appeared to solve the problem of funding the army and at the same time permitted the continued alienation of the state's revenues. They brought with them also an increasing alienation of the state's jurisdiction over its subjects, and a slow privatization of the juridical rights of the peasantry. Yet the relatively slow rate at which this process occurred, and the small size of the great majority of military *pronoiai* (the first documented example is from the second decade of the twelfth century, and involved a relatively small grant for the maintenance of three soldiers), suggests that this institution was not in itself the major factor in the alienation of state resources that Ostrogorsky once thought. Indeed, given the fact that the enormous landed estates of the central and eastern Anatolian magnates were lost as a result of the Seljuk occupation of these regions, the pattern of land-holding in the period from the early Komnenoi on appears to have been much less dominated by such vast ranches. Recent work suggests a much more complex pattern of small- and middle-sized estates interspersed with the occasional large holding of a major landlord, but also with a continuity of independent smallholders in many areas. Big estates there were, but these were properties resulting from the accumulation of lands by the wealthy, and had little or nothing to do with the granting of *pronoiai*. The principle of issuing revenue-grants or *pronoiai* for the maintenance of soldiers does not seem to have greatly affected this pattern. In short, the *pronoia* 'system' alone was only one element in a whole series of developments which reflected the state's increasing devolution of fiscal authority, either to maintain ideological unity and political loyalty, or to facilitate the maintenance and support of soldiers in the provinces.[106]

But while the legal status of some peasants in some areas of the empire was affected, as were the rights of non-*pronoia* landowners, in an evolution which again points up the antagonistic relations of wealth allocation between state and aristocracy, these are all factors of a secondary level, that is, they are concerned with the legal forms through which the distribution and re-distribution of surplus was achieved. In one sense, they are superstructural or conjunctural elements, and reflect in no way any fundamental changes in either the mode of surplus appropriation or the relationship of the producers to the means of production. In another sense, they function as part of the relations of production, as I have suggested already, expressing, therefore, the particular configuration of the totality of production relations which evolved in the context of the development of Roman and Hellenistic social, institutional and administrative mechanisms. In other words, the legal-juridical changes we have noted represent the particular, historically-specific forms available to this social formation, and through which changing relations of distribution could be expressed. What have changed are not the social relations of production between classes, but the political relations of distribution between fractions within the ruling class. And it must be added that such changes were accompanied by changes in the rate of exploitation of the producers, as each faction attempted to maximize or to guarantee its income.

This is an important point. For it is often overlooked that, even though there may often have been substantive quantitative shifts within the framework of a particular set of production relations, this does not have to imply a qualitative shift (and a transformation of the mode of surplus appropriation). The point seems often to be ignored by opponents of the broad application of the tributary/feudal mode. In the Byzantine case, the position of the peasantry with regard to the state, to private landlords, and its ability to maximize its juridical independence, all changed in the period from the sixth to the fifteenth century. Over the same period, the relationship between the state and its ruling elite also evolved, an evolution that was causally related to that in the position of the producing population. Power over the rural population fell increasingly into the hands of private landlords (including the Church and monasteries) after the later eighth century, and especially from the tenth century; and the competition over the distribution of surplus appropriated by both landlords and the state was gradually resolved in favour of the former. Thus a marked evolution of the institutional and juridical forms of the mode of surplus appropriation occurred, an evolution that expressed also the fundamental contradiction within the institutional mechanisms of collection and distribution of surplus as available to the Eastern Roman state. But the essential nature of that mode – the extraction of feudal rent in the political economy sense – did not alter at all.

Such shifts in institutional relationships cannot be ascribed to modal change, therefore, unless the institutional forms present in each particular state and social formation are to be regarded as arbitrarily constituted and independent of the mode of production itself. And this ignores their function as precisely those elements of the relations of production which express, in an infinity of local culturally-determined ways, the fundamental mode of surplus appropriation. They represent a key element in the conditions of existence of that mode of production, and cannot be regarded as irrelevant to its functioning and evolution. They do not determine the mode of production, they are its forms of expression. They represent the forms of social praxis through which it is maintained and reproduced.

The strength of the centralized Byzantine state, the degree of relative political and institutional autonomy it retained, and its commitment to 'its' resources can be seen in the power it was able to exercise until very late in its history in overriding the legal rights of private persons who were considered to have amassed too much property: by a process known as *hikanosis* ('equalization') the state could confiscate lands in excess of the taxable value attributed to a specific individual or institutional landlord, and re-attribute them, either to itself or to a new private landlord. At least one example of this is known to have affected supposedly inalienable Church lands early in the ninth century; and the practice is well-attested in technical fiscal handbooks of the tenth to the twelfth centuries. By the later eleventh century, the power of the magnate class was such that this policy became all but impossible to apply (except where a ruler could politically isolate a particular family), but still in the later tenth century the emperor Basil II (976–1025) was able to confiscate magnate lands whose owners posed a threat to imperial power.[107]

The centralized state continued to exist until 1453, as did a dependent bureaucracy of both non-magnates and magnates. Indeed, the enormous strength of the imperial ideological system, which demanded a centralized imperial state, and which was inextricably interwoven with the political theology of the Orthodox Church, made anything else inconceivable. And it should be remembered that, while the consideration of a mode of production remains primarily a theoretical abstraction concerned with economic relationships – forces, means and relations of production (although these all have a social dimension) – a social formation is a specific form or variant on a combination of such modes of economic structure, and ideology plays a crucial role in determining how it functions to reproduce itself, how it perceives itself, and – especially in respect of literary sources and visual representation – how historians can construct their knowledge of it. The state 'meritocracy' of the seventh and eighth centuries, which evolves into the magnate class of the tenth century and after, was ideologically bound to the notion of a bureaucratic and centralized state headed by a divinely-appointed emperor, long after that ideology had ceased fully to represent its objective class interests, and long after the development of factional interests and groupings within the ruling class. But since that ideology was focused above all on the position of the emperor as God's vice-gerent and appointee on Earth, rather than on any concept of the state as such, the ideological representation of the world was not perceived as contradictory within the context of the shifting relations of distribution.

The transition from ancient to medieval social, economic and cultural forms in the early medieval East Mediterranean area thus takes on a very different appearance from that which occurred in western Europe. Nor did it occur in this form in the territory of the eastern Roman empire alone – those lands which were lost to Islam were incorporated into a new state system, whose basic patterns of urban and agricultural exploitation were rooted in their Hellenistic past. Central government, the growth of localized administrative governmental elites, and the contradiction between landholding and serving the state existed here too, although the political and social forms through which they were given expression were different.

From the Byzantine perspective, therefore, the late sixth, and especially the seventh and the first half of the eighth centuries represent a re-focusing of power (and authority) and the successful re-direction by the state of antagonistic elements within the class structure to serve its own interests. The form this structure took was that of a centralized, autocratic and bureaucratic despotism, a more cohesive and tightly controlled version of the Dominate of the fourth-century Roman state. In essence, of course, it is the ultimate descendant of the ancient city-state, its subjects were the 'citizens' whose contributions supported the commonwealth in war and peace. Its historical evolution had taken it far beyond this, through the evolution of class antagonisms, the acquisition and loss of empire, the development of a complex ideological system which was, in a number of ways, to outlive even the demise of the state itself in the fifteenth century, and the crisis of late antique civilization in the West. But the later Roman and Byzantine states had their roots firmly in a social formation dominated by tributary relations of production, however heavily that may be disguised in the technical vocabularies of Roman law and Byzantine fiscal treatises. The Byzantine social formation can perhaps best be described as the tributary mode of production in the form of the bureaucratically centralized and massively expanded late ancient state, with all the institutional contradictions which this formulation implies.

It was in these institutional contradictions and in the changing relationship between the state, its economic base and the dominant class that the essential constraining mechanisms imposed by tributary relations of production on states and especially on their political autonomy are to be located. I will discuss the question of constraints on state autonomy in the next chapter. But it is worth noting here that the dynamic underlying the changes which can be observed – between the Byzantine state and its agents, the state/state elite and the producers, and in respect of the growth of an economically independent ruling class – can all be much more readily understood in the context of tributary production relations. For it is clear that it is precisely around the institutions of surplus appropriation and the contradictions within the methods of surplus distribution that the shifts and tensions in Byzantine political and social-economic relations are to be isolated.

In spite of some similarities, this view is not the same as the position held by any of the different groups of Soviet scholars, for example, whose views I summarized very briefly at the beginning of this chapter. For them, Byzantium represents either a declining slave mode of production, or a transitional or 'proto-feudal' mode, until the later seventh or eighth centuries (or the eleventh or twelfth centuries, depending on one's position). In this light 'real' feudalism (but actually understood as much through its superstructural forms as through the totality of its production relations in the strictly economic sense) did not develop until after whichever of these two key moments of transition one prefers.[108] The basically tributary/feudal nature of production relations throughout the later Roman period, and indeed throughout much of the ancient world, albeit at times displaced by the dominance of a slave mode in certain areas, is generally not taken into account. And once again, it is the structure of the state and its institutions, which mediates the social relations of production and the class contradictions within these social formations, which deserves attention.

A detailed analysis of such contradictions as they worked themselves out, and more particularly the analysis of the relationship between state institutions, governing or power elites, and ruling classes, is the subject of other chapters and other examples. In the meanwhile, we can conclude that Byzantine society was 'feudal', or rather, the Byzantine social formation was dominated by tributary/feudal relations of production. But this becomes clear only when the concept of the tributary/feudal mode is both clearly elaborated and carefully employed. In the traditional historical materialist terminology, Byzantium was feudal – but not because it appeared so.

4

Tributary States, Ruling Elites and State Autonomy

1. State Forms and Power

I have discussed already (chapter 2) some of the key defining characteristics of 'states' as agreed upon by a majority of commentators, and at a relatively high level of abstraction. In more concrete terms, states can be defined in the first instance as territorially demarcated regions (although this does not preclude the possibility of their lands being dispersed and geographically separated), controlled by centralized governing or ruling establishments of some sort, at least in theory, which will originally have dominated, and may continue to have a monopoly over, the use of coercion; and which have the power to assert their authority over their various territories by such means as and when necessary. How exactly such central authorities achieve these ends varies enormously from state to state and society to society. And in most historical states there have always been gaps in the nature of state authority – border or mountainous regions, for example, difficult of access and untouched by state supervision; 'tribal' groups nominally owing allegiance and occupying territory claimed by the state, but not always easily brought under the state's authority or control. Thus, in areas where geography favours a tribal pastoral and/or nomadic economy, conquest states have generally relied on these elements for their soldiers, certainly in the initial stages of their evolution; but this has also meant that, because of their mobility, their internal social cohesion and self-sufficiency, and the fact that their wealth is generally easily moved away from the reach of state officials, they are both able and sometimes inclined to resist any central authority that does not directly favour their own interests. Ideological commitment can overcome this, of course, at certain times, but it remains always a short-term means of cementing such power-relationships.

In addition, and as implied already, a state is represented by a particular political ideology or set of ideological currents, which serve to legitimate (at least in respect of the distribution of power at any given moment) its existence and the rule of its governing elites, and through which the population at large, or substantial sections thereof, may receive a specific identity – as subjects, citizens of such-and-such a state, city, kingdom or whatever, as adherents perhaps also of a common religious creed or value-system, and so on. But not all of these are necessarily internalized to become part of the self-identity of the social strata or groups in question; in many cases they remain externally-imposed, either by commentators who describe the social formation in question from their own, often very alien, point of view, or by internal commentators, usually members of a different social-cultural element, applying labels which are often symbolically highly-charged. For the historian, they are always problematic.

These features are usually found in complex combination, of course, and there are many variants on both status and belief which could be added. Perhaps most importantly of all states tend to erect, or try to erect, more complex ideological and legitimating systems for themselves, more impersonalized and institutionalized modes of surplus extraction than, for example, do clan or tribal groupings. An important element seems to be that the authority of the ruler is recognized as both legitimate and exclusive. States thus tend to move away from administration based on kinship and lineage relationships and the exploitation of kin-based modes of subordination – necessarily, as we shall see, if they are to maintain their existence and cohesion, on the one hand, their authority, on the other. And they tend to move towards the establishment of a permanent and self-regenerating body of administrators, which draws its recruits either from specific groups within the state (tribal groups, for example) or from those of a particular social or cultural background (although it must be noted that the degree to which this development is completed varies widely). They tend thus to evolve institutional structures – fiscal systems, military organizations and so forth – which establish their own sets of roles and discourses, divorced from the daily practices of 'ordinary' society. The state becomes a specialist, and dominant, set of institutions, which may even undertake the creation *ab initio* of its own administrative personnel, and which can survive only by maintaining control over the appropriation and distribution of surplus wealth.[1]

This last point is particularly important in respect of the potential for state formations to reproduce themselves, a potential which I would contrast with that of a particular dynasty or ruling family, with its retinues based upon personal loyalties and notions of honour, obligation and reciprocity, to maintain itself in power over a number of generations. The evolution of a bureaucratic elite which has a sense of its own function within the state/society, identifies with a particular set of ideological and symbolic narratives, and can recruit and train its personnel into the institutional roles and behavioural patterns relevant to the maintenance and even expansion of these structures is a crucial factor, as both Marx and Weber in the course of very different analyses pointed out. The relative success of the Roman and Byzantine, Chinese and Ottoman states in this regard, to name just a few examples, provide good illustrations of the first evolutionary possibility; the failures of the Frankish kingdoms (among many others) illustrate the second. Some states seem only with difficulty fitted into such a pattern, of course, since the problems of both regional and lineage identities (however spurious or artificial the latter may usually have been from a purely genealogical point of view), such as tribal or clan solidarities, for example, dramatically vitiated attempts by a central authority, even when supported by elements of a permanent civil or military bureaucracy, to maintain themselves over more than a few generations. A number of early Islamic states exemplify this, most notably, perhaps, the Umayyad Caliphate, in which the conflicts of interest between centre, tribal military support (fragmented by inherited ideological rivalries), underprivileged converts to Islam, and the remnants of traditional bureaucratic elites among the conquered urban populations (all four elements overdetermined by deep-seated religious ideological factionalism) combined to produce a situation in which the ruling Arab family and its clan support proved unable to mobilize the resources to fend off serious and ideologically well-motivated attack. In contrast, the Sassanian kingdom which dominated Persia from the third to the seventh century AD, and whose Iranian element proved so powerful an influence in the development of Islamic culture and political structures, provides a good example of a remarkably successful dynasty. For the actual power of this royal family depended very largely on two key factors. In the first place, there was the ideological commitment of a powerful group of regional clan or dynastic chiefs (the Sassanian 'aristocracy', from whom the royal house was itself drawn) to the legitimacy of the dominant dynasty (which claimed also a certain politico-religious authority sanctioned by both a claim to ancient lineage and military leadership). In the second place, and as can be found in all state formations, they supported the claims to legitimate power and followed the authority of that dynasty as long as the results of Sassanid rule were at the very least not in contradiction to their own interests, whether ideological, political or economic (usually all three). Interestingly, and as a result of a certain social and religious opposition to elements of the traditional nobility on the part of urban and oppressed rural populations, the Great King Khusru I was able, during the sixth century, to introduce a series of reforms of the fiscal structures of the state (involving an increased central control over revenues) and establish a more permanent standing army attached to the capital, consisting of leading elements of the middling and lower provincial elites, and hence binding them more closely into the system of royal patronage and central power. Of course, personalized dynastic rivalries, questions of honour, shame and competition are part and parcel of this picture, since they are always also context- and conjuncture-bound. Nevertheless, there is some evidence for the beginnings of an attempt to bring about a major shift in the pattern of power-relationships and the distribution of power in the Sassanid kingdom at this time.[2]

These considerations bring us back to the point that the success or failure of states to survive over a longer or shorter period depends ultimately upon the relationship between other actual or potential centres of social power (spatially or socially) and the rulers and their dependent elite, for control over the appropriation and distribution of resources (whether economic or ideological – it is important to stress that ideological power is just as functionally important here). In some cases, a central authority can survive for a long time purely through the manipulation of key ideological and symbolic elements in the cultural system of the social formation as a whole. South Indian temple culture and the attendant state structures, particularly as exemplified in the Chola and Vijayanagara empires, provide classic examples. They also illustrate the central importance of the priesthood and of ideological legitimation in such cases.[3] Indeed, South-East Asian states in general provide a range of fascinating examples of the ways in which economic relationships are given expression through ideological systems which present themselves and are understood as the dominant form of social relations at all levels of society; they fulfil also the function of social relations of production, a point emphasized in chapter 2. In particular, these states provide good examples of the processes of amalgamation and fragmentation of larger political units, as different rulers and dynasties were or were not able to establish and then maintain their authority over regions outside their immediate physical control.[4] Both centralized and de-centralized states of the federated and consolidated type existed. Yet in spite of their differences, it is clear that political authority, however it might have been legitimated, always depended upon control over the appropriation and distribution of surplus wealth, whatever the processes actually involved. And it is important to remember that these varied enormously, of course: state taxation and rent in the Byzantine world, ritual redistribution of the produce from temple lands in parts of India, service in the kings' armies in the Merovingian Frankish world, each representing very different forms of the same essential phenomenon, each depending in their own way on ideological and symbolic legitimation, but each involving the movement of wealth, in a variety of forms, from the producers via a range of different means to a political authority that could wield it, as far as conditions permitted, to maintain and reproduce its position, whether by coercion or conviction. In some societies, rulers actively invested in improvements in the forces of production (by building canals, irrigation works and so on) to qualitatively improve their own sources of revenue. In others, they were able to capitalize on the labour and, more importantly, on the ideological infrastructure, the 'moral economy' of peasant communities, to this end. Thus in India, for example, irrigation works were in many regions traditionally the responsibility of the community under its dominant lineages, so that state intervention and the consequent authority it is sometimes supposed to have lent the central power would be redundant.[5]

None of this is to say, of course, that state structures may not also represent, and be promoted by, individuals and dynasties intent upon the consolidation of a particular form of political control, in which absolutist rulers continue to determine policy and the forms which the consumption of surpluses should take under given circumstances. But it is at precisely this point that we need to examine in greater detail how autonomous such institutions and their personnel can actually be or become, and to what extent such individuals or dynasties, clans or factions, also embody a particular configuration of power-relationships, of which they are also agents or bearers. In other words, it is essential to bear in mind the fact that human beings are both constitutive of social practice and constituted by it: to claim that they are merely agents of the social structures they inhabit is as false and as misleading as to assert that they are purely constituting subjects and to deny that they are determined in the possibilities open to them by the weight of the cultural system around them.

States 'exist' at two other levels, of course, which are equally important. On the one hand, they have an ideological life which is not necessarily tied to their actual political and institutional efficacy or power. Political ideologies and other belief systems, once in existence, are perfectly able to adapt and to survive in conditions which have evolved well away from those within which they originally developed, provided the contradictions between the two are not too extreme or insurmountable in terms of social praxis and psychology. Those which respond to long-term functional needs in human society provide the best examples, and include religious systems in particular, such as Islam or Christianity, for example, which can, to a greater or lesser degree, free themselves from both the political and the social and economic conditions which produced them. But political ideologies too can be extremely flexible. They may provide a rationale for conflict where no visible or obvious reason in terms of competition for material resources exists, for example. And they can also be extremely powerful. Thus many states were, in effect, little more than territories ruled over only nominally by a king, in which actual power was exercised by a class of magnates whose position in origin may well have depended upon the central ruler and/or the conditions in which the state came into being (by conquest, for example) but who, because of their actual control over resources, and other historical conditions, were really and in practical terms independent. Yet in such cases we find that the idea of a centralized kingdom or state, together with the residual power of concepts such as honour, fealty, and so on, were enough to maintain at least a fictional unity of identity. So that, on the other hand, those outside such political formations (which were thus little more than a congeries of locally-competing sub-powers) continued to regard them for, say, diplomatic purposes, as unitary states.

By the same token, however, it is important to remember that every cultural formation embodies a whole range of symbolic and ideological sub-sets, whether represented in socio-economic vested interests, however garbed in the language of the dominant symbolic universe or *Weltanschauung*, or in more 'spiritual' symbolic structures, and that these in their turn play a central role in the ways in which a particular set of power-relationships comes into being, functions and is regenerated, or declines. 'Counter-ideologies' is a little too modern a term, but on occasion such sub-sets can provide alternative narratives to account for the perceived realities of various groups within the culture in question.[6]

The point is, then, that the real power of rulers was determined by problems of communications, of regional identities and traditions, of the difficulties inherent in administering and taxing a large territory, and of the slowness of coercive responses to opposition. Only the smallest medieval states, in particular those with clearly-defined geographical boundaries and limits to the authority of their rulers, could remain both centralized and efficient. The Norman kingdom of England is, possibly, one of the best examples, together with its contemporary, built on much the same principles and in the same way, the Norman kingdom of Sicily. But it is precisely in confronting the problem of the ways in which tributary states maintain central authority that the question of what Berktay has called the primary determinant of such states arises: how did such states, in the context of pre-capitalist technology, solve the problem of maintaining the producing class in subjection, while at the same time assuring itself of a surplus adequate to its own maintenance and reproduction? The universal answer, by whatever means it is eventually arrived at, is for the state elite/aristocracy to administer this double process directly through revenue assignments, fiefs, or other forms of allocation and distribution. As I will suggest below, the secondary determinant, and fundamental constraint upon tributary state autonomy, was the inherent contradiction in this relationship: between the interests of 'the state' (the ruler, bureaucratic elite, dominant aristocratic faction at court, or however the centre expressed its position *vis-à-vis* those in the provinces or outside its immediate physical control) and other factions of the ruling class in respect of control (a) over the appropriation of surplus and (b) over its distribution.

In respect of communications and the question of the maintenance of coercive authority, the nature of the problem faced by tributary states is clearest when we look at extensive imperial or colonial state systems, where the potential for continued expansion, on the one hand, and for maintaining a stable frontier, on the other, depends very much on a combination of factors: the degree of central authority and the modalities of control over provincial and frontier military commanders; the dynamism of peripheral or frontier exchange-relations and markets, together with the balance of economic interests along the borders and their hinterlands, and so on. In this respect, both Mann's work, and especially that of Luttwak, whatever their other limitations, have demonstrated convincingly just what the potential and the limits of pre-industrial territorial expansion by conquest actually were. But territorial expansion and coercive power in terms of distance is only one aspect of the whole. I would argue that the crucial factors in this complex were the political relations of surplus distribution and the ways in which the central authority failed or succeeded in controlling the resources adequate to the continued maintenance of its power.[7]

A final feature through which we can identify a state formation over the longer term is the fact that states tend to attribute to themselves a degree of permanence (often belied by their actual history) and hence expend more effort on codifying their public political ideology. In contrast to tribal cultures, for example, states often explicitly assume a continuity of purpose and abstract rationale which is quite independent of any ruler or dynasty or governing elite. The state becomes in itself the logic of existence, and along with ideological/religious institutions represents the form through which the vested interests present in the social formation can be understood and given expression. This is especially true in the case of politically successful states which have a history of conquest and expansion behind them. As they evolve, so the ideological narratives which account for and legitimate this history become hardened and serve to deaden any attempts to change or modify the way things are done (or at least, to determine the ways in which things are perceived to have been done in the past and therefore in which things ought to continue to be done). Structural problems are thus misrecognized, ideological lines of battle are drawn which serve to mask the real nature of the contradictions which have arisen. Both the history of the internal responses to change and 'decline' as perceived from within the Ottoman empire, on the one hand, the British empire in the 1940s (and the British Isles thereafter), on the other, are illustrative. And by the same token, as states consolidate their power and control over the society they dominate (although this descriptive separation of 'state' from 'society' is itself problematic, as we shall see in a moment), so the burden of administration and defence tends to increase, a phenomenon expressed precisely through the ideologically conservative consolidation of theories of legitimation.

These are, of course, sets of definitional criteria which remain fairly abstract. Not all states conform to all these desiderata. Some states appear to have existed in name only – although it is surprising how powerful an ideological element a name can be. And the conceptual and institutional dividing line between a state, on the one hand, and a region controlled by a powerful clan or tribal confederacy, on the other (which may itself be in the process of becoming a state), is often difficult to ascertain.

Indeed, the question of state formation is important if we are not to get bogged down in terminological dead ends. Social formations are always dynamic insofar as all social structures permit change and evolution, although they may not necessarily evolve without 'external' pressures which show up 'internal' structural contradictions. Tribal- and class-dominated territorial units may or may not develop into states in the sense defined above, depending upon local conditions, social and economic relations within the tribal group and between it and subordinate groups, and so on. Theorists of the origins of the state have tried to describe various moments along the graph of such developments through descriptive categories such as 'proto-state', 'early state' and so on. This is adequate in a synchronic context (although sometimes arbitrary), but often disguises the point that it is the ultimate fact of a state emerging which promotes or hinders the application of such descriptive terms.

It is difficult to conceptualize any complex social organism in its totality without doing it a certain amount of descriptive violence. One of the most difficult problems seems to me that inherent in describing states as 'dominating' or 'having power/control over' a society (and brings us back to the difficulties involved in the use of spatial metaphors such as 'base and superstructure' discussed in chapter 2). For this immediately implies a degree of separation between two distinct levels of social and political existence. This may well be heuristically helpful in respect of the institutionalization of certain sets of power-relationships and the social practices and behavioural patterns which maintain them. It describes, therefore, the perceived reification as a set of 'state' institutions and practices of a range of social discourses, and the differentness of the state (both for the modern observer and the for members of the society in question) as representative of sets of administrative/bureaucratic structures, for example, access to which is strictly controlled, from 'civil society' at large. On the other hand, it tends to conceal the fact that such structures are at the same time intimately bound into particular sets of relations of surplus production, appropriation and distribution, that they are therefore inscribed into and dependent upon the social relations of production of the society as a whole, but which they yet inflect and nuance according to particular institutional imperatives (to maintain and reproduce certain structures, sets of power-relationships and so on). This can perhaps be most clearly illustrated by looking at the activities of a social/economic elite whose own position serves both the interests of the state centre and at the same time their own prosperity and social dominance. In following certain institutionally- and socially-determined patterns of behaviour, they necessarily promote the reproduction of a given set of relations of production, and at the same time the set of power-relationships in which the continued existence of a particular form of the state is inscribed. No distinction can be made between the two, except for the purposes of responding to certain questions. Yet in order to analyse these structures, we are necessarily led to differentiate between 'state' and 'society' in an entirely artificial way. There is nothing new in this observation – it constitutes a fundamental element in the methodologies of the social sciences – but it is worth emphasizing at this juncture in order to pre-empt accusations that the separation, at certain points in the discussion, of 'state' from 'society' is taken to represent anything more than heuristic necessity.

Like all definitions, therefore, the notion of 'the state' must be used as a heuristic tool, not as a box within which to force the historical material willy-nilly, nor yet as a conceptual strait-jacket which ignores the fundamentally dynamic and dialectical nature of human social praxis. A useful reminder that this is the case is perhaps supplied by the fact that forms of rulership reflect precisely the already socially-inscribed nature of power relations, and whether or not we choose to describe these relations in terms of Weber's notion of patrimonial or professional bureaucratic structures, for example, should make no difference.[8]

There is a further point. States in themselves generally imply also class society, that is to say, social formations in which there is a clear difference in economic power between different groups in society, defined in terms of their relations to the means of production of wealth and its distribution, and hence occupying a specific position with regard to one another – thus, in pre-industrial society, between landlords and tenants, for example, or between tax-paying subjects or citizens and the apparatus of the state. Whether or not these differences are expressed also juridically, through different legally-defined statuses, for example, is important but secondary. More important are the ways in which such economically distinct classes are both united and divided by (often vestigial) lineage and kinship structures, local or regional identities, status-groups or political organizations, and ideological and religious affiliations (or a complex combination of these). Such structures cut across purely economic class divisions, and render any attempt to explain the political actions of individuals or groups in terms of their economic position alone, without regard for the praxis-structuring ideological context within which they operate (and perceive themselves to be operating) is quite useless. The impossibility of explaining the political and social loyalties of members of various Ottoman *millets*, or of members of the Ottoman 'ruling class', or yet again of Christian peasants on the eastern frontier of Byzantium in economic class terms alone is obvious, as I will show.[9] But this does not mean that economic relationships are not determinant of the configurations possible in a given social and cultural formation. It does mean that, in pre-capitalist social formations, the economic is always expressed through structures (sets of practices) which bear other roles too – kinship, religion, political organizations and so forth (which is what Marx intended when he remarked that 'the middle ages could not live on Catholicism, nor the ancient world on politics'). I have discussed this in more detail in chapters 2 and 3 above. And it also means that the political forms through which state power can be exercised, and the actual policies which rulers can reasonably pursue, will be determined to a large degree by the relative economic strength and ideological centrality of such structures at any given time.

Economic class divisions, as defined above, clearly exist in all societies which have moved beyond the most basic division of labour, between men and women, and the distribution of surplus through kinship and ranking or age-sets alone. But whereas in modern, capitalist society personal identity is largely, if not exclusively, determined by consciousness of economic position (and the process of social and cultural allocation from which it follows), in pre-industrial and pre-capitalist society, while economic position is determined by relations to the means of production, social identity is determined by other structural constraints (however these may also function as relations of production themselves, that is, as institutions and forms of social praxis through which production relations are expressed). Medieval European peasants generally saw themselves in terms of a regional and local identity – Christians from so-and-so village – as well as in terms of family identities and their actual economic status. Only under certain specific conditions did they act trans-locally as a class.[10] In the same way, Byzantine magnates only begin to act as a class in respect of their political and economic power (represented to them both through the prism of notions such as family honour and so forth, as well as through their awareness of a common interest in terms of political and economic power *vis-à-vis* the centre) from about the middle of the eleventh century, before which time (and to a degree thereafter) clan and kinship in conjunction with their generally antagonistic and competitive economic and status relationships with one another determined their political actions. Similar considerations apply to the Ottoman ruling class in its various factional and economically differentiated forms.

The complexity of the relationships between different sets of social practices is especially in need of emphasis. The 'objective' economic relations which I have set out in some detail in respect of class as a relationship of exploitation can be more-or-less identical with cultural and political identities in respect of status or rank or attributed function. But in the vast majority of cases this is not the case. Individuals always belong to more than a single set of role-structuring practices – a peasant is generally both a farmer and a member of a kinship community; he may also have a particular position in his village in respect of outsiders (the state, a local landlord, etc.). All these roles will in turn involve him in sets of wider relationships; and while not all peasants in the same community, to continue with the example, will necessarily occupy such a wide variety of positions, the existence of a few such persons will render more complex the relations between the community as a whole and the 'outside' world. Indeed, from a sociological perspective, it is perhaps methodologically too limiting to view peasant communities and society as so distanced or independent of the wider social context. The evidence for these more complex connections, cutting across those assumed for individuals of a particular social and economic position, may not always be plentiful, so that little concrete can actually be said with any certainty. But such relations, making peasant communities less isolated, more dynamic elements in a whole network of relationships functioning at different levels, should perhaps be assumed to exist, rather than vice versa. Where evidence is available, as we will see below, it clearly affects any possible interpretation of how the social relationships which 'supported' the state actually worked.

These are important considerations to bear in mind also because the state, while inevitably having the effect of providing a framework for (and hence limiting in various ways) the development of certain social and economic relationships, through its need to establish and then maintain a regular and predictable structure of surplus extraction, also had the effect of enabling or facilitating the evolution of new practices and relationships. This is especially clear, for example, in the way in which the East Roman/Byzantine state transferred the focus of its attention in fiscal matters away from urban centres to village communities, thereby radically altering the ways in which social relationships between landlords and tenants, on the one hand, and between peasant producers, the state and towns, on the other, functioned.[11] But there are other examples, as the cases of the Ottoman and Indian states dealt with below and in chapter 5 will suggest. In short, the state also created spaces in which new developments could take place – the role of tax-farmers in the Byzantine, Ottoman and Mughal contexts, for example, both as extractors of surplus and as a potential stimulant to changed patterns of investment or consumption of wealth, to changed structures of money-use on the part of both producers and state administrations, and so on. In some cases, the existence of a central fiscal administration may have given hitherto unimportant local leaders – village headmen, small-scale local landlords – a more significant role in the process of surplus appropriation and accumulation, leading to shifts in the political order of power at the local level and ultimately reacting back on the state itself. Again, in the Ottoman case, the growth of a local 'nobility' (the *a'yân*), together with the garrisoning of imperial salaried troops and Janissaries in the provinces on a permanent basis, radically altered the relationship between central government and regions (generally seen as to the disadvantage of the former); yet such changes were made possible precisely because of the state's perceived fiscal and military requirements.[12] In sixteenth- and seventeenth-century Indian states the role of pre-imperial village elites and rank-attributions had a significant influence on the ways the Mughal state, for example, and its regional predecessors and successors, could organize, just as the existence of centralized state apparatuses and their demands for surplus in turn affected the ways in which these local relationships worked, opening up new social space within which they could evolve. These all represent complex issues of social and economic history which I can acknowledge rather than pursue in detail. But they are crucial to understanding how states work, and it is important that they are not lost sight of.

None of this alters the fact of the existence of economically distinct classes, of course. But it must radically affect the ways in which we attempt to understand the social practices which expressed such economic relations. And the point is that, whatever the factors which divide a given social formation internally, the members of one level – mutually antagonistic though they may be sometimes be in the structural terms described above – are able to extract surplus from those of other levels by virtue of their control over the means of production and distribution of wealth. While power is often the issue, therefore, both for the social actors and for modern commentators, this is itself ultimately an expression of an economic relationship. The point is that the existence of a state directly affects how these different sets of practices interact and, therefore, evolve, so that they in turn come to affect the state structure which enabled certain of them to develop.

The actual mechanisms of surplus extraction vary enormously – but in the end, the possibility of coercion, embodied in legal institutions and the law, underlies most such relationships. And by virtue of its power to extract surplus, such a class gains also the possibility of increasing the rate of exploitation (the amount of surplus demanded in relation to that necessary for the social and economic reproduction of the producers) and thereby of exerting a considerable degree of control over the lives of the producers themselves.

This is particularly important, since states provide at the very least the possibility for an intensification of surplus appropriation, whether through the state apparatuses themselves or through the increased concentration of the powers of coercion in the hands of the ruling class. Not all states necessarily realize these possibilities, of course. But, as I will argue below, the potential established by the existence of a state to redefine the conditions (ideological as well as political and economic) under which surplus is appropriated means also that the conditions under which this occurs provide a focus of struggle over the distribution of such social wealth, both between exploiters and the exploited, and between different elements of the ruling elite.

In this respect, states can be differentiated from simpler clan and tribal territorial organizations, insofar as state fiscal apparatuses become less and less part of the relationship between ruler and subjects (or dominant clan/family and subordinate clans), and more a key element in the organizational logic and the contingent structural and ideological imperatives of the state establishment itself.

A final point remains to be mentioned in this context, and that is the effect state structures have on the social relations and relations of production from which they derive their existence. While it does not represent a primary consideration in the present book, it is nevertheless important to bear in mind the extent to which different types of state structure affect their societies. Byzantine and Ottoman state institutions appear to have had a much greater impact upon the fundamental structures of social relations, chiefly through their fiscal structures, than, say, those of the Frankish kingdom which, through much of its history, extracted surplus only indirectly and in the form of service and gifts which permitted the basic unit of peasant production to function without reference to the centre at all. As we will see in chapter 5, this directly reflects the extent to which the kings failed or succeeded in embedding their administrators at the level of local communities, as well as reflecting the social origins of royal functionaries, and the nature of the relations between the kings as representatives of a particular form of symbolic authority and the other 'big men' of the political confederacy. It meant that consumption remained highly localized, that the control over the appropriation and distribution of surplus wealth remained de-centralized, and that the producers of that wealth remained effectively outside the control of the central political authority. Only in the case of an unusually powerful assertion, through coercive force or threat of force, does this situation change; and then generally, in the context of such an embedded pattern of diffused power, over a relatively short period. This does not mean that the existence of an ideologically-defined (and occasionally physically effective) central authority had no effects on the society from which it derived its existence; only that the modes of expression of those effects are not necessarily obvious to the external observer, particularly in the context of a more-or-less autarkic peasant economy.[13] Exactly the same considerations apply, for example, to the ways in which the Mughal state was able to effectively intervene at the level of local relations of production, employing village or regional elites to fulfil 'state' functions which might in fact be merely a recognition, under different circumstances, of traditional methods of surplus appropriation and distribution.

2. States and the Tributary Constraint

While a state may achieve a considerable degree of autonomy from the explicit class interests of any dominant socio-economic group, it must also be emphasized that it inevitably also provides a framework within which such a class is able to reproduce itself, as I have suggested in respect of the possibilities for intensifying the rate of surplus extraction. Whether this occurs independently of the state or, as is often the case, through the state itself varies historically. As we shall see in the Ottoman example, the state, through its ruling dynasty, first re-directed the ideological interests of the dominant class (the traditional Turkish clan nobility) in its own favour; it then created an elite of its own (as a contradiction evolved between the interests of the Ottoman house and the rest of the ruling class) in the form of the *devşirme* and the slaves of the Porte, thus balancing the power and political independence of the former group. But the new order could not remove the power-base of the old ruling elite without at the same time creating a new dominant elite, initially totally dependent upon the rulers, but which itself embodied certain contradictions between the organizational requirements of the 'autonomous' state, on the one hand, and the logistical possibilities through which such requirements could be met, on the other. The inevitable process of de-centralization and power diffusion which followed seems to be a universal phenomenon, although the degree to which it evolved before further structural transformations become inevitable varied enormously from social formation to social formation.

It is in this context, therefore, that we must address the question of the nature of the constraints imposed on states by different modes of production – in the case of our examples, the tributary mode. In capitalist formations, it remains in the interests of states not to hinder or adversely intervene in the process of surplus extraction, and therefore in the fundamental relations of production of capitalist social formations, for the obvious reason that states themselves depend for their existence on just this mode of surplus appropriation and its institutional conditions of existence and reproduction. While governments or rulers may therefore intervene from time to time to modify the particular institutional or juridical forms characteristic of capitalist production relations in a given state formation (in order to alter the relations of surplus distribution, for example), they normally also act in a way consonant with the fundamental mode of capitalist appropriation. Capitalist states use tax, for example, as a means of redistributing surplus, which is produced by economic means through the creation of relative surplus value. The extraction of tax, as an institution for the redistribution of surplus value, is therefore an indirect or secondary form of surplus appropriation, a form which can only occur after the process of primary appropriation through the creation of relative surplus value has already taken place.

States in the capitalist world, therefore, are maintained ultimately not through their power to tax, but rather through the maintenance of those production relations which promote the extraction of relative surplus value. The state itself has little or no contact with these relations, except in a regulating or supervisory capacity, or in a period of temporary crisis.

In tributary social formations, this constraining or limiting factor exists, but it takes a somewhat different form. It is clear that state elites and ruling classes in pre-capitalist formations have an equally powerful vested interest in the maintenance of those relations of production to which they owe their position. Struggles over the distribution of surplus within dominant elites, and between exploiting and exploited classes, provide the dynamic elements through which institutional and organizational changes occur, to the advantage of one group or class or another. But all state formations dominated by feudal relations of production share one particular characteristic which, in the context of the dominant set of relations of production in the social formation as a whole, serves to differentiate them from state or social formations in other modes. This characteristic is the direct nature of primary surplus appropriation by the state, and the contingent modes of surplus distribution.

In the tributary mode, the relationship between the ruler or ruling elite and those who actually appropriate surplus on their behalf is always problematic. It is always a contradictory and potentially antagonistic relationship. In contrast to capitalist states, ones dominated by tributary production relations must attempt to appropriate surplus themselves, or ensure that an adequate portion of such surplus is passed on to them, to be certain of their survival. More than this, and in stark contrast to capitalist relations of production, tributary ruling classes and states function at the same level of primary appropriation, directly inducing the creation of surplus through their monopoly of various forms of non-economic coercion. As we have seen in chapter 3, they thereby directly affect the rate of exploitation and the conditions of surplus creation among the peasant economies they dominate. Peasants in different social-cultural formations have been able to resist such pressure and to defend their interests, to a degree, and according to specific situations, at various times. But this does not alter the fact that it was direct coercive pressure exerted by the feudal ruling class in part or wholly which determined the rate of exploitation and the possibilities for surplus extraction.

In the case of the tributary state, therefore, its power to extract surplus in the form of tribute/feudal rent depends entirely upon its power to limit the economic and political strength of other classes, but more particularly other fractions of the ruling class. In pre-capitalist societies dominated by tributary production relations, the very existence of state formations means that the relations of surplus distribution are inherently antagonistic, since the contradiction implicit in the institutional arrangements for surplus distribution and consumption – essentially, between the state and the agents it must necessarily employ as intermediaries – cannot be avoided. Capitalist states only rarely come into direct conflict with the bourgeoisie through whom capital is invested and generated, chiefly because these two elements clearly depend upon each other. Shifts in this relationship can be clarified through cyclical changes in the relative strengths of the two in time and space, as Mandel and others have suggested. In contrast, tributary or 'feudal' rulers and elites compete directly for control over the means of production, and hence the material basis for their autonomy, to the extent that one side may attempt (and even temporarily succeed) in destroying or so weakening the other that no further opposition is forthcoming. But in neither case does this involve a shift in the relations of production or in the mode of surplus appropriation. What does change is the identity of the exploiters with the power to coerce; in other words, as I argued in chapter 3, it is the political relations of surplus distribution which change.[14]

The constraints imposed upon tributary states, therefore, are constraints constituted both through the mode of surplus appropriation, and through the relations of surplus distribution, which in turn express the social relations of production in respect of control over the means of production (and the multiplicity of incidental factors which influence these relations, such as the geography, ecology and demography of the territories making up the state in question). How these constraints actually work themselves out, and how their effects are to be appreciated, can only be understood through an examination of the political relations of surplus distribution between states, elites and producers.

It is thus the direct and primary role of states and ruling classes in the process of surplus appropriation in tributary formations which informs both the nature of the class struggle between exploiting and exploited classes, as well as the structure of the political relations of distribution within the ruling class. This contrasts clearly with capitalism, where – as I have already noted – taxation is the means through which surplus re-distribution takes place, to the state's advantage, occurring therefore after the process of surplus appropriation through the creation of relative surplus value has been completed. It is a secondary process of appropriation, in other words, a process of re-distribution. Similarly, it contrasts with the slave mode, where it is crucially the supply of slave labour itself (which is to say, the availability and maintenance of a particular type of means of production), which determines the relationship between the ruling class, the state and the mass of non-slave producers.

It is clear that, in looking at the state formations selected for discussion in the present essay, the heuristic value of using the tributary mode as a guide to their internal articulation is considerable. For, as we will see in each case, the central determining element in respect of the degree of state autonomy achieved, and the crucial axis around which relations between producers and exploiters, and within the exploiting class itself, revolve, is represented by the mode of surplus appropriation and the forms or institutions of surplus distribution. These reflect accurately social and political relationships of resource control as they evolve and are transformed through the resolution of the contradictions which they embody and the antagonisms which they express.

3. The Ottoman State

The Ottoman state, and the Mughal state in India from the sixteenth century on (and which I will examine in the next chapter), are perhaps among the most interesting formations in this respect. The Ottoman state in particular has received a great deal of attention in recent years, largely because (also like the Mughal state) it has seemed to represent one of the better examples of a state formation which could be fitted into, or understood through, the 'Asiatic' mode of production. I do not intend to go into the whole debate around this concept here, except to say that, on balance, I do not think elaborations on the basis of Marx's original very tentative construct help us to understand any of the societies to which the Asiatic mode has been applied, partly because – as a number of commentators have pointed out – it conflates conceptual categories and empirical phenomena in a way which makes it quite difficult to employ heuristically. And since Amin's formulation of the tributary mode, within which the dominant relations of production and mode of surplus appropriation of both the feudal and the Asiatic mode can be subsumed, it has lost much of any relevance it may originally have possessed.

In fact, in its economic structure, which is to say in respect of its production relations and, more especially, its mode of surplus appropriation, the Ottoman state, and the social formations which fall within its bounds, can be understood unproblematically through the tributary mode. And it is interesting to note, incidentally, that until the Asiatic mode was imported into the historiography of the Ottoman state by Turkish critics of the traditional, positivist history-writing of scholars such as Barkan, earlier, and still valuable, discussions of Ottoman state and society, exemplified in the works of Köprülü and Lybyer had taken its feudal nature absolutely for granted (although it should be recalled that this meant chiefly a comparison with key elements of western European systems of subinfeudation, enfeoffment and so on).[15]

Our chief concern here, however, is the relationship between the state, its apparatus, and those who staffed it, on the one hand, and the ruling class or dominant elite of the Ottoman world, on the other. And we must immediately confront some of the legalistic myths of Ottoman historical studies: namely, that there was no stable, hereditary nobility within the Ottoman empire, and that, consequently, the state was also the ruling class;[16] and that the absence of private property in land, together with the importance of state slavery and the *devşirme*, or child levy,[17] meant that there could be no intermediate magnate class between the *re'âyâ* (subject) population and the state – in other words, that the state extracted surplus directly through its own agents.[18] How then did the Ottoman state function?

The seat of empire, the residence also of the Sultan, had been since the time of Mehmed II (1451–81) at Istanbul – the former Byzantine capital of Constantinople (the name Istanbul was itself derived from the medieval Greek *eis tin polin*, 'in/at the City'). Here, in the palace, were the chief palatine administrative bureaux, military and naval headquarters, along with the Sultan's residence and the harem. The territories of the state were divided for fiscal and military purposes into a number of *sancaks* or 'banners', under the command of *sancakbeyis*, in turn making up a number of provinces, under *beylerbeyis*.[19] Each *sancak*, or district, was in turn divided into *kazas*, or sub-districts. The *sancak* commander held both civil and military authority; and a provincial administrative staff made up from the 'ruling class', an Ottoman technical term to which I will return in a moment, dealt with fiscal and military registers, revenues and expenditures, justice (under the *kadi*, or judge) and police (under the *subaşı*, chief of police).[20]

The term *re'âyâ* signified 'protected flock', and comprised the majority population of the empire, regardless of religion, made up for the most part of subsistence peasant communities and pastoral nomads, with a small but important group of urban merchants and artisans. The nomads occupied an anomalous position, insofar as their military potential might be conscripted for short-term campaigns. On the other hand, the state consistently tried to fragment tribal groups and to convert them into dependent peasantries, since they represented a fundamentally ill-fitting element in this otherwise straightforward relationship of exploitation. Similarly, many *re'âyâ* peoples, especially the subject Christian populations of the Balkans, provided allied or auxiliary troops for the Sultan's forces, although this never brought them 'ruling class' status.[21]

The revenues of the state were collected under two main headings, religious taxes and customary levies, the former mentioned in and authorized by Islamic law (Arabic *Sharí'a*, Turkish *Şeriat*). These included the *öşür* (tithe – although amounting to a quarter or a fifth of cereal production in some areas), the *cizye* or *harac* (Arab *jizya* and *haraj*) tax on non-Muslims, and a range of lesser levies. The Ottoman *öşür*, although originating as a contribution to the community from the faithful, and inscribed in holy law, was in practice no longer a religious levy: it represented the basic land or produce tax, and therefore the bulk of the state's revenue. Its ancient origin in the *Şeriat* functioned as a fiction through which it was legitimated; and since there was no Muslim organization in the sense of the institutionalized Christian Church, its revenues went to the state.

The customary taxes (*'âdât*) or 'sovereign right' taxes (*rusûm-i örfiyye*) were based on pre-existing levies in the conquered territories as well as dues introduced by the Ottoman rulers themselves. They included additional, minor land taxes, pasturage dues, taxes on specific types of produce, customs dues, and so on. The main difference between these *örfi* taxes and the 'religious' dues lies in the fact that the former represented the ruler's authority as war-leader and conqueror, not delimited, in consequence, by holy law, and representing an additional and legitimate source of income for the state independent of

Islamic tradition and the authority of the *'Ulemâ*, the doctors and theologians of Islam. I will return to this below.

A third category, of 'extraordinary' taxes, the *avanz* or 'war-chest', eventually became regularized, but was levied separately from the other dues mentioned, collected on the basis of specially-maintained central registers of tax-payers by salaried officials or state agents rather than by *timâr*-holders based in the provinces, as was the case with most revenues.

These revenues were distributed in various ways. All sources of revenue were organized in units called *mukâta'a* or allocations, which were in turn grouped according to whether the holder of the *mukâta'a* kept the revenues or returned them to the central treasuries, receiving instead a fixed treasury stipend. The latter were usual, on the whole, only in the larger market centres – administrative units covering markets and petty commodity production, or the collection of customs dues. The former were more numerous and more usual. The commonest form was that of the *timâr*, an allocation of revenue in kind or in cash from the land, in which all of the said revenue was retained by the *timâr*-holder in order to support a service for the Sultan. It was the *timâr* which formed the basis for the regular provincial cavalry of the Ottoman state until the later sixteenth century. As well as the *timâr*, revenues and lands could also be assigned to *mültezim* or tax-farmers who, in the usual way, paid a variable annual sum to the treasury, but were permitted to retain for themselves any revenues above those required by the state. As we will see, this procedure gradually erodes the efficacy of that based on revenue-assignments or *timârs*, and comes to replace it almost entirely, generating at the same time the development of vast landed estates or *çifliks* farmed by a depressed peasantry of share-croppers and tenants. And it is important to note that, institutionally, the tension between these two forms of surplus appropriation reflects their common structural character. In effect, they operated at the same level, penetrated each other, and could quite easily (in one direction, for example, by a process of commutation of military service) be transformed into each other. A remarkably similar process occurred in the Byzantine state in the eleventh century, for example, when personal military service was increasingly replaced by a form of commutation in order to assure the state of a more disposable form of revenue income.[22]

The right to collect taxes was expressed through Ottoman-Islamic law as an attribute of the Sultan alone, won by right of conquest and force of arms. All sources of revenue belonged in theory to the ruler as his 'eminent domain', whether in his role as war-leader or as secular leader of the Islamic community. In that sense, all land in the empire was at his disposal: in accordance with Islamic legal authority and practice, conquered lands became state lands (*mîr*), granted out as secure holdings to its peasant cultivators. Such notions of 'eminent rights' are not, of course, confined to Islam alone. This was a formal attribute of many conquerors, or of rulers whose position was legitimated in some way by the fact of conquest, in many different societies at different times. William I of England claimed such rights after his victory in 1066, supported and legitimated by Papal authority and support for his undertaking.

The Ottoman state had a class structure similar to that of all tributary states. In law and theory, its population was divided into two groups or estates, representing in effect the economically dominant class and its dependants – a military class with a monopoly of the right to bear arms and receive revenues and allocations of lands; and an exploited and producing class, a hereditary and permanent tenancy of (predominantly) peasants and farmers. From the time of Mehmed II (1451–81) the 'ruling class', was known simply as 'Ottomans', but also as warriors, military men – *'askerî* – which effectively described their original duties and their origins. For it is important to remember that it was the latter aspect which was primary. Only with the final successes of Mehmed II in firmly establishing the *devşirme* class on an equal footing with the old Turkish nobility (see below) was the notion of the ruling class ideologically reconstituted – as 'Ottomans' – only then was the list of qualifications for admission to that class (as opposed to membership of the traditional, and tribal, older Turkish nobility, a warrior elite) elaborated; and only then was the term *'askerî* applied to all the members of this new, imperial ruling elite, even though many were not, of course, soldiers at all. But admission to this class qualified a person to bear arms and to hold a *timâr*; and the close connection between the elaboration of a state structure, on the one hand, and the process of class formation or consolidation, on the other, becomes very clear.

The chief general qualifications for entry into this class now became acceptance of Islam (although this was less important than has often been assumed), loyalty to the Sultan and the state, and knowledge of the 'Ottoman way', that is to say, the practices, customs and language of the ruling dynasty and state. This was, therefore, a 'compromised meritocracy', although patronage and clientage were built into it in respect of the selection and the training of recruits.

The 'ruling class' thus included all state servants and officers from the highest palatine official down to the lowliest Muslim soldier. While the term describes a political-theological estate, with differential economic and power implications internally, rather than a ruling class in the sense of a dominant class in the strictly economic sense, it is also clear that it marks out a clear difference in respect of basic relationships to the means of production and distribution of surpluses between it, and the subject populations, the *re'âyâ*.

Thus far the theory of the basic structure of the Ottoman state, as it is supposed to have pertained in the late fifteenth and for much of the sixteenth century, has been described. But to begin with, these political concepts, aspects of specific historical ideologies of rulership and power, must not be taken at face value – the crucial point is to determine how far, and why, some rulers were able to turn these rights at times into a political reality. The practices and economic relationships through which these claims could be realized (and the nature of the power resources of the ruler) are central. And the key element in all this is, as mentioned above, the mode and the main institutions of surplus distribution.

In day-to-day terms, the imperial lands could only be administered through the medium of agents or representatives of one sort or another. The crucial question for each political formation, as we have seen, is precisely what form this took, and this reflects in turn what was both possible and available to the central authority. To what extent were certain specific institutional forms imposed upon the rulers, for example, and to what extent were the rulers, in the context of political, cultural and other relevant factors, able to assert their own organizational structures?

Until the time of Murad II (1421–51) and Mehmed II (1451–81) the rulers held in many ways a relatively weak position, acknowledged as absolute rulers, yet with only a precarious hold over the Turkish clans and nobility, who still dominated the provinces and led the army. But it is important to note that from the earliest times, in the later thirteenth century, a sizeable number of Christian lords in northwest Asia Minor had rallied to Osman's banner, which certainly represented for them greater opportunities for booty and enrichment. Thus even at this early stage a division existed between the Turkish, Muslim element in the Ottoman lands, and the heterogeneous elements dependent directly on the Osmanli family and household retinue for their position. These elements, too, contributed in significant ways to the formation of the Ottoman state. The promise of conquests and the winning of new lands for themselves gave these various, mixed elements and their leaders a rationale for supporting and promoting the Ottoman dynasty in its expansionist endeavours, a rationale which was legitimated ideologically – at least, in the later tradition – through the notion of the *jihâd*, the Ghazi war against the infidel. To a large extent, it was these mixed elites who made the Ottoman state possible.[23]

Murad I (1360–89) and Bayezid I (1389–1402) both attempted to place some limitations upon the power and influence of the more independent element of this older elite by promoting both the household retinue and its dependants, particularly by promoting the 'slaves of the Porte' (*kapıkulları*) chosen from their *pençik*, one fifth of the booty traditionally taken by the leader from the spoils of war.[24] They had tried to develop a new military force, the *yeni çeri*, or 'new guard' (Janissaries), recruited from such sources, more dependable than both the older *müsellem* (cavalry) and *yaya* (infantry) troops, in effect a rotational levy owed by the Turkish warriors and clansmen of Anatolia, who had received lands in the process of conquest, and who were bound to serve in the ruler's campaigns; and the predominantly (but not entirely) Türkmen nomad cavalry who had formed the bulk of the Ottoman forces until the time of Orhan Ghazi (1324–59), serving together with lighter auxiliary troops, in many cases recruited for service in the Balkans from the conquered Christian populations for employment on the frontiers against enemies to the North. The rotational levy, a relatively ancient institution, was first developed in Seljuk times during the reign of Malik Shah (1079–92), and represented a half-way stage between tribal warrior structures and a disarmed and de-tribalized peasantry.

But the system of promoting slaves suffered a set-back after the battle of Ankara in 1402 (at which the Ottomans were utterly defeated by the army of Timur). Indeed, two clearly discernible factions had already developed at the Ottoman court under Murad I and Bayezid I; on the one hand, the Turkish nobles, in particular the marcher *beys* (the *Uç beys*, whose soldiers were often more loyal to their own leaders than to the Sultan – a tradition which is evident even in the early sixteenth century, see below), who still led the armies and headed the conquest of new territories, who held these territories, granted to them in return for their military support, as *timârs*, and which represented in effect vast clan territories or estates. It is important to note in this connection that, regardless of any theoretical prohibition on 'private' landed property inherent in Islamic law, this elite had effective possession and control of their territories and the incomes which these produced; and the central authority was rarely in a position to challenge this. On the other hand, the Christian vassals of the European and Balkan lands, who advised halting the advance against the Christians of the Balkans and turning against Muslim foes in Anatolia, represented an important counterweight, recognized and cultivated as such by the Ottoman Sultans already from the middle of the fourteenth century.[25] The policy of reining back the military advance in the Balkans favoured the interests of the Ottoman dynasty and the central state, of course, in contrast to those of the semi-independent Turkish elite and marcher lords; for through the conquests in Europe the latter received vast tracts as extended benefices, as mentioned already, expanding their own power and authority and representing thereby a potential threat to the Sultan's own central power and authority. Anatolia outside Ottoman control (still a very considerable area until Bayezid's campaigns in the 1390s), in contrast, represented both a source of political opposition – seven independent tribal emirates or confederations existed outside the Ottoman state – and it was not organized in extensive clan or chieftaincy *timârs* in the same way as the Balkans, much more recent conquests. Its absorption into the state would have promoted the interests of the rulers.

After the collapse of 1402 there followed an interregnum which lasted until the accession of Mehmed I, an accession secured only because Mehmed himself, in order to win the Turkish nobility and the *Uç beys* to his side, agreed to disband the slave guards regiments and to dismantle the *kapıkulları* system. Only under his son, Murad II, was this revived and built up once more, so much so that, paradoxically, the still dominant faction of Turkish nobles and clan chiefs, who hitherto had stood to gain a great deal from constant warfare along the frontiers – which it was their duty constantly to advance – began to favour a policy of peace and consolidation in order to limit the possibilities for further strengthening the slave element at court and in the army. The factionalism within the elite was now represented by the *devşirme*, or slave element, promoted by the Sultan, on the one hand, and the clan nobles and their kin, on the other. And these factions took on an increasingly ideological guise as the stakes rose. *Örfi* law by definition favoured the ruler (since it was through this channel that he could expand his power) and the *devşirme*, and for this reason the old Turkish nobility turned increasingly to the *Şeriat* (and its interpreters, the members of the

'Ulemâ) in its attempts both to halt the further development of the *devşirme* as well as to demand the re-affirmation of the traditional, tribally-rooted relationship between clans/tribes and Sultan. Under Mehmed II, the conflict came to a head. The older nobility pressed for peace on the European front, a case strongly represented by the Grand Vizir, Candarlı Halil, and a member of the traditional clan elite. But the campaign against Constantinople – a major propaganda move, but of little military significance – went ahead. It was an ideological and symbolic gesture designed to strengthen his own authority in Islam and at the same time the position of the *devşirme* and the *kapıkulları*.[26] And after his victory, Mehmed felt powerful enough to move decisively against the old tribal elites. Candarlı Halil was dismissed and executed, and there took place a wide-ranging purge of the older nobility: exile, execution, confiscations of *timâr* estates and provinces, the latter awarded to 'new men' of the *devşirme*. By the 1460s, Mehmed had achieved the situation generally thought of as typifying the 'Ottoman state' in the discussions referred to above. The Janissaries (*yeni çeri*, the 'new guard' mentioned already) were reformed, re-equipped, and had slave officers imposed instead of the old officer elite; the *devşirme* was massively expanded and, with the support of the Janissaries, the new slave units, and a loyal body of trusted slave administrators (including the Grand Vizir, now likewise a member of the *kapıkulları*, and the Sultan's representative), Mehmed was able to impose his will in a radical re-affirmation of his own absolute authority.

Yet, in a second series of confiscations, in the 1460s and 1470s, forced upon him partly by a shortage of resources and of soldiers, he seized the properties of both religious foundations (*wakfs*) and secular landholders and, having returned them to *mîr* (state land) status, used them as the base for an expansion of the provincial cavalry, the *sipâhis*. This policy was itself a consequence of the new-found position and power of the *devşirme* elite, whom Mehmed now had to rein back in order to safeguard his key position as arbitrator between the poles of the *Uç bey* (marcher lord) elite and the *devşirme* and its clients.

This was a crucial element in his politics. It is important to note that he did try to strike a balance between the two, between the representatives of the new elite created by his own and his predecessors' policies, and the traditional clan leaders and their retinues, for such a balance was the guarantee of his own absolute authority – and that of his successors. A number of the older and more prestigious nobles were left with their *timârs* intact, as well as their positions; and while he reduced the power of the *Uç beys* in command of the Türkmen and other troops directed at the enemies of Islam, by increasing their number and reducing the size of the their commands, he could not afford to replace them entirely, for they represented the front line in the jihad, both in the Islamic popular vision as well as in terms of military reality and the defence of the Ottoman lands.

The Sultan's role was, in consequence, the key. And the balance that was achieved depended very much on the character and ability of individual rulers. Mehmed II removed the aristocratic Candarlı Halil, and replaced him with a line of *devşirme* Grand Vizirs, men who had no connection with the old establishment and were utterly dependent upon the Sultan himself. Even so, his policies failed to resolve the factionalism built into this structure: his actions were not unopposed, either from the vested interests of the *'Ulemâ* faction, or from the Turkish Muslim nobility itself. In opposing the absolute authority of the ruler as reflected in *örfi* law, preferring instead the older relationship of lords to war-leader which had epitomized the early period of Ottoman expansion (and which became as a result much idealized), the Turkish nobility inevitably found itself in alliance with the representatives of the *Şeriat*, the holy law of Islam, which in itself represented potentially an alternative set of values and system of authority.

On Mehmed's death in 1481, there took place a serious reaction and partial reversal of his policies, accompanied by civil war. And in the struggle for the succession which followed, between the brothers Bayezid and Cem (ostensibly a political faction fight between two individuals), the problematic nature of the 'balance' established and maintained by Mehmed II, and the antagonism between the vested interests of the *devşirme* and the Turkish aristocracy or elite, became very clear. In order to counteract the increasing influence of the *devşirme*, for example, Mehmed II had in his last years appointed as his Grand Vizir Karamanı Nisanci Mehmed Pasha, a member of the older Turkish elite, not of the *devşirme*, unlike all his predecessors since the unfortunate Candarlı Halil. Mehmed Pasha's policies (which also favoured the interests of the *'Ulemâ*) were resented by the *devşirme*. So that on Mehmed II's death, a plot led by leading *devşirme* men, and with Bayezid as claimant to the throne, was able to win over the Janissaries and the *devşirme* leader of the Albanian campaign army, and defeat Cem, who fled to Rhodes. The Grand Vizir was killed by the Janissaries. In return for this support, however, and advised by his closest confidants, Bayezid promised to relax his father's policies and return much of the *wakf* and other confiscated property which had been seized from the *devşirme* and its clients in Mehmed's last years. In effect, the now powerful *devşirme* elite had become – in contrast to the period before the conquest of Constantinople under Mehmed II – the real conservatives, and sought to promote and consolidate the position they occupied. At the same time, Bayezid personally was greatly influenced by the conservative *'Ulemâ*, and the alliance between old Turkish elite and *'Ulemâ* was now replaced by one between the latter and the *devşirme*: both parties now had a joint interest in limiting the Sultan's power, based on the exercise of *örfi* law, in favour of a more traditional approach. The problem for the 'autonomous' state, in the sense of a 'state for itself' (strong foreign policy, firm control over resource extraction, allocation, distribution and consumption, independence of state interests in this respect from those of any dominant elite with sources of power outside such interests), was now expressed precisely through the ideological tension between *Örf* and *Şeriat*, between Sultan's authority as conqueror and holy law. The structures, both ideological and administrative, which had been moulded in the complex evolution of the Ottoman polity, and which were promoted to his own particular advantage by Mehmed II, provided the framework within which and through which these tensions and contradictions were to work themselves out.

The backbone of the army had now come to be constituted by the Janissary corps, along with the elite central cavalry and artillery divisions, on the one hand, and the *sipâhi* cavalry of the provinces, on the other. The former were directly supported by the treasury, the latter by *timâr* holdings. Since these holdings have been the subject of a great deal of discussion (and a degree of misinformation) with regard to the supposed absence of any 'hereditary nobility', it will be worth devoting some attention to them at this juncture.

Basically, the *timâr* holder was granted the right to collect the revenues of the district allotted to him as a living in return for performing state services – usually, but not always, military. *Timârs* were divided into five groups, from the lowest, which rendered an income of approximately 2000 *akçes*, or silver aspers, per annum, to the highest grade, producing as much as 40,000 *akçes*. Such holdings, or, rather, allocations, provided for the basic income of most of the imperial officials, civil and military, from simple *sipâhi* soldiers to the *sancak beys*, or governors of provinces. Allocations of revenue were also given in return for outstanding service, great devotion to duty and the Sultan, and as rewards for military prowess. A not inconsiderable number of *timârs* were also granted to religious functionaries or urban officials. But the vast mass of small *timârs* consisted in grants to *sipâhi* horsemen, intended to maintain the troopers and their retainers.

Now, in spite of the authority of the Sultan in respect of the withdrawal of a *timâr*, or of the regular or occasional rotation of the larger *timârs* (*hasses* or *ziamets*) in particular, an authority which never entirely lapsed or fell into disuse, there was always a very great degree of continuity of occupancy. The central portion of a grant (the *iptida* or 'beginning') generally passed upon application to a son on the father's death. In most cases, permission to continue in occupancy was granted. Only those revenues which the father had accumulated as a result of rewards for good service could not be passed on. Retired *timâr* holders often kept the basic portion of their holding as a pension, the remainder going to their son or to another *sipâhi* if there were no male offspring. The right to apply for and to hold a *timâr*, indeed, was hereditary within the *'askerî* class.

From the time of Selim I (1512–20), furthermore, there is some evidence to suggest that a remnant of the old Turkish clan and tribal elite of Anatolia and the Balkans was able to regain some of its ancestral holdings as *timâr* grants, thus enabling them to re-assert their economic position; a process which had been inaugurated under Bayezid II who was obliged by political and ideological pressure to restore many of the privileges of both the Muslim Turkish nobility and the *devşirme* elite which had brought him to power, as mentioned already.[27] At the same time, some of the indigenous nobles in the Balkans kept their lands and served the Sultan as *timâr*-holders even after their defeat, although they were generally quickly absorbed into the Ottoman ruling class, thus losing any cultural particularism. In addition, some of the wealthier or more powerful *timâr*-holders also possessed smaller plots or 'reserves' for private use, cultivated by day-labourers or share-croppers, and which were entirely at their personal disposal. This was most common among the powerful holders of the much bigger *ziamet* or *hass timârs*, in which huge demesnes farmed by a substratum of dependent peasants were often built up.

Those to whom *timârs* were granted were in addition also responsible for the collection of the land-tax, the periodic re-distribution of peasant holdings which might be ordained in the event of a particular holding becoming uncultivated or deserted, as well as the maintenance of civil order. Through the collection of fines and the receipt of customary prestations of labour, fodder, wood and so on, the *timâr*-holder could thus build up a considerable income or reserve in both cash and kind. Thus, in spite of his ultimate dependence upon the state for possession of his *timâr*, the timariot and his family were often able to maintain themselves relatively independently once an initial grant or allocation had been made. They were certainly an integral part of the local economy, not simply an imposition upon it, for they exercised on behalf of the state (and their own interests) a continuous supervision over and intervention in its affairs. They represented a crucial aspect of state control over the agrarian economy of the empire: the Ottoman land-codes show that peasant cultivators could do very little to change either their methods of production and their crops, or the rate of exploitation without state (that is, timariot) permission. And while the state also supervised thereby the timariots themselves, this had less to do with 'protecting' or 'defending the rights of' the peasantry – a popular interpretation among conservative historians of the Ottoman state – than with assuring an average rate of exploitation of peasant labour and the securing of the necessary surplus required by state interests as opposed to those of any third party.[28]

The *timâr* 'system' has rightly been seen as a fundamental element in Ottoman state power during the period from Mehmed II to the death of Suleiman in 1566. Two important observations can now be made. First, that although *timâr*-holders, and particularly the *sipâhis*, were allotted revenues rather than lands – like the Byzantine *pronoia* which I will discuss below – they nevertheless constituted the state in one of its most important surplus-consuming forms. They represented the legal fiction of a medium through which surpluses were transferred to the state; and this medium was in itself, and regardless of any internal rotation among *timâr*-holders, intended to prevent the alienation of the state's revenues to private sources, a permanent feature of the relations of production and surplus appropriation of the Ottoman state. While there was no hereditary aristocracy with permanently-held family property, there did exist a hereditary ruling class, internally differentiated as we have seen, located in town and country, fulfilling different state functions, which reproduced itself both by birth and by recruitment of new *devşirme* elements. The fact that this class as a whole supposedly had no particularistic familial and class identities, and that formally service under the Sultan brought with it slave status, does not mean that it was not a class in the economic sense or that it did not reproduce itself both biologically and, more importantly, through the institutional structures which were themselves integral to the existence of the Ottoman state itself, in this form: that is, that it appropriated, consumed and thereby 'passed on' to the state (that is, it retained as the state) surpluses from the producing population in the name of the Sultan. It thus represented structurally a potentially antagonistic force which, without the political control made possible by successful warfare, territorial expansion and internal equilibrium, could (and did, of course) challenge the central authority over the distribution of resources and surplus.

In this respect, the Ottoman state clearly rested on the same fundamental structural principles common to all tributary social formations, where an intermediate class represents the state to the producers, consuming a large portion of the surpluses it extracts in the name of a central political authority and an appropriate legitimating political ideology; and it contains the same structural contradictions in respect of control over the distribution of surpluses. The cyclical nature of the antagonistic relationship between central control and local consumption, centralizing demands and centrifugal tendencies, between the 'private' and the 'public' aspects of pre-industrial state administrative demands, a cycle which depends then upon the complex, local combination of political, ideological and economic factors for its form and expression, is thus equally a part of the history of the rise and decline of the Ottoman state.[29]

That the state intervened at the ideological level through customary and state law, and the Sultan's 'protection' to prevent over-exploitation by *timâr*-holders of the producers does not alter this essential point. For the state law (*Örf*), in contrast to religious law (*Şeriat*), reflected historically the ruler's right to legislate on the basis of custom. While the *Örf* represented in different parts of the empire the traditional mode of exploitation, evolved locally, and juridically-fixed by the new state, and at the same time the pragmatic approach to conquest and absorption into an evolving political structure characteristic of many Islamic states, it was also a crucial medium of control over both the peasantry and the timariots, re-inforcing and consolidating the power-relationships and the relations of exploitation which had evolved out of the original conquest (or absorption) and which depended ultimately upon coercion. So much is clear from the attitude of the mass of the *re'âyâ* population to the provincial governors and their officials and soldiers, representative and symbolic of this law, who appear from the later sixteenth century (but possibly before – the evidence is somewhat sparse before this time) to have been particularly feared and hated for their exploitative and extortionate rule, and who were compared unfavourably with the representatives of the religious law, the *kadi*s and other members of the Islamic learned community.[30]

Neither does the fact that there existed a degree of social mobility alter the economic class nature of Ottoman society. In practice, the (hereditary) subject peasantries provided only through the *devşirme* an element of the ruling class, whose members had in any case, and regardless of origin, thoroughly to internalize and assimilate the ideology of the Ottoman establishment.[31] Furthermore, the policies of the rulers in actually moulding the formation of this ruling class – by weakening traditional tribal and clan nobilities in favour of their own *devşirme* recruits, and through the institutionalized slavery that imperial service always brought with it – must be understood at more than just the political-ideological level at which it was, and often still is, represented: it embodied the struggle for power over and control of economic resources required to promote a particular ideology (that is, the *jihâd* and *ghazâ* [raid]),[32] and the dynasty that proclaimed it, and, more specifically, a struggle over the relations of surplus distribution within the ruling 'military' class of the expanding Ottoman state. For it must be clear that control over surplus distribution meant control over the resources of the state and hence political control as such. Yet in spite of its efforts and desires, the central authority never entirely removed the hereditary frontier nobility from its powerful position. Only in the later sixteenth century was it successful in lessening the power of this group; by which time the contradictions within the new system were already becoming apparent.[33] But what this means for state theory, of course, is that states can and do, under the appropriate conditions, influence the later moulding of economic classes. The inference from this, however, is not that they are supra-class structures themselves, or indeed in any way autonomous of the social formation in which they are rooted. On the contrary, it shows how integrally determined are states, and their political and economic strategies, by the conditions within which the appropriation and distribution of surpluses takes place. As I will suggest below, it also illustrates how states facilitate the development of new sets of social-economic relationships, promoted by their own institutional demands, relationships which in turn contribute paradoxically both to the maintenance of the state and to challenges to its power at the local or regional level of the distribution of surpluses and political authority.

The second observation concerns the relationships within this broad ruling elite, both between its provincial representatives and those at court, and between different factions at court: in particular, the rivalries which developed between those of *devşirme* origin and non-*devşirme* groups. Once again, the structural contradictions of surplus distribution within the dominant elite provides a dynamic element underlying Ottoman political and military decline, rather than the ideological forms through which these contradictions were expressed.

The story of these developments has been elucidated by several historians, and is long and complex.[34] The primary contradiction lay in the structure of the ruling class itself, a class which depended for its economic well-being and its ideological unity upon a continued policy of military and economic expansion. Once expansion ceased – as the state came up against a firmer European opposition north of the Balkans, and the Safavid Persian state in the East in the second half of the sixteenth century, and as it attained what represented its maximum viable extent in respect of both military and political control (crystallized in terms of communications and logistics) – these contradictions became apparent as the structure of Ottoman society and political organization were radically transformed by the effects of its initial successes.

The sixteenth century witnessed a number of concurrent developments, which coalesced in the 1570s and 1580s. Particularly significantly, there took place a breakdown of rural order which has traditionally been ascribed to a demographic upswing at the end of the sixteenth century, especially in Anatolia, in turn seen as resulting in a dearth of land. At the same time, an inflation caused by an influx of cheap Spanish silver both affected the hitherto relatively stable silver *akçe*, the standard silver coin of the Ottoman state, and reduced the values of the fixed incomes of the *timâr* holders, especially the *sipâhis* of Asia Minor. The degree and the supposed effects of this demographic expansion have been questioned, as have those of the import of silver and consequent inflation.[35] In the first place, population expansion cannot convincingly be generalized to the whole of the empire, although there was an increase in many regions, such as the western Anatolian coast, especially the hinterlands of large urban and commercial centres, such as Izmir. In the second place, the movement of large numbers of *re'âyâ* peasants from the land took two forms: on the one hand, it was promoted, at least initially, by the state itself, in its efforts to recruit ever greater numbers of mercenary soldiers with firearms into its service. On the other hand, many peasants fled to cities and defended towns in order to escape the endemic brigandage of the last years of the sixteenth century caused by the fighting between *celâli* bands and renegade *levend* (mercenary) soldiers, and the state's *kul* or slave soldiers. For the shift in international military technology towards infantry and firearms had left both the elite Janissary regiments and the traditionally-armed *sipâhi* cavalry at a considerable disadvantage in their confrontation with European, especially Austrian, armies. Thus from the 1540s and 1550s especially the state began both massively to increase the size of the Janissary corps (which an early seventeenth-century adviser to the Sultan noted had risen from 13,500 in 1574 to 43,000 by 1632), and to recruit ever greater numbers of mercenary soldiers with firearms from the *re'âyâ* populations. The demand for such soldiers became especially pressing during the war with Austria from 1593 to 1606. These *sekban* units, however, were recruited largely at the expense of the traditional *sipâhi* cavalry.[36] For in order to maintain the new units, the state needed the revenues consumed by the increasingly marginalized provincial horsemen. Some of these revenues were thus transferred to the central fisc to finance the recruitment of more Janissary and *sekban* units. Provincial governors – *beylerbeyis* or *vâlis* – received greater power as the control or supervision of revenue collection and assessment came increasingly into their hands. The state needed cash; yet the silver inflation only exacerbated the situation; and the *sekban* units themselves – recruited from the rural peasantry – tended to be hired for the duration of a campaign, rather than be supported, like the *sipâhis*, on the basis of a permanent arrangement.[37]

The state had, on the whole, no arrangements for supporting such units in peacetime, however. The result was that, when it attempted to disband them or proved unable to provide lands or other means of support, many of them turned to brigandage and extortion, terrorizing the localities they inhabited or passed through into providing for them. These bands were soon a major threat to Ottoman state power, representing a source of disruption both to established patterns of administration in the provinces, as well as to agricultural production and the state's ability to appropriate and distribute revenues according to its requirements. Peasant flight to fortified centres and the abandonment of land was one result. Devastating warfare between the ever-increasing numbers of Janissary units based permanently in the provinces to check these *celâli* was another.[38] This expansion of the *kapıkulları* or slave units across the cities and provinces of the whole empire was of particular importance to the patterns of power distribution and control over the means of distribution of surplus wealth in the ensuing years. Finally, the *levend* or mercenary units, once raised, and then returned from the theatre for which they had originally been recruited, often remained together under their leaders, hiring out their services to the highest bidder. This was particularly the case after the military defeat of the *celâli* at the hands of government forces in 1608, for having failed to win access to the *kapıkulları* and thereby achieve their political aims, such mercenaries turned increasingly over the course of the seventeenth century to service in the retinues of provincial governors and similar patrons, giving an independence of political action to such officials which they had only rarely possessed before. For they could now be independent of both the *sipâhi* elite of the countryside, who had a vested interest in the maintenance and enforcement of central authority in respect of their *timârs*, and the Janissaries and other slaves of the Porte established away from Istanbul.

The significance of these 'external' factors, however, has led even very recent commentators to conclude that the Ottoman system was entirely stable until such elements intervened. In fact, the internal stability was both the effect of a particular balance of economic and power-relationships, and relatively short-lived. In addition, it was laced with contradictions, both within the ruling elite, and between the Ottoman 'ruling class' and the leading elements of the *re'âyâ*: the efforts of *re'âyâ* military men to obtain *kapıkulları* privileges and status, for example, which can be shown to date from at least the 1550s, and the consequent hostility of the Janissaries; the dominant position of a number of *sekban* officers of *re'âyâ* origin, both in the provinces and, in the first half of the seventeenth century, for the central government; and the civil war-like conditions of many regions in the Balkans and Anatolia at times during the seventeenth century, as Janissaries and centrally-mobilized peasant and urban militias fought against *levend* or mercenary units; as well as the rise of the urban *a'yân* in the seventeenth century all illustrate this.[39]

The fiscal problems which the state had to confront in attempting to support the vast number of mercenary and slave soldiers contributed in addition to a crisis of the *timâr* system as a whole, since the smaller allocations could no longer support the cost of the regular campaigns demanded of them. Confiscations of *timârs* for failure to appear at musters were ignored or circumvented, while many *sipâhis* joined the *celâli* brigands. As the *timâr* system became increasingly marginal to the state's immediate military requirements, and as the demands of the central government as well as those of provincial authorities and governors for cash grew, so tax-farming increasingly became the chief means for the state to raise reliably the sums it needed. Tax-farming had always been present, of course, but it now dominated the methods by which the state appropriated surplus.

One of the long-term results of these developments, however, was the very opposite of what the state and the rulers of the later fifteenth and earlier sixteenth centuries had intended. For it found itself now unable to prevent the gradual evolution, more rapidly in some areas than in others, of provincial officers and rural notables with estates (originating among both greater and lesser *timâr*-holders as well as tax-farmers, themselves often officers within the administrative elite or their dependants and agents) who, apart from attracting economically depressed peasants to their properties, were able to exploit regular landlord–tenant relationships, primarily by virtue of the conversion of state revenues into farmed taxes collected at all levels by agents, both for the central fisc, as well as on behalf of local governors and other officials. The imprecision of the revenue registers from this time – the last years of the sixteenth century – which was an integral part of this process (and which reflected the difficulties inherent in adequately assessing revenues in a period of inflation) facilitated the formation of what were, in effect, estates and properties which remained, in theory, of *mîrî* status, but which became increasingly difficult to control from the centre. The process had already begun, but with the support of the rulers, during the middle of the sixteenth century, when a number of officers of the military-administrative elite were granted what were termed 'estate-like' revenues on a permanent basis from the normal state taxes. While the lands which went with these grants of revenue were not private property, they do seem nevertheless to have represented an important element in the building up of personal possessions in land and income among such elements of the state elite in the provinces, and in the conditions of the later sixteenth and seventeenth century described already they marked an important stage in the breakdown of the traditional system of revenue assignments proportional to state posts and under strict central control. The effective alienation of state revenues to the private consumption of members of the *'askerî* class meant also, of course, a weakening of state control over the land and the basic relations of production.[40]

The same process occurred in respect of *wakf* estates (in theory corporate religious foundations endowed by the pious – including the Sultan – whose property was also derived from *mîrî* land) which also grew in extent and number. For they represented a legal and age-old way of circumventing both Koranic prescriptions on inheritance and, more importantly, a mode of subtracting lands and revenues from the state. Under their administrating families or organizations, such estates tended to become their private and hereditary property, a phenomenon which repeats itself in all Islamic societies.[41] But in the Ottoman context of the later sixteenth century and after, it had particular repercussions. And as this phenomenon of estate formation and revenue expropriation was general throughout the ruling class, from the most powerful down, the net result was a decline in state revenues and state power, as its resources were progressively alienated to the nascent landholding elite.

As the *timâr* system declined, so the state relied increasingly, as we have seen, on the slave regiments and the *sekban* mercenary units, between whom there existed a fierce hostility. The Janissaries, now spread throughout the empire, consolidated their position and economic independence in the towns in which they were based by allying themselves with, working for, and sometimes becoming members of the new landholding elite. The result was an increasing ineffectiveness of the *timâr* system and its piecemeal transformation into an extended system of tax-farming (*iltizam*), partly influenced also by the Arab tradition as the Middle East and Egypt were incorporated into the empire during the sixteenth century. The vested interests of both court and provincial elites were embedded in this process. The state was left with its extraordinary levies, the *avanz*, over which it retained much greater direct authority, along with a range of similar extraordinary impositions, most of which tended over time, and as a response to the state's need for cash, to be raised as regular taxes. The crucial importance of the maintenance of centrally-controlled registers of tax-payers in this respect is apparent. Over the same period – that is, from the later sixteenth to the end of the seventeenth century – the position of the peasantry seems also to have worsened – the brief century and a half of state supervision and regulation, whatever its real nature, and as it is reflected in the land-laws or *kanûn names*, was over, and the oppression of the rural population by a self-interested landlord class, fragmented though it was in respect of its varied origins and political affiliations, became the norm.

Civil wars, and the consequent widespread economic and demographic disruption in Anatolia in the late sixteenth and seventeenth century were at the root of many of these developments, as must by now be clear.[42] Such wars were both symptoms of the problems facing the state, its inability to respond to them at a structural level (at least in respect of 'restoring' what was considered by some contemporary advisers to the Sultans to have been the 'traditional' establishment), and acted at the same time as further stimuli to the changes in the older arrangements. Although attempts at reform did occur – based chiefly on efforts to re-establish a 'golden age' of Suleiman and the mid-sixteenth century – they could not succeed. The function of Ottoman state ideology and political theory is in this respect crucial, for it presented a systemic rationale which both legitimated social relations and the state as these were refracted through it, yet was incapable of taking account of major shifts in its conditions of existence. While taking shifts of a local nature (both geographically and temporally) into consideration, as contemporary works of statecraft testify, it could offer no solutions, except to present itself as the only model upon which a secure state and a harmonious social order could be founded.

The *timâr* system continued to operate at varying levels of efficiency throughout the empire until its final abolition in the nineteenth-century reforms, and until the very end there is ample evidence to show that the state never conceded the struggle to retain control over *mîrî* land and the holdings or revenue-allocations of its *sipâhis*. But the decline of the *devşirme* due to demographic collapse in the seventeenth century, and the recruitment of *re'âyâ* peasants into the Janissaries and the court establishment, which occurred from the middle of the seventeenth century, now meant that there was no longer a significant institutional difference between the Sultan's erstwhile loyal slaves and non-slave Muslims. The court came to be polarized around ambitious individual leaders and their clients, depending in turn on the continued support of powerful provincial interests. Three dominant factions can be distinguished in the palatine establishment: the Janissaries and the provincial commanders, who used their troops to promote their own political and economic interests; the administrative bureaucracy; and the religious leadership and intellectuals, the *'Ulemâ*, fiercely opposed to reform, which would have brought with it the re-establishment and promotion of *örfi* law and the legal authority of the state at the expense of Islamic tradition. In spite of periodic efforts to confiscate and return to the fisc the provincial private estates that had evolved, the government could no longer prevent the establishment and consolidation of a provincial and hereditary aristocratic elite which, while existing within the fiction of the Sultan's absolute authority, nevertheless maintained its lands and its power until the nineteenth century.[43]

The role of the *'Ulemâ* or class of learned men was ideologically central in this respect, for it was responsible for organizing, propagating and defending Islam, interpreting and applying Islamic holy law, and training younger theologians and intellectuals.[44] As a group, they were differentiated internally according to their specific functions; but they represented a deeply conservative element in the ruling elite – especially those concerned with the interpretation of Islamic law, the Koranic tradition and the state traditions of Islam. They dominated education and the judiciary and, of course, gained financially from their control over *wakfs*. Together with popular religious orders, such as the Bektaşi dervishes, they provided one of the pillars of the opposition to the reforms of Selim III and of Mahmud II in the later eighteenth and early nineteenth century, reforms aimed initially at modernizing the armies and re-organizing older corps, but in so doing threatened the position of the *'Ulemâ*, who relied on the Janissaries for support. They constituted a reserve of fundamentalist and anti-reformist sentiment that could mobilize the Janissaries (that other pool of conservatism and vested interest), and block any attempt to introduce structural change in the balance of power between this elite, in its various forms, and the central authority. Naturally, the Sultans were still able to take action against individuals who, once isolated, could be successfully removed, but the power of this new elite as a class was never seriously challenged. By the later eighteenth century the *a'yân* (provincial notables) and the *derebey* nobles of Anatolia had established tax-concessions based around landed estates or *çiftliks* which deprived the state of vast revenues, lands which were, in effect, hereditary.

The growth in the power and influence of the *a'yân* families can be detected as early as the later sixteenth century.[45] The central authority needed to employ local leaders, whatever their origin (many were of *kul* or slave origin, for example, established as Janissaries in provincial towns and with well-established vested interests in local affairs), to organize and lead the popular militias raised from the *re'âyâ* to oppose the depredations of both the *celâli* and *sekban* mercenaries, as well as the Janissaries who exploited the peasants and imposed irregular levies and other demands upon them in both cash and kind. At the same time, such local notables also operated as tax-farmers for the central government, using their positions to build up their own wealth and, especially significantly, acting as representatives of local interests to the central government. Together with growing trade, both internally and externally, and expanding commercial wealth, as suggested by studies of towns and the generally monetized nature of rural–urban economic relations, such developments considerably weakened the state's fiscal as well as its administrative control over provincial affairs, and began to have an effect clearly from the 1630s.[46] But while the *a'yân* rarely cherished any ambitions for political independence, the Anatolian *derebeys* ruled many regions as semi-independent lords with their own administrative apparatus – imitative of the Sultan's court and bureaucracy – so that the parcellization of sovereignty constituted a major threat to the very existence of the centralized state. The threat to state authority was emphasized by the fact that many provincial governors employed their own private retinues, often recruited from brigand or mercenary bands, as I have said, hence attaining a greater degree of local independence.[47]

It is important to note a difference, however, between these later examples of provincial independence, in respect of their significance for the authority and effectiveness of central government, and the many examples of the state deliberately delegating authority to local elites after the conquest of a particular region. Thus not all cases of 'regional autonomy' should be seen as necessarily contrary to the state's interests, at least not in their original contexts. After its final annexation from the Shi'ite Safavid power following the battle of Caldiran in 1514, eastern Anatolia remained largely under its indigenous Sunni Kurdish chiefs, who could be assimilated into the ruling elite and relied upon to maintain Sunni orthodoxy and pursue the Sultan's anti-Shi'ite policies. There are a number of similar examples.[48]

But the process of decentralization, and the situation of regional semi-autonomy, which later developments represent, has been picked out by many commentators, and rightly so. For whatever the original conditions within which provincial elites came to act more or less independently of the centre, the long-term results of such autonomy were the effective paralysis of central power in respect of the real running of the state for considerable periods; the reliance of the state upon ideological motivation alone rather than upon economic control for the maintenance and reproduction of its authority and sovereignty, as well as a proportion of its revenues; and the gradual and piecemeal contraction of the empire territorially as it was progressively less able to muster adequate resources, trained manpower and effective leadership to counter external military pressures. Most important of all is the fact that the changes reflected also the context of the Ottoman power internationally: the growth of capitalist market relations in western Europe, and especially the speed of technological change, left the tributary Ottoman empire on the margins of what was soon to become the First World. The agrarian and then the industrial revolutions in England, the strength of the European powers, all served first to peripheralize politically, and then to colonize economically the Ottoman world for European markets and exports. The effort made from within this tributary framework of production and power relations to respond to this external challenge, however, was not qualitatively of the sort to lead to real structural transformation. Draconian reforms undertaken by Grand Vizirs, who managed, for a while, to impose a certain unity on the court, and thereby over the empire's resource-base, made reconquest and aggressive warfare possible on occasion – the great attack on Vienna in the 1680s, following a successful war against Venice, is a good example. But the structural impact of such reforms was limited, the successes illusory. By the middle of the eighteenth century, even though the *sipâhis* continued to occupy their *timârs*, albeit on a very much reduced scale, the local landlord class which had entrenched itself in the provinces, allied with provincial military commanders and governors, could defy the Sultan's government more often than not with impunity. But it is important to note that this 'defiance' only rarely involved any political confrontation or denial of the centre's power and authority. On the contrary, it involved tacit refusal to render dues and service owed, to carry out certain imperial commands (which could be circumvented by the invocation of alternative courtly factional activity and the use of patron–client relationships) and so on.

In all these developments, it is important to realize that the absence of juridically-defined private property, the continued possibility for the Sultan arbitrarily to confiscate fortunes and wealth amassed during a career at court, the lack of sanction for privately-held estates and the absence of a formal, titled nobility, are all phenomena belonging properly to the political arena of Ottoman state practice, without, of course, wishing to deny that they provided also both the context for the institutional forms which the Ottoman landed elite took, as well as the ideological authority for the Sultan to intervene directly in economic relations. And as we have already seen, this 'absence' was in practice, for much of the time, a reflection of Ottoman state theory: particularly in the period before the fall of Constantinople in 1453, but also thereafter, it is clear that effective possession of lands, and therefore control over the incomes to be derived from them, was in the hands of a fluctuating provincial elite made up of *timâr*-holders, tax-farmers, those dependent upon the income from pious foundations and, from the later sixteenth century on, members of the regional notables, the *a'yân*.

Yet at the same time, and along with Ottoman law, these theoretical constraints on property-owning had still served as constitutive elements in the evolution of the relations of distribution which dominated during the period from Mehmed II until the later sixteenth century. They represented, in other words, elements of the conditions of existence of that system. As the relations of distribution shifted, their functional economic relevance receded, while their political-ideological and symbolic relevance was modified to the changed political circumstances. Ideological systems generally (historically) respond only gradually and on a piecemeal basis to shifts or transformations in the conditions of their genesis and evolution. Modifications and shifts in weight or emphasis in the elements which make up a symbolic system can often shore up and endow political ideologies with legitimating value long after they have ceased to reflect the interests of the dominant class. Similarly, the symbolic elements inhering in established political-ideological narratives can be reinterpreted according to the perceptions and experiences of a new generation, and thus attributed with new functional relevance, hence providing, for different social/political groups, both continued legitimation and stimulus for change in received patterns of practice. This seems to have been the case with Ottoman imperial ideology: the old system, with its rigid division between *'askerî* and *re'âyâ*, a division re-inforced and hardened by the defeat of the *celâli* rebels in the early seventeenth century, could still be understood to provide the best representation of the perceived interests of both the state and the economically dominant class. This is especially clear in respect of the role of senior and middling bureaucrats and administrators at the capital who, while willing to embrace institutional reforms which did pose a threat to fundamental elements of the old system of fiscal and, more particularly, military administration, did so in order to preserve the authority and centrality of the ruler and the government, the central symbolic element of the state theory underlying Ottoman explanations of the origins and success of the empire, and a central power which represented both law and justice. As we have seen, the chief opposition came from the *'Ulemâ* and those whose interests could be held in common with them, an opposition which represented an alternative, and more traditionally Islamic, view of, and rationalization for, the existence of the Ottoman polity. Yet Ottoman political ideology successfully enabled the 'modernizing' element to maintain both the relative political independence of the central establishment and the relative territorial unity of the empire, at least where potential centrifugal and separatist tendencies were concerned. For the very success of the state in its early history, and its consolidation through the fifteenth and into the sixteenth century, were conflated together in a theory of the genesis and the function of the state, which lent to this ideological system a certain flexibility in respect of the interests of groups both within and without the government establishment at Istanbul.

But there is another important factor that needs to be taken into account, especially when the traditional view that the Ottoman state 'declined' from the later sixteenth century on, culminating in its complete political bankruptcy in the nineteenth century, has barely begun to be challenged. For it needs to be emphasized that, in spite of its fiscal problems and its defeats at the hands of European powers, the Ottoman state did survive, and did provide a context for the evolution of social and economic relationships for over three hundred years after the 'decline' set in. It is often implicitly assumed that it survived in spite of the socio-economic changes taking place within the constraints imposed by its existence (a point of view which usually entails a whole series of value judgements about the more 'advanced' nature of western economic developments, and the inevitability of their evolution). Instead, I would like to suggest that it survived because it did not come into fundamental conflict with these structures, even enabled their further development, a process which in turn contributed directly to the survival of the state, in respect of both the relative internal stability of its relations of production, and the political distribution of power in respect of local and central access to resources. A degree of equilibrium was thus achieved between the various factions within the ruling class, which comprised both the Ottoman elite and notables and others, of *re'âyâ* origin, who had effective possession of landed incomes or other sources of wealth. This does not mean that there were no structural tensions and that the relations of production were free of contradiction – that is obviously not the case, and the developments of the late eighteenth and nineteenth centuries make that very plain.

Inevitably, such a view involves jettisoning the nineteenth-century liberal Eurocentric notion of the 'strong' state which survives only if its interests coincide with those of the majority of its subjects, or only if it cruelly represses those 'progressive' elements which seek its overthrow. Central state power in the Ottoman world did 'decline' from the early seventeenth century in a variety of ways, so that the existence of the semi-autonomous *derebeys* of the nineteenth century give the impression of a state in name only. Yet it should be remembered that the position of these local warlords was made possible, and could only be maintained within the context of, the Ottoman state. The point takes us back to that made in chapter 2 and at the beginning of this chapter, namely, that states, by virtue of their very existence, need to be seen at all levels as both facilitating and enabling the evolution of new and sometimes alternative sets of economic and political relationships which must not necessarily threaten directly the state's own institutional survival.

The continued ability of the government to intervene was enough to cement the system of malversation and corruption which became a hallmark of Ottoman administration for later European commentators. Insecurity of tenure of office promoted the maximization of exploitation, personal gain and alienation of state revenues. But it is also clear that insecurity brought with it a heightened importance to the extensive household and the complex relations of patronage within Ottoman society. High officials placed clients or protégés in the establishment (and the choice of protégé often depended on shared ethnic and linguistic identity), such networks serving to protect individuals both from the ruler's whim as well as from his rational policy decisions, and to cement a degree of administrative continuity (but also vested interest) independent of the Sultan. By the same token, slave members of households entered such networks and reinforced them after they had been promoted or manumitted, continuing to rely upon the system of patronage and support through which they had been brought up or initiated into Ottoman social forms. Such households, eventually forming semi-independent bases of power and authority, came to function as complementary to the central household of the Sultan. The result was that, even in the sixteenth century, authority was in practice dispersed within the state much more widely than has sometimes been assumed, while the more important members of the ruling class (in the Ottoman sense) received a distinct identity outside that of service under the Sultan – even if this identity was only occasionally realized and given expression directly.[49] This is important, since it furnishes an insight into the *de facto* effects of the existence of a centralized state, with all that that entailed, in particular – and as stressed at the beginning of this chapter – in respect of creating 'new' spaces for the evolution of new sets of social and economic relationships. The ties binding provincial landlords and office-holders to tax-farmers (who might also be members of the state establishment), on the one hand, and to commercial centres and markets, on the other, had a clear effect on the ways in which the 'state' worked in the provinces. It was precisely the state's efforts to maintain some sort of order and authority in Anatolia during the *celâli* wars, for example, that gave a boost to the growth of a local nobility, the *a'yân*, which in turn radically transformed the nature of state–province relations, as I have noted already. Equally, it was the relationship between tax-farmers and fiscal administrators, and urban artisans and producers, which provided a major stimulus to the productivity and wealth of otherwise fairly remote and land-locked urban centres such as Kayseri. Just as importantly, the differences between various regions can be understood in the light of these developments in the context of particular characteristics (religious organization, self-perceptions, and so on) of local subject populations and especially their elites, who were partially integrated into the nexus of state–tax-payer–market activities. This can be seen especially clearly in the case of a major port and entrepôt such as Izmir (Smyrna) in the late sixteenth and seventeenth centuries, for example; but it applies equally, if on a somewhat different scale and in a different form, to the Christian communities and subjects of the Balkans.[50]

Whatever the complexities of its evolution, however, the fundamental point to emphasize is that, in spite of its continuities, both real and apparent, the first decisive factor in the internal political evolution of the Ottoman state was the struggle over the distribution of surplus appropriated from the rural producing populations of the empire, which took place within the ruling class. The struggle of the state – the Sultans and their advisers and whichever faction dominated at any given moment – to maintain its control over the means both of production and of distribution provides the context. A second crucial factor hinges on the degree of autonomy which the state was able to enjoy. Up to Mehmed II, the Sultans maintained a rigorous control over the administrative and military institutions which were tools of their policies, reflected through the ideology of holy war and Islamic expansionism. The *devşirme* elite in theory represented the centralized state power and functioned, against any opposition from provincial or tribal interests, to promote the ideology of the Ottoman establishment and dynasty. But even in respect of the source of its personnel and the effectiveness of the *devşirme*, the state up to and during the period from the reign of Mehmed II to the end of the reign of Suleiman I enjoyed no absolute independence of the interests of the older Turkish aristocracy, the *Uç bey* elite and other tribal elements who fought on the frontier, the warrior vanguard and founding elite of the Ottoman state. At the same time, and as became clear in the last years of Mehmed II, and in the war between Cem and Bayezid II, the consolidation of a *devşirme* elite tended to replace rather than merely balance the power of the Turkish tribal nobles.

The factionalism and political fragmentation of the dominant elite at court, the networks of patronage which increasingly from the later sixteenth century tied court and provinces together, were all factors which diminished the Sultan's systemic absolutism, weakened the fragile unity of the state elite, and turned the state itself into an arena for factional interests. The dominance of men appointed directly from the centre, after service in the Sultan's own household and the court, to higher provincial military and administrative positions reduced the value of provincial career structures and denied to many provincials the opportunities which they had previously had to advance themselves in the state's service. This was a feature which became increasingly apparent from the late sixteenth century on, stimulated by the increasing obsolescence of the provincial cavalry forces in the context of the times. At the same time, the increased power of provincial governors, partly a result of the fiscalization of *timârs*, meant that local networks of patronage and influence became increasingly important (as centrally-appointed officers depended more and more upon regional elites and social networks), stimulated in turn from the middle of the seventeenth century by the growth of the provincial *a'yân* class.

The contradictions within the state elite, on the one hand, and between state and local interests (which might also be represented by members of the state apparatuses themselves, of course), on the other hand, were expressed most clearly in struggles over the degree of the rate of exploitation, and the relations of surplus distribution.

But the relations of production in respect of the mode of surplus appropriation were not transformed, although the forms of surplus distribution and the rate of exploitation of peasant producers may have been. The ideological commitment of the Islamic ruling elite to the absolutist rule of the Sultans and the concept of the Ottoman state, on the one hand, together with the corporative substructures of the Ottoman social formation, which contained a disparate group of local cultural and social formations through the medium of regional religious and cultural identities (the so-called *millet* system[51]) under the umbrella of a universalist political ideology, on the other hand, these are what lent to the Ottoman state its deceptively static appearance, emphasized in addition by the rapid transformation of the western European states in the period from the sixteenth to the nineteenth centuries, with which – given the invasive effects of capitalist market relations upon the Ottoman economy and society – it was (and is) inevitably compared.

But it is significant that when, in the first half of the nineteenth century, the Sultan Mahmud II (1808–39) undertook a series of westernizing reforms, designed primarily to adjust the internal balance of power, re-inforce the position of the Sultan and re-centralize the government's political and economic control, it was only with the support of an 'enlightened' and 'progressive' westernizing faction at court, and through the inherent structural divisions between different institutional elements of the ruling class (religious, military, scribal and palatine services), and by dint of a lack of any solidarity among the *derebeys* of Asia Minor, that he could successfully force his policies through. And the lack of solidarity among the Asia Minor nobility was in any case the result of divisions within the ruling elite which followed the failed attempts at reform of Selim III (1789–1807). Mahmud was thus able to isolate key opponents and crush them quickly.[52] The Janissaries were destroyed and the *'Ulemâ* faction divided and weakened, again a result of internal divisions and rifts, for there existed reformist elements even here. Nevertheless, Egypt gained its independence; while the tax-farmers and *çiftlik* estates of the Balkans, and the quasi-hereditary *wakfs* subsisted. The trappings and formal institutional appearance of the older system were done away with, but under the new laws – heavily influenced by western legal principles of private property law – many tax-farms on state lands were converted into the secure holdings of secular landlords, thus cementing the position of the provincial landholding elite and preserving the underlying contradiction between central authority and provincial vested interests.[53] The changes which affected the Ottoman state during the eighteenth and early nineteenth centuries, especially its confrontation with the imperialist and industrializing states of the West, were much more ramified and complex than I have been able to present here; I have given only the briefest of summaries. But I will return to the implications of this survey for a theory of the state in the following sections and chapter.

4. State Power and State Autonomy

I have looked at the Ottoman case in some detail because it is very instructive from the point of view of the problems sketched out in the Introduction and in chapter 2 above. The Ottoman example is the case *par excellence* where a state elite which is nominally neither hereditary nor representative, nor drawn from a pre-existing socio-economic elite, dominates or appears to dominate a political formation headed by an absolute ruler. The state must thus appear autonomous from the society in which it is rooted, but over which it appears to stand. But the appearance of this structure, perhaps because of its very strangeness to the predominantly European historical or sociological observer, belies the nature of the relationships it embodies. Wherever we look, whether at the centralized empires of central and South America, or the ancient states of China and Asia, the relationships between state elites, ruling classes and rulers are complex, dialectical and – crucial for my point – determined by the question of the control over resources. The fact that these relationships appear as political and ideological elements should not conceal this. For whether it is a question of relations of production or of distribution of surplus, it is such relationships which underlie and are given expression through the dominant forms of political-ideological organization.[54]

These relationships are rarely expressed in non-capitalist contexts through economic categories, of course. On the contrary, they are voiced through symbolic systems and ideologies in which authority and power are the terms of reference, whether earthly or divine. Most importantly, power is not an abstract, nor is it a disembodied quality of political personalities and relationships – it, too, is rooted in the differential access of individuals, groups and classes to resources (which must include also the possibility or actuality of their being excluded from such resources), and hence is inscribed within economic relations. This applies equally, of course, to forms of charismatic power exercised at an individual level, as Weber also saw, for this is itself the expression of the mobilization of emotional narratives and contexts in which the question of access to or exclusion from social resources (however this might be expressed in specific cultural formations) – in other words, control or lack of control over the process and means of reproduction of spiritual and material life – is at stake. The search for power, as Mann has noted,[55] is a search for a means to an end – the (more) effective control or mobilization of certain resources in order to facilitate the achievement of certain goals: the maintenance of political authority, for example, and thus the reproduction of a particular set of social and hence also economic relations. The ways in which these relationships are expressed, naturally, is determined by the general field of cultural tradition and context, and by the specific modes of the distribution of power.[56] This, it seems to me, is the great value of the work of both Mann and Runciman: not to demonstrate the absolute autonomy of structures of power, whether collectively or distributively located, and whether of a broadly economic, coercive or ideological character, but rather to illustrate how these expressions of the fundamental relations of production in a social formation are to be apprehended. The detailed analysis of a historical social formation, its day-to-day functioning and its developmental trajectory, will not necessarily entail the reiteration of the embedded economic nature of relationships of power and authority, hierarchy and status, either in the vocabulary of the modern analyst or in that of the cultures under examination. But this does not mean that it is not the economic structure which provides the framework of action which these specific and culturally-determined practices express and realize.

This is not to say either that the argument from economic relationships takes place at such a level of abstraction or generality that it is of no analytic or heuristic value. I do not wish to collapse all of society into a vacuous category of 'the economic', and then argue on an a prioristic basis that it is therefore 'ultimate'. I do want to argue that analysis must proceed from the premise that social praxis is limited and constrained by economic relationships – relations of production – in the first place, and thus provide a direction for the search to locate the key points at which other expressions of social relations – power, for example – are located and coalesce. In the examples of states dominated by tributary/feudal relations of production presented here, this means looking in particular at the relationships and politics embodied in the methods and institutions of surplus appropriation and distribution, for it is here that the major site of class conflict – between producers and exploiters, as well as within the exploiting class – is to be found.

Nor is this to argue that the economic nature of social power as a product of relations of production need ever be made explicit by a culture; it is to argue that it is such relationships, and the contradictions, limitations and possibilities which they embody, that provide the dynamic and underlying social and cultural potentialities of a social formation, and the individuals who constitute it through praxis.[57]

But I suggest that this does not bring us back to a simple base and superstructure metaphor. First, we know that societies and the way they evolve are looked at in different ways according to what we want to understand about them – analysis is always functional and directed.[58] Second, we have seen that many social practices and institutions can function as relations of production – it depends what we want to know about a given institution, role or set of practices as to whether we wish or need to relate them to the ultimately economic context within which they are effective. What we need, therefore, is an organic rather than a spatial model of society: all the elements, superficial or not, are vital to the particular appearance and evolution of a society in a specific form. None of the elements stands on its own, but there is, nevertheless, a sense in which certain practices establish a pattern for the ways in which all the other forms actually operate. The economic relationships thus constitute a skeleton which determines both the limits and the basic configuration of a social formation. Just as the different primates have different skeletons, differently articulated but with bodies constructed from the same basic set of corresponding organs and tissues, so different social and economic formations represent different modes of production or combinations of modes of production, their differently articulated relations of production determining the general possibilities and limits of the social practices from which they are constituted. Like the skeleton, therefore, relations of production do not cause a social formation; but they do have a determining influence on its physical forms, its capacities to deal with external influences, and its limitations in respect of production, consumption and expenditure of energy. Unlike a skeleton, of course, social relations are dynamic and constantly in a state of flux, open to change and transformation – contradictions and incompatibilities evolve as they are overdetermined by both ideological factors and 'interests'. So I do not wish to press this analogy too far (although the human skeleton is also subject to change and process, too). It is intended merely to illustrate the difference in the way we are able to conceptualize the totality of social relations of production and relate their different elements dialectically, without using the base–superstructure metaphor, which is so liable to distortion or misunderstanding. Such an analogy makes it possible at least to see the determining nature of economic relationships, without at the same time suggesting that they are either causally prior or that they are not themselves determined in their mode of expression by other factors.

These considerations are important when we come to consider the question of relative or absolute autonomy of states and state elites. For it must first of all be clear that absolute autonomy is structurally an impossibility – the personnel and leaders of a state apparatus are always keyed in at some level or another to the social relations of production of their society, and hence into the pattern of cultural identities, no matter how distanced they may be from the actual work of production itself. The Ottoman example discussed above provides ample demonstration of this. Tied as it was, at least initially, to the absolute will of the Sultan, the *devşirme* elite was as bound to the conditions of reproduction of surplus extraction as the economically disabled and politically marginalized Turkish nobility, precisely because they were both the product of that system as it had evolved (by conquest) and because the interests of the *devşirme* elite in respect of the distribution of surplus wealth were, at first, antagonistic to those of the older elite.

But that state institutions and their 'organic' personnel can act autonomously from a non- or only partially-incorporated ruling class in the provinces (however the land and possessions of the latter are held from the point of view of juridical authority) should not surprise, and certainly does not run counter to a historical materialist position. Such autonomy is generally relatively short-lived, however, and does not represent an autonomy which seriously challenges the relations of production which make it possible, although it can certainly – as we have seen – introduce changes into the form and structures through which those relations of production are expressed. For both groups are dependent upon the same system of surplus appropriation and distribution. Indeed, it is difficult to see how any state leadership or elite can act for long in a way which fundamentally conflicts with the long-term interests of the majority of the dominant economic class in society, even when the political power of that class is heavily compromised by the configuration of power-relationships determined by the evolution of the polity. But this question does, inevitably, raise the problem of the qualitative difference between the power of the modern state and that of pre-industrial states. Telecommunications, surveillance and data-processing systems, rapid transportation, massively increased physical and particularly psychological coercive potential, together with the saturation of all social-cultural strata by advertising and 'information' systems, all these in the context of political and legal norms which actually permit (as in the UK today) a more or less complete autonomy of action to governments for limited periods, must necessarily qualify the interpretation offered here. But (although a separate discussion is really required) I would argue strongly that even here we can still only speak of a relative (even if extensive and long-lasting) autonomy of states or certain discrete state institutions (for example, security services, defence and so on). The relationships between governments and power elites, state fiscal and banking interests and those of international and local investment capital, to name but two elements, substantially modify and limit state autonomy. And I would also argue that, to suggest that the modern technocratic state system is fully autonomous is massively to misconstrue the role and constitution of ideology and the nature of the subsumption of political programmes within contemporary industrial society to the needs of international capital.

Even in cases where new state elites have attempted to introduce or impose radically new techniques of production and distribution of wealth, the role of the army and of coercion, and of factional and class or tribal alliances remain crucial to their success. The reforms and industrialization programmes inaugurated under Bismarck present a classic instance in which a 'small' and 'progressive' state elite was able to introduce a range of structural innovations through a process of authoritarian command politics legitimated in traditional nationalist ideology, class alliances and political bargaining. The social-economic group which ultimately gained most from this was the German bourgeoisie, but the ideology of cultural-ethnic unification together with a politics of imperialist competition and expansion, which necessarily involved the military and its officer corps, drawn from the declining feudal elite, provided also a function for ideologically still quite powerful elements which had only a limited economic interest in the transformations which the Iron Chancellor promoted.[59]

Many similar examples can be found from the history of the development of a system of capitalist world markets, and especially in the development of new national and nationalist elites in non-capitalist countries. It has generally been the state which, in emergent industrial and 'developing' countries, in the context of the international expansion of capitalist exchange and production relations, has acted to re-structure patterns of agricultural and industrial production. This has in almost all cases been in conjunction with key elements of a formative bourgeoisie, the army, and 'commercial profit' propaganda, and has led to substantial shifts in relations of production – chiefly from what can be seen as compromised tributary relationships (despite the presence of modern and bureaucratic administrative institutions in most cases staffed by elites educated in the industrial First World, or in institutions established by or modelled on such 'parent' structures) to capitalist relations of production, in respect both of the creation of an urban industrial workforce and of the imposition of a series of monocultural agrarian cash-crop regimes designed to meet the demands of debt-servicing, and the cost of industrialization and mechanization (usually legitimated within an ideology of 'progress'). The creation of a large, landless sub-peasantry is one consequence, the resultant urban overcrowding and deprivation another. And inflexibility in agricultural production combined with overuse of fertilizers designed to maximize short-term returns has in a number of cases resulted in a catastrophic collapse in subsistence levels and the ability of the land to sustain the levels of output required. But in examples such as these, where states and elites share a common interest in the political programme of 'transformation', it is important to examine very carefully the constitution and structure of the state apparatus itself, especially in respect of the vested interests embodied in its policies, and its situation in an internationalized market and banking context. Again, it will be seen that fundamentally economic relationships and pressures are in operation, even where represented through specifically local forms, ideological institutions and practices. To argue, however, that this is to admit the centrality of purely external causal stimuli is to ignore the point that capitalist relations, as far as they are entirely international in their effects, are as much an internal as they are an external element in the composition and structure of all economies.[60]

Conflicts between the state leadership and the dominant class, or a faction of the dominant class, generally means that the state acts in ways which favour other classes, or other factions of the dominant class, a point made by Miliband in reference to modern state formations.[61] In the example of the development of the Ottoman state, it was in the first instance the *devşirme* who profited from the struggle between the Ottoman ruler and the old Turkish nobility which had given him his empire; and indirectly, the *re'âyâ* subjects of the empire benefited, albeit for less than a century, from the anti-aristocratic policies of the Sultans and their slave administration and army; but this was essentially a structure developed to safeguard the state's control of resources, and in no way suggests that the state was somehow independent of society or the economic relations and vested interests on which its power rested.

It is the conflict over the distribution of resources which tends to promote disintegration or decentralization should the state elite lose, but which in contrast promotes a strengthening of central authority and a corresponding weakening of oppositional groups if it wins. But it needs to be emphasized that the political autonomy which is a consequence of the latter is itself clearly to be understood in the context of those particular relations of production and distribution.

5. The Byzantine State after the Tenth Century: a Crisis of Surplus Distribution

Both the Ottoman empire and its territorial predecessor, the East Roman or Byzantine state, demonstrate these points. In the Byzantine case, as we have seen in chapter 3, radical changes occurred during the seventh century in respect of the possibilities of maintaining the traditional forms of surplus distribution, whether through state taxes or private rent-taking, weakening the broad 'ruling class', the senatorial aristocracy. The changes which took place made it both necessary and possible for the state to intervene and centralize the administration of both fiscal and military affairs, and to control appointments to key positions; on the other hand, the Church mobilized its resources to redirect popular attitudes and to legitimate the shift in the relations of distribution which were occurring. The demise of the classical and late ancient municipalities, the failure of the established pattern of organization to defend the interests of the state against Islam in the 630s and after, all led to a strengthening of the autocratic power of the emperors and their political freedom of action, as I have suggested in chapter 3.

The emperors found themselves in a position where they could dictate and direct military and civil affairs regardless of all other groups in the empire (with the exception of the Church, and to a certain extent of the individual armies of the militarized provinces, or *themata*), through the medium of a class of administrators and imperial officials who were completely dependent upon the emperors for their positions and their future careers. Policies were determined by ideological constraints, together with the basic institutional demands of state survival, of maintaining an existence through what was by any standards a catastrophic situation in economic and military terms (the empire lost some two-thirds of its territory and perhaps three-quarters of its revenue to the Arabs in a period of some twelve to fifteen years from 634 to about 650). But the independent position of the imperial establishment was itself made possible by these political events and by shifts in the relations of surplus distribution within the empire brought about by a combination of very long-term social and economic developments stretching back to the third century (especially the decline of the autonomous municipalities), with the short-term crises brought on first by the Persian war (particularly from 603–26) and then the conquests of Islam. The possibilities for this autonomy of state or state elite are thus already inscribed within the social relations of production of the later Roman empire, but it was only realized when the state was able to intervene to adjust the structure of the relations of surplus distribution in its own favour. Equally, such conditions were not permanent. By the later eighth century, there is plenty of evidence to suggest that the members of the state bureaucracy and army, who had in the seventh century replaced the establishment dominated by the senatorial elite, were themselves coalescing into a new dominant class which offered a potential, and later a very real, challenge to state control over the appropriation and distribution of resources.[62]

Thus the new service elite which the state brought into being in this changed context (initially as a more efficient means of controlling the machinery of surplus extraction) rapidly developed into a service aristocracy and then a hereditary provincial and metropolitan nobility, able to alienate and divert resources from the state to its own interests. In the seventh and much of the eighth centuries – like the Ottoman state in the later fifteenth and first half of the sixteenth centuries – the Byzantine state could and did act relatively autonomously of the direct, short-term interests of a large section of the dominant social and economic class. But it did not act in a direction which actually impaired its power in respect of the prevailing relations of production. And in administering its resources through an intermediate group of officials who eventually developed into an independent and essentially antagonistic aristocracy of provincial and metropolitan landowning families, it demonstrated the fundamental problem facing pre-industrial states already referred to: the unavoidable need to invest an intermediate administrative group with the potential to alienate the state's revenue to its own advantage.

In the Byzantine case in particular, the problem facing the state becomes clear from the tenth century. From this time, the antagonism between the two sets of interests and the contradiction within the state which it represented became apparent; the imperial government had to take legislative action to protect the interests of small-scale peasant holdings when, in the 920s and 930s, a series of droughts and poor harvests reduced many communities to penury and forced them into the hands of large landowners, whose reserves of seed and of provisions and livestock could see them through such natural crises. As a result, the differences between the economic interests of the state on the one side and the magnates on the other (referred to already in contemporary documents as 'the powerful') were clearly set out. At the same time, these differences were papered over by a combination of ideological and social-economic factors: loyalty to the notion of empire and God-appointed emperor; an imperialist expansionism which seems to have gripped the military faction of the magnate class, directing their resources outwards rather than inwards; a bond of loyalty based on ties of clientage which developed between the military commanders and their families, which had provided the leaders of the armies over several generations, and their soldiers (made up of both provincial conscripts and professional and mercenary troops); and, from 963 to 976, the fact that two of the empire's greatest tenth-century generals successfully usurped the throne, ruling jointly with the minor Basil II.

In spite of their great wealth, the military magnates of Anatolia (who were primarily responsible for the reconquests in Syria and Iraq) still very much represented localized clan and family traditions and loyalties, competing amongst themselves for honour and prestige within the institutional framework of the state's military and bureaucratic apparatus. It was, therefore, not too difficult for a firm, authoritarian soldier-emperor such as Basil II (976–1025) with the help of a loyal guard of foreign mercenaries (the Russian Varangians) – who constituted an independent power-base for the ruler – to impose drastic sanctions on individual members of this class-in-itself and to introduce draconian anti-aristocratic legislation to protect the economic status of the peasantry, upon whom the state was absolutely dependent for surplus and soldiers. At the same time, Basil promoted a strategy which transferred imperial expansion away from the eastern front to the Balkan theatre, where by 1018 his forces had destroyed the powerful Bulgarian empire and re-occupied the Balkans up to the Danube (regions which had been out of Byzantine control, although always claimed by them as part of the empire, since the early seventh century). This rich new province, which the emperor kept firmly under state control by appointing non-aristocratic governors and commanders dependent on imperial patronage, provided him with the economic resources through which he could balance the vested interests and the power of the Anatolian nobility. It also meant that even after his death a series of much less capable emperors were able to lessen the reliance of the state on the military aristocracy by using this new source of wealth, gained through conquest, to pay for more foreign mercenaries and to promote further aggressive military undertakings in southern Italy and Sicily.

For while the conquests in Syria and Iraq had traditionally favoured the Anatolian magnates by bringing both greater security to their own estates and lands, as well as wealth, booty and lands in the reconquered territories, warfare in the Balkans had never promoted their interests. Few great magnate families came from this region, even after the subjugation of the Bulgarian empire and the death of Tsar Samuel in 1018–19. Economically, the new Bulgarian provinces were a rich source of agricultural produce, and served as a valuable counter-weight to the power of the magnates of Asia minor. And it was the existence of this new source of revenues which gave the metropolitan and predominantly (although never exclusively) 'western' state elite, in opposition to the mostly eastern and military elite of the provinces, the upper hand during the first half of the eleventh century.[63]

But the deliberate running down of the frontier armies (military service was commuted in some areas for a cash payment) by a 'civil' bureaucratic faction in the capital, a policy which directly affected both the power of the magnates (which it was intended to do) and the empire's ability to maintain a coherent defence against sudden attacks, polarized the factions in the state elite after Basil II's death and led ultimately to the seizure of the state by a representative of one of the aristocratic clans, the Comneni (initially between 1057 and 1059, later from 1081 to the end of the twelfth century). And it was from the mid eleventh century at first, increasing rapidly through the twelfth century, that the rulers turned to grants of state revenue, in effect lands, in *pronoia* (literally 'in care') in order to raise and maintain soldiers. For although many of these grants were small, the clear alienation of resources from direct state authority had begun, and the process of de-centralization – structurally an unavoidable aspect of all pre-industrial state administration – re-asserted itself.[64]

As we have seen in chapter 3, *pronoia* allocations varied in size, most being limited to single soldiers, some being allocated to higher-ranking persons for the support of a larger force. Notionally non-heritable, and revocable at the emperor's will, many tended eventually to pass from father to son. But the important point was that the state could no longer exact resources effectively through its civil bureaucracy, nor could it rely upon the old peasant militia or 'thematic' troops (*thema* being the technical word for both a provincial army and the region from which it was drawn) due to the decline in the position of the provincial rural populace under the pressure of big landlords and state tax-collectors. It was thus forced to rely upon the consumption of its resources by its soldiers and administrators directly, and for the administration of its affairs in respect of surplus appropriation upon the latter and the class of magnates – whether the civil or the military faction (although the two are not always so readily distinguished). In this context in particular, ideological factors provide a key element in the continued unity (and indeed existence) of the reduced Byzantine empire. This is clear after the restoration of imperial power at Constantinople in 1261, following the collapse of the Latin empire established after the Fourth Crusade in 1203–4. A common language, literary and political culture, and above all Orthodoxy and the concept of the divinely-protected sole empire retained their power and authority long after the final demise of the Byzantine state with the fall of Constantinople to the Ottomans in 1453.

The Byzantine state thus provides a further example of the problematic nature of the idea of 'state autonomy'. A formally bureaucratic empire state with a complex civil and military apparatus, an advanced legal and judicial system; it was a state which was nevertheless constrained very clearly by the exigencies of both its geographical position and its historical setting, in which we can perceive very clearly the limits which the structure of the social relations of production and surplus distribution between different elements of the elite set on state power.

So far, we may perhaps generalize thus: the relative autonomy of state politics – the 'organizational imperatives' of a given state apparatus as determined by both functional and ideological demands – meant that the political ideology, individual psychologies and personal identities which had developed in each specific cultural tradition dominated the motives and institutions of the staff and leaders of the state apparatuses. But on the other hand, it meant also that the state elite had itself as a class, or a fraction of a class, a vested interest in maintaining that set of institutional practices which were necessarily and systemically in its own best interests. In tributary states, the crux of the matter turns on the nature of surplus distribution and the relations between those responsible for the collection of surplus and those responsible for its distribution and consumption, since control over the mechanisms of distribution meant also control over the resources of the state as a whole. To retain the maximum degree of control, tributary states must strive to maintain a distance between these two groups – when one group carries out both functions, the state is generally unable to maintain its economic and therefore political freedom of action. There is no doubt that the Ottoman elite understood this field of common interest very well.[65]

This does not mean that the elites to which I have referred were internally undifferentiated blocs with no contradictions and conflicting fields of political and economic practice. But in both the Ottoman and Byzantine examples, the power elite – the politically dominant fraction of the ruling class – can be distinguished in respect of its economic position in the relations of production and its political position in respect of the relations of distribution of surpluses.[66]

The problem for the state centre begins when the balance of power – specifically economic power – tips against it, so that the alienation of resources and challenges to the politics of the centre reduce its ability to direct and control the whole. Generally speaking, states have found only two options to prevent this occurring. They can (i) extract surplus in cash and ensure that it is forwarded from the provinces to the centre, from where it can then be re-distributed as the state requires. Alternatively, they can (ii) arrange for the extractors of surplus to be also the state's military and civil functionaries, consuming surplus directly; this system requires that the state be able to supervise or otherwise apply strict checks on the process of extraction and consumption of surpluses. Different versions or permutations of both these methods can be found in all tributary states, and as we have seen, represent the main options tried by both the Byzantine and the Ottoman rulers at different times. Both options are determined by the need for states to maintain control over the institutions of surplus distribution. Most significantly, however, these options represent the fact that, in pre-capitalist societies dominated by tributary production relations, the very existence of state formations means that the relations of surplus distribution are inherently always antagonistic, since the contradiction implicit in these institutional arrangements, between the state and its agents, cannot be avoided.

States may retain a degree of residual power determined largely by the strength of a particular political-ideological system, of course. The ability of the Byzantine state to maintain a degree of independence of the ruling class until relatively late in its history provides a graphic example.[67]

But it needs to be stressed that this residual power does not necessarily represent solid political power founded on a firm control of resources. Just as with the Ottoman state under its absolutist rulers, it is important to distinguish between the latent and active exercise of power, between the possibility of using power in a way which reinforces an ideology without threatening a vested interest, and the application of power, and hence control over sufficient resources, effectively to oppose and defeat such a vested interest. To a greater or lesser degree, this is dependent upon the strength of the dominant political ideology and legitimating discourses wielded by the central authority, as well as on the international economic context. In the first case, Byzantine magnates (until the middle of the eleventh century) and Ottoman state officials, members of the elite, concurred with the exercise of the ruler's absolute power because it reinforced an existing political system in which they could perceive their own interests and with which they could identify (however independent of the state or ruler they may in practice have been), and because it clearly did not threaten their economic interests, both as individual members of a social class and as representatives of particular clan or family configurations (however implicit this identity may have remained). The possibilities for Ottoman officials to advance their careers in the provinces as well as in the capital, for example, combined with the entrenched household patronage networks discussed above, are important aspects of any explanation of their relative independence from, but continued support for, and obedience to, the central government after the seventeenth century.[68] In the second case, where a Sultan such as Mahmud II had to act with extreme caution in the context of the increasing marginalization of the Ottoman state and its being drawn into the nexus of western market relationships and commercial exploitation (with the fundamental threat that such a process involved for the establishment), in order to promote any shift at all in the internal political balance of power, the Byzantine rulers after 1081 (when Alexios I seized the throne) found that only a system of aristocratic clan alliances could maintain the political and ideological apparatus of their state. The centralized, bureaucratic state survived, on a decreasingly effective scale, until its demise at the hands of Mehmed II in 1453, as indeed did a dependent bureaucracy of non-magnates and a less dependent landed elite. It was the enormous residual strength of the imperial ideological system, which was predicated upon the survival of such a state, demanded its continuous existence, and was inextricably interwoven with the political theology of the Orthodox Church, which made any other trajectory inconceivable. Crucially, the ideological focal point was the God-appointed emperor. And long after it ceased to represent the interests of the landed elite, it continued to represent their perceptions of how things were. The contradictory nature of this ideological edifice was not understood as long as ideological attention was fixed upon this symbol, the emperor.

But this no more means that there exists an absolute autonomy of ideas and ideologies than it does that there is an absolute autonomy of the political. Although the Byzantine imperial ideology retained its hegemonic appeal, it was nevertheless consistently modified in a piecemeal manner in order to render it, or key elements therein, commensurate with its social conditions of existence; that is to say, in order that people could continue to make sense of their world within the framework of their symbolic universe and the social praxis it represented for them and reproduced. It is not without significance (and perhaps a certain irony) that both elements of the Byzantine ruling elite and the Church, as well as Mehmed II himself, came to regard the conquering Sultan as the legitimate successor of the Byzantine emperors. A similar general development in the field of ideology and the shifts which took place in the narratives of social practice can be observed in the Ottoman experience. Only when brutally confronted by the technologies and aggressive economies of the industrializing western European powers did this change, as has been described above; and only then was a forlorn effort made by the Sultans to imitate the institutions of the dominant and threatening economies of the West.

5

State Formation and the Struggle for Surplus

1. The Frankish Kingdom: a Compromised State

So far, I have looked at two states in which, at different times and for different reasons, the dominant or governing elite has been able, for a while, so to dominate the process of surplus appropriation that it could act autonomously of other interest-groups or classes in society. But the relations of production determined the form which that apparent autonomy took, the contexts in which it occurred, and the structural limitations on its evolution. Crucial to the ways in which this occurred was the struggle between the state as represented by a given elite, and other leading elements of the social formation, those who might, or did, compete with the state or the state class for control over the exploitation of resources and, in particular, the distribution of wealth. In addition, and as I emphasized in chapter 4, the existence of a state 'centre' always co-exists at the local level with what are in effect 'alternative' structures, sometimes working in parallel with the central administration, sometimes actually made possible by the existence of a central administration, with all its needs, and the ways in which these needs can be realized locally in respect of surplus extraction and in the context of those relationships which pre-dated the establishment of the state centre in question. Looked at from this point of view, it is clear that this involves also the continuing evolution of states. But the answer to the question of who controls the appropriation and distribution of resources, and how, ultimately determines whether or not states dominated by tributary production relations are able to survive as functioning bureaucratic-administrative structures, or whether they begin to fragment and lose control over their territory and sources of revenue. In this chapter, I will look briefly at further examples of this particular problematic.

Large states clearly suffer from the potential economic and cultural superficiality of state control and authority, which depends as much upon efficient administration as it does upon logistical problems, distance, geo-political and climatic factors, and so on. Particularist and anti-pluralist religious or political ideologies, shared cultural and linguistic identities, regional and trans-regional economic substructures independent of, but permitted by, the existence of the state, such features may all serve to hold them together as states even when political and military fragmentation reduces central power – this was the case with Byzantium from the eleventh and twelfth centuries. Such features affect smaller units equally, however, as the example of the Frankish kingdom in Gaul and the western Germanic regions in the early medieval period demonstrate.

The backdrop to Merovingian Gaul is provided, of course, by the late Roman context and the piecemeal establishment during the fifth and sixth centuries of the Germanic successor kingdoms. In Gaul and the regions west of the Rhine in the last twenty years or so of the fifth century the Salian Franks, an expansionist tribal confederacy, succeeded in establishing a unitary kingdom under their leader Clovis (481–511), primarily through military means, but with the sanction of at least a substantial part of the pre-existing Gallo-Roman elite and the Church (which had favoured Clovis even before his conversion), a kingdom which formed the basis for both the later Carolingian empire and the medieval kingdoms of France and Germany. Divided though this kingdom often was during the sixth century, a state replaced the territorial tribal chieftaincies of the Salian Franks during this period, a state which adapted to the requirements of its Frankish political elite important aspects of late Roman administrative structures. Like the Ottoman state, the Merovingian kingdom was formed through conquest; but unlike the Ottoman state, its leaders had no mechanism at their disposal, and only a distant pre-existing tradition, of centralized government. For the late Roman administration had itself become highly devolved, so that local magnates and bishops played as central a role as did imperially-appointed military and fiscal officers in respect of the raising (and the consumption) of state revenues. Partly this reflected the developing conflict of interests and outlook between the residual imperial government and the senatorial and ecclesiastical landed elite of the western provinces. But the successor kingdoms adopted this dispersed pattern as the administrative norm, even if they themselves held a notional monopoly of executive power.

Merovingian kings were thus always kings of the Franks, rather than of a country or state – although the concept Francia soon came to signify the territories under their sway. The kings' authority was founded upon personal ties of loyalty to them and to their family or kin-group, and upon wider-ranging kinship relations. Insofar as these were perceived as the only justification for mutual support in both war and peace, the kingdom was in effect wherever the king and his retinue were. Warbands and retinues were thus of crucial importance in the formation of the kingdom and the establishment of the 'state'. The warband of the kings themselves constituted a key component in the nascent royal nobility.[1] It was these latter whom the kings appointed to the administrative-military positions throughout the early kingdom, giving them land in return for their service. At the same time, however, both posts and the properties attached to the duties of such posts tended often to be dispersed, so that the higher-ranking members of the leading groups often held lands and exercised functions simultaneously in different parts of the kingdom at once.[2] The officials, who belonged also to the king's retinue, had their various centres of authority and power dispersed across the whole kingdom, and might be drawn from a variety of ethnic backgrounds, not necessarily Franks, and certainly including Romans. Their positions were remunerated by grants of land, which in some cases may have been temporary, but which in most cases were probably for life or longer. By virtue of placing members of his family and retinue as officials throughout his lands, the king was able to draw upon a wide network of loyalty, and enforce his authority wherever he found himself. In theory, this system, which was based ultimately on purely personal ties, both enabled the kings to remove power from traditional tribal or clan leaders and provided the ideological justification for punishing those who challenged their authority. In practice, however, as we will see in a moment, the mixed Frankish–Germanic and Gallo-Roman elites of the different regions which made up the Frankish kingdom seem often to have possessed both an independent ideological identity as 'nobles' or leading families, often accompanied by allodial (private) landed property, and from the earliest stages of the establishment of the Merovingian kingdom, so that royal power was less solidly based than might at first seem to be the case.

The early Merovingian kingdom seems to have been essentially a kingdom of ranked or hierarchical retinues or warbands grouped about a particular local leader, the king, at least in the most heavily

Germanized regions of the North and East. A great deal of archaeological research has taken place on the settlement sites and especially the cemeteries of the period c.480–750 AD, and the results of this work, when tied in with the extant narrative and other literary sources, suggest a gradual evolution over the sixth and into the seventh century, of a state and society in which the king's retinue slowly evolved into a relatively small group of great families and their kin who had been able to accumulate property over a wide area.[3] Dependent to a degree upon them for their lands and their livelihood were a substantial number of lesser warriors, upon whom in turn depended large sections of the rural population, although it must be remembered that many peasants remained still independent of such ties. A relatively open, ranked society, in which Germanic warrior-farmers held land, alongside members of the royal retinue, both those with royal offices and others (with the Gallo-Roman rural population in part subordinated to the former), thus characterized the earlier and middle sixth century. Aspects of this social structure can be detected in the arrangement and grave-goods of the so-called Reihengräber (row-grave) cemeteries of north-eastern France. These show more often than not a number of graves of varying degrees of wealth grouped around the more luxuriously-appointed tombs and graves of what can be taken to be a local notable family.[4] As this 'ranked' society, which seems to have been very mobile, evolved more stable patterns of local power and wealth transmission, so the nature of the cemeteries changes: tombs and graves begin to be centred in or near churches, which came to represent the permanent settlement of landlords on or near their estates. And these changes in turn have been connected with the emergent stabilized and stratified social structure of the later seventh and eighth centuries – neatly summed up by Steuer as the change from an open, ranked society, in which kinship and personal ties were paramount, to one of more clearly-defined social and economic classes, into which individuals were born, and which in turn determined the significance and structure of personal loyalties.[5] The systematic robbing of cemeteries (with the exception, generally, of the wealthiest or most important graves and tombs) at the close of the Merovingian period (first half of the eighth century) has been interpreted as a reflection of the clear dominance of powerful lords and the increasing subordination of the various social strata of dependants, for it seems to be evidence of a marked disregard for traditional burial practices and respect for ancestors.[6]

While these observations apply to the Frankish and Germanic populations, especially in the North and East, it must be remembered at the same time that the cultural division between the Romanized southern regions of Gaul and the North was enough to permit the survival of a wide range of Gallo-Roman traditions, as we shall see in a moment. It would be incorrect to paint too uniform a picture. While the conditions described above were generalized from the early sixth century, it should not be forgotten that the weight of tradition, in respect both of social as well as of political organization, gave the South of Gaul a somewhat different character from that of the original area of Frankish conquest and domination.

Administration in the Merovingian lands was based on the old cities, headed locally now by a royally-appointed count, who was responsible for both civil and military administration. There is some slight evidence to suggest that elements of the late Roman military administration of the Gallic provinces continued to function at some levels under Merovingian royal authority, until perhaps the later sixth century – leaders referred to as *tribuni* with their *milites* or soldiers occur in sources such as the Book of Histories of the later sixth-century writer Gregory, bishop of Tours. It has been argued that some late Roman units, highly localized and well integrated into the urban and rural social contexts from which they were recruited, continued to exist and to provide a military force independent of the warrior retinues of the Merovingian and Gallo-Roman elites.

The kings appointed their counts, but counts were in many cases checked more by the presence of a local bishop or a regional duke than by any centralized supervisory procedures. Bishops often provided the crucial link between the older, indigenous population and the newcomers – Franks, Burgundians or Goths. They were a source of justice as well as of charity, and their spiritual and economic power made of them formidable potential opponents of secular administrators. By the same token, it was the adoption of Christianity in its Chalcedonian, or Catholic, form, which gave the first Merovingian kings the support of the bishops and made the stabilization of their kingdom possible.

Dukes were likewise royal appointments, at least at first, before such titles became *de facto* hereditary during the later sixth century and after and, because they were associated directly with the royal retinue, they had probably a great deal more power than the counts. The latter were more numerous, but had authority usually over relatively small districts and numbers of soldiers, and were often selected from local men.[7]

Power in the Frankish kingdom was never intensive, except on a highly localized basis – the selective application of armed force. The kings were able to enjoy their privileged position chiefly because they retained an ideological and symbolic relevance as the traditional dynastic lineage of warrior-kings of the Franks. But there is no evidence to support the idea that all land in the kingdom was royal land, to be disposed of by the kings as they thought fit. We have already encountered this concept, common to many cultures, in the case of the Ottoman state. In practice, anyway, land could only be administered and exploited through intermediaries and local delegates of royal authority. And not only was political authority highly decentralized within the kingdom, the latter was itself sub-divided on several occasions in order to provide separate but equitable inheritances for the sons of kings.[8] A clear tension existed between the notion of the state – essentially part of Roman thinking and its cultural traditions – and the idea of lordship and personal ties of loyalty – a combination of both Germanic tradition and late Roman social practices.

The rapid cycle of fragmentation and re-unification which marks the later seventh and early eighth centuries promoted an increase in the independence of local counts, and especially of royal dukes and provincial magnates of similar standing, men who were able through royal immunities and other means to consolidate that independence at the expense of both royal authority and royal revenue. Indeed, although grants of land both for service and as a means of rewarding loyalty in general were originally given only for a lifetime, there is every reason to think that very many of them became hereditary in practice quite rapidly, giving the nascent magnate class a power-base in land and retinues that made them potentially independent of the kings.[9]

The exact nature of the 'aristocracy' at this early period, and into the Carolingian era, however, remains unclear. Steuer, for example, has argued that the original tribal notables and the retinue of the kings themselves constituted the chief element, and has interpreted differences in wealth in the Reihengräber cemeteries as differences of family wealth within a rank- or lineage-group of warrior/peasant families and clans, rather than as differences between aristocrats and non-aristocrats.[10] This would appear to fit quite well with what we can surmise, from an anthropological point of view, early post-conquest Frankish (and Germanic) society in general may have looked like. By the middle and later sixth century, however, it is apparent that clear social divisions in terms of wealth, power and access to land had evolved, so that the late sixth-century narrator Gregory of Tours can give fairly detailed accounts of the considerable wealth of many of these magnates. From the 540s, Gregory refers to the different magnates in their political role as an identifiable interest group. But in spite of this process of stratification and social differentiation, it is important to bear in mind that agnatically-orientated patrilineal family descent-groups do not appear in the sources until the tenth and eleventh centuries, certainly in the Germanic territories. Until this time (and as prosopographical analyses have suggested) it was wider circles of cognate and collateral lineage and kinship bonds which mark noble and aristocratic interests and self-identity. The archaeological evidence as interpreted most recently by Steuer, referred to already, would appear to re-inforce this impression. This is not to say that individual family descent-lines were unimportant, simply that they become dominant only after the tenth century. The Germanic societies which imposed their rule on Gaul can thus be seen from this anthropological standpoint as representing the final stages of a dissolving segmentary lineage formation, in which exploitation and appropriation of wealth secured by means of lineage rights and traditions came to be replaced by, first, the establishment of retinues around war-leaders and kings, which tended to break down purely kin-based loyalties, a process accompanied by, secondly, the internal polarization and gradual fragmentation of the lineages themselves. The Frankish kingdom thus represents, in effect, a single political authority imposed upon competing modes of production, in which elements of both tributary and lineage modes of surplus appropriation and distribution met, but in which the greater economic potential of the tributary mode to extract resources and apply coercion proved to be the more powerful of the two.

This process is paralleled, of course, in many historical examples – the early stages of the establishment of the Ottoman empire, for example, or of the Mongol empire under Chingis, to name but two. Interestingly, this fragmentation of lineage structures did not occur in India, at least not in the medieval period, for reasons which I will discuss in the next section.[11]

But the Frankish/Gallo-Roman elite – leading men of the king's retinue, 'nobles' in the loosest sense of the term – was of very mixed origins. South of the Loire the majority of the royal counts seem to have been of Gallo-Roman extraction. And although personal ties of loyalty to the king existed too, it was more by virtue of their own social origins as members of families which had belonged to the senatorial elite of the later empire that they achieved such positions. Equally, men of very humble origins could rise through royal service to positions of considerable power. Such was the count of Tours, Leudast, for example, whose father had been a slave.

The kings depended on their counts for the maintenance of their authority; and they depended at the same time on the dukes and magnates of the land – all those in positions of wealth and power – for the effectiveness of that authority. To retain their loyalty, or at least to obtain their acquiescence, lands and other forms of wealth had to be regularly distributed. Yet it was this aspect of royal largesse which transformed these members of the original royal retinue into a socially distinct class of magnates and lords. At the same time, the counts were in a position to usurp property rights in their districts of authority and to establish their own economic bases, independent of the king's will.[12] The leading offices of state remained non-hereditary, in theory, and the support, at least nominal, of either the king or the mayor of the palace was essential during the sixth century to the security of most members of this emerging magnate class. But it was through this very insecurity and the ideological perception of their needs in this regard that the beginnings of diffuse, spontaneous and local personal ties of vassalage began to develop between powerful men and their dependants and clients, given also the conditions of endemic physical insecurity of the times.

James has outlined two main periods in the development in the relationships between kings and magnates during the Merovingian era: that stretching from the time of Clovis to the 650s (the reigns of the sons of Dagobert I); and that of the slow emergence of the Arnulfings, as mayors of the palace, as the leading magnate family, and of their unification of the kingdom under their own rule. In fact, effective royal power may already have been weakened by the events of the years from 610 to 620, when the mayors of the palace emerge for the first time clearly as key figures and representatives of the magnates and lords as a distinct group with particular interests and political aims (even if they were far from unified in these respects). Between that time and the later years of the seventh century is a period of competing power-groups centred on the different mayoral factions, factional struggles which resulted in the emergence of the

Arnulfing mayors of the palace of Austrasia as dominant (the period culminating with the establishment of one of their number, Pippin, the father of Charles the Great, as first 'Carolingian' king in the year 751).[13] During the first period, it is possible to observe through the sources the growth of an established class of lords and magnates, however dimly. By the year 600 they were able to act on a regional basis and in regional groupings or factions to intervene directly in dynastic politics, using as their spokesman in Burgundy a leading noble who became mayor of the palace in that sub-kingdom. In Austrasia at the same time they were represented by, among others, two of the wealthiest and most powerful magnates of the area, Pippin, later to become mayor of the palace, and bishop Arnulf of Metz (the family alliance achieved by the marriage of Pippin's daughter to Arnulf's son producing, of course, the family eventually known as the Carolingians). Increasingly from this time it was the mayors of the palace, leading members of the magnate class, who controlled royal politics. The kings remain as both rulers and figureheads, representatives of a royal dynasty which bound the kingdom of the Franks together nominally through a mixture of ideological tradition and political expediency.

The importance of the mayors of the palace, and the increasing prominence in royal politics of the magnates from this time, reflects not only the long-term evolution of this class over the course of the sixth century, but also the political conjuncture of the early seventh century, when, in 613, Chlothar II defeated Brunhilda, the mother of Childebert II and one of the most powerful figures in Frankish royal affairs of the time (and a key instigator in the devastating civil wars which her struggle to survive and to defeat her enemies entailed). As the price for their support, the magnates extracted increased privileges from Chlothar, together with a considerable strengthening of the authority and power of the mayors of the palace.

From the 620s, therefore, the mayors of the palace in Austrasia (eastern France[14]), Neustria (western France) and Burgundy seem no longer to have been merely palace officials in charge of royal courts; they effectively governed the kingdoms as well, with the support of the magnates, of course.[15] From this point until the reconquest of the various independent regions of Gaul under Charles Martel and Pippin (between the 730s and 750s) Frankish history is partly the history of the gradual rise to dominance of the Arnulfings over other mayoral houses (Neustria and Burgundy), as well as of the increasing importance of the provincial magnates, powerful landed nobles with near independent political status. Charles Martel, who campaigned widely and regularly throughout Francia in an effort to bring the provincial nobles under his authority (or that of his nominal king), rewarded his followers with confiscated lands and established himself as undisputed master of Austrasia and Neustria. But the magnate families even in these regions retained their landed power bases and remained potentially a threat to any centralizing agency. In peripheral regions this was even more so, and only by regular campaigning – just as in the time of the Merovingian kings of the first half of the sixth century – could authority be imposed and maintained. Indeed, it is important to remember that by the later seventh century there is evidence in the sources for a trans-regional cultural and political consciousness among the leading magnates (which includes also the leading bishops and Churchmen of the kingdom), so that interests (and political alliances) were shared, or disputed, at the highest level across the whole kingdom. And from an ideological point of view, it is clear that residual notions of the old Roman state, together with the continued existence of a system of local and royal justice, on the one hand, and the ideological strength of Merovingian royal tradition, on the other, served still to focus attention quite clearly on the court. Frequently, regional magnates, both ecclesiastical and secular, appealed to the kings and their advisers to resolve conflicts – a fact which, as has been suggested, hardly supports the view that Merovingian rulers were entirely powerless at this time.[16]

In contrast to the kings, therefore, whose counts were responsible for the traditional levies which co-existed with any older late Roman military units which had survived, and which eventually replaced them, the mayors of the palace and their vassals had much greater, locally-rooted, intensive power, although based on a personal, patrimonial rule. By the later seventh century the levies had become little more than an untrained peasant host of little or no real military value, in contrast to the better-equipped soldiers and horsemen of the powerful lords.

The power of the Merovingian kings was finally eroded away altogether; this occurred in part through the fact that a tension developed between the loyalty owed by the leading freemen and magnates to the king as representative of the Merovingian dynasty and the bonds of vassalage and dependence between the mayors of the palace – the *de facto* rulers of the kingdom – and their supporters. It should be stressed that such bonds were related as much to economic factors – access to and control over resources – as they were to notions of honour and respect. Conflicts of interest between counts and local landlords and notables also contributed. The net result was that the mayors of the palace of Austrasia, as we have seen, were able to extend their power and authority both by a process of regular campaigning and conquest, and by building up a greater number of vassals supported by grants of land, or benefices, from which soldiers and retainers could be maintained.[17]

The Merovingian kingdom of the sixth century had been what some analysts have dubbed a proto-state: that is to say, the exercise of royal authority was based on traditional lineage and warfare loyalties with no real possibility of royal control being enforced through the counts once they no longer had at their disposal an effective fighting force or royal support. In fact, this picture is complicated by the somewhat different nature of the relationship between the Gallo-Roman notables of the South and the kings, where lineage and kinship played a less prominent role. Nevertheless, as long as the kings were active and popular campaigners, and their war-hosts took to the field every year, they could enforce compliance by the threat or application of direct coercion, and this seems generally to have been sufficient to maintain a degree of order and obedience, enough at least to maintain internal order and the continued appropriation of revenues. As long as the kings could maintain peace and some form of order to the extent that the interests of the magnates upon whom they depended were assured, then they received the support of those magnates. But once this military activity declined, both the threat of coercion and the ability of the kings to maintain order receded, and so royal authority receded also. And it must be seen that royal coercion began to fail as magnates and wealthy lords found the wherewithal to oppose the kings, even if passively, simply by not turning up or not sending soldiers or warriors, or enough of them, when the kings demanded. It would be incorrect to see the rise of the lords and magnate class in general as a result of royal weakness – on the contrary, the two developments were inextricably connected.

In anthropological terms, therefore, the Merovingian kingdom can be conceived of very much as an elaborate 'big man' chieftaincy, dependent upon the royal household, certain lineage solidarities and the kings' role as war-leaders for its cohesiveness. Their state was in practice the result of the imposition of a compromised tribal kingship upon a rural peasantry and its landlords. A dissolving lineage mode of production had been in effect imposed upon a pre-existing set of tributary production relations, a process which hastened the transformation of the former into the latter.

From the institutional point of view, some Roman structures survived, of course, as we have seen, and particularly in the realm of royal justice and taxation the Merovingian kings maintained a degree of administrative continuity for a long time. But as has been shown, even though the very notion of statehood in its Roman form meant for the Germanic successor states the ability to raise tax on the basis of non-personal, institutionalized relationships, royal taxation was regarded as both heavy and as an unjustifiable additional burden. Its continued existence served to emphasize the supreme authority of the kings, of course, and to recall the shadowy past of a Roman state authority which they had inherited. But bishops and laymen fought, often successfully, for exemption; and tax rapidly became only one, minor, element of the royal resources, to be granted away in immunities to royal favourites or to those whose support the king needed. It continued to be raised until the end of the seventh century in a number of localized forms, but this reflected as much the institutional stasis of tradition as embodied in the activities of local counts, as it did central control.[18]

The replacement of the Merovingian dynasty by the Carolingians in 751 was a problem only in respect of traditional attachments to an old dynasty. In real terms, the mayors of the palace, now kings (with papal support, a key ideological pre-requisite), had exploited a radically different and much more effective network of power relations, and it was this establishment of successive layers of dependence which cut the ground from under the old royal household and its provincial representatives.

Of course, Carolingian and later French and German rule remained patrimonial, in Weber's sense, and highly dependent upon the ruler's personality for its efficacy. The structures of subordination and vassalage which developed in the Merovingian period constituted the basic framework of power relations, within the terms of which both 'private' and 'state' political power and authority were constrained. Indeed, the Carolingian kingdom hardly fared better in the end than its Merovingian predecessor, succumbing to the strains engendered by an over-stretched geo-political structure administered by an under-resourced royal administration. For in spite of the early successes of the system of *missi dominici*, royal messengers sent out to supervise the local powers of the king's realm, effective power still depended ultimately on royal campaigning and the regular assertion of royal rights and vassals' obligations. Patrimonial power and charismatic leadership were not adequate bases for a permanent and effective bureaucratic administrative apparatus, the more so in view of the lack of any real, centrally-controlled fiscal system which would give the ruler a permanent, independent and legally enshrined 'state' income. The inability to establish a bureaucracy is perhaps one of the most important points in this respect. Such intermediate agencies generally evolve, through their own, culturally-specific institutionalized practices and rituals, an ideology of service, on the one hand, and are able both to recruit new members through the appropriately determined channels, and effectively reproduce themselves (and are thus at least partly independent of the ruler or the dominant elite), on the other hand. Without such an agency, it was clearly impossible for the Frankish rulers to act autonomously or to pursue policies which in any serious way diverged from the interests of the dominant political elite. The reasons for the failure lie in the intensely personalized nature of political power relationships, in which service was to an individual rather than to a corporate body or conceptually reified institution such as the state, in contrast, for example, to the situation in the eastern or Byzantine empire. They also lie in the human and social sources of Charlemagne's administrators who, for the most part, were drawn from the ranks of the powerful, and represented the same element as the ruling elite of the Merovingian period. Literacy – a prerequisite for any effective administrative apparatus – may have been more common under the Carolingians, and the rulers may have relied to a far greater extent on written legislative acts to further their policies. But familial loyalties and entrenched and interlocking relationships of both patronage and vassalage, together with the entirely personal nature of the relationship between Charlemagne and his *missi dominici* (in most cases only marginally dependent upon the king for their economic security), meant that an organized bureaucracy, independent of 'feudal' relationships in the juridical sense, had really no chance. The failure of any such structure to develop combined with traditional Frankish inheritance practice to destroy Charlemagne's empire even more rapidly than that of the Merovingians. As the unitary Carolingian state broke up into its constituent political-geographical parts during the ninth century, it was precisely this network of relationships which provided the dynamic elements in the slow evolution of the kingdom of France, on the one hand, and the conflicts between the German emperors and the duchies or principalities of Swabia, Saxony and Bavaria, on the other.

Thus it was the combination of the alienation of state (that is, royal) lands to the servants of the kings, reducing the power of the former to raise revenues and control their own service nobility, together with the superficiality of the royal administration and the fragmented and localized patterns of loyalty and social solidarity, which rendered an effective, self-regenerating, non-personalized mode of rulership and a centralized administration more or less unviable, much though the Franks admired Roman institutions. Patrimonial rule can be highly effective in a state formation with a sophisticated bureaucratic tradition – as in the eastern Roman or Byzantine empire, for example; but the extensive and fragmented patterns of power in post-Roman Gaul deprived it of any long-term, regenerative efficacy.[19]

The Frankish kingdom was thus never entirely centralized nor properly bureaucratic. It relied upon traditional loyalties (that is to say, upon established ideological practices) to a specific dynasty or ruler, which in the case of the early Merovingians extracted revenues simply by imposing upon a pre-existing structure of taxation and corvées a group of officials with local powers. In respect of the mode of surplus appropriation, therefore, nothing changed. What did change were the officials who carried out the collection of revenues (and even here there may well have been substantive continuities, especially in respect of the tenants of Gallo-Roman landlords) and the authority for whom the surplus was extracted. Royal officials merely collected a raked-off surplus, but their diffused power in society as a whole came to be as much based on personal relationships of patronage and, later, vassalage as it was on royal authority. This was not in itself in strong contrast to the early Carolingian regime, whose vassals, the magnates of the later Merovingian period, won over by warfare or by other means, represented the first and most obvious level of the ruler's reach into the social relations of production. But the Carolingians recognized the nature of their power, which evolved out of just such relationships, and exploited the situation accordingly. It was a combination of these ties of vassalage to the mayors of the palace, with the religious-cultural and partly ethnic identities of the Frankish and Gallo-Roman landholding and office-holding elite which made the later Merovingian kingdom what it was, and the Carolingian kingdom possible. It was these same structural features which prevented the Carolingian kingdom from developing permanent state fiscal and administrative structures. The Visigothic kingdom of Spain offers close parallels.[20]

While the process of state formation may have been different in the Merovingian and Carolingian cases respectively, both suffered from the same fundamental problems of control over resources and their distribution essential to their further existence and to the power and authority of their rulers. Both succumbed in effect to the same fate, resulting from the same general structural causes. Both can reasonably be described as 'segmentary states', signifying territorially sovereign polities, with nominal central, yet patrimonial, rule, with a number of peripheral centres of power and administration; with a ruler's monopoly over force, yet with the legitimate use of coercion open also to peripheral authorities, and with the potential for the more peripheral powers to detach and transfer their allegiance from one 'centre' to another.[21] Both these formations were dominated by tributary relations of production, and both were constrained in their evolution by the forms of surplus appropriation and the political relations of surplus distribution which they either inherited or developed. The absence of any strong bureaucracy or administrative institutions through which the kings could maintain an institutionalized control over the direct appropriation of surplus to their own advantage meant that the process of delegation and fragmentation of state authority inexorably promoted the collapse of central rule, and made anything more than a conjunctural or cosmetic autonomy of royal politics a structural impossibility.

When we look at other regions of the European and Asian worlds, it is apparent that, in spite of a multiplicity of forms and appearances, there are actually only a limited number of structurally-possible systems within which pre-industrial societies could create states – that is to say, states which move beyond the stage of tribal confederation and attained a degree of permanence and continuity dependent upon sets of self-reproducing structural relationships. In the Frankish case, we are faced initially with a post-Roman society based on what I have described in chapter 3 as essentially tributary relations of production, whatever the phenomenal forms through which these were represented, and overlaid by lineage clan groups or confederacies in the process of being transformed into, or subordinated by, 'big-man' chieftaincies founded upon warbands and booty, conspicuous gift-giving and retinue-building. The settlement in Gaul, and the conquests and extension of Merovingian power, together with the institutional and administrative means of exacting wealth which the first Merovingian kings adopted, generated at the same time a new class of warrior magnate families (partly derived from the older clan elites and leaders, of course), who invested their wealth both in secular property and in warfare, on the one hand, and in the Church on the other – bishoprics and the ecclesiastical lands, in the first instance (especially in the areas where Gallo-Roman culture survived most strongly), monastic foundations in the second. The combination shaped what historians have generally identified as the early stages of an institutionally specific European feudal structure. But from the point of view of the state and its institutions, neither the Merovingian nor the Carolingian kingdoms ever reached the stage of mature statehood.

2. Tribute, Surplus and Autonomy: the Mughal Empire

In looking at the three medieval state formations so far discussed, each of very different cultural appearance, I have tried to highlight the key point in respect of the two related questions with which chapters 3 and 4 are concerned: in the first place, can states, or state elites bound up with the perceived interests of a given state formation at a given period, act independently of the interests of dominant socio-economic classes? And, in the second place, to what extent must states eradicate or subjugate (militarily, economically and ideologically) (a) aristocratic or other elements in society which possess control over or access to wealth sufficient to facilitate their opposition to, or competition with, the state for control of resources, in effect, for control over the process of surplus distribution; and (b) traditional structures of kinship and lineage, if they are to ensure their long-term survival and the creation or maintenance of conditions conducive to their political-institutional reproduction?

I have tried to answer the first question largely in the negative. but it is clear that under given, short-term conditions, it is perfectly possible for state elites or rulers to act against the majority vested interests of the leading social groups within a state, however much that possibility is determined by conditions established by the relations of production at a given moment. In the second case, however, the answer depends much more on the specific evolutionary and conjunctural track of the state in question and the social and cultural formations over which it exercises power. It represents a problem of a more concrete historical order. It is also a question which has lain at the heart of much comparative historical sociology: the dialectic between centrifugal and centripetal tendencies, a central theme for Max Weber, for example, characterized in terms of the constant battle between centralized, despotic regimes, on the one hand, and decentralized, particularistic structures, on the other, a struggle between 'feudalism' and patrimonialism. The first is used by Weber to define political relations of power, rather than social relations of production, but its intention is clear enough. And in these chapters, I have been looking at the ways in which such relationships worked themselves out in three very different socio-economic and cultural formations, albeit within the political economy context of tributary production relations as defined in chapter 3.

Thus, in the case of those three states, the central power tried, sometimes successfully, sometimes less so, to suppress or check the growth of potential rivals for resources and therefore power. And it is absolutely clear that the basic dynamic of evolution moves between centripetal and centrifugal poles, whatever the culture-specific modalities and historically-determined institutional structures through which this movement takes place. Kinship structures played a role in the Ottoman and Merovingian cases, for example, for there the ruler's power was founded in the first place upon conquests and wealth won for him by social groups still retaining many of the key traits of clan and tribal structure, however much they were being transformed, socially differentiated and hierarchized or ranked through warfare and the formation of retinues.

In some political formations, however, the structures of kinship and lineage have proved much more tenacious and have indeed consistently hindered and complicated any process of institutional embedding of state structures. The history of Indian society and cultural formation is particularly informative, although it is also exceedingly complex and, of course, overlain by a number of thorny ideological debates and questions. For example, the extremely complex, multi-level segmentary lineages of Indian society throughout the sub-continent in the medieval and pre-modern periods can certainly be shown at certain periods to have been affected in the short term by efforts at state centralization and the direct intervention by centrally-appointed officials of the state into local economic affairs for fiscal purposes. The state thereby contributed to a reduction in the power of lineage and kin at local levels, where they functioned as important elements of the social relations of production.[22] On the other hand, the relationship between locality and state in India is to a large extent overdetermined by the nature of this all-pervasive caste and lineage system, which defines belonging and social relationships both at the generic level of (attributed) class-occupation (priest, warrior, peasant/merchant and servant) as well as at the level of the ranked lineage group, and is highly inflected in respect of local variations in status and practice (so that 'caste' as popularly employed in western literature actually signifies two cross-woven sets of structures, class in the sense of occupation – *varna* – and lineage identity and attribution or 'caste' – *jati*).[23] Lineage structures, and rank or status attributions, which are at the same time commensurate throughout most of India with fundamental patterns of economic organization, and distribution of wealth at the level of the village or locality,[24] are able to survive periods of economic subordination at the hands of strong state intervention, but have proved able, once such state structures are weakened, to re-assert themselves remarkably rapidly. Political functions and political organization were based on such structures, and the rise and fall of local potentates or rajas were equally determined by the complex relationship between centralizing states and local lineage systems, and between and within the latter. When state power was weak, lineage elites could increase their power and authority, at the expense both of the state and of neighbouring or subordinate lineages. When the state was strong, such local magnates had either to submit to the central authority and accept the function delegated to them, if any; or they were suppressed. But, as we shall see, the very notion of central state power needs to be carefully qualified, especially in respect of the points discussed at the beginning of chapter 4, for example: the nature of the mode of surplus appropriation and especially of surplus distribution, the degree of supervision of the central power over its provincial and more distant representatives, and so on. Assumptions about the efficacy of Mughal political authority have done much to produce an overly neat and uncritical vision of an autocratic system which succeeded in exploiting its resource-base to the greatest potential on the basis of rigid and efficient centrally co-ordinated institutional arrangements. But, as Perlin has recently made very clear, the very existence of state structures, with all their fiscal and institutional demands and effects, in turn both limits certain types of political and power relations while at the same time facilitating either the evolution of new forms, or alternatively attributing older structures with new possibilities for their further development – and all this in turn must necessarily react back upon the ways in which the state can maintain itself and evolve. I have made similar points already in chapter 4 in particular; but the evidence for the Indian context (however underdeveloped its treatment, if we accept Perlin's analysis) is extremely valuable in this respect.[25]

Nevertheless, the peculiarly tenacious nature of these kin structures, which, as I have noted, determined also patterns of wealth production and property or resource allocation and distribution (including patterns of marriage), has puzzled many commentators, and led Marx, for example, and others since him, to suppose a rather static set of production relations. It has also led to ramified debates among sociologists, anthropologists and historians on the origins, evolution and mechanism of the whole system, debates which are still very much alive.

There is, however, an important difference between the northern and southern Indian zones, for the description offered so far relates only in its broadest and most general outlines to the whole of the sub-continent. In the North, for example, the *kshatriya* institution, and the warrior elites it generated, was crucial to the social and political shape of the region. It was *kshatriya* lineages, with their extended agnatic and affinal roots, which provided the numerous competing local elites and more powerful overlordships. To quote Stein, 'the usual political condition in northern India during ancient and medieval times was its relatively short-lived dynasties and its division into a great number of small territories under kin-linked warrior families of high ritual status'.

In the South, in contrast, there was no *kshatriya* class to speak of. The marked regional climatic and soil variations led to the evolution of distinct economic and socio-cultural types, distinguished ecologically by the differences between wet and dry zones, and those intermediate districts which exhibited features of both; and socially by intensely localized territorial segmentation – the extensive lineage structures of the North are not present here. Instead, the highly localized social landscape is dominated by three broad status-class groupings: of *brahmans*, *shudra* and lower castes, the former, with the 'respectable' castes of the *shudra* class, making up the dominant social elite, the latter being further divided between antagonistic 'left-' and 'right-hand' groupings, to a degree identical with certain occupational divisions and, as one scholar at least has suggested, with specific vested economic interests and, therefore, economic class relationships. The *brahmans* wielded great influence, both in ritual/religious terms and in terms of political and economic practice, so that, while the intensely localized patterns of social, economic and cultural reproduction promoted a high degree of political-economic exclusivity and fragmentation, the influence of the brahmanic class promoted a countervailing tendency towards supra-local organization. The result has been the evolution of regionalized social and economic units organized into wider 'segmentary' political structures re-inforced, as we shall see, by *brahman* influence and Hindu ritual vested in over-kings who can overcome at a symbolic and ritual level the tensions between these localized foci of social and political praxis. At the same time, these ritual (and 'transactional') networks serve as channels of surplus re-distribution to the advantage of the centre in respect of the periphery.[26]

In the context of these relationships (which vary considerably from region to region in their actual institutional forms), territorial states seem unable, except for relatively brief periods, to maintain their dominance over local kin-determined economic and political structures, and in particular to assert their authority and maintain their sovereignty for long over the underlying endemic social-economic competition between antagonistic lineage interests; although it must be clear too that their efforts at different times and in different regions likewise affected the lineage structures, in particular in respect of their internal differentiation. One reason for this in the North, it has been suggested, lies in the extent of what has been dubbed the 'web of attributional genealogical linkage', which ties in local communities to a much wider set of lineage identities and loyalties. The effect of this is to permit kin identities to survive, even though states may have been able to suppress local magnates representing lineages and to deprive the lineages themselves of their local political functions. In the South the semi-autonomous and localized social subsystems seem to have been able to tolerate a form of ritual and general overlordship more easily – perhaps a reflection of the strength of sub-regional identities and institutions – with the result that what some have chosen to dub 'segmentary' state formations came more easily into being (although equally easily dissolved in the face of regional and sub-regional opposition).[27]

As with the Ottoman state, however, it needs to be pointed out that the same reasons underlay both the weakness of centralized states and their continued existence. For the existence of state apparatuses and the local structures which represented 'alternative' sets of social practice were as often as not complementary as much as they were contradictory (or at least, complementarity and antagonism were dependent on the context and process of their respective development), so that their interplay permitted the maintenance of the conditions of existence of both.

The reason for the failure of territorial, centralized states in India to endure as effectively centralized powers for very long thus lies both in the micro-structure of local social relations of production, and in the inability of states to remove such structures and replace them with a state-orientated administrative and fiscal establishment. Whether Indian states, similarly to the Merovingian kingdom, tended merely to superimpose political, military and ritual authority over regions distant from their centres of power, with little attempt (except for the Mughals) to embed that power on a permanent basis at the local level, is debatable. But traditional localized modes of economic and political administration were never effectively replaced by any machinery created specifically by and for the state (although the Mughal fiscal reforms of the later sixteenth century were influential in respect of revenue assessment). States did not, on the whole, reach down very far into the interstices of the society they dominated. Even the powerful Mughal state relied for the most part on a system of delegation to the traditional representatives of lineages and kin-groups for local and village administration and revenue collection – however much these in their turn may have been under the supervision of (or in competition with) the state's soldier-administrators in the provinces. The amount of revenue demanded varied, of course, but in general little was done to change traditional patterns and methods of provincial fiscal administration. There were exceptions and attempts at reform, but these were relatively short-lived.[28]

The role of trade and industry constituted a further important factor. Long before the medieval period the demands of local and supra-local elites for luxuries, for the maintenance of retinues and armies, for buildings and other construction work, had been an important stimulus to trade and commerce. Coastal regions had attracted foreign traders and merchants from the earliest times, and had acted as channels for the export of a wide range of products, both in bulk terms and in respect of luxury goods. As a number of scholars have pointed out, while the centre of gravity may have moved over time from region to region, the sub-continent tended on the whole to absorb surplus wealth from outside, producing goods such as cotton and silk, dyes, spices, narcotics, timber, ivory, pitch and a number of other products, and importing relatively little – certain ores, slaves, horses. This trade, through numerous localized merchant elites, was integral to, if mostly parasitic upon, the relationship between urban and rural production. Merchant groups themselves, whether indigenous or foreign, acted as a mediating force between rulers and more distant centres of urban as well as rural production. In addition, the demands of local and intra-regional commerce promoted the relatively high degree of monetization of Indian exchange relationships, although the form of the exchange medium varied enormously across time and from region to region, as well as according to the level at which transactions were conducted. In respect of the ways in which dominant elites and rulers were able to exploit resources and influence the distribution of wealth, as well as in respect of the degree of independence from local entrenched socio-economic sub-systems which the rulers of larger political formations were or were not able to achieve – in short, in respect of the contouring of patterns of power – merchant groups and the existence of well-established trade routes and markets represented an important constitutive element. In some areas, external markets created demands sufficient to promote the development of flourishing long-term cash-crop economies, especially in respect of cotton and other textiles, or rice, for example, and later in respect of tea. It is obvious that such factors, according to the particular historical context, could play an important role in the formation, consolidation and fragmentation of political systems. Perhaps crucially, such factors functioned as both alternative and complementary sources of wealth and, therefore, of power to those which were founded solely on the appropriation of agrarian surpluses, and further intensified the highly regionalized nature of Indian economic structures. And it was not only merchant groups who were involved. There is some evidence for the investment by wealthy *mansabdar*s and members of royal households in trade for profit: some owned shipping, others actively involved themselves in maritime trade on a considerable scale. While the state income from duties on trade may well have been limited, private profit-taking must have contributed to a degree to the wealth at the disposal of those who invested in commerce of one sort or another. And there was in addition the fact, only comparatively recently appreciated, that the re-distribution of surplus wealth appropriated as tax by the state often followed pre-existing commercial networks and was actually facilitated thereby, thus creating a degree of interdependence of the one upon the other such that, just as in the later Roman period, some trade may well also have been facilitated by the state's own fiscal network and transportation system. The central authority certainly presented itself as closely interested in the well-being of traders and those involved in commerce, and in at least one official document encouraged its officials not to neglect their interests. Finally, but particularly significant, is the fact that from the fifteenth century there occurred an expansion of international commerce which played an important role in the ways in which the Mughal administration was able to conduct its fiscal affairs, and the ways in which other political centres could acquire wealth and either resist Mughal power or evolve structures not bound in to the Mughal system of surplus appropriation.[29]

Thus far I have been describing aspects of Indian state and social formation at a rather high level of generality. I should like for a moment, therefore, to dwell on the Mughal empire and its structures in order to illustrate the points made above. For, like the Ottoman state examined above, the Mughal empire has traditionally been associated with efficient central authority and a fluidly effective machinery of surplus appropriation via an obedient class or group of state-appointed military and civil officials. This image has recently been substantially challenged, and the picture now emerging is of a much more diffused network of power-relations and a much less effective central authority. The rather artificial picture of Mughal state structures and the role of Akbar as a great reformer and innovator can be modified by taking more explicitly into account the origins and evolution of Mughal power. For like the Ottomans, the Mughal dynasty evolved out of a context of warring Islamic dynastic factions, and the first Mughal rulers, Babur and his son Humayun, merely adopted and adapted the structures of military organization and surplus appropriation they inherited in the regions they conquered. Babur himself was nominally heir to the principality of Farghânâ, and although he was able, by supporting the Safavid Shah Ismâ'il against the Uzbek Khan, to gain Samarkand for a while, the Uzbeks regained the upper hand shortly after and Babur was forced to retire to his secure territories around Kabul. His involvement in north Indian affairs was stimulated by an invitation from the dissident governor of Lahore, who was in conflict with the Sultan of Delhi, Ibrâhim Lodî. Babur's troops defeated the Lodî forces in 1526 and he occupied Delhi in the same year. But as a result of the conflict between his son and successor Humayun and the Afghan Sher Shah, Delhi and much of the Mughal conquests were lost until the late 1550s, when first Humayun and then Akbar were able to exploit the weaknesses in Sher Shah's son's rule to restore their position. In a series of wars with neighbouring Muslim and Hindu rulers, Akbar then succeeded in establishing a firm authority, partly shored up by family alliances, based at Delhi. Expansion by military and diplomatic means followed more-or-less unbroken until the late seventeenth century as the empire extended its sway deep into the Deccan. But the degree to which Mughal authority depended upon effective coercion and embedded fiscal administrative institutions has been increasingly called into question as the complexity of the interacting political and economic relationships upon which Mughal rule was based has come to be recognized.[30]

Like the Ottoman state, the Mughal state maintained its armies by a system of grants of revenue to state cavalry soldiers, who were thus given the means to support themselves and a certain number of horsemen. These cavalrymen, similar in function to the Ottoman *sipahis* and higher-ranking officers in the fifteenth and sixteenth centuries, functioned also as administrators of the districts assigned to them, representing the state at the local level. But there the similarities with the Ottoman system end, for the higher-ranking Mughal assignee, or *mansabdar*, had a more or less free hand in his relations with the communities under his authority (at least as far as custom and the amount of coercive power at his disposal established certain structural limitations), and could collect his revenues by any one of several different methods.[31] The reforms of Akbar (1555–1605) have traditionally been held to have introduced a number of changes into the system that had evolved since the original conquests in the early sixteenth century, a set of practices which, as we have seen, were inherited directly from preceding regimes. The fundamental pattern, based upon traditional Islamic administrative structures, was of a central administration divided into several departments. Particularly important was the general fiscal bureau responsible for taxation and revenues (in turn subdivided into various different competences) and a department responsible for maintaining the armies and keeping a register of the various revenue assignments. In addition to the regular *sipahi* cavalry, compulsory levies from subordinate princes also served in the armies; and an important element, concentrated around the Sultan, consisted of slave troops, as in other Islamic states. Although the terminology was altered, it was essentially this pattern of administration at which Akbar's reforms were directed.

It is important to emphasize the crucial intermediate role played by local – Hindu and Muslim – notables and regional elites in the growth of the Mughal state, upon whom the centre also depended for the effective re-distribution of a portion of the surplus. It is not surprising that in the pre-Mughal Sultanates of North India, just as in the growing Ottoman state, points of tension are evident between the vested interests of the conquering elite of war chiefs and the interests of the Sultans, often in association with a military and civil bureaucracy of servitors (slaves) and with non-Muslim but subject princes – very similar, in effect, to the sets of political relationships which evolved in the fourteenth- and fifteenth-century Ottoman world.

It would be a mistake to attribute none of the changes which affected Mughal state administrative practice to Akbar, of course. The structure of revenue assignment was adjusted, for example, so that payments had to be made, at least for a time, centrally and in cash. Officers of state were divided into thirty-three grades, from the highest holders of revenue assignments (*jagirdars*, in possession of a *jagir* or *iqta*), in possession of very considerable holdings, down to the lesser cavalry officers or simple *mansabdars*. Akbar also converted many *jagirs*, larger assignments, back into fiscal land in an attempt to prevent the alienation through excessively large accumulations of such possessions in the hands of individual lords, and such lands were placed under the authority of centrally-appointed fiscal officers.

These changes took place in a very specific historical context, however, and in particular one in which Akbar found himself forced to defend his position both against his half-brother Mirza Hakim, ruler of Kabul and its territories, and against interference from the Uzbek Khans; it should also be borne in mind that Akbar's conflicts with neighbouring powers were a prime reason for the continued expansion of the Mughal domains on the sub-continent, and that his victories brought with them not only vastly increased revenue potential (and therefore the possibility of employing such revenues to re-affirm his own authority, both ideologically and militarily), but also a series of much greater problems of political control. The conquest and absorption of Bengal, Gujarat and Sind, for example, in the 1570s and 1590s respectively, meant a vast increase in Akbar's territory, and in the case of Gujarat, control over a wealthy commercial and industrial region. And it was precisely in the process of responding to this constantly changing situation that Akbar's reforms have to be understood: it is perhaps more useful to view them as a series of transformations of the relationships between centre and periphery, than any consciously-guided attempt to introduce reforms into a pre-existing and subjectively less efficient system.

Recent work has indeed suggested that the notion of a series of reforms substantially misrepresents both the effectiveness of whatever changes Akbar is thought to have introduced, as well as misrepresenting their character. For in the first place, it appears clear that Akbar's reign and those of his immediate successors were just as prone to effective opposition and separatist tendencies among outlying subordinate potentates; while in the second place, they faced equally divisive challenges from contenders for a share in absolute power, especially at times of succession, as had their predecessors Babur and Humayun, for example. Aurangzeb even agreed to the subdivision of the empire under his sons, hardly a sign of established and unchallenged centralizing tendencies. And equally significantly, Akbar himself, while challenged (or at the least threatened) on more than one occasion by his half-brother Mirza Hakim, did not remove the latter from his position as ruler of the region around Kabul, nor challenge his continued control over the revenue-assignments of that region; and, while Mirza Hakim was presented in certain contemporary court accounts as an awkward subordinate of the emperor, it seems in fact that he was a great deal more independent than this.[32]

The *mansabdars* of all grades, like the Ottoman *sipahis*, held no hereditary title to their assignments, which could be cancelled by the emperor at any time. In practice, of course, most *mansabdars* remained life tenants, but their assignments could not be inherited by their heirs, unless the emperor explicitly ordered (or agreed to) this. They secured their future, in consequence, by arranging marriages with other members of the administrative-military class and by obtaining appointments for sons and relatives.[33] But the *mansabdars* were not the only people with access to or authority over land. There was a considerable stratum of hereditary 'rent'-takers, or *zamindars* (this Persian term came to replace a wide range of traditional local words for the same social position), generally members of locally-dominant *jati*, or lineage-caste groups referred to already.[34] The term itself was used by the central administration to cover a wide range of local titles and terms, titles which generally involved rights and privileges in respect of incomes, judicial authority, political and communal leadership, and so on.[35] Their entrenched local power, buttressed by their own, often very considerable, armed retinues, was, of course, threatened by the imposition upon their districts of state assignments to *mansabdars*, the effects of which varied from place to place. Most members of this *zamindar* stratum seem to have been themselves incorporated into the state apparatus below the various degrees of *mansabdar*, although some obtained *mansabdar* status too, in certain cases receiving confirmation of their rights in the form of major official grants of revenue, or *jagirs*. The state certainly intervened to formalize *zamindari* rights, where possible, and to enforce the transfer or replacement of *zamindars* who proved unwilling to co-operate with state demands for revenues. One study for North India, for example, has shown how, by the early eighteenth century, conflicts of interest over revenue between local *zamindar* elites and the state forced the latter to expropriate *zamindari* rights and to assign them to a different (and rival) local power elite. Nevertheless, there is ample evidence to show that, in many cases, the rajas and *zamindars* were left as virtually autonomous local magnates and rulers over districts for which they paid a 'tribute' to the emperors, but which was exacted on the basis of customary relations of power. The considerable customary rights they enjoyed in their locality (which could include also a wide range of prestations in cash or kind as well as, in many areas, in the form of labour, which was often of considerable importance both to local rulers and to the state[36]) were supported by the traditions enshrined in the relationships between different strata within lineage groups.[37] And although the Mughal state generally employed the *zamindar* elites as subordinate instruments of its own tax-collecting (and here the fineness of the difference between 'rent' and 'tax' becomes particularly apparent), the latter and their dependants were themselves able to appropriate a considerable proportion of the surplus produced by the peasantry, a surplus that, while it was often limited by custom to a particular proportion of the total in most regions, was less easily reclaimed by the state through the same institutional and juridical means as that taken from the *mansabdars* after they had appropriated the due revenue from their assignments. Importantly, when the state or its agents the *mansabdars* increased their demands for revenues from the *zamindars*, the latter more often than not offered no resistance, merely passing the burden on to the peasant producers.

The system of surplus extraction was not uniform across all the lands of the empire, of course. Apart from territories remaining more or less autonomous under local rulers or elite sub-castes, or those placed in addition in *mansabs* or *jagirs*, there were districts or communities subjected to assessment for the imperial treasury alone, and districts subject to *mansabdars* alone, with no local elite acting as intermediaries. Often, communities registered under a range of such different headings for fiscal purposes were found in the same region, so that the pattern of fiscal administration cannot be understood on the basis of geographical divisions and blocks of territory alone.[38] While the system of revenue assignments may have functioned quite well under rigorous central supervision, such supervision was extremely difficult to maintain over such a far-flung empire, and (given the tensions between local elites and state officers in normal times) will have failed when conditions of political insecurity and increasing pressure on the revenues of the state in respect of military expenditure led, in the later seventeenth and eighteenth centuries, to the development of farming revenue assignments. But, as we have seen, even under the supposedly strongly centralized regime of Akbar, such central authority was never as strictly enforced (or enforceable) as some historians have wanted to think. At the same time, the threat of transferral of assignments inevitably encouraged the maximization (under whatever local constraints existed) of tax revenue, producing a short-term cycle of oppression and peasant reaction, followed by armed intervention and coercion. Indeed, the evidence suggests that the state was able to maintain its policy of regularly transferring *jagir* assignees (*jagirdars*) only partially and incompletely, thus exacerbating the problem. There is evidence from several regions, for example, to suggest that already at the beginning of the seventeenth century imperially-appointed *jagirdars* and lesser officials were entrenching themselves locally and putting down roots, thus dramatically compromising any attempt on the part of the central authority to maintain a strict control over its provincial representatives. In addition, the theoretical limitations imposed upon the more powerful *mansabdars*, especially as regards the accumulation of wealth and the appropriation of judicial authority over the local population, were limited by factors such as distance from the imperial centre and by the ability of *jagirdars* to exploit local economic and social circumstances. And the accumulation of wealth provided them with the possibility of obtaining similar posts and positions for their offspring and other members of their family or clientele. A state elite thus came into being which was largely independent of state service after two generations or so. In this respect, it is important to stress that this elite represented in only the very loosest sense of the term a state bureaucracy – those elements which served directly the central power at the imperial court, perhaps; yet for the most part the *mansabdar-jagirdar* stratum was hardly involved in the 'administration' of the state in the narrower sense of the word. The so-called *mansab* and *jagir* 'systems', which have so often been portrayed as a reflection of the efficient functioning of the centralized Mughal autocracy, appear in fact to have been not a system, but rather a set of evolving institutional power-relationships strongly determined in their *modus operandi* by highly localized and regional traditions and relationships of surplus appropriation, distribution and exchange which pre-date the Mughal polity.[39] It is the fluidity of these relationships which needs to be stressed, and which a dynamic model of social relations of production should emphasize. Indeed, the Mughal and Ottoman cases illustrate just how misleading tendencies to think of historical structures as systems, that is to say, in a purely synchronic sense, can be. To speak of systems in this ill-considered way (as with the Byzantine 'theme system' for example, or the Ottoman *devşirme* system, or indeed the 'feudal system') is to promote precisely the idea that social relations exist in a kind of homeostatic state in which change evolves only as a result of 'dysfunctional' elements – a resort to an implicit form of structural-functionalist interpretation which cannot explain change, only describe it.

As the state and its elite became increasingly uncertain of ensuring a constantly high proportion of the surplus (in competition with localized elites), many *mansabdars*, especially the more powerful, found that it was more profitable, more certain and more economical, in respect of their personal incomes, to farm their assignments, a practice which developed gradually, particularly in Bengal, from the last years of Shah Jahan and the reign of Aurangzeb, that is, from the 1650s and 1660s on. And the conversion of state revenues, or claims to a substantial proportion of the produce for specified districts, by this route into proprietary rights over the land itself (a development well under way by the middle of the eighteenth century), and by the *de facto* succession of sons of *mansabdars* to their fathers' assignments, signalled the demise of effective central control, compromised though it always appears to have been. In addition, many *zamindars* gained for themselves the right to operate as tax-farmers for both their own lands and *zamindari* rights, and those of other, neighbouring and often less powerful *zamindars*. At the same time, *zamindari* rights could be bought and sold, and this stimulated the development of a market in landed rights and the surpluses these could produce.

In the Punjab, for example, it has been shown that, during the first half of the eighteenth century, the central authority became increasingly less relevant to the needs of the Mughal governing elite, which formed a distinct body of lords of Turanian origin, whose maintenance of power and authority, in respect both of local Indian lineage elites and the Mughal rulers, depended upon the re-direction of imperial revenues destined for the frontier armies, and the endowment of members of their own group with the income from state fiscal lands. Ruthless oppression of the local elites and lesser state officials ensured their dominance. At the same time, the greater prosperity of the region, a prosperity which resulted from the relative peace and stability of Aurangzeb's reign (d. 1707), gave local *zamindars* the possibility of defying such overlords, who could in turn demand more military and fiscal resources from the emperor with which to combat this threat. Local autonomy was the actual result.[40]

It is worth pointing out, of course, that revenue-farming is not necessarily a bad thing.[41] Several commentators have noted that, to the contrary, tax-farming can lead to greater investment in production, since revenue-farmers are in the nature of things interested in maximizing their profits over the longer term as well as on a short-term basis. Thus they may (directly or indirectly, in terms of the fiscal pressure exerted upon the producers) encourage a quantitative expansion of the land brought under cultivation, where conditions permit this. In some areas, revenue-farmers were clearly closely connected with commerce and the export trade, thus contributing to an integration of the surplus wealth generated by rural production and that generated through trade in a merchant-trading market which was able at times to rival that of European traders and investors, in the seventeenth century certainly. Revenue-farmers could, of course, exploit their sources of income to the point of ruin, but this must have been very unusual, if only because – like state tax-assessors and -collectors, they had for the most part to work within pre-existing sets of power relations, and were certainly not the only ones able to use coercion. This will have been even more so when local elites were able to purchase the revenue assignment for their district, however exploitative their role may have seemed to contemporary European observers. As we shall see, this was certainly the case in the South; there is no reason to assume that the same logic did not apply in the territories dominated by the Mughal power.

The basic income of the state came from the land. The system of revenue assessment had evolved through a number of stages, initially taking the form of a simple crop-sharing, whereby the state demanded a certain portion of the harvest, according to the quality of the land and the year's produce. This evolved into the so-called *zabt* system, whereby tariffs for each region were established, based on average yields and quality of harvests, and upon the basis of which a cash assessment could be based. Beneath this relatively uniform system – traditionally taken to have been finally consolidated under Akbar, but in fact representing only a relatively superficial administrative uniformity – a wide range of local variations and customary systems survived, of course, so that considerable regional variations can be observed in the sources. In theory, the state preferred to assess the revenue due to it on the basis of individual cultivators or taxpayers, and in some cases this was done. But for the most part the basic unit of assessment was the village (or its equivalent – not all settlement was in the form of nucleated communities, of course, since land-use and geography clearly played a role in fixing settlement-patterns), and it was usually the state's agents, members of local or regional elites, who were made responsible for the collection of the assessment. These could be tax-farmers or *zamindars*, on the one hand, or the village headman, on the other, according to local conditions. As long as the state obtained what it demanded, local tradition and local interests determined who paid most, and how.

The peasantry could clearly be grossly exploited under such conditions, and in spite of the efforts of individual rulers to prevent it (and in spite of a strongly paternalistic element in some Mughal rulers' self-image: a document issued to an imperial official in the years 1707–12, under 'Âlam Bahâdur Shâh, stresses the emperor's concern for the agrarian population).[42] Those who served the central authority in this capacity received sometimes very considerable rights to draw on the produce of cultivated land, and had the fields or territories in which their rights lay assessed at (often much) lower rates than the standard. There is no doubt that the fiscal burden on the poorer farmers was very great, and that social differentiation within communities was often very marked. This was further heightened by the high degree of monetization of the state's economy: revenues (if we exclude the vast range of local demands from *zamindars* and others upon the agricultural population) were mostly collected in cash, which reflected both the relatively high level of commercialization and specialist agricultural production as well as good access to markets.

The highly monetized economy reflected several factors. The vast bureaucracy of the empire, the attendant services it demanded or stimulated, and the great demand for a wide range of luxury goods and services to maintain the ostentatious consumption and display of the ruling elite meant that a reasonably stable precious-metal coinage as well as a trustworthy low-denomination coinage was essential to the smooth exchange of social wealth between the producing population and the consumers of that wealth. More importantly, this was in turn made possible by a long-standing tradition of monetized exchange and particularly by the considerable demand stimulated by increased contacts with European markets as a result of first Portuguese (and later Dutch, French and English) merchant enterprise.[43] Indeed, it was this favourable balance of trade between the sub-continent and Europe, and the flow of silver to India, which made the Mughal silver currency possible – the rupees minted from 1556 on were largely coined from Spanish and Portuguese silver *reals*.[44] As the world market for textiles, silks, spices and other products expanded, so the import of both copper (which formed the basis of the coinages of much of North India until the introduction of the Mughal silver) as well as silver and gold increased.[45] But there existed even before direct major European involvement a widespread and very flourishing network of trading contacts across South Asia, linking Chinese, Japanese, Philippine and Indian ports and centres of agricultural and industrial production together, and with the Iranian, Arab and East African regions.[46] And it is clear that well before the Mughal period the extraction of surplus at all levels was well-integrated into a monetized system of exchange, using a wide variety of currency media – copper, gold, cowries and a range of other token currencies, a 'system' entailing sets of overlapping pools of money-use extending from the level of state activity via large-scale commercial exchange and tax-farming, right down to village economies.[47] From the last years of the reign of Akbar, the state itself increasingly insisted upon the payment of the produce tax in cash; and it was in the period covered by the reigns of Sher Shah (1540–5) and Akbar that the tri-metallic currencies of the Mughal state – copper or billon, silver and gold – began to dominate. But a range of alternative currency forms remained in use right up to the early colonial period, specially at the most local levels of exchange, both as currencies of account and practical exchange media.[48] Beginning in the 1590s, the silver rupee (*rupaya*) became the official unit in which the Mughal state demanded the payment of tax. But apart from tax, the use of the state's coin alone was hardly enforceable, given the enormous diversity in the ways in which surplus was rendered and consumed across the various regions of the Mughal domains. Yet from an administrative point of view, the Mughal fiscal officials were able to maintain a uniformity of standards across the numerous mints, a major achievement in itself, and one which inevitably lent both stability and authority to the currencies in circulation. This was important both for the ability of the central power to convert locally-appropriated surpluses into cash for taxes, as well as for the drawing into the market of bullion which could be fed into the system through state-supervised or controlled mints.

By the middle of the seventeenth century, the rupee had become the dominant element in official transactions throughout Mughal-controlled territories, with the copper coinage functioning primarily as a means of low-level exchange, even though it has been shown that production of the latter increased considerably over the seventeenth century and into the eighteenth.[49] The supply of silver was obtained entirely through exporting produce or manufactures, however, and although the influx of European silver in the later sixteenth and seventeenth centuries does not seem to have had particularly marked effects on prices – partly because there appears to have been a parallel increase in demand for finished products and raw materials from outside the sub-continent at the same time – this nevertheless meant that fluctuations in access to the international market in precious metals had direct effects on the Indian coinages as well as the fiscal operations of Indian states at this time. The crucial role of Europeans, initially welcomed precisely because of their demand for Indian products in return for silver, can be easily appreciated in this regard. Just as with the Ottoman case discussed in chapter 4, it is important to examine the internal relations which form the context for the import of foreign silver before drawing over-hasty conclusions regarding its supposed massively inflationary effects.

The existence of a well-established silver currency worked also to the advantage of both local and long-distance commerce. Of course, fluctuations, sometimes quite marked, took place in the relationship between the different elements of the currency. Yet on the whole the system experienced a remarkable stability, a result both of state policy (a reflection of its function in state fiscality and surplus appropriation) and of its importance in independent commercial and exchange activity.

The central importance of a highly-monetized economic life meant, of course, that tax-farming, the development of a market in the rights to agricultural produce and ultimately in land itself (by the early eighteenth century), as well as the development of fairly sophisticated structures for credit and loans, went hand in hand. It also meant that the relationship between the resource-extracting class of local and regional notables in the empire and the commercial and urban markets, upon which the former depended for both luxury goods and services, diluted the political and fiscal link between the centre and its resource-base.[50]

There are in some ways a number of similarities between the Mughal and the Ottoman systems both in terms of the fundamental structural principles upon which they functioned (especially the ways in which the state tried to separate its agents from any control over revenues and means of distribution of surplus) and in terms of the processes through which they were transformed, a reflection of their common Islamic and Turkic/Turanian cultural and political traditions, and of the nature of the contexts within which their states came into existence. In both cases, it is interesting to note that tax-farming was one outcome of pressure on the state's resources (although the roots of the pressure were in each case somewhat different); in both cases, and in spite of efforts to prevent its occurrence, a ruling elite or localized ruling elites were able to establish a power base independent of the ruler's personal control and the fiscal administrative mechanisms designed to check such a development, even though their independence was also threatened by localized conflicts over revenue assignments.[51] But a major difference was the fact that the Mughal elite always remained outnumbered and at the same time subject to the cultural influence of the indigenous elites, so that an absolute ideological hegemony was never established. While the Ottoman rulers certainly had to struggle against Shi'ism, in Asia Minor in particular, as a vehicle of political-cultural opposition to their absolutism, the Muslim confrontation with Hinduism, the deeply embedded structures of lineage inscribed in the system of *varna* and *jati* already described, and the entrenched position of the numerous localized strata of *zamindars*, meant that the Mughal state had little chance of embedding itself without thereby losing its identity in a proliferation of local variations on the original theme.

Akbar's abolition of the *jizya*, the Islamic tax on all non-Muslims, is indicative of the problems faced by Mughal rulers; for it was precisely the threat of opposition from the Rajputs, one of the leading military elements of Hindu society, and the pressing need to present the emperor as having the interests of all his subjects at heart, whether Hindu or Muslim, which made such a step necessary.[52] In contrast, and except along its northern periphery, the indigenous ruling elites conquered by the Ottoman state were usually either already Muslim, or quickly adopted Islam as a means of political and social survival. This was only rarely the case with Hindu elites, although many individual examples are known (the founders of the Vijayanagara empire in the fourteenth century, for example, had been converts to Islam, but had later apostatized and returned to their own cultural tradition). It is once again in this respect highly significant that, given the political situation within his territories, and his relations with Muslim powers to the North-West, especially the Uzbeks, who posed a potential threat to him both militarily and ideologically, Akbar recognized this problem and addressed it directly, even if there is a clearly opportunistic element present. Until the 1570s, the court literature of his reign presented him as an orthodox Muslim ruler, presenting his rivals in an unfavourable light designed to assert Akbar's own credentials as a leader and Islamic hero. But from the late 1570s, he appears already to have expressed some doubts about certain key elements of Islam. In 1579 he issued a decree, signed by leading members of the *Ulema*, in which he was credited with the title and powers of a just ruler, claiming the highest authority in doctrinal disputes and thereby, in effect, the power and position of a Caliph. In reality, Akbar himself relied on his own appointees for decisions in such matters, so that the decree remained something of a formality with little practical effect. But it did directly challenge the traditional structures of religious teaching and interpretation. And in 1581, modifying orthodox Islam even more dramatically, he established the 'Divine Faith' (*Din-i Ilahi*). In this new, highly syncretistic system, Akbar was himself the prophet of the new faith, which rejected all forms of idolatry. Rooted in Islam, it yet borrowed heavily from Hinduism and from the Parsis (Zoroastrians), as well as from Christianity, in its ceremonial aspects. Perhaps predictably, the new faith never spread beyond a very limited circle at court. Indeed, many Muslim lords with their followers broke into open rebellion against Akbar's new heresy, as they were bound to view it, so that from 1581 until 1585 he was engaged in suppressing the revolt of the Afghan lords of Bengal, and other magnates who had rallied around Akbar's brother – who was presented as the representative of orthodoxy in Kabul.

The *Din-i Ilahi* seems to have been intended as a focus of loyalty centred upon a cult of the ruler, which stood above the two main religions of the empire, an ideological device which could unify the disparate elements of the central and provincial elites. While it failed insofar as Akbar's successors did not show much interest in its furtherance in their personal lives, it constitutes one among the many elements which imbued the Mughal throne with a degree of ideological permanence and respect similar in many ways to that attached to the Ottoman sultanate or the Byzantine imperial throne. Similar, if less long-lasting, results had been achieved to a degree by the Chola kingdom and, later, the Vijayanagara kingdom in the South of the sub-continent, although this had depended more on the actual symbolic power ascribed to the kings themselves – chiefs and sub-kings were pleased to partake in the reflected ritual authority of their divinely-sanctioned, and brahmanically-supported power. In contrast to other dynasties, however, the Mughals retained a vested residual power and authority long after their real political power had evaporated away entirely.[53]

Akbar's reforms, in particular his fiscal administrative innovations, had little long-term effect, with the exception of a more rigorous establishment of the principles for the actual assessment of revenues due; and in their main lines the traditional ways of revenue-raising re-asserted themselves during the reign of his successor Jahangir. In spite of Mughal expansionism on the political-military front, the empire remained even at its height a segmentary warrior overlordship imposed by a Turkic-Turanian Muslim minority upon pre-existing traditions of social-economic organization, which the central power did little to change. The state, even at its strongest, never succeeded in entirely controlling many of the so-called 'tribal' peoples nominally under its suzerainty. Good examples come from Sind, where the state tried persuasion and the appointment of clan and tribal leaders to the appointment of large revenue assignments, military coercion and a policy of sedentarization, in order to bring the nomadic and semi-nomadic peoples more thoroughly under its control. It never succeeded, and there are examples from many other regions – not all of them so peripheral to the central power – which emphasize the problems.[54]

The vast bureaucracy, which administered the day-to-day running of the state's requirements, was largely independent of the emperors themselves. But this bureaucracy was in itself only partly made up of Muslims – from the middle of the seventeenth century over twenty-five per cent of the military-administrative establishment was of Hindu composition – and was no guarantee against either local separatism or fragmentation. And as we have seen, the majority of the state's agents or intermediaries in respect of tax and tax-assessment were members of entrenched local elites.[55]

It is precisely the relative ease with which peripheral districts could secede and change their allegiance – a factor of the essential superficiality of Mughal rule outside its core territories – that explains the rapid loss of central authority in the course of the latter years of the reign of Aurangzeb and the half-century that followed (c.1690–1750s). Most of the secessions which took place were relatively non-violent, since the Mughal rulers could do little to prevent them taking place.[56]

For the empire remained an empire of coercion, and in this respect it can be contrasted to a degree with the Ottoman state. The state represented, in effect, the surplus-appropriating activities of a small elite of officials and their households and retinues, imposed upon a basically unchanged pattern of rural cultivators and surplus appropriation, supervised through the *mansabdar* system. The pressing need to maintain a high yield from taxation, both to cover military expenditure and household and retinue costs and consumption, meant a constant need to maintain or increase the rate of surplus extraction. Some estimates suggest that in many regions this expropriation was so great that the producing population barely had enough for their subsistence, and sometimes was made absolutely destitute.[57] The power of the *jagirdars* and lesser *mansabdars* to increase the proportion of surplus demanded, which the *zamindars* or those in comparable positions then passed on down to the producing population itself, meant a sharp polarization between the small number of extremely wealthy state officers, even though they were regularly transferred from region to region, as we have seen, and both the ordinary rural populace and lesser elites. On the other hand, lower ranking *mansabdars* with small retinues were often unable to enforce their demands on local elites and *zamindars*. They therefore oppressed all the more those who could not resist and who had no local potentate to protect them. The weaker peasants, and sometimes whole communities, often fled as a result of this situation to the territories of those potentates who could provide a measure of protection, and resist imperial fiscal oppression. It is important to stress that this phenomenon applied as much to the lands of indigenous chieftains and princes as it did to those of the state's class of *mansabdars*, so that Habib's notion of an agrarian crisis brought about by a cycle of oppression and peasant flight from the lands of state assignees alone can no longer be regarded as representing the whole story.[58]

In spite of the ruthlessness of the revenue collection (communities which resisted were often razed or massacred, or enslaved) under powerful *mansabdars* and central government, it is clear that the state's ability to extract revenues and to enforce its authority depended on the balance of power between local and regional elites and the greater *mansabdars*, together with the ability of the latter to continue to maximize the extraction of surplus in order to maintain soldiers. The absence of any unifying ideological system, however, together with the systemic competition between the Mughal *mansabdar* elite and the indigenous elites, and the constant and oppressive demands upon the producers from both these groups, meant that the whole system was inherently unstable and riven with contradictions.[59]

The *raison d'être* of the Mughal domination came, as a result, to be identified with two elements. In the first place, the relative political stability and consequent economic expansion which affected both commercial and rural spheres[60] meant that the dynasty received a degree of passive acceptance, at least so long as these conditions prevailed. As I have pointed out above, the existence of the central authority with the demands generated by its institutional apparatus created the possibility for a whole range of political-economic relationships to evolve within the framework of Mughal power. Only when the vested interests of these two different, and potentially antagonistic, levels of resource control, surplus appropriation and redistribution, and social power come into clear conflict, does the tension in respect of access to resources become a serious contest. In the second place, conquest and expansion, and the possibility for both personal and imperial enrichment, represented a common interest for both Hindu and Muslim elites of all lands in state service, and lent a certain common political purpose to the otherwise fragmented and factional political and military ruling class.[61]

But the weakness of the central power was compounded by wasteful wars of succession. As former provinces dropped away, either to become independent or to be absorbed into competing formations (the Maratha empire in particular[62]), some of which were able to base their new strength precisely on those 'alternative' structures which had hitherto co-existed with those of the central state apparatuses, so Delhi was left with fewer and fewer territories from which to extract revenues and maintain an administration and an army. Many former territories remained technically part of the empire, owing a nominal allegiance to the emperors. But this meant little in practice, although its ideological importance, in respect of legitimating a particular ruler's authority, was, as I have mentioned, considerable. In 1739 however, the Persian ruler Nadir Shah, who had successfully destroyed the Safavi dynasty, took Punjab, Sind and Kabul, which left the empire with very little indeed. The sack of Delhi, and defeat at the hands of the Marathas in the 1740s and 1750s, left the Mughal rulers little more than the district of Delhi itself and a few local dependencies.

In spite of its collapse in the eighteenth century, however, and in spite of the structural weaknesses to which I have pointed – in particular, the inability of the central authority to establish a permanently-rooted local administration and bureaucracy in its provinces, which would carry state policies in respect of fiscal administration, regardless of the vagaries of central politics – the Mughal empire cannot be described as a state which failed. Neither in the sense that it broke down soon after its founder had died – it clearly did not – nor in the sense that it left no bureaucratic traces is it easily dismissed. Akbar's fiscal and administrative reforms, while they may not have been as carefully devised and planned as some historians have thought, and while they foundered on the rocks of both his successors' lack of concern and the vested interests of key groups in the ruling elite, did leave traces, which were clearly identifiable when the British seized formerly Mughal territories, especially in respect of local land- and tax-assessment, and the legendary 'just' rulers – in particular, Akbar himself – who were associated in local tradition with the principles upon which this administrative machinery was founded.[63] Nevertheless, the Mughal empire provides a very clear example of the way in which the history of states dominated by tributary relations of production is determined by the framework evolved locally in each social formation, or group of social formations, for the appropriation and distribution of surplus. Both the history of the relations between the Mughal state rulers and their agents, on the one hand, and of that between these agents and the indigenous ruling elites, on the other, is the history of the struggle for control of the appropriation, distribution and consumption of surplus wealth. Any political autonomy of action gained by rulers was clearly constrained by these characteristics.

3. Medieval Indian Alternatives: Vijayanagara

In the southern Indian region the various Muslim and Hindu states experienced much the same pattern of state formation and collapse. The most important of these from the fourteenth century until the middle of the seventeenth century was the Vijayanagara Hindu empire which dominated the southern Indian peninsula. But in spite of a central administrative seat (at the city of Vijayanagara itself) and the introduction by one ruler of a new mode of land and tax assessment during the early sixteenth century (although whether by centrally-appointed 'state' officials, or representatives of the local elites who had conceded their ultimate political-military authority to the Vijayanagara emperor, remains uncertain), it always remained a loose confederation of competing chieftaincies and commercial centres (on the coast), which appear to have remained internally relatively autonomous, owing only military service and certain other obligations to the emperors. As we have seen, this was to a degree a reflection of the geo-political and economic divisions which characterize the southern part of the sub-continent.[64]

Like empires in the North, the Vijayanagara empire was the result of military conquest and assimilation. It owed its existence initially to the fact that the first rulers were able successfully to oppose Muslim expansion southwards where previous confederacies and states had failed. But its armies came to include both Muslim and European mercenaries, and this inevitably meant an increased dependency of the ruler on cash and land with which to reward the services of these soldiers. As we shall see below, this placed the Vijayanagara emperor in a rather vulnerable position.

It was in addition ideologically reinforced by, and heavily dependent upon, the vast number of localized Hindu religious centres, with their complements of *brahmans* and devotees. For the ideological structures of Hindu society were a central pillar of the existence of the Vijayanagara empire. The temples and monastery-like seminaries had a high moral standing, and local sentiment and devotion was totally bound into the religious narratives and symbolic universe of Hinduism. Since deities could select as well as defend those whom they wished to worship them, the acceptance by monasteries and temples of Vijayanagara overlordship (in return for donations and grants of wealth in various forms) was a crucial step in the consolidation and maintenance of Vijayanagara power.

Larger states in the North had generally also been held together by direct coercive means as much as by any development of a permanent bureaucracy, and there is no reason to doubt that the role of religious centres and of ritual authority had been a significant element there, too. Indeed, most states which lasted more than a couple of generations appear to have evolved legitimating structures as rapidly as possible, centred on both the symbolic and ideological system of the conquerors as well as, at times, an effort to assimilate aspects of the traditional ideologies of the conquered populations. In the case of the Mughals, the tension between a dominant and imported Muslim elite and its Hindu territories always remained problematic, although visible efforts were made, as we have seen, to generate a more universalist ideology by Akbar. But in the context of South Indian geo-political and ecological divisions, the function of ritual incorporation within a common symbolic universe – or, to express it differently, the perception of divine acceptance and promotion of a specific political leadership, and the implications this had for the social praxis of elites in particular – took on an especial significance. I will return to this below.[65]

The empire developed only the most fragile bureaucracy or administrative apparatus to serve its needs, relying rather on traditional local organization – lineage chieftaincies and clan structures – under the supervision of regional lords, or *nayakas*, appointed to specific districts which they exploited directly and from which they drew the income to support their soldiers, retinues and households. Some of these were drawn from the traditional lineage elites, many were imported from other, more distant regions. In the core territories, such men owed their position to the Vijayanagara rulers; at a greater distance, however, local autonomy was the norm, even if the emperors were able to intervene militarily to coerce obedience or co-operation at times. The *nayakas* represented the rulers insofar as they owed them allegiance in return for the confirmation of their positions – their military power, as well as any traditional and hereditary rights and lands they may have held or obtained – an allegiance which, in its turn, reflected well on those who placed themselves under the protection of the Vijayanagara emperors, tied in as it was to the ideological networks of Hinduism and the temples. Many of the greater *nayakas* were often in effect independent rulers of their territories, certainly after the time of Krishnadevaraya (1509–29: see below).[66]

Like its predecessor, the Chola state, the Vijayanagara empire was structured as a series of concentric zones, focused around a political core. This central region was the source of immediate state or royal income, while the areas furthest away from the centre of military and political coercion were attached primarily through occasional military expeditions and by connections of a ritual nature. The royal rituals were centred on key religious centres and temples, through whose authority the rulers re-inforced their legitimacy and claims to overlordship, and in return for which they undertook to support such institutions through a variety of endowments, regular gifts in cash and in kind, grants of labour services, and so on. And it was precisely through involvement in such rituals that members of dominant social groups could be incorporated within what was, in effect, a network of royal and spiritual patronage. At the same time, they legitimated their own, more highly localized authority and power, so that the system as a whole served to legitimate a particular set of political institutions and power relations, and a set of social-economic relations: both the mode of surplus appropriation, in the general sense, and, particularly, the mode of surplus distribution.

The concept of 'ritual polity', intended to describe just these sorts of relationships, has been applied to a number of South Indian state formations in recent years. The Chola and Vijayanagara empires have been singled out in particular for detailed treatment. It should be stressed, however, that there is a danger in this approach of turning a specifically-structured system of social praxis, which reflects and maintains also a given symbolic universe, into an idealist notion of theocratic, 'Asiatic' stability, in which the rise and fall of states and power elites is determined by 'religion', and in which economic relationships are created by the demands of religious observance and beliefs or perceptions. In fact, it is clear that rulers were generally quite aware of the process of religious-political manipulation necessary to the maintenance of their power, and especially of the need to maintain control over resources in order to invest in this ritual system on a grand scale in order to continually legitimate their position. Power-relationships were, quite simply, expressed indirectly and through the mediation of a ritualized concept of *dharma* or 'righteousness', through which both divine support and earthly political legitimation, and therefore supremacy, were secured. It was the loss of the 'dharmic' authority which encouraged the re-location of ritual ties, a diminution in resources, and a consequent loss of political-military coercive power.

In this respect, it is important to remember that there are many other examples of states evolving a closely-integrated ritual and ideological identity with specific religious structures, a mutual identity of interests which benefited both parties by legitimating the secular authority in the eyes of the mass of believers and through which the spiritual authority usually received considerable advantages in respect of land, income from gifts and endowments, and so on. The Byzantine state provides an excellent example, especially from the eleventh century, when the state, that is, the rulers and their relatives, as well as members of all social classes, bestowed enormous amounts of wealth in a variety of forms upon monasteries in particular, to the extent that, in its final years, the empire relied upon the wealth of the Church and its organization to provide some of its military (as well as its spiritual) defences. It is perhaps significant that this relationship becomes especially apparent at a time when the empire begins to succumb, albeit gradually, to increasingly dangerous and threatening external pressures.

But the Vijayanagara empire represented one modality of what has been referred to as the 'segmentary state', a constantly shifting pattern of principalities and internal coalitions under the notional hegemony of an initial military conqueror, whose power was maintained through a balanced combination of military coercion and fiscal demands, and ritual domination. Only during the reign of Krishnadevaraya, which lasted until his death in 1529, was there any attempt at military and administrative centralization, a policy which, while later abandoned by his successors, nevertheless introduced important changes into the political structure and power-relationships at the regional and local levels. Krishnadevaraya established fortresses manned by troops under *brahman* commanders (who had no local ties, and depended therefore entirely upon the ruler for their authority) throughout the central core of his territories, primarily in order to contain the independent power of the local chiefs. At the same time a new stratum of lesser chiefs – the 'poligars' of later British parlance – whose power again derived entirely from royal delegation of military service, was brought into prominence as guardians of forts and suppliers of infantry soldiers at the local level. Over the whole system he placed trusted military commanders – *nayakas* – who represented his authority in the regions around the central core, collecting revenue and tribute, and forwarding a portion of it (although the evidence shows that it was often only a very small portion) to the ruler. These new, powerful royal representatives replaced the rulers of the sub-states and chiefly territories who had originally been merely tributary to Vijayanagara, but whose territories were now to be incorporated under state control in a more thoroughgoing way.

The great power of the new *nayakas*, however, and the internecine strife over the succession after the death of Krishnadevaraya, soon returned the situation to what it had been before his reforms, but with a new ruling stratum now in a position to compete with representatives of the older elites. The rulers retained only the most superficial authority over the *nayakas*, who were in several cases able to establish more-or-less independent sub-states under nominal Vijayanagara suzerainty. Even at its apogee, the Vijayanagara state remained a confederation united by the threat of central coercion, the personal ties of loyalty between rulers and *nayakas*, and by the transformations in local social and economic relationships promoted by the emperors from the time of Krishnadevaraya on. The imposition of outsiders on regional or district rulers interrupted to a degree the pattern of traditional clan and lineage structures in respect of power-relationships by inserting a second focus of surplus appropriation and distribution. In spite of both military and ideological pressures, however, the older, traditional clan and lineage elites, with their rulers and chiefs, were never properly subordinated to the Vijayanagara royal establishment. The centre could assure a surplus, therefore, chiefly in an indirect way, in the form of military service and political co-operation from its subordinated confederates, apart from that which could be extracted from the core territories, where even here local lineage elites proved difficult to contain. In this respect, the crucial role which the Vijayanagara rulers attributed to ritual and to perceptions of their symbolic function as paramount representatives of dharmic power can readily be understood, particularly in view of the ways in which this 'transactional' network of ritual observance involved necessarily a considerable transfer of wealth from the local rulers, whether royal representatives or semi-independent sub-rulers, to the temples and other religious foundations which gave their support to the emperors' rule. The ideological structure and its accompanying practices represented, in effect, a medium for the redistribution of surplus wealth to the advantage of the central political elite.

For one of the binding elements which held the Vijayanagara state together was the common efforts of both local chieftains and lineage elites as well as kings to loosen their ties with the communal (lineage, community-bound) foundations of their power, an aim achieved partly through seeking ratification and ritual legitimation for their position with a higher authority – in this case, the Vijayanagaran kings – and partly through economic means, through trading alliances with merchant groups established in commercial centres, hence providing themselves with an income independent of their lineage and community roots and the relations of production which these represented.

The role of revenue-farming needs especially to be emphasized, since many traders were involved, hence promoting a more rapid conversion of agricultural products into a commercial form than would otherwise have been the case. Several scholars have recently argued for the positive role of tax-farmers in this respect, and I have also pointed out that – contrary to the traditional picture of such persons as universally grasping and oppressive (partly a reflection of sources originating among a literate state elite) – they were often very aware of their vested interest in not over-exploiting a long-term resource, and indeed acted as a positive stimulus to certain types of rural production, particularly where a ready outlet to a commercial market was thereby made available.

Surplus wealth appropriated from the primary producers was thus also redistributed through the considerable investment in consumable luxury goods, conspicuous display and ritual expeditions through which dominant elites affirmed their cultural, economic and political position and legitimacy, thus supplying the means of existence for a large stratum of artisans and merchants. Town and market centres were thus also centres of petty commodity production, while further investment in non-local, long-distance trade stimulated the integration of dominant lineage elites into the network of market exchange relationships. And the existence of such external trade, and the demand for the goods it brought, eased the way to the annexation of this trade by more powerful (European) trading and commodity-producing interests.

Class divisions existed within lineage organization, of course, a point referred to already in connection with Merovingian society; but these externalized economic relationships increased the possibility for lineage elites to consolidate their economic position as appropriators of surplus from the members of their own lineage groups, and at the same time offered them an economic base unconnected with these social-ideological structures. Just as the *zamindar* elites of the Mughal lands tried to safeguard their local political and economic independence, while at the same time using their function in the interstices of Mughal fiscal administration to consolidate their own position as exploiters of rural producers, so the elites of South India used the opportunities provided both by the existence of a higher-order political authority and by local commercial activities to establish themselves on a more secure and permanent basis as a class, in the technical, political economy sense of the term, differentiated from others both economically and ideologically.

These features, especially from the sixteenth century and the appearance of European traders, represent also the beginnings of a much more widespread shift in the relations between commercial centres, their hinterlands and external markets, which I do not have time to go into here. But they clearly had important results for the social relations of production of rural society, and in particular for the town–country nexus, with all the consequences which followed for the nature and effectiveness of state power and the relationship between the local and centralized elites and the producing population.[67]

The rise of the Vijayanagara empire in the fourteenth century and its fragmentation and collapse through the later sixteenth and early seventeenth centuries represent not the failures of a corrupt central government or an incompetent bureaucracy, for every district had by long tradition a local, village-based administration, which could serve both distant state centres as well as more local foci of power. It reflected rather the vagaries of military alliances, political gain and ideological identity, together with the highly localized nature of lineage-based power-holding and rent-taking. It was this latter feature, which meant that relations of production were only affected at the local level (the role of elites), that is particularly significant. For while these elites received enhanced status through association with the state, they were also enabled to evolve a role more independent of local society. With the economic advantages bestowed upon them by involvement in trade and commercial investment, not only were the bonds that tied them into the web of relations of production which had generated them in the first place relaxed, but they were also able to become politically and economically less dependent upon the state which had promoted their interests in the first place. The easy detachment of Vijayanagaran chieftaincies and principalities, which the period of 'decline' actually represents, makes this much clear. As Stein has emphasized, and in spite of accusations of exaggerating the strength of the ritual and ideological elements in Vijayanagara power, even at its height the empire was only united in the loosest sense and centralized only very incompletely.

It is worth emphasizing that the implications of such an assessment are to support the view that it was not simply the arrival of European commerce and investment, or military technology and organization, which caused these transformational shifts, although they certainly exacerbated their effect and dynamically affected the structures of social and economic relationships with which they came into contact. Equally, and as Stein's analysis implies, it is to argue that the static model of a 'segmentary' state needs to be modified very considerably in this context (at least) to account for both internal tensions and the resolution of structural antagonisms and contradictions. The relationships I have sketched out clearly represent an 'emergent', or dialectical, process of historical change.[68]

There is an additional factor, however. The ideological structures of Hinduism, and its contingent social practices, which marked every aspect of Hindu social and political life across the whole subcontinent, tended under certain conditions to render the functions normally assumed and required of any state structure, especially those of maintaining order and internal cohesion, dangerously redundant. If we assume that states provide both centralized authority and, more importantly, normative rules for legal, social and economic relationships, then it becomes clear that in the Hindu context these characteristics of state organization are already present in the internal order of religious and social life – the lineage structures and caste attributions alone provide for much of this. Following the literature which has dwelt on this aspect, Mann has recently summed up some of these features as the 'intense ritual penetration of everyday life', although we must constantly bear in mind that such 'ritual' consists in social praxis, not simply in ideas or attitudes, and was itself constitutive of, and reproduced by, social reproductive practice and, to a degree, the social relations of production. And this may have contributed also to the relative failure of state systems to embed themselves in Indian social formations.

Here, I would make two observations. In the first place, it seems to me that it is less the fact that such interactional networks exist that is important, than determining the role they play: in South Indian society, such ritualized networks functioned also as networks of distribution and redistribution of surplus wealth, organized in favour of a particular centre at a given moment. But in the second place it would not be unreasonable to argue that the 'ritual penetration' of a society in respect of specific sets of social practices, which are themselves the expression of the structure of social relations of production, is common to all pre-capitalist social formations. It is not necessarily these particular practices, however, which have come to be the dominant expression of relations of production in all societies – as Godelier has pointed out, each social-cultural formation represents these economic relations in different forms, the location and origins of which must be the subject of specific empirical analysis. In the case of South Indian cultures and their dominant symbolic universe, it was the particular combination of a specific ecological context, kinship structure and religious configuration which promoted the unique importance and centrality of these ritual, transactional networks. But this importance was crucially enhanced by the political demands of state centres and rulers in respect of control over surplus distribution. For, as we have seen in chapter 4, states which are unable to maintain adequate direct control and participation in the process of primary surplus distribution (through direct taxation, for example) must attempt to survive by promoting their interests through alternative, secondary means of surplus re-distribution. Such means include the devolution of military and other authority, for example, to the level of the fief or an equivalent institution, or – as in the South Indian case here under discussion – through transactional networks of redistribution reinforced and operated through primarily religious structures.

Of course, both Islamic and Christian rulers in East and West legitimated the extraction and distribution of surplus – which is to say, in effect, the continued existence of their respective states – through political theologies, ideologies which highlighted the necessary duty of the state and its rulers to defend the faith and to promote the variety of associated activities which this entailed. At the same time, they had to be seen to re-inforce and re-affirm their particular symbolic universe through ritualized expressions of faith and the redistribution of considerable amounts of surplus wealth to religious foundations of various types, or through certain ideologically legitimating ritual actions. In the Byzantine world, the complex ceremonial of the imperial palace, the detailed hierarchy of ranks and offices, and the daily acting-out of rituals designed expressly to recall and to imitate the harmony and peace of the heavenly order were all fundamental expressions of the symbolic order. The close relationship between the emperor (with the state) and the Church, and the supervision by the Church of popular beliefs and kinship structures, for example, created an equally impressive ideological and symbolic system of legitimation. Yet, in this particular historical formation, and in contrast with the South Indian examples, it did not itself express also, or serve as, a key institution of surplus distribution necessary to the economic survival of the state institution. Similar networks can be seen in the Islamic world, in western Christendom, and in the Chinese empire. And in the case of both Christianity and

Islam, ritual incorporation (that is to say, conversion) served as a fundamental tool of political integration and domination. The 'segmentary' states of South and Central America provide closer parallels to the South Indian case, for here temple-centred redistribution of surplus and tribute was a crucial means through which surplus appropriation and political authority were maintained.

In short, therefore, it is the specific context and history of the South Indian region which lends to the transactional networks of ritualized surplus redistribution, and the political relationships which they reflect, their particular structural importance.[69]

The cultural-ideological domination of the brahmanic tradition, with its accompanying network of devotional, educational, legal and socio-economic functions, meant that for the mass of the population of the sub-continent (except for those who converted to Islam in the aftermath of the Turkic invasions of the eleventh and twelfth centuries and the establishment of the Sultanate of Delhi) civil order, justice and social equilibrium could be guaranteed up to a point without a secular authority. Centralized state power was enhanced when local magnates or regional potentates conflicted and generated destructive and economically disruptive wars. Powerful secular rulers could end or prevent this. But the combination of Hindu religious structures and organizational principles, with the ramified networks of lineage identities and the associated practices, meant that the state remained, for the most part, a structure of local and regional elites, kept together by a process of coercion, symbolically-derived status advantages, and externally validated narratives of authority and access to power and wealth. In this sense, it rarely, if at all, put down roots in society. Even where not all these elements were present to the same degree, the general tendency remains the same. In South Indian states, therefore, the relationships expressed through the ritual and religious institutions and accompanying practices, while also acting as means of expression of a perceived cosmic order, functioned also, crucially, as relations of surplus redistribution and of the distribution of political and economic power. As one commentator has noted, 'The concept of the ritual polity thus focuses attention directly on the intermediate and local levels of power, and calls for a clearer understanding of productive and distributive processes that supported a class society.'[70]

After an initial period of military conquest and coercion, it was thus a complex and dynamic interaction between ideological perceptions and the concomitant social practice, on the one hand, with the perceived economic interests – the class interests, in the political economy sense – of local elites, on the other hand, which made the Vijayanagara state possible and which, of course – once a certain stage in the evolution of the resultant economic and social relationships had been reached – promoted its fragmentation. This was not, of course, the result of deliberate long-term strategies. What it does represent is what Runciman, for example, would call a process of 'competitive selection' and 'role recombination' in social praxis. In this case, that process was one in which the struggle of particular elites to maintain or extend their control over the means of production and distribution, by increasing their share of the social wealth produced through rural production and by greater participation in local and longer-distance market activities, constitutes a fundamental element.[71] Once more, it is clear that the causally central moments in the evolution of the Vijayanagara power are to be located around the specific forms taken by the localized structures of production relations and, specifically, the mode of distribution of surplus wealth. When the complex system of clan alliances upon which Vijayanagara military and political pre-eminence depended began to fragment, the rulers were unable to realize the surplus they had hitherto received, whether in tribute and tax, on the one hand, or in military service and political gifts, on the other. Just as significantly, however, they were unable to invest to the same degree as hitherto in religious foundations and in maintaining the ritual network so central to the continued legitimation and reproduction of their power ideologically. Competition for dominance had, indeed, already begun within the Vijayanagara empire in the 1530s – a point which Stein emphasizes, since it reveals both the politically segmented nature of this state, and the importance of ritual networks as the key to political-ideological unity and coherence.[72]

4. Indian 'Feudalism' and the State

I have hardly been able to do justice to these examples of Indian state formation, either in respect of the recent literature on the themes discussed here, or in terms of the enormous complexity of the developments and transformations which took place during and before the period from which I have drawn my examples. Not only changing economic situations – in particular, the development from the sixteenth century of a considerable international trade and commerce, wider-ranging still than the network of well-developed trade relations which was already in existence – but the complex history of the modes of agrarian exploitation, need to be detailed more precisely in order to provide more than a superficial account. In addition, the qualitative changes in the relation between 'state' centre(s), towns and centres of commerce, and rural peasantry, particularly as different states attempted to introduce centrally-controlled fiscal structures at the regional level (although the success of such initiatives has hardly begun to be explored, especially in the South), all contributed towards increased economic differentiation within villages and localities, and consequently increased the possibility for the state to intervene in local affairs. And it is at this point that the non-specialist meets certain problems in respect of the historiographical tradition. Stein, for example, who has made an extremely important contribution to the history of southern Indian political and social development, has tended to reduce the influence of the state at local level almost to nothing, seeing it chiefly in terms of ritual power networks between kings, local dominant lineages and brahmanic centres. In contrast, and as has been pointed out before, historians concerned with the North have tended to ignore this level of social organization, concentrating instead on the Mughal state and its centralizing, political apparatuses at the expense of regional intermediaries.[73] Neither approach is, of course, mutually exclusive, and, indeed, they reflect the nature of the sources employed, or available, as much as any pre-existing intellectual traditions. Ultimately, it must be a question of seeing how these structures interact dynamically in time across the whole sub-continent, rather than limited parts, and how they generate different results, according to their respective geo-political contexts. From this point of view, of course, the qualitative differences between southern and northern states, and between these and the central region of the Deccan and Maharashtra, deserve to be contextualized in order to avoid the all too common particularization of 'India' into an abnormal phenomenon, uniquely different from all other state and social formations. As I hope this brief account will have shown, the differences between Indian and non-Indian states – between Ottoman and Mughal empires, for example, or between the particular functional roles of a given set of social and ideological practices (the 'ritual' transactional networks of South Indian states, for example) – reflect historically-determined political-economic and socio-cultural trajectories, and both are fully susceptible to analysis.[74]

Certain key features of Indian state formation can be emphasized.

In particular, it seems that the 'caste' system (to use the term once again in its crudest and least specific sense) cannot stand alone as an explanation for the supposedly static nature of Indian social relations of production – while they remained extremely stable, they were never static. And, as Stein and many others have now shown for both North and South, it is important to contextualize the dynamic and changing pattern of relations between rural society, commercial centres, local chieftains (whether or not we see them as 'peasant chieftains', following Stein, or as members of localized dominant elites – the *zamindars* in the North, for example – and thus admit a differentiation of class), dominant lineages, and major centres of royal power, over a period of more than a thousand years. Last, but by no means least, geography played a crucial role in determining the course of, and potential for, large-scale state-building. The plains of the Indus and Ganga rivers form a great arc across the northernmost third of the sub-continent, a zone which, while much more arid at its western edge than in the centre and East, has few substantial internal divisions and forms – as the historical record testifies – a geo-political whole. Central India, the Deccan and the southern section of the sub-continent represent a clearly contrasting region, consisting of a series of hills, plateaux and valleys, interrupted by a number of riverine and coastal plains, and making up a much greater number of distinct and divergent geo-political units and sub-units. These features must be taken into account in any discussion of the historical differences in state formation and organization between the North, on the one hand, and the central and southern regions, on the other.

On the question of tributary relations of production (or 'feudalism') in the Indian context, about which so much has been written, I should like to make two basic points.

In the first place, I have defined the tributary mode of production in chapter 3 not in terms of political relations of distribution or social hierarchies and legal structures, but in terms of the mode of surplus appropriation which characterizes pre-industrial agrarian class society, that is to say, a society in which peasant producers in direct possession of their means of production are compelled through non-economic coercion to surrender a portion of their produce in the form of tax or rent. This is to argue for tributary production relations as a macro-historical category (or, in Perlin's terms, a macro-logical category), its value being (as with 'capitalist production relations') to home in on the fundamental organizational principles of the mode in its infinite historical and geographical variety, but without – as I hope I have made clear – insisting upon any necessary similarity or comparability of the phenomenal forms through which these principles are given expression. By these means it becomes possible to examine the empirical data from a given epoch or society and do more than merely describe the phenomena represented in the sources, whether literary, for example, or archaeological in character. It becomes possible to use the heuristic construct of mode of production and, more particularly, the specific defining characteristics of each mode (mode of surplus appropriation, mode of combination of producers with the means of production, mode of surplus distribution) as a means of testing hypotheses relating to causal relationships and the structures underlying or giving form to the phenomena represented and refracted through the sources, without resorting to *ad hoc* empiricist hypotheses. And crucially, the application of the concept of mode of production impels us to look for complexity in historical social formations – other forms of production relations may exist in addition to those characterized by, for example, tributary relations, and it will depend upon whether or not the social formation as a whole is dominated by one or another set of such production relations as to whether it can be said broadly to represent one mode or another. In fact, it would seem that most class societies contain elements of at least one other mode of production, and that these modes generally overlap in their economic and social effects. It is the analysis of the ways in which they overlap, and the contradictions and antagonisms which such overlapping generates, which gives each specific social formation its particular appearance and constitution; and it is the analysis of these antagonisms, and their expression, which constitutes one of the tasks of the historian in examining a given society.

Modes of production, therefore, do not descriptively specify particular types of social formation, a point I have already stressed at length in chapters 2 and 3, and they cannot, in consequence, be constrained by concrete historical realities such as political boundaries. They provide a heuristic and analytical conceptual framework within which we can come to grips with the causal and integrational relationships which give colour and texture to the historically-given forms presented by, or perceived through, the material that modern historians have constituted as evidence. Finally, they furnish us with concepts designed to reveal the dynamic and changing pattern of social structure in space and time, as the individuals constituted by their socio-culturally determined conditions of existence reconstitute and reproduce those conditions through the dialectic of social reproductive practice.

In the second place, there seems to me little doubt that, on the basis of their production relations, Indian socio-cultural formations in both North and South India can be apprehended through the concept of the tributary mode, throughout the medieval and early modern period, and indeed well before. All the crucial elements are present. What has complicated matters has been the ways in which the lineage/caste system functions at the level of village community and the regulation of production relations, and the problem of dealing with the centralized 'Asiatic' state. Since it does not appear to be like western European feudalism at the level of political forms, Indian society is assumed by many, therefore, not to have been feudal. Once again, two incommensurable descriptive systems are compared and, logically enough, the result is that one of them is found to be inadequate.

As I have pointed out in chapters 2 and 3 above, this is not a particularly logical or fruitful way to approach the problem. To a large degree, the discussion has been obfuscated by different applications of the term 'feudalism', a point I have already stressed, and which has been made by others before. Those who criticize Marxist approaches, for example, do so not on the grounds that socio-economic relationships as defined by historical materialist research did not prevail, but because the political-juridical relations of power do not correspond with those of 'classic' feudal societies: where there are no bonds of vassalage, formal enfeoffment, and tied peasant or serf populations, there can be no feudalism. This is, of course, wilfully to confuse two quite separate sets of criteria. The same confusion exists among Marxists, too, as we have seen in chapters 2 and 3 above.[75] From the historical materialist context a political economy definition of 'relations of production' and their articulation with 'the forces of production' (a combination which is characterized in the case of each mode by a specific mode of surplus appropriation and a particular set of possibilities for the distribution of that surplus) as the central criteria upon which analysis should be founded seems much more useful than one based on political forms – which will be different in most respects in every state, whatever the supposed or actual structural similarities between them. Political forms are less clearly useful for generating an analysis which is more than merely descriptive, than are relations of production in the wider sense.

The question of the role of urban centres and trade has also played a significant role in the discussion, and since I have so far said relatively little in this respect, it will be worth dwelling on the issue for a moment. Stein, for example, is reluctant to concede the existence of tributary relations of production in India (in the context of his discussion referred to always as feudalism) on the grounds that urban-based trade, commerce and commodity-production were relatively well-developed at various times, and represent forces economically antagonistic to a feudal context.[76] But this is to ignore the total context in which they are thought to possess any transformative power, and, more importantly, to ignore the possibility that potentially contradictory production relations might co-exist in a state of tension for some considerable time before any conflict or real antagonism forces shifts in the patterns of social relationships to the ultimate advantage of one set or the other. What made a difference in the western European case – where urban centres clearly did play a role in the dissolution of feudal relations of production over the long term – was the particular context and evolutionary form of European feudal and state structures, in which the peculiar nuances of the relations between lords, urban centres and markets, and kingly authority, in the context of both economic expansion and certain technological changes, wrought a whole series of complex changes in the practices which expressed the social relations of production. This is in no way to imply that European developments were bound to produce sets of relationships within which the possibilities for the development of capitalist relations were inscribed, nor to suggest that Europe was in some way uniquely different, qualitatively, in the nature of its social relations of production. It is merely to re-inforce Marx's point, that the same underlying sets of economic relations will be expressed through an infinite variety of forms according to different historical or geographical circumstances. In particular, this is not to deny that capitalist relations of production would have developed elsewhere. But the simple fact that they developed in one place first qualitatively alters the ways in which they might then evolve in other social formations.[77]

Tributary relations of production can in fact only be transformed or replaced by capitalist relations of production when there takes place a proletarianization of the peasantry, that is, when a large proportion of the producing population is separated from their means of production, hence creating a free and available supply of labour which can then be exploited within capitalist production relations.

A concentration of money, or wealth in other forms (such as credit instruments, for example), in the hands of merchants, together with petty commodity production in both villages and towns, and long-distance trade, does not by itself lead to capitalist relations or indeed the break-up of feudal relations of production. The 'capital' available to merchants and traders is always only potentially capital, insofar as, without a proletariat whose labour-power can be transformed into relative surplus value, it functions merely as a medium of simple exchange.[78] This is apparent when we consider the situation in western Europe until the fourteenth and fifteenth centuries, when it was only with the discovery of the New World and the opening up of the African and South Asian littorals and their hinterlands to European merchant activity that a major discrepancy between the wealth generated by feudal production relations, and that produced by long-distance mercantile exchange, developed. Even then it is important to note that, up to the sixteenth and seventeenth centuries (and later in many areas), long-distance trade was itself of a highly traditional type – as Amin expresses it, it brought into contact social formations that were mutually ignorant of one another, exchanging products the costs of production of which were not known in the society to which they were delivered.[79] Where those social labour costs were unequal, one society is in effect benefiting from the transfer to it of surplus produced in the other. This relationship characterizes European trade with Asia and Africa in the later medieval and early modern periods. And it is only when the visible profits from commerce make goods available in such a way that the dominant class had to increase its surplus (both in order to compare economically and politically with the newly powerful merchant elite, and to invest itself in such commerce) that it began to invest in market-orientated agricultural production or stock-raising, reducing the size of the rural population that the land had to support directly in order to maximize its revenues from this source. In other words, the break-up of tributary production relations hinges on a particular conjuncture in western European social, economic and cultural history, when the traditional mode of surplus appropriation could no longer render the surplus necessary for the traditional ruling class to compete with a rising mercantile elite. And it was in just this context that the towns of western medieval Europe could play such a key role, since the particular institutional evolution of tributary relations of production and mode of surplus appropriation (which we can refer to in their specific and local form as feudal) in this region had excluded urban centres from any structurally necessary economic role. As a result, they had much greater economic and political autonomy, albeit threatened in various areas by centralizing rulers in the twelfth and thirteenth centuries in particular. Their role as centres of independent merchant activity meant that, as peasants evicted or fleeing from their landlords estates took refuge there, they formed a labour force which the merchants and artisans of the towns could exploit, so that commodity production and wage-labour flourished.[80] Combined with the newly-discovered Atlantic trade and its world-wide extensions in the sixteenth century and after, trading activity underwent a qualitative transformation, and the flow of increased wealth into the old feudal societies began decisively to affect the balance between old and new forms of wealth and power. Landlords needed money to compete and to remain economically and politically viable in the changing circumstances; capitalist agriculture, producing through wage labour for a market in agricultural commodities, hastened the process as a whole.

The story is too well-known to bear repeating here. But it is worth emphasizing once more that the break-up of the particular form of tributary relations of production which had evolved in the West, feudalism, was not simply a result of either the existence of towns and merchants, or long-distance trade, or both. It was the result of a particular historical configuration of tributary production relations over a particular period. And, as is generally admitted, once dominant in the West, capitalism was exported through the imperialist demands which the process of primary accumulation sets in motion in the context of a potential world market, to influence and re-direct the evolution of all other social formations, whatever the form their particular combination of modes of production actually took.

Now it is clear that in neither the Mughal nor the Vijayanagara empires (nor, for that matter, in the Ottoman world), where long-distance trade occupied an important, if by no means dominant, role in surplus appropriation and accumulation, did this 'window' ever open. Partly, this was because expansionist European traders arrived in time to dominate Asian trade and to invert the pre-existing relations of commercial exploitation between the Indian sub-continent and its periphery. In addition, the different ways in which the institutional forms of tributary relations were structured in India – in particular, the self-contained and semi-autonomous nature of rural production relations, the integration of merchant and trading groups into a balanced set of social relationships through lineage identities and demands – are central elements in this picture. There may well have been high levels of exchange and of petty commodity production, to the extent that members of some regional elites were largely dependent upon particular commercial relationships for their wealth. But I would argue that the existence of money is in itself not to be equated with capital, nor the existence of commodity exchange and petty commodity production to be taken as a sign of capitalist relations of production. Indeed, one could argue that just as western European tributary relations of production – feudalism – were characterized by particular institutional forms – vassalage, the fief, parcellization of sovereignty, and so forth, institutions which were peculiar to its own historical antecedents and evolutionary trajectories, which expressed primarily the mode of distribution of surplus – so Indian tributary relations of production are characterized similarly: only here these characteristics or typical forms, through which the social relations of production were represented, are to be located in the particular ways in which lineage structures – caste – on the one hand, and urban centres, on the other, served to express some facets of the mode of surplus appropriation and surplus distribution.

The debate in respect of Indian 'feudal' relations has been helpfully polarized in recent years around two key questions: how did states form and reproduce themselves? And how did the different elements (village, temple, town, bureaucracy, assigned revenue-holder, king and court) articulate together to produce the 'typical' Indian state and social system?

An especially problematic area has been that of Indian particularism (not unencouraged by Marx himself). This resulted partly from the fact that the incorporative ideologies of localized lineage-groups, on the one hand, or property-exploitation groups on the other, have masked the actual economic class differences (that is, the differential relationships of members of different caste [*jati*/lineage] groups to the means of production) between and within them, giving the impression of a more or less classless rural society, which in the absence of a strong centralized state effectively ran its own affairs, and in the presence of the latter needed no intermediaries to function on its behalf in respect of the channelling of resources from the tax-base to the state and its apparatus (and with towns perceived as a further 'external' factor). These attitudes apply to both North and South, although it is most clear in the historiography of the South. It has served both to obfuscate similarities between these regions, and within them, and has also led to an exaggeratedly optimistic view of the efficiency of, for example, Mughal rule in the North.[81]

While it is certainly true that castes were internally self-regulating in respect of a wide range of activities – economic, social and juridical – it is equally clear that members of dominant castes could and did 'exploit', in the political economy sense, the activities of members of other, subordinate, castes, as well as members of their own caste or lineage group who, naturally, did not in the great majority of cases share the same economic and social fortunes as those at the top of the social pyramid. Whether this was a question of an internal hierarchical ordering of sub-castes or of the dominant position of individual members of dominant lineages who attained local power – such as district rajas and regional maharajas – does not matter at this level of abstraction. It is also clear that in much of India, the *zamindars* or most important members of dominant sub-castes and castes (in the North) and the *nayakas* and regional chiefs in the South (all those, in other words, who had hereditary rights to positions through which they could dominate local relations of surplus distribution to a greater or lesser degree) held very great power, and all behaved as, and were effectively treated and regarded as, regular landlords in respect of their (often hereditarily fixed) rights to a portion of the agricultural produce which during the later seventeenth and eighteenth centuries in the North came to be associated with rents and established rights over the land itself and its occupants. But even where juridically-defined property in land was absent, customary rights to appropriate produce through coercion (whether enshrined in legal and/or customary form, or through physical violence) were universal. On these criteria alone, and in spite of enormous local variation, it seems reasonable to speak of tributary relations of production as dominant in Indian society until very recently.[82]

This is not to deny, either, the 'communal' elements of Indian lineage or caste organization in respect of the production and distribution of surplus, so that while we may speak of the dominance of tributary relations of production, we can admit that the forms which expressed those relationships were often institutionally a legacy of a 'lineage mode' which may, indeed, have preserved a considerable degree of integrity at the basic level of peasant production, at least in respect of labour techniques and task allocation, and particularly of the distribution of the means of subsistence within the community of producers. But it functioned under, and was subordinated to, the greater economic and coercive potential of tributary relations of appropriation and distribution. It seems quite possible, therefore, given these elements, to see in Indian society the co-existence and articulation of both a lineage mode of distribution of the means of subsistence, and a tributary mode of surplus appropriation and distribution, a symbiosis which lends to Indian social formations their particular configuration and appearance.

In the foregoing, I have attempted to survey two Indian state formations very briefly from a comparative point of view, using the tributary mode as a basic framework for the delineation of key structures common to both Indian and other state forms. In particular, the relationship between state elites or rulers and dominant economic classes as mediated through the mode of surplus distribution has been of importance. While the specificities of Indian social forms cannot be ignored, they should not detract from an effort to generalize and to look for causal relationships found elsewhere.

Thus it is quite clear that an analysis of the formation and evolution of the Ottoman state provides a number of parallels with the history of the Mughal state, and that, in the context of their very different social formations, both were subject to similar structural limitations on the extension and maintenance of state power. This was a reflection of several factors that have to be considered together: their common Turco-Turanian, and more particularly their Islamic, background, with a shared institutional and military tradition; the struggle of a ruling class or dynasty to maintain its authority through coercion, on the one hand, and fiscal and legal structures, on the other; the problems faced by all territorial states in efficiently allocating yet maintaining control over resources; and the problem of generating and maintaining a unifying, hegemonic ideological system which would substantivize state authority and foundation myths, thus serving both to legitimate the position of the ruling dynasty and to represent opposition to that rule as deviant. In this respect it is clear that the Indian context created greater difficulties for conquerors or state-founders, although the relative success of the Mughals, in spite of the comparatively short-lived period of their real hegemony (some one hundred and fifty years), was considerable.

The point of these examples has been to suggest that military expansion and conquest, whether or not in conjunction with subordinate but semi-independent sub-rulers, princes or magnates, and even with the support of the established religious-political system, are not sufficient to maintain the dominance or hegemony of a ruler and his armies, except through frequent coercive measures which, inevitably, can only be effectively carried out over limited areas at a time and for limited periods, activities which in turn set up a cycle of demand for and consumption of surplus. This is exacerbated when the state in question is merely one of a number of competing formations which may be in a more-or-less constant state of war – the South Indian examples are particularly illustrative in this respect. Only with a process of administrative-structural 'embedding' of state machinery in society can this be achieved. States where formalized, self-reproducing bureaucratic-administrative apparatuses exist, or are established, and where the fiscal-administrative machinery of the state directly intervenes in the process of surplus appropriation and distribution – hence affecting, or at least able to affect, the forms of the relations of production – such states have a much greater chance of surviving for a longer time. This may reflect also the existence of a political-ideological system which identifies the key values of the culture as a whole in terms of its own moral-ethical structures, and identifies the continued existence of this symbolic universe with the continued existence and preservation of the state. The example of Hinduism, in which the notion of a centralized state could become more or less functionally irrelevant, demonstrates the fundamental importance for an understanding of social praxis and political structures, on the one hand, and on the other the dialectic between praxis and ideology, of the ways in which the world was (and is) perceived and acted upon.

The universal problem faced by all states is that of the control of resources. But whether states are able to develop bureaucratic means of doing this, or whether rulers come to rely on the loyalty of individuals to the throne or the person of the ruler, in administrating such resources, the problem of supervising or controlling such agents inevitably arises. Given the pre-industrial levels of communications, transport and surveillance at their disposal, tributary states were confronted both with the need effectively to control their producing populations, and ensure the effective appropriation of surplus to reproduce their apparatus. The inherent contradiction between the need for the state to collect its revenues directly, and the inevitable process of delegation and the competition over surplus offered by dominant social-economic elites (the ruling class, in other words, in whose interests the state at one level functioned and was reproduced), renders the nature of the limits on state autonomy fairly clear.

How autonomous can tributary states as centres of political power actually be, therefore, in respect of the interests of their bureaucratic apparatuses, and of dominant socio-economic elements within the different social and cultural regions of the state territories?

The examples I have cited in this chapter seem to permit only one conclusion: even under the most ruthlessly efficient pre-modern state regimes, state political power was necessarily limited by the constraints of social and economic structure in its ecological and geographical context. In particular, and as we have already said, states (by which I mean here either rulers and their immediate entourage, or state elites on a wider basis) must either directly implement the appropriation and distribution of surplus wealth, or appoint agents of one sort or another to accomplish this on their behalf. In pre-industrial societies there is no alternative to this, and this process brings them into potential conflict both with the producers, and with aristocracies, or the group of agents or intermediaries, established or selected by the state for this purpose. The latter constitutes an element which, by virtue of its position, either within society outside the state centre, or within the state apparatus itself, can be transformed into a major competitor for control of resources, competition manifested in struggles over the appropriation and, politically, the distribution and redistribution of surplus wealth. Constraints on state power (and autonomy) are therefore determined both by the limits of exploitation of pre-capitalist rural production (which is obvious), and, more importantly, by the nature of the social and political relations of distribution of surplus. The issue of control over the collection and distribution of surplus (which does not affect the mode of surplus appropriation of that surplus) was, therefore, crucial. It determined both the political relationships (power relations) within states and those pertaining between states and the ruling class, as well as the possibility for states to act independently of the interests of such a ruling class. But it was in its turn overdetermined in its effects by the inflections of each specific state and social formation, and the institutions, both social and administrative, which evolved.

For short periods, most rulers, or ruling elites, can exercise a degree of political autonomy independent of the social interests of otherwise powerful social-economic classes, whatever the institutional form such classes may have taken in any given society. But, as these examples appear to suggest, such periods depend upon a very particular combination of political-military-ideological circumstances, which are themselves configured by the specific forms of the relations of production in a particular society. Not directly, of course (or at least, not necessarily so), nor obviously or visibly, either to contemporaries or to the modern observer. And this would suggest that, as I have mentioned already, the level of analysis at which Mann operates, for example, and at which his heuristically and descriptively insightful categories of power and power distribution are invoked, is more profitably employed when fitted into a basic limiting framework of possibilities already established by the social relations of production of the cultural zones with which we are dealing.

The purpose of this chapter, then, has been to suggest quite simply that the notion of 'absolute autonomy' of the political in medieval (and ancient) state formations is misleading. I would argue also that the same applies equally for modern, industrialized state formations. Only the nature of the exercise of power, and the vastly more advanced technologies of intelligence-gathering, surveillance and social control, as well as the patterns of cultural subsumption within a reifying, materialistic ideology of the market and the consumer, disguises and conceals the actual operation of command structures and the diffusion and intensity of power relations across a wide range of different levels of social praxis in capitalist formations. More importantly, such processes actively hypostatize economic relationships into other forms and, just as the nature of the exploitation of labour-power is concealed and transformed by the commodity-form, so the sources and context of power-relationships are concealed and transformed by the commodification of social praxis.

In the struggle over control of resources, over political independence and the maintenance of their authority, different approaches were tried in different tributary states. I have suggested that the chief constraining elements in this type of formation are to be located in the mode of surplus appropriation, at which point the state has to confront directly the actual producers and any other social elements which may be competing for control over that surplus. The problems encountered in trying to resolve the contradictions these situations revealed or promoted also bring to light the crucial importance of ideology, both in respect of the political ideologies of states, and the ideological systems, or patterns of belief, in different cultures, in determining the possibilities open to states or rulers in achieving their ends.

6

Conclusion: Absolute or Relative Autonomy?

I have tried to outline in the foregoing some of the key elements in a historical materialist approach to the analysis of pre-capitalist – and specifically, tributary – state formations and how they functioned in terms of their access to and control of the means of production, mode of surplus appropriation, and forms of surplus distribution necessary to their institutional existence and reproduction. I have suggested that it remains both legitimate and heuristically useful to view the relations of production – the 'economic base' in Marx's words – as the primary determining, but not necessarily causal, element in social formations. In respect of the state itself, I have argued further that within the general field established by these relations of production, it is centrally the mode of surplus appropriation together with the mode of surplus distribution which determine the possibilities for state development. On this basis, and employing a coherent set of concepts of modes of production, and the range of historically-attested political and economic relationships which they represent, a sound heuristic framework is available through which states can be analysed not simply with a view to describing their structural relationships, but with the possibility of understanding the dialectical nature of those relationships and the elements – practices, roles, institutions – through which they are constituted. By the same token, such a framework makes it possible to understand the contingent value of different practices which lends to them their particular appearance and form. For without the determining economic relationships, there seems to me a real danger that other practices come to be divorced from the very contexts within which they are generated and inscribed, to be attributed with a causal power independent of the context which determines the extent of their effectivity. Such is the case with the religious structures of South

India, granted in Stein's work on Vijayanagara a greater causal primacy as religious structures (as opposed to their aspect as elements in the relations of production) than they warrant with regard to their function and position in that formation.

'Power' has played a key role in recent debates, both those concerning states and the development of hegemonic political authority, and those concerned with the operation of specific social agencies and networks of relationships (as in the later work of Foucault, for example). Mann has argued for a model of power-relationships in which control of military, economic, ideological and political resources is essential to their effective exercise and reproduction. As a descriptive account, I have no reason to disagree with this formulation. Where I would distance myself from his position, however, is in the level at which the economic operates, as I have defined it here and as it is traditionally understood within historical materialist analyses. And my main ground for disagreement lies in the fact that power in the political, military and ideological spheres is ultimately dependent upon access to and control over the distribution of economic resources, although particular ideological traditions can function more independently, and within a particular dynamic of their own, once the conditions for their existence and reproduction have been secured. Military power, for example, can be employed to extend political and therefore economic and ideological power; but such power must in itself first be grounded in control over resources sufficient to maintain and reproduce it within its original engendering context, whether or not that control is itself mediated through a range of ideological features. Political power can be understood in much the same way – it must first be grounded in resource control before it can extend its purchase on social or geographical regions outside its own immediate field of reference. Indeed, political power is itself one mode of resource control, since it represents in effect sets of practices which ensure access to and facilitate control over various types of resource, and hence is of an unavoidably economic nature. Ideological power, I would argue, while ultimately grounded likewise in the control and manipulation of economic resources, operates more independently (and more unpredictably) than the first two, as I have already implied.

Power is thus not an abstract, but an embedded set of practices contingent upon specific sets of relationships, moments, and constellations of ideas, and rooted ultimately in the relations of production which generate those moments and social institutions.

This is not to deny the role of the individual. On the contrary, it is to provide precisely the framework through which beliefs and ideologies can be understood to take their strength and dynamism, and to suggest a way of understanding how narratives – discourses of belief and legitimation – can be at the same time both the product of a given set of relations at a particular moment, and yet appear to float free of the relationships for a time once they have become available and articulated.[1]

The fact that, for example, some political leaderships are able for a while to pursue policies and promote strategies which are in fact fundamentally in contradiction to the interests of a dominant class in society does not, of course, mean that absolute political autonomy is a real possibility. Such policies inevitably end in political or social-economic shifts which rapidly bring the world of the political back within the limits set by the social relations of production and the particular aspect of those relations – in the case of social formations dominated by tributary/feudal relations of production, we have seen that the mode of surplus appropriation and particularly surplus distribution is crucial here.

For the state itself is always inscribed within exploitative relations of production and must necessarily constitute an arena which facilitates the promotion of the interests of the state elite and/or the dominant class, or at the very least, as I have said already, does not intervene permanently in a way which damages such interests. When states or their rulers attempt to maintain and institutionalize such a balance, their efforts usually depend on the ability of the ruler or ruling elite, rather than on the actual attainment of a structurally self-regenerating equilibrium – if only because the conditions within which such structures have to operate are subject to unpredictable changes. Of course, these are 'external' factors. But they are internal to the relations of production as a whole, whether one includes aspects of those relations which exist and function outside the territorial control of the state or not. The Ottoman state provides an excellent illustration.

In all the cases discussed, the form of rulership and the power of the dominant political-theological ideological system was crucial, although its cultural manifestation differed radically from society to society. But in the last analysis, the multiplicity and variety of specific forms which each of these social formations exemplifies, as historically evolved variants of tributary relations of production, are limited in the possibilities open to them for further development and transformation by the social relations of production themselves, and particularly by the primary and secondary determinants of tributary state forms: in the first place, the means available to maintain the producers in subjection and to appropriate surplus appropriate to the demands of the state in the context of pre-industrial technology; and in the second place, the need for the state to function as a primary appropriator of surplus, and the contradiction implicit in this role, between the state centre and its agents (whether an aristocracy of birth or a bureaucratic elite of some sort). Thus the relations of production are determinant not of the specific forms – a point about which Marx was quite insistent, for example[2] – but of the limits and possibilities for their functional evolution. From the analysis of the various state forms undertaken in this book, we may conclude that the degree of relative political autonomy for states or rulers or ruling elites in tributary social formations is normally inscribed within the political relations of surplus distribution, and that state power may not necessarily reflect any direct and clear relationship between itself and the interests of a dominant class. On the other hand, we must also conclude that the appearance of political autonomy in feudal societies is a reflection of the particular possibilities open to different historical social formations dominated by tributary production relations in respect of the actual appropriation and distribution of surplus, that is to say, in respect of both social-cultural and ecological-geographical factors.[3]

In particular, the direct nature of primary surplus appropriation by the state or ruling class means that competition over the distribution of resources between potentially antagonistic elements, and over the institutional forms through which the mode of surplus appropriation is expressed, point to the two key areas of the relations of production in which conflict occurs. In all the state formations we have examined, it is on these elements that conflict has been focused: in other words, around the various historically determined logistical possibilities for physical control, coercion and supervision of the producers; the form actually taken by surpluses (labour services, military service, provisions for state officials and soldiers, maintenance of roads, post-stations, cash, agricultural produce, and so on); and the institutional means available to the state to raise and employ these surpluses in its own interests. Thus, while all states and state elites are constrained by the mode of appropriation of surplus dominant in their particular society, it is the direct, primary nature of surplus appropriation by states and ruling class in tributary social formations which informs both the nature of class struggle between exploiters and exploited, as well as the nature of the political relations of distribution of surplus within the ruling class. These relationships, and the institutional forms through which they are expressed, constitute the fundamental constraints on tributary state formations in respect of their political autonomy from the ruling class and its interests. As we have seen, this contrasts with capitalist societies, for example, as well as with the slave mode. In capitalism, taxation is the means whereby the state re-distributes surplus value already produced and distributed between the owners of the means of production and those who sell their labour-power in return for a wage/salary; in the slave mode, the supply of slave labour itself is the crucial determinant in the structure of relations between the ruling class, the state and the mass of non-slave producers.

Of course, there do exist certain universal features within state structures which can be observed in both pre-modern and modern states. These are, on the one hand, the establishment of more-or-less highly institutionalized means through which states are able to retain control over their means of political and economic reproduction (in particular legal systems, through which exploitative economic and power-relationships are legitimated), including a mediating group or class through whose agency the state physically appropriates surplus and maintains its authority. On the other hand, they include the conflicts which arise between factions of the state elite, or between state and service elite and a less dependent dominant class, or subordinate aristocracies or ruling elites of particular regions within the state's area of hegemony. These conflicts are always connected with the distribution of surplus wealth. Again, political ideologies and legal structures constitute an important set of enabling conditions, which affect the outcome of such struggles. In this sense, therefore, while it is clear that there is a multiplicity of forms and appearances of states which can exist under given sets of political-economic conditions, reflecting in turn the dominant mode of production and the way it is articulated with elements of other modes, there are actually only a limited number of structurally-possible systems of the appropriation and distribution of surplus wealth within which states can form and move beyond the stage of tribal confederation, attaining thereby a degree of permanence and continuity dependent upon sets of self-reproducing relationships and institutions. It is instructive to compare societies where states actually fail to reproduce themselves with those that are more successful. But it is also clear that the social relations of production cannot predict exactly either the form of such structures, or their developmental trajectory: the infinite variety of local factors, as Marx noted, makes this a task for detailed empirical research. That the relationship between the political economy of a society and the mode of expression of its political and power structures is not necessarily 'economic' should not surprise. The relative autonomy of the state and the logic of its organizational structures are perfectly real. But they must themselves be understood as dialectically generated characteristics of a particular set of relations of production, of a particular set, therefore, of political economy potentialities.[4]

The force and the direction of state theorist critiques of historical materialist approaches to the state, to the structures of power, and to the possible autonomy of the political has been based upon attempts to show that Marxist perspectives are either, or both, class reductionist and economistic, preconditions which prevent them addressing the nature of the relationships between politics, coercive power and ideology. As I have tried to show, this ignores a great deal of modern Marxist research and discussion, just as it ignores in fact the fundamental propositions set out by Marx and Engels themselves, whatever the empirical failings of some of their historical researches and that of some of their successors might have been. Marxist theory is itself a historical phenomenon, and the fallacy of basing a serious critique of historical materialism solely on the work of certain reductionist representations whose origins and evolution can be historically traced must be apparent, the more so when alternative, more sophisticated, theoretically more coherent and empirically more fruitful models had already begun to be mapped. For the modes of distribution of economic, coercive and ideological power – to use Runciman's terms – are already framed by the economic relationships within which they are reproduced. The fact that they may appear to float free of the social context which generated them, even if they also act back upon that context (a condition which Marxist theory must anyway insist upon) and hence lead to new structures and relationships, cannot alter the determining effects of the social and, therefore, the economic context. Indeed, it would be reasonable to argue that much recent state theory has itself actually produced a sort of 'state reductionism', whereby both the role of the individual and that of the relations of production are neglected. And as one commentator has already pointed out, some of the best state-centred arguments in effect concede the fact of relative autonomy, insofar as they admit that states cannot act in ways which are either unconstrained by social forces or arbitrary.[5]

I suggested above that it is the culturally contextual effects of the dialectic between economic and other structures or sets of social relations which lend to social formations or states dominated by the same mode of production their unique character and make possible so many different trajectories and evolutionary possibilities. Such possibilities are constrained by the contradictions inhering in antagonistic – class – production relations, at the most general level. But it is these developmental possibilities, as they are realized in the process of change, that historians study.

I want to conclude by emphasizing some central points. First, whatever their appearance, tributary states are not simply superstructures laid over societies. Where they do function in a way that is only marginally integrated into the relations of production and distribution of surplus wealth, they generally collapse or fragment, or are transformed from within over a relatively short period, to be replaced by more effective and more thoroughly diffused sets of institutionalized structures of power, or by a series of equally short-lived repetitions of the same superficial and conjuncture-bound political relationships. Second, tributary state apparatuses are never entirely autonomous in respect of the societies they dominate. Even where they function only at the level of expropriation and coercion, their effectiveness and their evolution is determined within the framework of the social relations of production, in turn characterized by the particular form of structural constraint peculiar to the tributary mode of production. In the Ottoman example, where strenuous efforts were made to create a state elite entirely divorced from the subject population, such efforts ultimately failed: the administration always had to operate within a framework set by the tributary mode of surplus appropriation and the institutions of surplus distribution. In addition, the institutional dynamic of the state apparatuses themselves, once established, evolved in ways which could not have been foreseen. The combination of pre-industrial communications, the limited possibilities for the application of intensive power across large territories, and the existence of interest-groups within the state apparatuses themselves inevitably had an effect – quite apart from the effects upon the whole of a variety of external and uncontrollable influences. In both the Ottoman and the Mughal states, the ruler never succeeded in eradicating entirely or displacing local nobilities and the tribal, ethnic or lineage ideologies they maintained. When central authority weakened, for whatever reasons, such factors immediately came to bear upon the qualitative relationships between state and elites, and between elites and producing class.

None of this is to suggest that politics are determined as simple reflections of economic and social relations. On the contrary, it is empirically very clear that people regularly adopt institutional roles and act in ways which reflect no obvious or relevant economic relationship, and that ideological systems can structure a cultural response to perceived situations directly. And so we must allow for approaches which ask questions about the effects of political-ideological processes as practices and as emergent structures, whose effect is not determined by the conditions which originally generated them. But it must on the other hand be remembered that such processes, and their consequences, are limited or constrained in two ways. In the first place, they are bound by what is actually possible within historically-specific expressions of social relations of production. In the second place, constraints are imposed in respect of what is attainable within a specific set of relationships between state and social formation. What, then, is the limit on the effects such processes may have before they rupture existing relationships and promote a crisis in which the contradictions they represent between novel and traditional sets of social practices become too obvious to avoid? However autonomous we might wish to think either the state or some of its structures, or politics, may be, the constraints I have described will be decisive. This is neither economic reductionism nor determinism, but it is to accept and to argue for the heuristic and explanatory value of starting any analysis with what I would maintain is the fundamental and determining framework of social praxis, namely the social relations of production.

Notes

1. Introduction

1. F. Engels, *The Origin of the Family, Private Property and the State*, in K. Marx and F. Engels, *Selected Works*, Moscow/London 1968, pp. 461–583, see 577ff.

2. K. Marx, *The Eighteenth Brumaire of Louis Bonaparte*, Marx and Engels., pp. 94–179, see 169ff.

3. Gregor McLennan, *Marxism, Pluralism and Beyond*, Cambridge 1989, esp. pp. 258–75.

4. For some useful surveys, see H.J.M. Claessen, P. Skalník, eds., *The Early State*, The Hague 1978; *The Study of the State*, The Hague 1981; R. Cohen, E.R. Service, eds., *Origins of the State: the Anthropology of Political Evolution*, Philadelphia 1978. On the non-unitary or 'overlapping' nature of social practice, see the somewhat overstated reminder of M. Mann, *The Sources of Social Power*, vol. 1: *A History of Power from the Beginnings to AD 1760*, Cambridge 1986, pp. 1–2; and for a survey of current social-anthropological and archaeological approaches to the question of such overlapping circles of influence, see the collection *Centre and Periphery in the Ancient World*, eds. M. Reynolds, M. Larsen and K. Kristiansen, Cambridge 1987, and especially the introductory chapter of M. Rowlands, 'Centre and Periphery: a Review of a Concept', pp. 1–11.

5. Mann, *The Sources of Social Power*, sums this up well in his notions of collective and distributive, extensive and intensive, authoritative and diffused power. See pp. 6ff.

6. Among the most important contributions are T. Skocpol, *States and Social Revolutions: a Comparative Analysis of France, Russia and China*, Cambridge 1979; Mann, *The Sources of Social Power*; W.G. Runciman, *A Treatise on Social Theory*, vol. 2: *Substantive Social Theory*, Cambridge 1989; M. Mann, 'The Autonomous Power of the State: its Origins, Mechanisms and Results', in J.A. Hall, ed., *States in History*, Oxford 1986, pp. 109–36. In a rather different vein, but nevertheless presenting a totalizing account of the development of human societies across history, see Ernest Gellner, *Plough, Sword and Book*, London 1988; and on all of these, Perry Anderson, 'A Culture in Contraflow, 1', *New Left Review* 180, 1990, pp. 41–78.

7. For recent challenges to some traditional assumptions within historical materialist writing, see, for example, J. Elster, *Making Sense of Marx*, Cambridge 1985; J. Roemer, *A General Theory of Exploitation and Class*, Cambridge, Massachu-

setts 1987; and McLennan, *Marxism, Pluralism and Beyond.*

8. See especially Mann, 'The Autonomous Power of the State', and Hall's introduction to *States in History.*

9. Compare the remarks made by G.E.M. de Ste Croix, *The Class Struggle in the Ancient Greek World*, London 1981, pp. 31ff.

2. State Theory and the Tributary State

1. Michael Mann, *The Sources of Social Power*, vol. 1: *A History of Power from the Beginnings to AD 1760*, Cambridge 1986; W.G. Runciman, *A Treatise on Social Theory*, vol. 2: *Substantive Social Theory*, Cambridge 1989. A third recent publication deals similarly with such phenomena, although its scope is, in fact, more limited, and it presents no new theoretical insights. See J.A. Tainter, *The Collapse of Complex Societies*, Cambridge 1988. The classic study is that of Barrington Moore Jr., *Social Origins of Dictatorship and Democracy*, Harmondsworth 1967/1973; the most important work of the recent generation, critical of both Moore's approach and the Marxist tradition, is T. Skocpol, *States and Social Revolutions: a Comparative Analysis of France, Russia and China*, Cambridge 1979, who further developed a theory of 'states in themselves'. Ralph Miliband has surveyed the discussion insofar as it concerns capitalist states: 'State Power and Class Interests', *New Left Review* 138, 1983, pp. 57–68; for a powerful critique of Skocpol, and especially of the state theorist and 'institutionalist' approaches, see P. Cammack, 'Statism, New Institutionalism, and Marxism', in R. Milibrand and L. Panitch, eds, *Socialist Register 1990*, London 1990, pp. 147–70.

2. See M. Mann, 'The Autonomous Power of the State: its Origins, Mechanisms and Results', in *States in History*, ed. J.A. Hall, Oxford 1986, pp. 109–36.

3. W.G. Runciman, *A Treatise on Social Theory*, vol. 1: *The Methodology of Social Theory*, Cambridge 1983, pp. 20 and 236ff.

4. See especially Skocpol; as well as the contributions to Hall; R. Cohen and E.R. Service, eds., *Origins of the State: the Anthropology of Political Evolution*, Philadelphia 1978; H.J.M. Claessen, P. Skalník, eds., *The Study of the State*, The Hague 1981; H.J.M. Claessen, P. Skalník, *The Early State*, The Hague 1978; and J.H. Kautsky, *The Politics of Aristocratic Empires*, Chapel Hill 1982.

5. Modern empirical analyses of, and serious interest in, states and their origins owe a great deal to the pioneering efforts of F. Engels, *The Origins of the Family, Private Property and the State*, first published in 1877 (English trans. E. Leacock, London 1972), which presents an evolutionist approach to states as the necessary political apparatus through which class antagonisms are checked and the dominant position of the ruling class is maintained as the social division of labour develops. Engels also believed that states could be formed through a process of conquest and the development of chiefdoms which gradually develop the institutional apparatuses of states and hence come to represent once again the interests of a dominant elite. See F. Engels, *Anti-Dühring*, publ. 1877/78, Eng. trans. New York 1939, pp. 197ff. For recent Marxist discussion of the state as well as of the accusations of reductionism and determinism, see H. Draper, 'The Death of the State in Marx and Engels', in Ralph Miliband and John Saville, eds., *Socialist Register 1970*, London 1970, pp. 201–307.

6. J.A. Hall, ed., *States in History*, Oxford 1986.

7. The standard detailed theoretical exposition of this approach remains N. Poulantzas, *Political Power and Social Classes*, Paris 1968/London 1978. It should be noted that the notion of 'the last instance' was invoked by Engels (in his letter to J. Bloch, in K. Marx and F. Engels, *Selected Works*, London 1968, pp. 682–3) in an effort to avoid a deterministic and reductionist account. Engels laments the fact that the notion that 'the *ultimately* determining element in history is the production and reproduction of real life' had already been turned into 'the economic element is the only determining one'. 'Marx and I are ourselves partly to blame for the fact that the younger people sometimes lay more stress on the economic side than is due to it. We had to emphasize the main principle vis-à-vis our adversaries, who denied it .... Unfortunately, however, it happens only too often that people think they have fully understood a new theory and can apply it without more ado from the moment they have assimilated its main principles, and even those not always correctly. And I cannot exempt many of the more recent "Marxists" from this reproach, for the most amazing rubbish has been produced in this quarter, too.'

There have been numerous critiques of Althusser's approach, which do not bear listing here. For representative discussions, see the remarks with literature in note 40 below; as well as T. Benton, *The Rise and Fall of Structuralist Marxism*, London 1984; and Perry Anderson, *In the Tracks of Historical Materialism*, London 1983, pp. 37ff.

8. For a comment on the treatment of the political in Braudel, see G. McLennan, *Marxism and the Methodologies of History*, London 1981, pp. 136ff.; and see in particular Christopher Hill's critique of the Annales approach to the political in 'Braudel and the State', in *The Collected Essays of Christopher Hill*, vol. 3: *People and Ideas in Seventeenth Century England*, Brighton 1986, pp. 125–42. For useful accounts of the different moral-philosophical strands in Marx's thought and the ways in which these have, or have not, been appreciated by later Marxist writers, see Jon Elster, *Making Sense of Marx*, Cambridge 1985. For Gellner's critique, see 'Soviets Against Wittfogel: or, the Anthropological Preconditions of Mature Marxism', in Hall, ed., *States in History*, pp. 78–108 (repr. from *Theory and Society* 14, 1985); for an illustrative guide to Gellner's work, see the essays collected in E. Gellner, *State and Society in Soviet Thought*, Oxford 1988 (which includes a slightly revised version of this essay under the title 'The Asiatic Trauma', pp. 39–68). But Gellner's criticisms often rest on a wilfully blinkered understanding of the potential of Marxist analysis and its political project, a point made in the excellent exposé by Ellen Meiksins Wood, 'Marxism and the Course of History', *New Left Review* 147, 1984, pp. 95–107, see pp. 99–100. Similar points apply in respect of several criticisms from within the historical materialist position, too: in particular, accusations which are themselves grounded in the facile reduction of a complex of notions in Marx's writings to a single, monocausal element, or the myopic refusal to see the possibilities for a more pluralist (without being relativist) causality in Marx's analyses, are tendencies which have been justly, and quite effectively, laid bare by Norman Geras, 'Seven Types of Obloquy: Travesties of Marxism', in Miliband and Panitch, eds., *Socialist Register 1990*, pp. 1–34. None of this is to deny, either, the threat to a historical materialist approach posed by the dogmatic and entrenched neo-Stalinist social science of the years preceding the Gorbachev era in the Soviet Union and Eastern Europe in particular, and still evident in Western Europe and the United States to a degree.

9. See Meiksins Wood, *inter alia.*, on this: 'Marxism and the Course of History', p. 102.

10. G.A. Cohen: *Karl Marx's Theory of History: a Defence*, Oxford 1978; and 'Reconsidering Historical Materialism', in J. Chapman, J.R. Pennock, eds., *Marx and Legal Theory*, New York 1983; and see D. Laibman, 'Modes of Production and Theories of Transition', *Science and Society* 48/3, 1984.

11. On these issues, see the brief survey by McLennan, 'Marxist Theory and Historical Research: Between the Hard and Soft Options', *Science and Society* 50/1, Spring 1986, pp. 85–95; and in particular J. McCarney, 'The True Realm of Freedom: Marxist Philosophy after Communism', *New Left Review* 189, Sept.–Oct. 1991, pp. 19–38. The idea of a 'weak impulse', taken up in McCarney's article, was outlined by Erik Olin Wright, 'Gidden's Critique of Marxism', *New Left Review* 138, March–April 1983, pp. 11–35, see p. 28. For a somewhat more positive interpretation (based on the notion that the social relations do not 'fetter' the forces of production themselves, but rather their use and application), see C. Bertram, 'International Competition in Historical Materialism', *New Left Review* 183, 1990, pp. 116–28, see pp. 122ff., following a series of arguments first set out by J. McMurtry, *The Structure of Marx's World View*, Princeton 1978, pp. 205ff.

12. A leading protagonist of a realist materialist approach has been Roy Bhaskar: see 'Emergence, Explanation and Emancipation', in P.F. Secord, ed., *Explaining Human Behaviour: Consciousness, Human Action and Social Structure*, Beverley Hills, 1982, pp. 275–310; *A Realist Theory of Science*, Brighton 1978; *Scientific Realism and Human Emancipation*, London 1987; and note in addition D. Hillel-Ruben, *Marxism and Materialism: a Study in Marxist Theory of Knowledge*, Brighton 1979. See also the arguments of Terry Lovell, *Pictures of Reality*, London 1980, esp. pp. 9–28. The debate on this problem and on the 're-thinking' of Marxism in Britain and North America has been summarized by G. McLennan, 'History and Theory: Contemporary Debates and Directions', *Literature and History* 10/2, 1984, pp. 139–64. For three important contributions, with the general direction of whose discussion and with whose conclusions the present writer is in broad agreement (although there are some important differences in emphasis and interpretation between them), see A. Callinicos, *Making History: Agency, Structure and Change in Social Theory*, Cambridge 1989; J. Larrain, *A Reconstruction of Historical Materialism*, London 1986; and G. McLennan, *Marxism, Pluralism and Beyond: Classic Debates and New Departures*, Cambridge 1989. Larrain's view, like that of McLennan, argues that a 'reconstructed' historical materialism (although I suggest 'reformulated' might be a more appropriate term) can retain a strong concept of the structurally determined nature of social change and history, while at the same time maintaining the centrality of human agency, praxis and class struggle, the outcome of which is not in any way pre-ordained.

13. McLennan, 'History and Theory', pp. 156–62.

14. See especially Hillel-Ruben, *Marxism and Materialism.*

15. See Meiksins Wood, 'Marxism and the Course of History', pp. 100ff.

16. See Elster, *Making Sense of Marx*; and especially E.O. Wright, 'Giddens' Critique of Marxism', pp. 24ff.

17. See, for example, P. Burke, *Sociology and History*, London 1980. The work of Skocpol, Mann, Runciman and others represents some of the more substantial versions of this comparativist critical approach. For a much earlier response to the criticisms implicit in these works, see G.V. Plekhanov, 'On the Question of the

Individual's Role in History' (1898) in G. Plekhanov, *Selected Philosophical Works*, vol. 2, Moscow 1976, pp. 283–315; and see Larrain, *A Reconstruction of Historical Materialism*.

18. See Elster, *Making Sense of Marx*; and J. Roemer, *A General Theory of Exploitation and Class*, Cambridge, Massachusetts 1982, with the useful remarks of A. Carling, 'Rational Choice Marxism', *New Left Review* 160, 1986, pp. 24–62. For a more hostile critical assessment, see E. Meiksins Wood, 'Rational Choice Marxism: Is the Game Worth the Candle?', *New Left Review* 177, 1989, pp. 41–88.

19. Anderson, *In the Tracks of Historical Materialism*, see p. 24. It is ironic that, as British and North American historical materialist history and historical sociology, having profited from the critique inaugurated by French structuralist Marxism, experience something of a strengthening and revival, among intellectuals at least, French Marxist history is in full decline – for reasons which reflect both the social and economic, as well as the political evolution of French society from the 1950s until the present day. See the useful survey of G. Ross, 'Intellectuals Against the Left: the Case of France', in Miliband and Panitch, eds., *Socialist Register 1990*, pp. 201–27.

20. These points are developed further in, for example, A. Giddens, *Central Problems in Social Theory*, London 1979.

21. See the excellent discussion of Callinicos, *Making History: Agency, Structure and Change in Social Theory*, pp. 9ff.

22. See J. Haldon, 'Ideology and Social Change in the Seventh Century: Military Discontent as a Barometer', *Klio* 68, 1986, pp. 139–90, where I have set out some basic arguments for such a theory.

23. In Marx and Engels, *Selected Works*, pp. 96–179, see p. 96.

24. Callinicos, *Making History*, p. 236.

25. Hall, ed., *States in History*, p. 5. Hall's critique is in fact rather crude, and hardly qualifies to be taken seriously. On the other hand, it is not untypical of many similar attacks, and for that reason should be shown up for what it is. It appears to be founded on the assumption that (1) Marxists base their arguments entirely upon the discussions of Marx, Engels and Lenin, and are taken, or strongly implied, to assume that these discussions are more-or-less unproblematic, free from internal inconsistency, doubt, possible alternatives; in consequence, it can be implied that any analyses based on such work is therefore already clearly falsified by more recent work (a position not dissimilar to that of Gellner); and that (2) Marxism has no history (of development, questioning, criticism). Where Lenin elaborates a somewhat different argument from Marx, for example, on certain issues, then his argument 'is scarcely Marxist at all'! See J.A. Hall and G. John Ikenberry, *The State*, Milton Keynes 1989, p. 8. Hall takes it (apparently – the dismissal is made very briefly) also that Marxist theory in the lands of the former Soviet Union, Eastern Europe, Western Europe and the USA represents a more or less undifferentiated block. Ironically, the impoverished nature of these views is made clear by the fact that they ignore a central theme of Hall's own work: politics. And he concludes that Marx's work has been 'the single most important source of the loss of interest in the state in modern social science' (*States in History*, pp. 3–4) – thereby neatly leap-frogging from Marx-Engels-Lenin, over the Stalinist period, and up to today. The absurdity (and remarkable ignorance) of such views, sadly, is not limited to Hall alone, as Cammack has recently demonstrated in a recent forensic attack and critique of such writings ('Statism,

New Institutionalism, and Marxism', cited note 1 above). Hall's remarks, in fact, clearly represent not a first-hand intellectual confrontation with historical materialist theory, but rather a second- or third-hand dismissal of Marxism based less on theoretical discussion than on political-ideological hostility. In contrast, the work of both Skocpol and Mann, the latter especially, presents a less dogmatic, more pluralist and more constructive approach, as McLennan's survey, *Marxism, Pluralism and Beyond*, pp. 226ff. clearly demonstrates. Yet for all that, both can be legitimately accused of a similar interpretative over-simplification of historical materialist principles of analysis. Marxists do *not* posit a reductionist, reflection-theory explanation of either politics or state functions: as I will argue in the course of this book, to assume this is to read into Marx and Engels, on the one hand, and contemporary Western European and North American Marxist analyses, on the other, the political and interpretational priorities of Stalinist dogmatism – a political-ideological mode which was, of necessity, inimical to any close analysis of state elites, the reproduction of state power and its economic mechanisms and the role of charismatic leaders. Contemporary Marxism has certainly suffered (and continues to suffer) from this legacy. But anyone familiar with the writings of, say, Plekhanov, or the less well-known Bogdanov, quite apart from a more 'open' reading of Marx and Engels, will have no difficulty in concluding that a historical materialist approach as such, as opposed to a practical exemplification of highly selective and de-contextualized extracts from their writings, or a particular version extracted from Stalinist historiography, is quite adequate to the tasks for which state theorists have claimed it unsuited.

26. Compare the remarks of G. Thompson, 'The Relationship Between the Financial and Industrial Sectors in the United Kingdom Economy', *Economy and Society* 6/3, 1977; and Tom Nairn, 'The Future of Britain's Crisis', *New Left Review* 113–14, 1979, pp. 43–69, esp. pp. 55ff.

27. Mann, 'The Autonomous Power of the State'; Claessen and Skalník, 'The Early State: Theories and Hypotheses', in *The Early State*, pp. 3–29; R. Cohen, 'State Origins: a Reappraisal', in *The Early State*, pp. 31–75; together with the papers in section 3 of the same volume.

28. Mann, 'The Autonomous Power of the State', p. 112.

29. A.R. Radcliffe-Brown, *African Political Systems*, eds. M. Fortes, E.E. Evans-Pritchard, London 1940, pp. ixff. For the state as an 'institutional form', see Skocpol, *States and Social Revolutions*, p. 27. A basic criticism is that Marxists have quite simply failed to give the state the attention it deserves: T. Skocpol. 'Political Response to Capitalist Crisis: Neo-Marxist Theories of the State and the Case of the New Deal', *Theory and Society* 10/2, 1980, see p. 200. For a trenchant critique of these views, however, see Cammack, 'Statism, New Institutionalism and Marxism', pp. 149–55, who shows up the one-sidedness and selectivity of this view.

30. Mann, 'The Autonomous Power of the State', p. 110. See A. Giddens, *A Contemporary Critique of Historical Materialism*, London 1982.

31. As I have tried to show in one case-study dealing with the social and political crisis in the East Roman/Byzantine world in the later seventh century: Haldon, 'Ideology and Social Change in the Seventh Century'. Recent debates over what has been dubbed 'rational choice Marxism' show only too clearly how necessary it is to relate inter-individual practices, attitudes and the construction and patterning of psychologies (micro-foundational analysis) to longer-term

tendencies and the structural effects which the interplay between individuals, groups, roles and institutions has in respect of the trajectory followed by any given aspect of a social formation. And these in their turn must then be related to the theoretical and conceptual categories which are designed to provide a framework within which these effects of social practices can be observed, and a heuristic guide through which they and their effects can be understood. It goes without saying that I do not wish to imply a methodological individualism here: macro-phenomena cannot be reduced on a one-to-one basis to their micro-foundations. But there can be no doubt that the specification of the multiplicity of causal relationships which together constitute trends, tendencies, 'structures' and 'events' is an essential foundation for historical and sociological understanding – a point which Marx and Engels recognized quite clearly, even if it has not always been appreciated by all their (theoretical) successors. See Elster, *Making Sense of Marx*; Roemer, *A General Theory of Exploitation and Class*; the survey by Carling, 'Rational Choice Marxism'; and the critical appreciations by A. Levine, E. Sober, E. Olin Wright, 'Marxism and Methodological Individualism', *New Left Review* 162, 1987, pp. 67–84; Wood, 'Rational Choice Marxism: Is the Game Worth the Candle?'; and Callinicos, *Making History*; McLennan, *Marxism, Pluralism and Beyond*.

32. See K. Marx, *The Eighteenth Brumaire of Louis Bonaparte*, in Marx and Engels, *Selected Works*, pp. 96–179, see pp. 169ff.; and *The Civil War in France*, ibid.. pp. 271–309, see pp. 285ff. These points have been made forcefully and in detail by Miliband, 'State Power and Class Interests'.

33. Engels, *The Origins of the Family, Private Property and the State*, in Marx and Engels, *Selected Works*, esp. pp. 577ff.

34. As argued by Miliband, 'State Power and Class Interests', pp. 65–7.

35. For some aspects of the debate in respect of the modern state, see the arguments of Miliband and Poulantzas in *New Left Review* 58, 1969; 59, 1970; 82, 1973; the comments of E. Laclau, 'The Specificity of the Political: Around the Poulantzas–Miliband Debate', *Economy and Society* 5/1, 1975; and those of Poulantzas in *New Left Review* for 1976.

36. Marx, *Capital*, vol. 3, Moscow and London 1972, p. 791.

37. The formulation begs the question, of course, whether states do always develop in the context of class antagonisms. The answer is empirically testable and unequivocally in the affirmative. Virtually all the comparative historical and social-anthropological work which has examined the question of the origins of states, whether 'primitive' or 'secondary', and from whatever theoretical standpoint, bears this out. See, from a Marxist perspective, Jonathan Friedman, 'Tribes, States and Transformations', in M. Bloch, ed., *Marxist Analyses and Social Anthropology*, London 1984, pp. 161–202; and from a non-Marxist (although not a non-materialist) viewpoint, Mann, *The Sources of Social Power*, pp. 82ff.; Runciman, *A Treatise on Social Theory*, vol. 2, pp. 185ff.; and R. Cohen, 'State Origins: a Reappraisal', in Claessen, Skalník, eds., *The Early State*, pp. 31–75, see esp. pp. 32ff., along with the other essays in the same volume. Note especially M.H. Fried, *The Evolution of Political Society*, New York 1967; and 'The State, the Chicken and the Egg: or, Which Came First?', in Cohen and Service, *Origins of the State: the Anthropology of Political Evolution*, pp. 35–47. The exception is E.R. Service, *Origins of the State and Civilisation*, New York 1975, who argues that the state originated in a process of mutual or contractual relations between different groups and ecological niches in a given social-cultural context, in which the state represents

the interests of all to their general best advantage. While this may certainly provide an ideological rationale for many state formations both today and in the past, such a narrow and functionalist view has met with little real support.

For Miliband's comment, see 'State Power and Class Interest', pp. 66–7. And it is worth noting, as Perry Anderson has pointed out ('A Culture in Contraflow, I', *New Left Review* 180, 1990, pp. 41–78, see p. 61), that even Mann's political source of power as represented in the state's capacity for 'centralized territorial regulation', and which serves as the basis for its political autonomy, is itself implicitly rooted in adequate military, economic and ideological power – in other words, political autonomy is determined by the state's control over resources which, in their mode of extraction and distribution, are bounded by the dominant relations of production. The question here, of course – and as I will argue in the next chapters – is not over the essential fact of this dominance of production relations; but rather, the ways in which these relations themselves are expressed and operate to constrain state autonomy in the different circumstances of each social formation, in turn understood within the framework of the dominant mode of production and the structural constraints it imposes. The problem revolves not around whether production relations constrain state autonomy, but how and why they do this in a specific way according to each mode of production.

38. Whether such divisions are expressed juridically, of course, for example through a hierarchy of legally-defined statuses, is, to a degree, a secondary issue. More importantly, the way in which economic classes are either united or divided internally – by lineage and kinship structures, status groupings and political organizations, local and regional identities or ideological and religious affiliations – is crucial. Because such structures cut vertically across economic divisions, any attempt to explain the politics of societies in terms of economic class position alone, regardless of the praxis-structuring ideological contexts within which people operate, will be valueless. In almost all pre-industrial social formations the general economic structure – the relations of production of society as a whole – is both partially constituted by and at the same time fragmented by such vertical divisions, sometimes setting one element of an economically-dominant group against another, often dividing peasant and pastoralist society along localized kinship and identity lines, and hence uniting at a regional or even more local level both exploiting and exploited classes ideologically. Dominant economic classes may thus suffer politically at the hands of either the state (perhaps allied with other classes) or an alliance of normally politically and economically subordinate classes. But this does not mean that economic relationships are not determinant of the configurations possible within a given social formation. It does mean that, in pre-capitalist society especially, the economic is always expressed through structures – sets of practices – which bear other functions too, as we have seen. And it also means that the political forms through which state power can be exercised, and the policies which rulers can reasonably pursue, will be determined by the relative economic strength and ideological importance of such structures at any given moment. This can be seen very clearly, for example, in the excellent analysis of the internal politics of Greek city-states and the rise of the Roman republic and empire of G.E.M. de Ste Croix, *The Class Struggle in the Ancient Greek World*, London 1981. The 'asymmetrical' nature of class relations in pre-industrial society is a point particularly emphasized by Mann, *The Sources of Social Power*, pp. 216ff., but it is hardly new to Marxist analyses.

39. Runciman, *A Treatise on Social Theory*, vol. 2, pp. 150ff.
40. Ibid., pp. 12ff. and 148ff.
41. Ibid., p. 153.
42. Marx, *Capital*, vol. 3, p. 791.
43. Ibid., pp. 791–2.
44. Marx, *Capital*, vol. 1, p. 85 and note 2. But it is important to note that the notion that pre-capitalist modes cannot be economically rooted in the same way as capitalism has crept back in. See, remarkably, Anderson's argument for a superstructural constitution of feudal relations of production: *Lineages of the Absolutist State*, London 1974/1979, pp. 401ff.
45. F. Engels, letter to J. Bloch (in Marx and Engels, *Selected Works*, pp. 682–3).
46. Engels, letter to F. Mehring (in Marx and Engels, *Selected Works*, pp. 689–93), see pp. 690–91.
47. A whole range of efforts to elaborate a more sophisticated version of this model has been undertaken, beginning perhaps most clearly with Lenin, who in his 1908 attack on Bogdanov, entitled *Materialism and Empirio-Criticism* (in *Collected Works*, vol. 14, Moscow 1962), tried to develop what amounts to a reflection-theory of ideology and the state (in contrast, in fact, to his more analytical discussion of political organization). Plekhanov tried similarly to develop a more thoroughgoing account, but in the process produced what some have seen as a reified spatial and sequential model of 'levels' and 'totalities' (see G.V. Plekhanov, *Fundamental Problems of Marxism*, Moscow 1908/London 1969/1970, p. 70). But Bogdanov had already begun to develop what was actually a much more sophisticated and nuanced model of social and economic structures and the nature of determination by the economic in his *Short Course on Economic Science* (*Kratkii kurs ekonomicheskoi nauki*, Moscow 1897), which was the subject of Lenin's critique, referred to already. See R.C. Williams, *The Other Bolsheviks*, Bloomington 1986, pp. 38ff.

The most recent attempt to defend the 'base–superstructure' metaphor is G.A. Cohen, *Karl Marx's Theory of History: a Defence*. Criticism of this model was voiced more forcefully by L. Althusser and E. Balibar, *Reading 'Capital'*, London 1971, and N. Poulantzas, *Political Power and Social Classes*; and *State, Power, Socialism*, London and New York 1978. Althusser established a model in which the levels of economics, politics and ideology, made up of specific practices, form a structural totality, in which the idea of determination is replaced by that of structural causality. The economic level remains determinant 'in the last instance', however, since it is the economic which determines which of the levels is dominant by establishing the limits of the relative autonomy of the other levels and allotting them functions necessary to its own reproduction. But it has been frequently pointed out that, while this alternative model challenges crude economic determinism, it actually leaves little changed in respect of the economic 'level'. Indeed, the relative autonomy of non-economic levels depends on their function as necessary to the reproduction of the economic level, and actually creates a split between their conditions of reproduction and those of production in general. This ignores a fundamental aspect of historical materialist notions of the dialectical and processual nature of human praxis. See M. Glucksmann, 'A Ventriloquist Structuralism', *New Left Review* 72, 1972; and the contributions to S. Clarke *et al.*, *One-Dimensional Marxism*, London 1980.
48. See M. Godelier, 'Infrastructures, Societies and History', *Current Anthropol-*

ogy 19/4, 1978, pp. 763–71 (also published under the same title but with a slightly different text in *New Left Review* 112, 1978, pp. 84–96). The idea has been taken up by several writers dealing with pre-capitalist social formations, generally of the segmentary lineage or the sectional type: see again, with examples, Godelier, 'Modes of Production, Kinship and Demographic Structures', in Bloch, ed., *Marxist Analyses and Social Anthropology*, pp. 3–27, esp. pp. 13ff.

49. See Bhaskar, 'Emergence, Explanation and Emancipation'; and *Scientific Realism and Human Emancipation*, London 1987. For Engels, see his letter to J. Bloch of Sept. 1890, in: Marx and Engels, *Selected Works*, pp. 682–3. It seems to me that the formulation with regard to human subjectivity, cultural constraint and intentionality as expressed here, and especially in respect of the use of the notion of experiential organization through narrative reconstruction, referred to above, can adequately account for the problems addressed by, for example, the work of Pierre Bourdieu and his followers in the 1970s and 1980s, which confronted the problem of the maintenance and reproduction of power-relationships from a structuralist Marxist perspective, in an effort to counter the 'discursive relativism' and fortuitous nature attributed to causal effects promoted by Foucault's work. Bourdieu argued in particular for a transfer of analytic and explanatory theory away from 'production' or what was termed the 'production-fetishism' ascribed to traditional Marxist discussion, to the terrain of 'reproduction' as interpreted through the fields of cultural investment and cultural capital, social context and the practices necessary for the reproduction of certain sets of socio-economic and cultural identities. See P. Bourdieu, *Distinction*, Paris 1979, and *La noblesse d'Etat*, Paris 1988.

50. Mann, *The Sources of Social Power*, p. 31, where he argues that this is not a necessary and teleological, but rather a developmental and contingent process. But I do not wish to return to a productive forces determinism in which the primacy of the productive forces alone is fundamental (as implied in Cohen, *Karl Marx's Theory of History*). Rather, it is both the productive forces and the social relations of production through which they are exploited, harnessed, developed or neglected which underlies this developmental trend. See E. Hobsbawm, 'Marx and History', *New Left Review* 143, 1984, pp. 39–50; and especially Wright, 'Giddens' Critique of Marx', see pp. 24–31, where a non-teleological model of the tendency of the forces of production to develop is ably summarized.

51. For the remarks made by Hall, see *States in History*, pp. 1ff.; and see Norman Geras, 'Ex-Marxism Without Substance: Being a Real Reply to Laclau and Mouffe', *New Left Review* 169, 1988, pp. 34–61, see pp. 40–41; note also N. Mouzelis, 'Marxism – Post-Marxism?', *New Left Review* 167, 1988, pp. 107–23, see p. 117 on the question of the political and its 'downgrading' by Marxists.

52. Runciman, *A Treatise on Social Theory*, vol. 2, pp. 148ff. and 182ff. See the review by C.J. Wickham, 'Systactic Structures: Social Theory for Historians', *Past and Present* 132, August, 1991, pp. 188–203.

53. Runciman, *A Treatise on Social Theory*, vol. 2, pp. 160ff.

54. See Frank Perlin, 'Concepts of Order and Comparison, with a Diversion on Counter Ideologies and Corporate Institutions in Late Pre-Colonial India', *Journal of Peasant Studies* 12, 1985, pp. 87–165, esp. pp. 96ff. and 101; M. Godelier, *Perspectives in Marxist Anthropology*, Cambridge Studies in Social Anthropology 18, Cambridge 1977, p. 24.

55. See, for example, the arguments of some of the Soviet Byzantinists

discussed in chapter 3 below; and the articles of Harbans Mukhia, 'Peasant Production in Medieval Indian Society', *Journal of Peasant Studies* 12, 1985, pp. 228–51; and 'Was There Feudalism in Indian History?', *Journal of Peasant Studies* 8, 1981, pp. 273–310.

56. Perlin, 'Concepts of Order and Comparison', pp. 90–92 and 97–101, categorizes the first two of these usages as 'micrological', the third as 'macrological'.

57. These basic types are presented by Marx in *Pre-Capitalist Economic Formations*, ed. E. Hobsbawm, London 1964, although, as is well known, he discussed them elsewhere as well, often adding or changing details of his argument as his views on the structure and dynamic of the capitalist mode evolved.

58. There is a clear exposition of Marx's notions in this respect in G. Therborn, *Science, Class and Society*, London 1976, pp. 355ff. Marx himself made a series of clear statements about these relationships: see, for example, *Capital*, vol. 3, p. 791, already quoted at length above.

59. *Capital*, vol. 2, Moscow and London 1977, pp. 36–7.

60. See the discussion of Godelier, *Perspectives in Marxist Anthropology*, pp. 23–4.

61. Compare Godelier on the 'socio-economic formation' (*Perspectives in Marxist Anthropology*, pp. 62–9).

62. See Perlin 'Concepts of Order and Comparison', pp. 101–4.

63. In this respect, Runciman's account of historical causation is not far from that of 'pluralist' Marxists such as D. Sayer, *The Violence of Abstraction: the Analytic Foundations of Historical Materialism*, Oxford 1987; R. Gottlieb, 'Feudalism and Historical Materialism: a Critique and Synthesis', *Science and Society* 48/1, 1984.

64. Runciman, *A Treatise on Social Theory*, vol. 2, pp. 40ff., 295. I have sketched out a similar approach to practice, perceptions of reality and the structuring role played by narratives, in 'Ideology and Social Change in the Seventh Century'. See Callinicos, *Making History*, pp. 39ff.

65. See Mann, *The Sources of Social Power*, p. 6; M. Foucault, *The History of Sexuality*, London 1979, pp. 81ff.

66. For the major recent discussions see B. Hindess and P.Q. Hirst, *Pre-Capitalist Modes of Production*, London 1975, and the debate which followed, exemplified in the review by T. Asad, H. Wolpe, in *Economy and Society* 5, 1976, pp. 470–506. In respect of particular historical problems, see C.J. Wickham, 'The Uniqueness of the East', *Journal of Peasant Studies* 12, 1985, pp. 166–96; Halil Berktay, 'The Feudalism Debate: the Turkish End – is "Tax vs. Rent" Necessarily the Product and Sign of a Modal Difference?', *Journal of Peasant Studies* 14, 1987, pp. 291–333; J.F. Haldon, 'The Feudalism Debate Once More: the Case of Byzantium', *Journal of Peasant Studies* 17, 1989, pp. 5–39, all of which provide recent literature and discussion of the key problems.

67. See chapter 3 below.

68. See Berktay, 'The Feudalism Debate: the Turkish End', p. 311.

69. See S. Amin, *Unequal Development*, Hassocks 1976, pp. 13–16; (implicitly) against, see Elster, *Making Sense of Marx*, pp. 257ff. and (explicitly) Wickham, 'The Uniqueness of the East'.

3. The Tributary Mode

1. This debate has its origins in the discussions of theorists such as Bukharin and Plekhanov in the early part of this century on the works of Marx and Engels.

See G.V. Plekhanov, *The Development of the Monist View of History*, Moscow 1956; N.I. Bukharin, *Historical Materialism: a System of Sociology*, Moscow 1921/1925. In the 1950s the debate reached a high point in western Marxist circles in what has become known as 'the transition to capitalism' debate: see R. Hilton, ed., *The Transition from Feudalism to Capitalism*, London 1976/1978, where the key issues are to be found. It has been given new impetus by historians of the Annales school and especially by Marxist structuralist thinkers, foremost among whom was, of course, Althusser (see L. Althusser, *For Marx*, London 1969; L. Althusser and E. Balibar, *Reading Capital*, London 1970). These produced the critique of Hindess and Hirst (see B. Hindess and P.Q. Hirst, *Pre-Capitalist Modes of Production*, London 1975) which attempted to elaborate a general concept of mode of production, as well as concepts of specific modes of production, and the question of transition from one mode to another. In spite of much criticism, their work stimulated a greatly-overdue re-appraisal of much taken for granted in Marxist history-writing and theory.

2. For descriptive-analytical surveys, see the essays in H.J.M. Claessen and P. Skalník, eds., *The Early State*, The Hague 1978; H.J.M. Claessen and P. Skalník, eds., *The Study of the State*, The Hague 1981; L. Krader, *The Formation of the State*, Englewood Cliffs 1968; S.F. Nadel, *A Black Byzantium*, London 1942; and from a more centrally Marxist perspective, E.O. Wright, *Class, Crisis and the State*, London 1978; D. Gold, C. Lo, E.O. Wright, 'Recent Developments in Marxist Theories of the State', *Monthly Review* 27/5–6, 1975. From a strongly Althusserian perspective, see N. Poulantzas, *Political Power and Social Classes*, London 1975/1978.

3. See most recently two important contributions from Chris Wickham: 'The Other Transition: from the Ancient World to Feudalism', *Past and Present* 103, 1984, pp. 3–36; 'The Uniqueness of the East', *Journal of Peasant Studies* 12, 1985, pp. 166–96; and the critique by H. Berktay, 'The Feudalism Debate: the Turkish End – Is "Tax vs. Rent" Necessarily the Product and Sign of a Modal Difference?', *Journal of Peasant Studies* 14, 1987, pp. 291–333). Note also G. de Ste Croix, *The Class Struggle in the Ancient Greek World*, London 1981; P. Anderson, *Passages from Antiquity to Feudalism*, London 1974; and the review of the latter by Hirst (P.Q. Hirst, 'The Uniqueness of the West', *Economy and Society* 4/4, 1975, pp. 446–75).

4. The classic western statement is P. Lemerle, *The Agrarian History of Byzantium: from the Origins to the Twelfth Century*, Galway 1979, pp. 89 and 115. For the more recent Soviet position, see K.V. Khvostova, *Kolichestvennyj podhod k srednevokovoj sotsial'no-ekonomicheskoj istorii* (The quantitative approach to medieval socio-economic history), Moscow 1980.

5. An argument elaborated by G. Ostrogorsky, *Pour l'histoire de la féodalité Byzantine*, Brussels 1954, and since followed and developed by others. For a brief summary of part of the debate, see Anderson, *Passages*, pp. 279ff. It is important to note, however, that Ostrogorsky's thesis was the foundation upon which the ideas of a number of Soviet scholars on this theme came to be based.

6. For an analysis and fruitful discussion of the conflicting and alternative definitions of the term feudalism, and the tendency of protagonists of both approaches to obfuscate the issue by failing to recognize the different functions of, and criteria underlying, these variations of usage, see Frank Perlin, 'Concepts of Order and Comparison, with a Diversion on Counter Ideologies and Corporate Institutions in Late Pre-Colonial India', *Journal of Peasant Studies* 12, 1985, pp. 87–165. For Shtaermann's view, see Ye. M. Shtaermann, *Krizis antichnoi kul'turi* (The crisis of ancient civilization), Moscow 1975.

7. M.Ya. Syuzyumov, 'Nekotorye problemi istoricheskogo razvitiya Vizantii i zapada' (Some questions on the historical development of Byzantium and the West), *Vizantiiskii Vremennik* 75, 1973, pp. 3–18.

8. M.Ya. Syuzyumov, 'Problemi asinkhronogo razvitiya v Drevnosti' (Problems of asynchronic development in Antiquity), *Antichnaya Drevnost'i Srednie Veka* 13, 1976, pp. 30–48.

9. A.P. Kazhdan, *Vizantiiskaya kul'tura* (Byzantine culture), Moscow 1968, pp. 263ff. But for a critique of the 'prime mover' theories, which underlies this purely internalized model of change, see G. McLennan, 'Marxist Theory and Historical Research: Between the Hard and Soft Options', *Science and Society* 50/1, 1986, pp. 85–95.

10. A.P. Kazhdan, 'K voprosu ob osobennostyakh feodal'noy sobstvennosti v Vizantii 8–10 vv.' (On the question of the specific forms of feudal property in Byzantium, 8th–10th centuries), *Vizantiiskii Vremennik* 10, 1956, pp. 48–65; and *Derevniya i gorod v Vizantii 9–10 vv.* (Village and town in Byzantium in the 9th and 10th centuries), Moscow 1960.

11. These views are best summarized in the work of G. Litavrin, *Vizantiiskoe obshchestvo i gosudarstvo v X–XI vv. Problemi istorii odnogo stoletiya 976–1081* (Byzantine society and state in the 10th and 11th centuries. Problems in the history of a century, 976–1081), Moscow 1977. See also the survey of G.L. Kurbatov, G.Ye. Lebedeva, *Vizantiya: problemi perekhoda ot antichnosti k feodalizmu* (Byzantium: problems of the transition from antiquity to feudalism), Leningrad 1984, which emphasizes both the importance of slavery in late ancient production (up to the seventh century) and the dominance of feudal relations of production from the later eleventh century. See also Z.V. Udal'tsova, K.A. Osipova, 'Formirovanie feodal'nogo krest'yanstva v Vizantii (VII–XI vv.)' (The formation of the feudal peasantry in Byzantium, 7th–11th centuries), *Istoriya krest'janstva v Evrope. Epokha feodalizma*, I: *Formirovanie feodal'no-zavsimogo krest'yanstva* (History of the peasantry in Europe. The feudal epoch, I: the formation of a dependent feudal peasantry), Leningrad 1985, pp. 428–61.

12. See G. Litavrin, 'Otnositel'nye razmeri isostav imushchestva provintsial'noi vizantiiskoi aristokratii' (The structure and extent of Byzantine provincial aristocratic properties), *Vizantiiskie Ocherki*, 1971, pp. 152–68, for a survey of views, with literature; and the numerous articles of Z.V. Udal'tsova, esp. 'K voprosu o genezise feodalizma v Vizantii (postanovka problemi)' (On the question of the genesis of feudalism in Byzantium [definition of the problem]), *Vizantiiskie Ocherki*, 1971. Note in particular M. Ya. Syuzyumov, 'Suverenitet, nalog i zemel'naya renta v Vizantii' (Sovereignty, tax and feudal rent in Byzantium), *Antichnaya Drevnost'i Srednie Veka* 9, 1973, pp. 57–65.

13. Anderson, *Passages*, pp. 273ff.

14. See note 3 above.

15. S. Amin, *Unequal Development*, Hassocks 1976, pp. 13ff.

16. See Wickham, 'Uniqueness of the East', p. 171; P. *Anderson, Lineages of the Absolutist State*, London 1974/1979, pp. 462ff. and 484–549; H. Lubarz, 'Marx' Concept of the Asiatic Mode of Production: a Genetic Analysis', *Economy and Society* 13, 1984, pp. 456–83. In spite of Anderson's and others' justifiable pleas that the Asiatic mode should be abandoned, it continues to find favour with some anthropologists and social scientists: see, for example, A. Southall, 'The Segmentary State in Africa and Asia', *Comparative Studies in Society and History* 30, 1988, pp.

52–82, esp. p. 54, note 13; and for a defence of the Asiatic mode (based on problematic definitions of rent, tax and tribute, in my view), see K. Currie, 'The Asiatic Mode of Production: Problems of Conceptualising State and Economy', *Dialectical Anthropology* 8, 1984.

17. See Berktay, 'The Feudalism Debate'. The notion of a feudal mode in the general sense has been discussed by O. Lattimore, 'Feudalism in History', *Past and Present* 12, 1957, pp. 47–57. For Marx's comment, see *Capital*, vol. 3, London and Moscow 1972, p. 790.

18. This is where I believe Cohen to be wrong in his critique of Hilton, for example, since the genesis of relations of surplus appropriation, while it may retain an ideological and juridical significance for the forms through which the mode of surplus appropriation is expressed (which I will take up again below), cannot adequately be employed to understand either the actual process of exploitation or its later history in a concrete, historically-attested social formation. See Hilton, ed., *The Transition from Feudalism to Capitalism*, p. 14; and 'Capitalism: What's in a Name?', *Past and Present* 1, 1952, pp. 32–43; G.A. Cohen, *Karl Marx's Theory of History: a Defence*, Oxford 1978, pp. 83–4. Marx clearly considered the possible variants of rent, as 'tribute' and as 'state tax', to be perfectly admissible within his schema of the feudal mode, since the determining element was the actual process of surplus appropriation. See *Capital*, vol. 3, pp. 791–2, 796ff.

19. See Marx: *Capital*, vol. 3, p. 771; *Theories of Surplus Value*, vol. 3, Moscow 1972, p. 400.

20. See Marx, *Capital*, vol. 3, p. 791. It is important to bear in mind the difference between the specific notion of a slave mode of production, and that of societies in which slavery as an institution is usual. In the former case, slavery is a central feature in the extraction of surpluses and dominates the relations of production as a whole; in the latter, while slaves may be extremely numerous, they are marginal to the main processes of surplus extraction. See the remarks of Anderson, *Passages*, pp. 21ff. and 24–5; and the discussion below.

21. See Marx, *Pre-Capitalist Economic Formations*, ed. E. Hobsbawm, London 1964, pp. 97ff. For a clear exposition of the fundamental contradictions between a mode of surplus appropriation based on slavery, one based on tenant labour, and one based on the sale of the labour-power of individuals as a commodity within capitalist relations of production, see C. Meillassoux, 'Historical Modalities of the Exploitation and Over-exploitation of Labour', *Critique of Anthropology* 13/14, 1979, pp. 7–16. For the main characteristics of the ancient mode, and other alternative post-'primitive communal' inflections on this evolution, see Marx, *Pre-Capitalist Economic Formations*, pp. 71ff. and 92ff., and the comments of E. Wood, 'Marxism and Ancient Greece', *History Workshop Journal* 11, Spring 1981, pp. 3–22. The key moment in the transformation of the 'ancient' mode into the feudal or slave modes is, to begin with, the process of subordination of citizen to citizen consequent upon the generation of objective antagonisms between different groups of citizens in respect of their relationship to the means of production. Under certain conditions, where for example democratic political organizations were founded upon a relatively widespread use of slave labour in agricultural production, this can lead to a degree of social and economic equilibrium within the citizen body – a point made by de Ste Croix, *The Class Struggle in the Ancient Greek World*, pp. 283–300, esp. pp. 286–8. But the state

eventually becomes the legislative and executive organ of a ruling class of citizens, which can henceforth use it to maintain their own position. In the second place, the use of slave labour in an estate-based economy tends to increase dramatically the economic power of the elite, who are best able to profit from this type of labour investment. In the ancient and Hellenistic worlds, this produced the dominance of a slave mode at times, for it was just this sort of exploitation which gave the political-military elite of the Roman Republic and early Principate its pre-eminent position, even though slavery by no means dominated agricultural production in the Roman world as a whole in purely numerical terms. See the comments of Wickham, 'The Other Transition'; and his review of A. Giardina, ed., *Società romana e impero tardoantico, III. Le merci. Gli insediamenti*, Rome and Bari 1986, in *Journal of Roman Studies* 78, 1988, pp. 188–93; de Ste Croix, *The Class Struggle in the Ancient Greek World*, pp. 133ff.

22. See, for example, Cohen, *Karl Marx's Theory of History*, pp. 34f.; Hindess and Hirst, *Pre-Capitalist Modes of Production*, pp. 221ff.

23. In contrast to the position outlined here, A. Callinicos, *Making History: Agency, Structure and Change in Social Theory*, Cambridge 1989, p. 49 follows Wickham in arguing that the difference between tax and rent does imply a modal difference. On the importance of the direct and primary role of the state in the process of surplus appropriation, in respect of its relation with other elements of the ruling class as well as in respect of the process of surplus distribution, see chapter 4 below.

24. See, for example, Hindess and Hirst, *Pre-Capitalist Modes of Production*, pp. 221–55 (although they are not always consequential in their discussion: see, for example, pp. 243 and 252); also Elster, *Making Sense of Marx*, Cambridge 1985, pp. 257–8.

25. *Capital*, vol. 3, pp. 790–98, see pp. 790–91.

26. Ibid., pp. 794–6.

27. Ibid., pp. 796–8.

28. Ibid., pp. 793–4, 795–6 and 797.

29. Ibid., p. 791.

30. Wickham, 'Uniqueness of the East', p. 168. Note also p. 186, where the point is made that in respect of demesne labour-service 'supervision tends to be counterbalanced by peasant customary practice'; and 'where [the lords] do try to influence production, they do not always succeed; it is the peasant ... who actually does the producing'.

31. These points are not controversial, as the discussions of the various forms of taxation in the states discussed below and in chapters 4 and 5 will make very clear.

32. Peasant rebellions in medieval England, in Europe in the ninth century and after, in early modern Poland, and many other cases, illustrate this point. See, for example, the survey in R. Hilton, *Bond Men Made Free*, London 1973, pp. 64ff; W. Kula, *An Economic Theory of the Feudal System: Towards a Model of the Polish Economy 1500–1800*, London 1976, pp. 46ff.

33. Wickham, 'The Uniqueness of the East', p. 184.

34. A similar range of objections to the differentiation of tax from rent at a modal level has been set out in detail by Berktay, 'The Feudalism Debate', esp. pp. 301ff.

35. For an example of a non-Marxist historian who has also equated rent with

tax, see E. Patlagean, '"Economie paysanne" et "féodalité byzantine"', *Annales ESC* 30, 1975, pp. 1371–96 (but for doubts as to the adequacy of mode of surplus appropriation and extraction in the sense argued here, however, see T. Asad, 'Are There Histories of Peoples Without Europe?', *Comparative Studies in Society and History* 29/3, 1987, pp. 594–607, esp. 598ff.).

36. *Capital*, vol. 3, pp. 791–2.

37. As we have seen, Marx several times noted the potentially infinite variety of forms of modes and their combinations in specific historical formations: see the passages quoted above. For Amin's tributary mode, see Amin, *Unequal Development*, esp. pp. 13–16, from which the quotations cited here are drawn.

38. See especially K. Hopkins, *Conquerors and Slaves*, Cambridge 1978, and M.I. Finley, *The Ancient Economy*, London 1973; *Ancient Slavery and Modern Ideology*, London 1980; together with the detailed analysis and argument of A. Carandini, *L'anatomia della scimmia*, Turin 1979, pp. 128ff., 140ff. and 166–79. O. Patterson, 'On Slavery and Slave Formations', *New Left Review* 117, 1979, pp. 31–67 and E. Wood, 'Marxism and Ancient Greece', take up the theoretical aspects of the problem, as does Carandini. See also de Ste Croix, *The Class Struggle in the Ancient Greek World*, esp. pp. 133ff. and 505–9. For a good short-cut to Carandini's views, see C.J. Wickham, review of Giardina, ed., *Società romana e impero tardoantico*, vol. 3; and D. Rathbone, review of A. Giardina and A. Schiavone, eds., *Società romana e produzione schiavistica*, Rome and Bari 1981, in *Journal of Roman Studies* 73, 1983, pp. 160–68.

39. Wickham, 'Uniqueness of the East', pp. 187–9; de Ste Croix, especially, on the ancient world, *The Class Struggle in the Ancient Greek World*, pp. 52–5.

40. This appears to be one of the conclusions to be drawn from the work of Carandini and others in Italy, as well as that of Hopkins and Finley, all of whom agree (explicitly or implicitly, and often on different arguments) that the crucial importance of slavery as a mode of production (as opposed to a legally-defined status) in the period from the second century BC to the second century AD was both regionalized (representing the source of wealth and power of the Italian ruling class which dominated the Roman state at that time) and was tied in with market production. That is to say, that the evolution of intensive plantation slavery was stimulated by the existence of a market and of the possibility of considerable profits in return for the necessary investment in slaves. While intensive and efficient, it depended – like all forms of capital investment – also on the market for its raw materials, which of course included slaves. Problems of capital outlay and of supply and demand affected this system, therefore, more drastically than they affected the traditional tenant holding or small freeholder; its brittleness meant that it could be a much riskier enterprise. Not all social formations in which slavery played a major role depended on markets, of course. But then warfare and conquest, which both fuel markets and provide direct sources for slave recruits, tend to have only a restricted development before the supplies are exhausted or begin to fluctuate too violently to permit forward economic planning. Since slaves do not, on the whole, reproduce themselves as a workforce, turning them into tenants and providing them with their own means of subsistence and reproduction is one solution to this problem, and this typifies the development of the Roman state from the third century at least. But this is then no longer plantation slavery and the slave mode of production.

This last point is especially important, since it has been shown that slavery as a condition continued well into the medieval period in the West, where until the eleventh century at least a good proportion of the agricultural population seems to have been of servile status, especially on the larger estates of the Church or of private landlords. See the survey of P. Bonnassie, 'Survie et extinction du régime esclavagiste dans l'Occident du haut moyen âge (IVe – XIe siècle)', *Cahiers de Civilisation Médiévale, X[e]–IIe siècles* 28, 1985, pp. 307–43. As far as the evidence permits us to say, such slaves seem to have lived side by side with peasants of varying juridical status; but they generally owed very much heavier labour-services to their landlords (see A. Verhulst, 'La genèse du régime domaniale classique en France au haut moyen âge', in *Agricoltura e mondo rurale in Occidente nell'alto Medioevo* (Settimane di Studio del Centro Italiano di Studi sull'alto Medioevo, XIII), Spoleto 1966, pp. 135–60, esp. pp. 153ff.). As in the classical world they could be sold by their owners on the market; and, as in the classical world, the source of such slaves was both warfare (in this case, endemic in central and western Europe from the fifth to the eleventh century) and the poverty and marginal subsistence economics of peasant life everywhere. But it does seem that the great majority of these slaves were tenants with allotments, providing for their own subsistence. In many cases, they were able to marry (not legally with a person of free status, although this too seems often to have occurred) or at least establish a recognized relationship, or *contubernium*, and reproduce themselves (see Bonnassie, 'Survie et extinction du régime esclavagiste', p. 321 and notes; Ch. Verlinden, 'Le "mariage" des esclaves', in *Il matrimonio nella società altomedievale* (Settimane di Studio del Centro Italiano di Studi sull'alto Medioevo, XXIV), Spoleto 1977, pp. 569–93). They thus had effective possession (however precarious) of their own means of subsistence, and were worked effectively as an unfree peasantry. Although the rate of exploitation was high, there is evidence from some regions from the ninth century that free peasants sometimes owed even heavier services than some servile tenants: see A. Verhulst, 'La diversité du régime domaniale entre Loire et Rhin à l'époque carolingienne', in *Villa-Curtis-Grangia: Economie rurale entre Loire et Rhin de l'Epoque gallo-romaine au XIIe–XIIIe siècle*, eds. W. Janssen and D. Lohrmann, Munich 1983, pp. 133–48, see pp. 136–7; J.-P. Poly, 'Régime domaniale et rapports de production "féodalistes" dans le Midi de la France', in *Structures féodales et féodalisme dans l'Occident Méditerranéen (X[e]–XIIIe siècles), Bilan et perspectives de recherches* (Collection de l'Ecole française de Rome, vol. 44), Rome 1980, pp. 57–84, see pp. 75–80; P. Bonassie, 'Du Rhône à la Galice: genèse et modalités du régime féodale', in ibid., pp. 17–44, see pp. 27ff.

The crucial point is, therefore, that such slaves were only rarely entirely alienated from the product of all their labours. Subsistence even in servitude was provided by the slaves themselves; and while biological and social reproduction were clearly hedged about with a range of juridical and physical hindrances, alienated plantation-labour is not what the forms of medieval slavery seem to represent. Once again, therefore, while it is certainly possible to speak of the medieval West up to the tenth and eleventh centuries (and depending upon the region in question) as a culture in which slavery remained ethically and juridically an important feature, and in which it figures as a significant element of the producing population, it does not represent the slave mode of production. Whatever their status and treatment, such servile tenants represented only one segment of an oppressed agrarian labour force given responsibility for its own subsistence and reproduction (see Poly).

Equally, demesne services seem to have no connection, and slavery only a limited connection, with the slavery of late antiquity. The demesne – which develops gradually and at different rates and in specific regions from the seventh century on – seems to be a specifically post-Roman, Merovingian phenomenon, as Verhulst has argued ('La genèse du régime domaniale', and 'La diversité du régime domaniale', cited above). Medieval labour services which are based entirely on the work of non-tenured servile labourers reliant entirely on their landlord for their subsistence needs may represent the slave mode, of course. But free and propertyless labourers might also sell their labour-power – on a seasonal basis, for example – both for cash as well as for returns in kind; and this does not, of course, represent slavery, but rather one element of the equation which eventually became capitalist relations of production. Elements of antagonistic modes can always co-exist within the same social formation – but only one can be dominant.

With regard to the dominant mode of production in the later Roman period, there is little evidence to support the idea that slavery still played the central role, as it undoubtedly did into the second century AD. But de Ste Croix argues this position and, while conceding that in respect of agricultural production it probably no longer dominated as the chief source of the income of the ruling class, he suggests that the role of supervisors, administrators and overseers of slave status can be interpreted to mean the continued dominance of slave relations of production in the Roman state (*The Class Struggle in the Ancient Greek World*, pp. 144ff.). This seems somewhat forced, and is anyway unnecessary to the general line of his argument, stemming – so it would seem – from a reluctance to employ the notion of feudal relations in this particular historical context. It certainly contradicts his own principle, enunciated at pp. 52ff., that the dominance of a mode of production is determined, not by how the bulk of the labour of production is carried on in a society, but rather by how the dominant classes ensure the extraction of the surplus upon which their political and economic pre-eminence is founded. The fact that many bailiffs and estate managers may have been of slave status, while conceding at the same time that most of the labour force were subsistence peasant farmers of one type or another, hardly affects this – the institutional continuity cannot be equated with the mode of surplus appropriation or the ways in which the producing population was combined with the means of production.

41. See Wickham, 'The Other Transition', p. 6; J.F. Haldon, 'Some Considerations on Byzantine Society and Economy in the Seventh Century, *Byzantinische Forschungen* 10, 1985, pp. 75–112, see pp. 104ff.

42. See Hindess and Hirst, *Pre-Capitalist Modes of Production*, pp. 18ff. and 79–108; Marx, *Pre-Capitalist Economic Formations*, pp.71ff. The most recent work on this mode has come from French structuralist Marxists and their critics. See E. Terray, *Le marxisme devant les sociétés primitives*, Paris 1969; the essays in M. Godelier, ed., *Perspectives in Marxist Anthropology*, Cambridge 1977; P.-Ph. Rey, 'Class Contradictions in Lineage Societies', *Critique of Anthropology* 13/14, 1979, pp. 41–60; P. Bonte, 'Classes et parenté dans les sociétés segmentaires', *Dialectiques* 21, 1977, pp. 103–15.

43. See Marx, *Pre-Capitalist Economic Formations*, pp. 71–82.

44. And as Wickham, 'The Uniqueness of the East', p. 183 and Berktay, 'The Feudalism Debate: the Turkish End', pp. 302–3 both note, tax and rent often

coincide in actual historical examples. See Marx, *Capital*, vol. 3, pp. 790ff.

45. A.P. Kazhdan: *Vizantiiskaya Kul'tura*; and *Sotsial'nii sostav gospodstvuyushchego klassa v Vizantii XI–XII vv.* (The social structure of the Byzantine ruling class in the 11th and 12th centuries), Moscow 1974.

46. G. Litavrin, *Vizantiiskoe obshchestvo i gosudarstvo*, pp. 264–90. But it must be recalled that Soviet scholars, among them Litavrin, have usually avoided attempts to equate such institutions directly with a western equivalent, at least in recent years, preferring to speak instead of their social and economic structural similarities. At the same time attempts to draw up complex typologies to describe the different variations on the feudal theme and the uneven development of different feudal social formations have occupied much discussion. See Ya. M. Kobishchanov, 'Tipi i sistemi feodal'nikh obshchestv' (Types and systems of feudal societies), in *Tipologiya razvitogo feodalizma v stranakh Vostoka*, Moscow 1975, pp. 40ff: V. Grohova, 'Mesto Vizantii ve tipologii evropeiskogo feodalizma' (The place of Byzantium in the typology of European feudalism), *Vizantiiskii Vremennik* 40, 1979, pp. 3–8, among many examples. Note that this general criticism applies to the remarks of Anderson also, who is particularly opposed to a concept of a generalized feudal mode (*Lineages of the Absolutist State*, pp. 401ff.)

47. Anderson, *Lineages of the Absolutist State*, pp. 402–3.

48. Ibid., p. 404

49. See again Berktay's exposition of this fundamental point, 'The Feudalism Debate'; for Marx's texts, see *Capital*, vol. 1, pp. 217; vol. 2, pp. 36–7; vol. 3, pp. 791–2.

50. Anderson, *Lineages of the Absolutist State*, pp. 403 and 404.

51. See the review by Hirst, 'The Uniqueness of the West', and Wickham's critique incorporated in 'The Uniqueness of the East'.

52. Anderson, *Lineages of the Absolutist State*, p. 420, for the absence of any inherent drive to capitalism embodied in feudal production relations; and on the establishment of a taxonomy of institutional forms, p. 404.

53. Points made most recently and strongly by Berktay, 'The Feudalism Debate: the Turkish End', pp. 317ff.

54. Marx's letter to Mikhailovsky, 1877 (transl. in Marx and Engels, *Selected Correspondence*, Moscow and London 1935, pp. 311ff.). Cf. also Engels's letter to J. Bloch of September 1890, in which a similar point is made: empirical analysis of specific societies, guided by the general theory, is what is needed, not the blind imposition upon the historical understanding of a non-historical theory (Marx and Engels, *Selected Works*, pp. 682–3). Note the remarks of Hobsbawm, in his introduction to *Pre-Capitalist Economic Formations*, pp. 62ff., quoted by Berktay, 'The Feudalism Debate: the Turkish End', p. 318, n.36.

55. Ashok Rudra, 'Pre-Capitalist Modes of Production in Non-European Societies', *Journal of Peasant Studies* 15, 1987–8, pp. 373–94.

56. See Harbans Mukhia, 'Peasant Production and Medieval Indian Society', *Journal of Peasant Studies* 12, 1985, pp. 228–51.

57. De Ste Croix, *Class Struggle in the Ancient Greek World*, pp. 43f.

58. Best summed up in a much-quoted passage from his 'Introduction' in *A Contribution to the Critique of Political Economy*, ed. M. Dobb, Moscow 1977, pp. 20–21: 'In the social production of their existence, men inevitably enter into definite relations, which are independent of their will, namely relations of production appropriate to a given stage in the development of their material

forces of production. The totality of these relations of production constitutes the economic structure of society .... At a certain stage of development, the material productive forces of society come into conflict with the existing relations of production or – this merely expresses the same thing in legal terms – with the property relations within the framework of which they have operated hitherto. From forms of development of the productive forces these relations turn into their fetters'.

59. See, for example, J. McMurtry, *The Structure of Marx's World View*, Princeton 1978; W. Shaw, *Marx's Theory of History*, London 1978, both of whom consider that the forces of production are relevant only to recent (or capitalist) history.

60. A. Levine, *Arguing for Socialism*, London 1984, pp. 164ff; A. Levine and E. Olin Wright, 'Rationality and Class Struggle', *New Left Review* 123, 1980, pp. 47–68; and esp. Callinicos, *Making History*, pp. 52–95, who presents a detailed account of the arguments surrounding Cohen's attempt to re-introduce the forces as a central and causal element in Marxist explanation.

61. For a recent discussion of some aspects of this problem (and of the question of the forces of production which, Rudra notes, tend to be ignored in the debate in question here) see G. McLennan, *Marxism, Pluralism and Beyond*, Cambridge 1989, pp. 59ff., esp. pp. 77–85. On the feudal 'prime mover' in particular, see Hilton, 'A Comment', in *The Transition from Feudalism to Capitalism*, pp. 109–17, esp. pp. 115–16; and especially Kula, *An Economic Theory of the Feudal System*, who provides one of the clearest available expositions of the economic dynamic of tributary ('feudal') production relations. For a clear account of the nature of the relationship between forces and relations of production, which likewise eschews a determinist inevitabilism in this connection, see the discussion of E.O. Wright, 'Giddens' Critique of Marx', *New Left Review* 138, 1983, pp. 11–35, esp. 24–31.

62. For the 'overlapping' character of all socio-economic and cultural structures, together with a discussion of the ways in which these reciprocal influences are hierarchized according to the relative strengths of the state, social, or cultural forms in question, see M. Rowlands, 'Centre and Periphery: a Review of a Concept' pp. 1–11; and Lotte Hedeager, 'Empire, Frontier and the Barbarian Hinterland: Rome and Northern Europe from A.D. 1–400', pp. 125–40; in M. Rowlands, M. Larsen and K. Kristiansen, eds., *Centre and Periphery in the Ancient World*, Cambridge 1987.

63. *Capital*, vol. 3, p. 794.

64. F. Tinnefeld, *Die frühbyzantinische Gesellschaft. Struktur – Gegensätze – Spannungen*, Munich 1977, pp. 56–8 for the late Roman period in the East. Also the survey of E. Patlagean, *Pauvreté économique et pauvreté sociale à Byzance, 4e – 7e siècles*, Paris 1977, pp. 263–340; and particularly that of D. Eibach, *Untersuchungen zum spätantiken Kolonat in der kaiserlichen Gesetzgebung unter besondere Berücksichtigung der Terminologie*, Cologne 1977, pp. 132–204.

65. M.F. Hendy, *Studies in the Byzantine Monetary Economy, 300–1450*, Cambridge 1985, pp. 631ff.

66. For example, Anderson, *Passages from Antiquity to Feudalism*, pp. 270–71 following R. Browning, 'Rabstvo v vizantiiskoi imperii (600–1200 gg.)' (Slavery in the Byzantine empire, 600–1200 AD), *Vizantiiskii Vremennik* 14, pp. 38–55. But see the detailed analysis of H. Köpstein, *Zur Sklaverei im ausgehenden Byzanz*, Berlin 1966, esp. pp. 26ff., 110ff. and 132ff. For a survey of the literature on this theme

until 1966, see ibid., pp. 22–6; and H. Köpstein, 'Die byzantinische Sklaverei in der Historiographie der letzten 125 Jahre', *Klio* 43–5, 1965, pp. 560–76. See also the extensive discussion in G.E. Lebedeva, *Sotsial'naya struktura rannevizantiiskogo obshchestva (po dannim Kodeksov Feodosiya i Yustiniana)* (The social structure of early Byzantine society [according to the Theodosian and Justinianic codes]), Leningrad 1980, who fails, however, to distinguish adequately between slavery as a mode and slavery as an institution.

67. On the various forms of taxation and state corvées in the Byzantine state, see F. Dölger, *Beiträge zur Geschichte der byzantinischen Finanzverwaltung besonders des 10. und 11. Jahrhunderts*, Byzantinisches Archiv 9, Munich 1927 and Darmstadt 1960, pp. 48–60; also H. Ahrweiler, 'Recherches sur l'administration byzantin aux IXe–XIe siècles', *Bulletin de Correspondance Hellénique* 84, 1960, pp. 1–109 (repr. in Ahrweiler, *Etudes sur les structures administratives et sociales à Byzance*, London 1971, no. VIII); J.F. Haldon, *Byzantine Praetorians*, Bonn and Berlin 1984, pp. 319ff.

68. Thus Anderson, *Passages from Antiquity to Feudalism*, pp. 265ff., seems to take the whole period from the fifth to the seventh and eighth centuries as undifferentiated by internal or other changes.

69. I use the word elite deliberately since, while most members of the Roman ruling class were members of one grade or another of the senatorial order, not all those who held senatorial titles were necessarily members of the ruling class in the political and economic sense. Indeed, many *clarissimi* (members of the lowest – and the only hereditary – grade of senator) were economically relatively weak and were often tenants of other landlords, with no property of their own. See A.H.M. Jones, *The Later Roman Empire, 284–602*, Oxford 1964, pp. 554–7.

70. Ibid., pp. 1065–7.

71. Ibid., pp. 554ff.; and 'The Social Background of the Struggle between Paganism and Christianity', in A. Momigliano, ed., *The Conflict between Paganism and Christianity in the Fourth Century*, Oxford 1963, pp. 13–37; also G. Dagron, 'Aux origines de la civilisation byzantine: langue de culture et langue d'état', *Revue Historique* 241, 1969, pp. 23–56 (repr. in Dagron, *La romanité chrétienne en Orient*, London 1984). The position is well summed up in a polemic by Synesius of Cyrene read to the emperor Arcadius at Constantinople in 399: 'Synesii De Regno', in J.-P. Migne, *Patrologiae Cursus completus, series Graeca*, Paris 1857–66 and 1880–1903, XLVI, cols. 1053–1108.

72. See Jones, *The Later Roman Empire*, pp. 177ff. and the still useful account of J.B. Bury, *History of the Later Roman Empire from the Death of Theodosius I to the Death of Justinian*, New York 1958, pp. 126ff. It should not be forgotten either that the eastern empire was able to shrug off the barbarians onto the West through a combination of bribes and threats, an option not available in Italy and Gaul, where the factional interests of the civil and military establishments had no common policy. See Bury, *History of the Later Roman Empire*, pp. 160–85, and Jones, *The Later Roman Empire*, pp. 183ff. For the best recent account of the 'crisis' of the early fifth century, see G. Albert, *Goten in Konstantinopel. Untersuchungen zur oströmischen Geschichte um das Jahr 400 n. Chr.* (Studien zur Geschichte und Kultur des Altertums, N.F. 1), Paderborn-Munich-Vienna-Zurich 1984.

73. In spite of some over-generalizations, and bearing in mind the theoretical reservations expressed already, Anderson, *Passages from Antiquity to Feudalism*, pp. 96–102, provides a good synthesis. See Wickham, 'The Other Transition', pp. 15–18 and 23–5 with the relevant recent secondary literature, for a discussion of

the contradictions within the social-political order of the western half of the empire in the later fourth and fifth centuries; and, in greater detail, de Ste Croix, *The Class Struggle in the Ancient Greek World*, pp. 465ff. For a recent general survey of some of these aspects, see J. Herrin, *The Formation of Christendom*, Princeton 1987, pp. 19–53.

74. On the political events, Jones, *The Later Roman Empire*, pp. 217–37; E. Stein, *Histoire du Bas-Empire*, I, Paris and Bruges 1959 and Amsterdam 1968, pp. 351–64; II, Paris and Bruges 1949 and Amsterdam 1968, pp. 7ff. and 177ff.

75. For these developments see Hendy, *Studies in the Byzantine Monetary Economy*, pp. 475ff.; Jones, *The Later Roman Empire*, pp. 207f. and 235f.

76. G.T. Dennis, ed., 'The Anonymous Byzantine Treatise on Strategy', in *Three Byzantine Military Treatises*, Washington DC 1985, pp. 1–136, see p. 13: 'The financial system was set up to take care of matters of public importance that arise on occasion, such as the building of ships and of walls. But it is principally concerned with paying the soldiers. Every year most of the public revenues are spent for this purpose.'

77. Procopius, *Wars*, ed. Dewing, II, xxii–xxiii.

78. See G. Ostrogorsky, *A History of the Byzantine State*, Oxford 1968, pp. 68–82 for a survey. For the text, see J. and P. Zepos, *Jus Graecoromanum*, Athens 1931 and Amsterdam 1962, I, Coll. I, nov. xi: Imp. Tiberii, *Peri kouphismon demosion* (a. 575). Tiberius began his reign formally in 578, but because of Justin II's illness, actually took over some time before this date.

79. For a brief political-military history of the period, see Ostrogorsky, *History of the Byzantine State*, pp. 83–95 and 100–17; and in more detail, A.N. Stratos, *Byzantium in the Seventh Century*, I, Amsterdam 1968; II, Amsterdam 1972; III, Amsterdam 1975. For the proportion of the revenue lost, see Hendy, *Studies in the Byzantine Monetary Economy*, p. 620.

80. I have discussed many of these changes and developments elsewhere. See 'Some Considerations on Byzantine Society and Economy in the Seventh Century', pp. 77ff. on cities and their slow decline into the seventh century. For shifts and new emphases in ideology and the power/authority equation, see 'Ideology and Social Change in the Seventh Century: Military Discontent as a Barometer', *Klio* 68, 1986, pp. 139–90, and chapter 5 below; and most recently, *Byzantium in the Seventh Century: the Transformation of a Culture*, Cambridge 1990.

81. See A.H.M. Jones, *The Greek City from Alexander to Justinian*, Oxford 1940, pp. 259ff.; E. Kirsten, 'Die byzantinische Stadt', in *Berichte zum XI. Internationalen Byzantinisten-Kongress*, Munich 1958, pp. 10ff.; D. Claude, *Die byzantinische Stadt im 6. Jahrhundert* (Byzantinisches Archiv 13), Munich 1969, pp. 176ff.; Patlagean, *Pauvreté économique et pauvreté sociale à Byzance*, pp. 156–235. Note also A.H.M. Jones, 'The Economic Life of the Towns of the Roman Empire', *Recueils de la Société Jean Bodin* 7, 1955, pp. 161–92 (repr. in Jones, *The Roman Economy: Studies in Ancient Economic and Social History*, ed. P.A. Brunt, Oxford 1974, pp. 35–60). For further literature see Haldon, 'Some Considerations on Byzantine Society and Economy in the Seventh Century', pp. 78ff.; and most recently, W. Brandes, *Die Städte Kleinasiens im 7. und 8. Jahrhundert*, Berlin 1989, for a full analysis of the archaeological and textual evidence for the decline of the late antique city and the development of the situation revealed in the sources for the later seventh and eighth centuries.

82. Jones: *The Later Roman Empire*, pp. 712ff.; and 'The Cities of the Roman

Empire: Political, Administrative and Judicial Functions', *Recueils de la Société Jean Bodin* 6, 1954, pp. 135–73; E. Frances, 'La ville byzantine et la monnaie aux VIIe–VIIIe siècles', *Byzantinobulgarica* 2, 1966, pp. 3–14, see pp. 5–10; Kirsten, 'Die byzantinische Stadt', pp. 25ff.; G.L. Kurbatov, *Osnovnye problemi vnutrennogo razvitiya vizantiiskogo goroda v IV–VII vv.* (The fundamental problems of the internal evolution of the Byzantine city in the 4th–7th centuries), Leningrad 1971, pp. 154ff., the last providing a good survey. See also de Ste Croix, *The Class Struggle in the Ancient Greek World*, pp. 465–74.

83. See especially J.-M. Spieser, 'L'Evolution de la ville byzantine de l'époque paléochrétienne à l'iconoclasme', in *Hommes et richesses dans l'Empire byzantin, IVe–VIIe siècles*, Paris 1989, pp. 97–106, esp. pp. 103ff.

84. The best survey is that of Jones, *The Greek City from Alexander to Justinian*, p. 89. See also his comments in *The Later Roman Empire*, pp. 716–19.

85. For the development of the new capital and its effects on its hinterland and the larger region about it see C. Mango, 'The Development of Constantinople as an Urban Centre', in *Seventeenth International Byzantine Congress. Major Papers*, New York 1986, pp. 118–36; for the ideological and cultural focus on Constantinople, see especially H. Hunger, *Reich der neuen Mitte. Der christliche Geist der byzantinischen Kultur*, Vienna, Graz and Cologne 1965; on the attraction of Constantinople and the palatine hierarchy for provincial elites, see F. Vittinghof, 'Zur Verfassung der spätantiken Stadt', in *Studien zu den Anfängen des Europäischen Stadtwesens*, Reichenau 1955–6, pp. 11–409, esp. pp. 27ff. and Spieser, 'L'Evolution de la ville byzantine', p. 106.

86. See J.W. Hayes, 'Problèmes de la céramique des VIIe–IXe siècles à Salamine et à Chypre', in *Salamine de Chypre, histoire et archéologie: état des recherches* (Colloques internationaux du CNRS no. 578), Paris 1980, pp. 375–87; C. Abadie-Reynal, 'Céramique et commerce dans le bassin Egéen du IVe au VIIe siècle', in *Hommes et richesses* I, pp. 143–62, esp. pp. 156–8.

87. See for the Syria/Palestine region the valuable survey of Hugh Kennedy, 'The Last Century of Byzantine Syria: a Reinterpretation', *Byzantinische Forschungen* 10, 1985, pp. 141–83.

88. Kirsten, 'Die byzantinische Stadt', p. 20; Jones, *Later Roman Empire*, pp. 758ff.; H. Aubin, 'Vom Absterben antiken Lebens im Frühmittelalter', *Antike und Abendland* 3, 1948, pp. 88–119 (repr. in P. Hübinger, ed., *Kulturbruch oder Kulturkontinuität von der Antike zum Mittelalter*, Darmstadt 1968, pp. 205–58).

89. See in particular the analysis of Hunger, *Reich der neuen Mitte. Der christliche Geist der byzantinischen Kultur*.

90. There is a vast literature on both the sources and their interpretation and on the related question of the nature of the 'monetary' economy of the Byzantine world. See Haldon, 'Some Considerations on Byzantine Society and Economy in the Seventh Century', pp. 78–94, for a summary; and for a detailed review of the literature, W. Brandes: *Die Städte Kleinasiens*; and 'Die byzantinische Stadt Kleinasiens im 7. und 8. Jahrhundert – ein Forschungsbericht', *Klio* 70, 1988, pp. 176–208. I have dealt with the question at length in *Byzantium in the Seventh Century: the Transformation of a Culture*.

91. In general on *coloni*, and the various sub-groupings, see Tinnefeld, *Die frühbyzantinische Gesellschaft*, pp. 45–55; Jones, *The Later Roman Empire*, pp. 795–803; for a good general survey, see also Patlagean, *Pauvreté économique et pauvreté sociale à Byzance*, pp. 263–340 ('la terre et la société'); de Ste Croix, *The Class Struggle in*

the Ancient Greek World, pp. 226–59; Eibach, *Untersuchungen zum spätantiken Kolonat in der kaiserlichen Gesetzgebung*, pp. 47ff. For the status of *coloni*, see R. Günther, 'Coloni liberi und coloni originarii: einige Bemerkungen zum spätantiken Kolonat', *Klio* 49 , 1967, pp. 267–71; also Eibach, pp. 132–204, critical of Jones' traditional view. For an analysis of the changes described here, see Haldon, *Byzantium in the Seventh Century*, pp. 125–72.

92. See J. Gascou, 'Les grands domaines, la cité et l'état en Egypte byzantine', *Travaux et Mémoires* 9, 1985, pp. 1–90, see 22–7; and W. Goffart, *'Caput' and Colonate: Towards a History of Late Roman Taxation* (*Phoenix* suppl. vol. 12), Toronto 1974, pp. 87ff. for the position of such *coloni* in relation to their landlords and the estates to which they were bound.

93. Haldon, *Byzantium in the Seventh Century*, pp. 132–53.

94. See in particular the comments of M. Kaplan, 'L'exploitation paysanne byzantine entre l'antiquité et le moyen âge (VIe–VIIIe siècles): affirmation d'une structure économique et sociale', in V. Vavrínek, ed., *From Late Antiquity to Early Byzantium*, Prague 1985, pp. 101–5; idem, 'Remarques sur la place de l'exploitation paysanne dans l'économie rurale', in *Akten des XVI. Internationalen Byzantinisten-Kongresses* 2/2, Vienna 1982, pp. 105–14, see pp. 107ff. with sources.

95. For taxation in the tenth century (assessment, application, extraction), see Dölger, *Beiträge zur Geschichte der byzantinischen Finanzverwaltung besonders des 10. und 11. Jahrhunderts*; G. Ostrogorsky, 'Die ländliche Steuergemeinde des byzantinischen Reiches im X. Jahrhundert', *Vierteljahrschrift fur Sozial- und Wirtschaftsgeschichte* 20, 1927, pp. 1–108; Ch. M. Brand, 'Two Byzantine Treatises on Taxation', *Traditio* 25, 1969, pp. 35–60; J. Karayannopoulos, 'Fragmente aus dem Vademecum eines byzantinischen Finanzbeamten', in *Polychronion. Festschrift Franz Dölger zum 75. Geburtstag*, Heidelberg 1966, pp. 317–33; N. Svoronos, 'Recherches sur le cadastre byzantin et la fiscalité aux XIe–XIIe siècles: le cadastre de Thèbes', *Bulletin de Correspondance Hellénique* 83, 1959, pp. 1–166.

96. For the best general analysis of Byzantine rural relations in the period from the sixth to the eleventh century, see now M. Kaplan, *Les hommes et la terre à Byzance du VIe au XIe siècle*, Paris 1992.

97. For the effects of these factors in the late Roman period, up to the later sixth century, see Jones, *The Later Roman Empire*, pp. 773–81.

98. On the effects of severe winters and bad harvests on peasant society, see esp. R. Morris, 'The Powerful and the Poor in Tenth-century Byzantium: Law and Reality', *Past and Present* 73, 1976, pp. 3–27.

99. For the senate and senatorial elite and its structure in the sixth century and before, see Jones, *Later Roman Empire*, pp. 523ff.; Tinnefeld, *Die frühbyzantinische Gesellschaft*, pp. 59ff. On the system of precedence in the later seventh century and after, and the shifts in the composition of the ruling elite, see F. Winkelmann, *Byzantinische Rang- und Ämterstruktur im 8. und 9. Jahrhundert*, Berlin 1987 and J.F. Haldon, 'A Touch of Class?', *Rechtshistorisches Journal* 7, 1988, pp. 37–50. The problem is discussed in detail in Haldon, *Byzantium in the Seventh Century*, 153–72 and 387–99.

100. See the remarks of G. Ostrogorsky, 'Observations on the Aristocracy in Byzantium', *Dumbarton Oaks Papers* 25, 1971, pp. 1–32.

101. It is precisely these transformations of the specific forms taken by the mode of surplus appropriation which persuaded so many historians that 'real' feudal relations commenced only from this time – the late eleventh and twelfth centuries.

See Ostrogorsky, *Pour l'histoire de la féodalité byzantine*, for example. For a detailed analysis of the ruling class at this period, see Kazhdan, *Sotsial'nii sostav gospodstvuyushchego klassa v Vizantii XI–XII vv.*

102. R. Morris, 'The Powerful and the Poor in Tenth-Century Byzantium'.

103. See Ostrogorsky, *Pour l'histoire de la féodalité byzantine*; and for a more recent assessment, H. Ahrweiler, 'La Pronoia à Byzance', in *Structures féodales et féodalisme dans l'Occident méditerranéen (X^e–XIIIe siècles), Bilan et perspectives de recherches* (Collection de l'Ecole française de Rome, 44), Rome 1980, pp. 681–9. For the debate among western Byzantinists on the *pronoia* and whether or not it is to be accorded a 'feudal' status, see A. Hohlweg, 'Zur Frage der Pronoia in Byzanz', *Byzantinische Zeitschrift* 60, 1967, pp. 288–308; P. Lemerle, 'Recherches sur le régime agraire à Byzance: la terre militaire à l'époque des Comnènes', *Cahiers de Civilisation Médiévale, X^e–XIIe siècles* 2, 1959, pp. 265–81; N. Oikonomidès, 'The Donation of Castles in the Last Quarter of the Eleventh Century (Dölger, Regesten, No. 1012)', in *Polychronion. Festschrift Franz Dölger zum 25. Geburtstag*, Heidelberg 1966, pp. 413–17 (repr. in Oikonomidès, *Documents et études sur les institutions de Byzance (VIIe–XVe)*, London 1976, XIV); G. Ostrogorsky, 'Die Pronoia unter den Komnenen', *Zbornik Radova Vizantoloshkog Instituta* 12, 1970, pp. 41–54.

104. For a historical materialist survey of the economic and social structure of the empire in the period from the ninth to the twelfth centuries, see especially A. Harvey, *Economic Expansion in the Byzantine Empire, 900–1200*, Cambridge 1989. Harvey retains the difference between tax and rent as having a modal significance, but this is otherwise the best survey available in English for this important period. For the specific situation of the peasantry in the tenth and eleventh centuries, see G. Litavrin, 'Zur Lage der byzantinischen Bauernschaft im 10.–11. Jahrhundert (strittige Fragen)', in V. Vavrínek, ed., *Beiträge zur byzantinischen Geschichte im 9.–11. Jahrhundert*, Prague 1978, pp. 47–70. The author concentrates primarily on the juridical and economic condition of peasant holdings and their relationship to private landlords and the state. For the later Byzantine peasantry (thirteenth century and after), see A.E. Laiou-Thomadakis, *Peasant Society in the Late Byzantine Empire. a Social and Demographic Study*, Princeton 1977.

105. On the ruling class in the tenth and eleventh centuries, see Kazhdan, *Sotsial'nii sostav*, esp. pp. 226ff. on the 'mixed' economic basis of magnate power. For the political and factional conflicts, see Sp. Vryonis, 'Byzantium: the Social Basis of Decline in the Eleventh Century', *Greek, Roman and Byzantine Studies* 2, 1959, pp. 159–75 (repr. in Sp. Vryonis: *Byzantium: its Internal History and Relations with the Muslim World*, London 1971, II); and *The Decline of Medieval Hellenism in Asia Minor and the Process of Islamization from the Eleventh through the Fifteenth Century*, Berkeley, Los Angeles and London 1971, who presents a rather black-and-white account. For an excellent recent analysis, which emphasizes the fluidity of the various competing power cliques and the constant re-ordering of their elements as individuals and family groups re-assessed their position and interests, see Jean-Claude Cheynet, *Pouvoir et contestations à Byzance (963–1210)*, Paris 1990.

106. See Harvey, *Economic Expansion in the Byzantine Empire*, pp. 72ff., who points out that the *pronoia* was in itself not a new institution – the word was used already before its use as a revenue allocation to mean also other forms of income from, for example, monastic institutions, which were granted to private persons (traditionally referred to as *charistikia*). See also K.V. Khvostova, 'K voprosu o strukture pozdnevizantiiskogo sel'skogo poseleniya' (Concerning the structure of late Byzantine rural communities), *Vizantiiskii Vremennik* 45, 1984, pp. 3–19.

107. See Oikonomidès, 'De l'impôt de distribution à l'impôt de quotité à propos du premier cadastre byzantin (7e–9e siècle)', *Zbornik Radova Vizantoloshkog Instituta* 26, 1987, pp. 9–19, see 16–17; and Ostrogorsky, *History of the Byzantine State*, p. 306.

108. See, for example, the survey article of Udal'tsova, 'Nekotorye osobennosti feodalizma v Vizantii' (Some peculiarities of feudalism in Byzantium), in Vavrínek, ed., *Beiträge zur byzantinischen Geschichte im 9.–11. Jahrhundert*, Prague 1978, pp. 5–30.

4. Tributary States, Ruling Elites

1. See M. Mann, 'The Autonomous Power of the State: its Origins, Mechanisms and Results', in J.A. Hall, ed., *States in History*, Oxford 1986; the essays in H.J.M. Claessen and P. Skalník, eds., *The Early State*, The Hague 1978, especially R. Cohen, 'State Origins: a Reappraisal', pp. 31–75; A.R. Radcliffe-Brown, *African Political Systems*, eds. M. Fortes and E.E. Evans-Pritchard, London 1940.

2. See most recently K. Schippman, *Grundzüge der Geschichte des Sasanidischen Reiches*, Darmstadt 1990; for older accounts, A. Christensen, *L'Iran sous les Sassanides*, Copenhagen 1944, and the relevant sections of R.N. Frye: *The History of Ancient Iran*, Munich 1984; and in *The Cambridge History of Iran*, 3/1, Cambridge 1983, pp. 153ff. The evidence for the 'reforms' of Khusru is extremely difficult to interpret, and there is a great deal of discussion and disagreement about the exact nature of the changes he is supposed to have inaugurated: cf., for example, F. Altheim, R. Stiel, *Finanzgeschichte der Spätantike*, Frankfurt a.M. 1957, pp. 31–53. See now, for a detailed discussion, Z. Rubin, 'The Reforms of Khusro Anushirwan', in Averil Cameron and L.A Conrad, eds., *States, Resources and Armies: Papers of the Third Workshop on Late Antiquity and Early Islam*, Princeton 1994.

3. The problem of tribal identities historically and in the contemporary Middle East is complex and extended. For good discussions, see esp. M. Godelier, 'The Concept of the "Tribe": a Crisis Involving Merely a Concept or the Empirical Foundations of Anthropology Itself?', in *Perspectives in Marxist Anthropology*, trans. R. Brain, Cambridge 1973, pp. 70–96; and the collection *Tribes and State Formation in the Middle East*, eds. Philip S. Khoury and Joseph Kostiner, Berkeley and Los Angeles 1990. From a somewhat different perspective see also M.H. Fried, *The Notion of Tribe*, Menlo Park, California 1975; and also M.D. Sahlins, *Tribesmen*, Englewood Cliffs, New Jersey 1968; P. Crone, 'The Tribe and the State', in Hall, ed., *States in History* (but note also the critical discussion of Richard Tapper, 'Anthropologists, Historians, and Tribespeople on Tribe and State Formation in the Middle East', in Khoury, Kostiner, eds., pp. 48–73). For an historical analysis of the structural contradictions within early Islamic states see, for example, I.M. Lapidus, 'The Arab Conquests and the Formation of Islamic Society', in G.H.A. Juynboll, ed., *Studies on the First Century of Islamic History*, Carbondale, Illinois 1982; P. Crone, *Slaves on Horses: the Evolution of the Islamic Polity*, Cambridge 1980. For some comparative discussions of late Roman, Sassanian and early Islamic state structures, see Cameron and Conrad, eds., *States, Resources and Armies*. On the Cholas of South India, see, for example, G.W. Spencer, 'The Politics of Plunder: the Cholas in Eleventh-Century Ceylon', *Journal of Asian Studies* 35, 1976, pp. 405–19; on Vijayanagara, see chapter 5, below.

4. For some alternative viewpoints on the dynamic underlying state power, stressing the ideological structures through which state systems and relations of

exploitation and/or appropriation are expressed, see esp. C. Geertz: *Agricultural Involution*, Berkeley 1970; and *Negara: the Theatre-State in Nineteenth-Century Bali*, Princeton 1980; and the account of J. Tambiah, 'The Galactic Polity: the Structure of Traditional Kingdoms in South East Asia', *Annals of the New York Academy of Sciences* 293, 1977, pp. 69–97. For a review of some recent work combining both anthropological and historical perspectives, see G.C. Bentley, 'Indigenous States of Southeast Asia', *American Review of Anthropology* 15, 1986, pp. 275–305.

5. For example, the Pyu and Pagan 'dynasties' of Burma in the 7th–13th centuries AD, whose power depended upon the maintenance of agricultural output and of exchange relations with the commercial centres of the coast, appear to have invested heavily in centrally-promoted irrigation schemes. See M. Aung-Thwin, *Irrigation in the Heartland of Burma: Foundations of the Pre-Colonial Burmese State*, DeKalb 1990. In contrast, the village-economies of southern India often generated and maintained investment in the productive infrastructure at the community level, stimulated both by the vested interests of dominant lineages and by market exchange relationships with both the state, on the one hand, and with commercial and trading interests, on the other. See Burton Stein, 'The Economic Function of a Medieval South Indian Temple', *Journal of Asian Studies* 19, 1960, pp. 163–76. See chapter 5 below for further discussion.

6. I have tried to demonstrate the ways in which these intertwining elements can be disengaged in order to demonstrate the causal relationships at play during a period of social and ideological transformation in 'Ideology and Social Change in the Seventh-Century: Military Discontent as a Barometer', *Klio* 68, 1986, pp. 139–90, in which the role of soldiers and their social origins is analysed in respect of their intervention at the level of state politics and imperial ideology.

7. For Halil Berktay's point, see 'The Feudalism Debate: the Turkish End – is "Tax vs Rent" Necessarily the Product and Sign of a Modal Difference?', *Journal of Peasant Studies* 14, 1987, pp. 312–13; and on territorial extent and pre-industrial communications and transport, see also M. Mann, *The Sources of Social Power*, vol. 1: *A History of Power from the Beginning to AD 1760*, Cambridge 1986, pp. 272ff., following E.N. Luttwak, *The Grand Strategy of the Roman Empire*, Baltimore 1976.

8. Weber elaborated a fairly complex schema of types of political power and authority: see esp. M. Weber, *Wirtschaft und Gesellschaft. Grundrisse der verstehenden Soziologie*, Tübingen 1972, see pp. 468ff. and 580ff.

9. And as has been shown in the excellent analysis of ancient (Greek and Roman) political-economic history by G.E.M. de Ste Croix, *The Class Struggle in the Ancient Greek World*, London 1981.

10. See the discussion of R.H. Hilton, *Bond Men Made Free*, London 1973, pp. 61–2, 114ff.

11. See chapter 3 above

12. See below; and note D. Goffman, *Izmir and the Levantine World, 1550–1650*, Seattle 1990, pp. 26ff.

13. See the useful insights of C.J. Wickham, 'Problems of Comparing Rural Societies in Early Medieval Western Europe', *Transactions of the Royal Historical Society*, 6th ser., 2, 1992, pp. 221–46.

14. The ways in which feudal landlords could intervene directly in the production process, redefining the amount of surplus demanded and consequently affecting both the amount of labour time invested by the producers and

the amount remaining to them as subsistence and as marketable or exchangeable surplus, has been well analysed in W. Kula, *An Economic Theory of the Feudal System: Towards a Model of the Polish Economy 1500–1800*, London 1976. I would contend that tributary (i.e. feudal) states can act in just the same way, making the incidence of taxation (whether in kind, cash or labour, or all of these) as one of the possible forms of feudal rent a fundamental element in the rate of exploitation of the producing population.

The relationship between capitalist states and the bourgeoisie is lucidly presented and discussed in Ernest Mandel, *Marxist Economic Theory*, London 1968, pp. 310–11 and 498ff.

15. For the Ottoman state as exemplifying the Asiatic mode, see Ç. Keyder, 'The Dissolution of the Asiatic Mode of Production', *Economy and Society* 5, 1976, pp. 178–96; H. İslamoğlu, Ç. Keyder, 'The Ottoman Social Formation', in A.M. Bailey and J. Llobera, eds., *The Asiatic Mode of Production: Science and Politics*, London 1981, pp. 301–24; H. İslamoğlu, *The Ottoman Empire and the World Economy*, Cambridge and Paris 1987, introduction. For a useful general comment on the Asiatic mode of production, see P. Anderson, *Lineages of the Absolutist State*, London 1974/1979, pp. 462–549; and for a survey of some aspects of the debate, see the remaining essays in Bailey and Llobera, eds, *The Asiatic Mode of Production*. For the discussion of an Ottoman feudalism, see A.H. Lybyer, *The Government of the Ottoman Empire in the Time of Suleiman the Magnificent*, Cambridge, Massachusetts 1913, esp. pp. 100ff.; and 'Feudalism (Saracen and Ottoman)', in *Encyclopaedia of the Social Sciences*, vol. 6, London 1932, pp. 211–13; and, for a survey of the intra-Turkish debate, Berktay, 'The Feudalism Debate', esp. p. 293 and notes 3, 4. Most recently, see the excellent analysis of Turkish historiography from Köprülü to the present in H. Berktay: *The 'Other' Feudalism: a Critique of Twentieth Century Turkish Historiography and its Particularisation of Ottoman Society*, doctoral thesis, Birmingham University 1990; and 'The Search for the Peasant in Western and Turkish History/Historiography', in *New Approaches to State and Peasant in Ottoman History*, London 1992, pp. 109–84. For a good survey of the current state of Ottoman studies in this respect, see S. Faroqui, 'In Search of Ottoman History', *Journal of Peasant Studies* 18, pp. 211–41.

16. So formulated, for example, by Anderson, *Lineages of the Absolutist State*, pp. 365–66; see also Ş. Mardin, 'Power, Civil Society and Culture in the Ottoman Empire', *Comparative Studies in Society and History* 11, 1969, pp. 258–81.

17. The *devşirme* developed in the first place through the collection of the ruler's traditional fifth portion (*pençik*) of the booty taken in war in the form of young captives, who were then trained for the personal service of the Sultan. Under Bayezid I (1360–1403) this appears to have evolved into an institution for the collection of young Christian boys, who would be brought entirely within an Ottoman context, trained to the Sultan's service, and from among whose number the Janissary corps and much of the personnel of the state apparatuses were drawn. See V. Ménage, 'Devshirme', in *Encyclopaedia of Islam*, eds. H.A.R. Gibb, B. Lewis *et al.*, Leiden 1960ff., vol. 2, pp. 210–13; H. İnalcık, 'Ghulam', ibid., 1085–91; J.A.B. Palmer, 'The Origins of the Janissaries', *Bulletin of the John Rylands Library* 25, 1953, pp. 448–81; D.D. Papoulia, *Ursprung und Wesen der 'Knabenlese' im osmanischen Reich*, Munich 1963. The average age of *devşirme* recruits was between 14–18 years, although it appears to have been very variable. See also Lybyer, *The Government of the Ottoman Empire*, p. 48.

18. See S. Runciman, *A Treatise on Social Theory*, vol. 2, *Substantive Social Theory*, Cambridge 1989, p. 28; K.H. Karpat, 'The Land Régime, Social Structure and Modernization of the Ottoman Empire', in W.R. Polk, R.L. Chambers, eds., *Beginnings of Modernization in the Middle East: the Nineteenth Century*, Chicago 1968, p. 74.

19. From the sixteenth century this older (military) title was accompanied by that of *vâli*, or governor; and from the later years of the sixteenth century, the large provinces under *beylerbeyis* were referred to also as *eyalets*, originally denoting a semi-autonomous district, a development which reflected the increasing local powers of these governors. See İ. Metin Kunt, *The Sultan's Servants: the Transformation of Ottoman Provincial Government 1550–1650*, New York 1983, p. 96.

20. For a description of the Ottoman administration from the fourteenth to sixteenth centuries see especially H. İnalcık, *The Ottoman Empire: the Classical Age 1300–1600*, London 1973, pp. 76–118; S. Shaw, *History of the Ottoman Empire and Modern Turkey*, vol. 1: *Empire of the Ghazis: the Rise and Decline of the Ottoman Empire, 1280–1808*, Cambridge 1976, pp. 112–32; *The Cambridge History of Islam*, vol. 1: *The Central Islamic Lands*, eds. P.M. Holt, A.K.S. Lambton and B. Lewis, Cambridge 1970, pp. 300ff.; and H.A.R. Gibb and H. Bowen, *Islamic Society and the West*, vol. 1: *Islamic Society in the Eighteenth Century*, London 1950–7, pt. 1, pp. 45ff. and 314ff.; Kunt, *The Sultan's Servants*, pp. 9–29. For a useful comparative survey, see I. Togan, 'Ottoman History by Inner Asian Norms', in *New Approaches to State and Peasant in Ottoman History*, pp. 185–210.

21. İnalcık, *Ottoman Empire*, pp. 65–9; A.D. Alderson, *The Structure of the Ottoman Dynasty*, Oxford 1956; see Shaw, *History of the Ottoman Empire and Modern Turkey*, pp. 112ff.; and especially C.V. Findley, *Bureaucratic Reform in the Ottoman Empire: the Sublime Porte 1789–1922*, Princeton 1980, pp. 13ff.

22. A good general survey of the key elements of the fiscal system, the development of tax-farming, and the role of local *a'yân* in the growth of large estates, can be found in H. İnalcık, 'Military and Fiscal Transformation in the Ottoman Empire c.1600–1700', *Archivum Ottomanicum* 6, 1980, pp. 283–337 (repr. in H. İnalcık, *Studies in Ottoman Social and Economic History*, London 1985, V), see pp. 311ff., esp. 328–33 on tax-farming and estate growth; and pp. 313–17 on the ways in which the state was compelled, from the late sixteenth century, to increase and regularize the *avarız* taxes in order to ensure the resources for its central armies and *sekban* infantry units.

23. The heterogeneity of the early Ottoman elite and the Sultan's retinue are discussed in R. Lindner, *Nomads and Ottomans in Medieval Anatolia*, Bloomington, Indiana 1983, pp. 12, 22–5 and 32ff.; and for doubts as to the value of the later ideological legitimation of the early Ottoman conquests by Ottoman writers through the concept of the *Ghaza*, see esp. p.24. Christian *timâr*-holders are still to be found in the early sixteenth century, for example, a point which serves to emphasize the very varied origins of the Ottoman elite. See İ. Metin Kunt, 'Transformation of *Zimmi* in *Askerî*', in *Christians and Jews in the Ottoman Empire*, 1: *The Central Lands*, eds. B. Braude and B. Lewis, New York 1982, pp. 55–67.

24. The use of slaves or 'servitors' was an Islamic secular tradition reaching back in the form represented by slaves as soldiers and state officials to the earliest Abbasid times. But it is important to note that it was for the most part limited to non-agricultural and service spheres of activity: soldiers, personal servants, clerks, administrators, intellectuals, scholars and so on. Slaves could traditionally be educated to a high standard if desired, and intentionally employed as the loyal

and totally dependent servants of a ruler. Considered as a member of the master's household, the slave acquired thereby the social status of the master and the household. The Sultan's slaves were thus an element of the 'ruling class', according to Ottoman notions, because of their particularly enhanced status. Indeed, there is some evidence from the mid sixteenth century that some slaves in private households had actually volunteered for their positions, willingly surrendering their free status in return for the privileged status of slave in a respected household, and the possibilities for social advancement which this opened up to them. See Kunt, *The Sultan's Servants*, p.45.

It needs to be emphasized, however, that men of *devşirme* origin often retained a strong sense of their original ethnic and regional identity. Those employed in the palace were highly political, and regularly appear to have used their linguistic and ethnic origins to gain patrons or help clients; and these local identities also gave them an interest in the affairs of their one-time home district, as recent research has shown. Further, hostile or competing groups within the *devşirme* elite itself developed around such identities. And so, in spite of their technical dependence upon the Sultan, there existed a great deal of room for manoeuvre and independent political and economic activity. Of course, the morphology of these relationships must have varied over time, and it is probable that such freedom of manoeuvre was not always so apparent as in the seventeenth century, for which a good study exists. Nevertheless, the point is that the assumed monolithic control of the ruler over the *devşirme* ought not to be taken for granted at any period. See İ.M. Kunt, 'Ethnic-Regional (*Cins*) Solidarity in the Seventeenth-Century Ottoman Establishment', *International Journal of Middle East Studies* 5, 1974, pp. 233–9; P.G. Forand, 'The Relationship of the Slave or the Client to the Master or Patron', *International Journal of Middle East Studies* 2, 1971, pp. 59–66.

Mehmed II's expansion and refinement of the *devşirme* system represents the most developed form of this tradition, and it was taken up elsewhere thereafter, notably by the Safavid Persian rulers in their efforts to escape the influence of the Kızılbaş Türkmen tribes – a strategy closely resembling that of the Ottoman rulers in respect of their relationship with their own Turkish nobility. See *The Cambridge History of Islam*, vol. 1, pp. 401–18. The status of slaves of the Sultan was, in fact, an honour which brought a number of advantages and privileges, a point noted by İnalcık, *The Ottoman Empire*, pp. 87–8. The best general survey of the development of the Islamic *mamlûk*, or slave soldier, tradition, the growth of the ideologies through which it was both made necessary and legitimated (the conflict between the prescriptions of the *Sharîʿa* regarding secular power, Islamic notions of the tribe as state, the need for the Abbasid Caliphs to protect their interests from various court and religious factions within the state, among others) is Crone, *Slaves on Horses*, esp. pp. 74–81. For a general analysis of slavery as an institution and the various forms it has taken under different historical and cultural conditions, see O. Patterson, 'On Slavery and Slave Formations', *New Left Review* 117, 1979, pp. 31–67; expanded in his *Slavery and Social Death: a Comparative Study*, Cambridge, Massuchusetts 1982; and for the very different connotations of the concepts of 'free' and 'unfree' as they have developed in the West, in particular in comparison with the Islamic world, see O. Patterson, *Freedom*, vol. 1: *Freedom in the Making of Western Culture*, London 1991.

25. See *The Cambridge History of Islam*, vol. 1, pp. 274ff. and 284–6; Shaw, *History of the Ottoman Empire and Modern Turkey*, pp. 22ff. Note that the term *timâr* (or *iqtâʿ*

in the traditional Arabic terminology) might be applied to two different things: traditionally, it referred to the granting of very wide districts or regions to individuals as governors. In the early Ottoman context, this means that the leaders of the Turkish warriors and clans became the provincial *beys* of the newly-conquered lands, holding them as *timârs*, from which they, their soldiers and their families were to be supported and rewarded. In this case, the ruler made little or no effort to intervene in the internal running of the areas in question. As long as he received the region's military support and some revenues, all was well (see below). The second sense of the word is applied to the smaller, more closely supervised grants through which the developed Ottoman state of the fifteenth century raised its cavalry soldiers and administered its revenues. See *The Cambridge History of Islam*, vol. 1, pp. 153–4; Lybyer, 'Feudalism', pp. 210ff.; and esp. Kunt, *The Sultan's Servants*, pp. 12–14, who notes the interchangeability of these technical terms until the mid sixteenth century.

26. *The Cambridge History of Islam*, vol. 1, pp. 300ff., 304–5 and 308–9; N. Beldiceanu, 'Recherches sur la réforme foncière de Mehmet II', *Acta Historica* 4, 1965, pp. 27–39; Shaw, *History of the Ottoman Empire and Modern Turkey*, pp. 57f.; *Encyclopaedia of Islam*, vol. 2, pp. 300ff. and 304–5.

27. *Timârs* were divided into three parts: one designated for the maintenance of the holder himself, known as *iptida*; one for the maintenance of retainers; and one referred to as 'bonuses' (*terakki*), awarded to individuals on the basis of their service or other qualities, not passed from father to son, whether or not the latter had the revenue-assignment renewed and confirmed on his father's death or retirement. The sources varied in their details from region to region, although the central authority did try to make the different local customs and traditions conform to a single model. In some cases, however, the state included within its fiscal income all the basic and religious taxes; sometimes the *öşür* was excluded, sometimes other levies were excluded as well. The most comprehensive discussion is that of N. Beldiceanu, *Le timâr dans l'état ottoman (début XIVe–début XVIe siècle)*, Wiesbaden 1980, although Beldiceanu follows a strongly traditional line and categorically rejects any notion that the *timâr* had anything to do with feudalism (but defined in the sense of a hierarchy of primarily juridical relations rather than in its economic sense). On the reaction under Bayezid II, see *The Cambridge History of Islam*, vol. 1, pp. 308–9.

28. For a good survey, see Bruce McGowan, *Economic Life in Ottoman Europe: Taxation, Trade and the Struggle for Land, 1600–1800*, Cambridge 1981, esp. pp. 52ff. On Ottoman land-codes and the intensity of state/timariot supervision, see Ö.L. Barkan, *XV ve XVI'nci Asırlarda Osmanlı İmperatorluğunda Zirai Ekonominin Hukuki ve Malı Esasları* (legal and financial principles of the Ottoman Empire in the XVth and XVIth century), Istanbul 1943. *Re'âyâ* peasants were dependent on their local timariots over a wide range of issues, including legal transactions related to their lands and their freedom of movement, and – while the normal form of tax was rendered in cash – they rendered services also in kind and in labour, varying both geographically and chronologically. See Kunt, *The Sultan's Servants*; Berktay, *The Other Feudalism*; and for detailed remarks, S. Faroqui, 'Rural Society in Anatolia and the Balkans during the Sixteenth Century', I, *Turcica* 9, 1977, pp. 161–95; II, *Turcica* 11, 1979, pp. 103–53.

29. This returns us once more to the 'fief' in its generic form, one pole of the centre–periphery continuum: the movement of state formations through various

phases of power/authority devolution, from strict central supervision to total alienation of resource consumption is a common feature of all social formations which can be called tributary (or 'feudal') with respect to their relations of production. It reflects, as I have noted, the problem of central governments or ruling elites in terms of communications, transport, the mode of distribution and consumption of surpluses, and political control, each of which represents in turn a whole range of sub-sets of variables. This is brought out nicely in the discussion of the 'fief' in medieval Islamic states by C. Cahen, 'L'évolution de l'iqta' du IXe au XIIIe siècle: contribution à une histoire comparée des sociétés médiévales', *Annales: Economies, Sociétés, Civilisations* 8, 1953, pp. 25–52, although again, taking the western European descriptive model for his definition of 'feudalism', Cahen is himself of the opinion that this Muslim institution bears no connection to the feudalism of the medieval West.

30. On the relationship between *örf* (from Arabic *'urf*, 'precedent') and *Şeriat*, and the hostility of provincial *re'âyâ* to governors and their staffs, see especially M. Akdağ, *Calâlî İsyanları (1550–1603)* (The Celali rebels [1550–1603]), Publications of the Faculty of Language, History and Geography of the University of Ankara no. 144, Ankara 1963. It is important to understand that there were implicit in *örf* law two potentially contradictory sets of power-relations. On the one hand, the assimilation into Ottoman practice (and, indeed, Islamic practice in general) of pre-existing traditions and customs gave the state administration a particularly pragmatic aspect, an inevitable result of the necessity of dealing with such a variety of legal and customary usages and norms among the conquered populations. This was not new – much the same occurred under the Abbasid régime, for example, or in Mughal India; it provided the ideological focus for much of the opposition to the later Umayyads; and the tension remains still as a focus for opposition to what are perceived as the 'secularizing' and even westernizing politics of many modern régimes in Islamic societies. On the other hand, while there is no theological contradiction between *Şeriat* and *örf*, since the former was, and is, understood formally to embrace the latter, the fact is that Sultanic rights and revenues, as defined in *örfi* law, were seen as distinct from those defined in Islamic law. In the context of the autocratic centralist policies of a ruler such as Mehmed II, it is easy to see how the tension between the vested interests of the *devşirme* on the one hand and the traditional tribal or non-*devşirme* elites on the other came to be reflected through the formation of political-ideological groupings based around these different foci of vested power and symbolic authority. See esp. the comments of İnalcık, *The Ottoman Empire*, pp. 70f., and the article '*kânûn*'in *Encyclopaedia of Islam*, vol. 4, Leiden 1978, pp. 556–62, esp. p. 560. For some general considerations on this, see Ira M. Lapidus, 'The Separation of State and Religion in the Development of Early Islamic Society', *International Journal of Middle East Studies* 6, 1975, pp. 363–85, and especially J.N. Nielsen, *Secular Justice in an Islamic State: Mazâlim under the Bahrî Mamlûks 662/1264–789/1387*, Uitgaven van het Nederlands Historisch-Archaeologisch Instituut te Istanbul, 55, Istanbul 1985, pp. 2–15; 20ff., and 26–33, who discusses the whole question of the inherent opposition between Sharia and state law in its historical evolution.

31. See especially the examples quoted in Findley, *Bureaucratic Reform in the Ottoman Empire*, pp. 36–8.

32. See *The Cambridge History of Islam*, vol. 1, pp. 269ff. and 283–91. The concept of *ghazâ* or 'raid' in the context of the *jihâd* has been described as the

(theological) basis of the Ottoman state; and while it certainly constituted the dominant legitimating motif in respect of Ottoman expansion against both non-believers and 'heretics', its importance in the original conquests – certainly as it is depicted by P. Wittek, *The Rise of the Ottoman Empire*, London 1938 – has been challenged, most recently and cogently by Lindner, *Nomads and Ottomans in Medieval Anatolia*.

33. See Kunt, *The Sultan's Servants*, on the prominent provincial families and households, the complex system of patronage that linked Istanbul to the provinces, and the consequent infiltrative (and therefore weakening) effects these structures had on the degree of central authority in the provinces. The clear contradiction between the interests of the state and those of the Anatolian nomads is apparent in the brutal repressive campaigns of Selim I the Grim against the Shi'ites, both sedentary and pastoral, in the first years of the sixteenth century; as it is also clear in the gradual sedentarization of the nomads and their subordination to the fiscal machinery of Istanbul. See again Lindner, *Nomads and Ottomans in Medieval Anatolia*, pp. 51–74.

34. For good surveys, see Shaw, *History of the Ottoman Empire and Modern Turkey*, pp. 169–216; *The Cambridge History of Islam*, vol. 1, pp. 342–53; İnalcık, *Ottoman Empire*, pp. 41–52. On the dominant elite in particular see Findley, *Bureaucratic Reform in the Ottoman Empire*, pp. 43–68; and the careful analysis of Kunt, *The Sultan's Servants*, which examines the composition and evolution of the *ümerâ*, the chief stratum of the *ehl-i seyf*, the 'men of the sword', that is to say, the military-administrative elite. C. Fleischer, *Bureaucrat and Intellectual in the Ottoman Empire; the Historian Mustafa Âlî, 1541–1600*, Princeton 1986, discusses the intellectual currents and ideological narratives through which the divisions and vested interests of competing groups were represented. Note also C.A. Bayly, *Imperial Meridian*, London 1989, for discussion of the effects of trading and merchant wealth which further complicated the factional interests and loyalties at both the provincial and central levels.

35. See Ö.L. Barkan, 'The Price Revolution of the Sixteenth Century: a Turning Point in the Economic History of the Near East', *International Journal of Middle East Studies* 6, 1975, pp. 3–28; but note H. İnalcık: 'Impact of the *Annales* School on Ottoman Studies and New Findings', *Review* 1, 1978, pp. 69–96 (repr. in İnalcık: *Studies in Ottoman Social and Economic History* IV), see pp. 90–5; and 'Military and Fiscal Transformation', pp. 306 note 52 and 312ff.; and especially H. Sundhausen, 'Die "Preisrevolution" im osmanischen Reich', *Süd-Ost Forschungen* 42, 1983, pp. 169–81, both of whom point to the fact that the state effected deliberate revaluations of the silver in relation to its gold currency in order precisely to control unofficial price-fixing and price fluctuations, and to preserve intact the relationship between the state and *timâr* incomes and agricultural produce. The Ottoman empire found itself in the position of a middle-man in the export of silver bullion to South Asia. On the general background, see P. Vilar, *A History of Gold and Money 1450–1920*, London 1976, p. 101; and F. Braudel, *The Mediterranean and the Mediterranean World in the Age of Philip II*, 2 vols., London 1978, vol. 1, pp. 517–42, esp. pp. 539–42; also F. Braudel and F.C. Spooner, 'Prices in Europe from 1450 to 1750', in *The Cambridge Economic History of Europe*, vol. 4: *The Economy of Expanding Europe in the Sixteenth and Seventeenth Centuries*, eds. E.E. Rich and C.H. Wilson, Cambridge 1967, pp. 378–486, see the graphs at pp. 470ff.

36. The importance of changes in military technology and their effects on

Ottoman warfare: see McGowan, *Economic Life in the Ottoman Empire*, p. 57; and esp. V.J. Parry's chapter on 'Warfare', in *The Cambridge History of Islam*, vol. 2: *The Further Islamic Lands, Islamic Society and Civilisation*, Cambridge 1970, pp. 835–50, who stresses that it was not simply the use of new technologies as such, which the Ottomans could, and did, acquire and assimilate piecemeal; but rather the development of new tactical formations as the prerequisite for the deployment of this technology, which the Ottoman armies – depending as they did for their tactical structures on socially-embedded organizational forms – were unable to emulate without major reforms. When such reforms were proposed, along with the fundamental structural changes that were their concomitant, the result was a wave of conservative opposition – see below; and Parry, pp. 849–50. On all these issues, see the survey of İnalcık, 'Military and Fiscal Transformation', esp. pp. 288–303. For the *levend* groups, W. Griswold, *The Great Anatolian Rebellion, 1000–1020/1591–1611*, Islamkundliche Untersuchungen 83, Berlin 1983, pp. 157ff. provides an excellent discussion.

37. See Kunt, *The Sultan's Servants*, pp. 79–88; and on the increase in the numbers of centrally-maintained forces see R. Murphey, ed., *Kanûn-Nâme-i-Sultânî li 'Azîz Efendi. Aziz Efendi's Book of Sultanic Laws and Regulations: an Agenda for Reform by a Seventeenth-Century Ottoman Statesman*, Cambridge, Massachusetts 1985, pp. 6–12 and 45ff.

38. See in particular Griswold, *The Great Anatolian Rebellion*; Akdağ, *Celâlî İsyanları (1550–1603)*, for the *Celali* rebellions; also the discussion of M.A. Cook, *Population Pressure in Rural Anatolia, 1450–1600*, London 1972. Cook argues that, even if demographic pressures certainly played a role, other factors – such as the absence of the military from large areas of Anatolia at this time (in wars against both Persia and Austria) – played an equally important role, especially if it is borne in mind that the nature of Ottoman control and authority rested as much on military and political coercion and supervision as it did on ideological legitimation and law. That there occurred a growth in population in the middle of the sixteenth century is not in doubt. What is questionable is that this, rather than demographic dislocation and movement, was at the root of these developments. See H. İslamoğlu, 'State and Peasant in the Ottoman Empire: a Study of Peasant Economy in North and Eastern Anatolia during the Sixteenth Century', in İslamoğlu, *The Ottoman Empire and the World Economy*, pp. 118ff. and the summary of the arguments of Faroqui, Eder and Cook in İnalcık, 'Impact of the Annales School', pp. 84–9 with literature. For a good account of the nature and effect of brigandage on local economy and society, see Goffman, *Izmir and the Levantine World 1550–1650*, pp. 25–33; and on rural society in general, Faroqui, 'Rural Society in Anatolia and the Balkans'; İslamoğlu, 'State and Peasant'.

39. See S. Faroqui, 'Town Officials, *Tımâr*-holders, and Taxation in the Late Sixteenth-Century Crisis as Seen from Corum', *Turcica* 18, 1986, pp. 53–82 and especially S. Faroqui, 'Political Tensions in the Anatolian Countryside around 1600: an Attempt at Interpretation', in *Türkische Miszellen: Robert Anhegger Festschrift*, eds. J.-L. Bacqué-Gramont, B. Fleming, M. Gökbcrk and İ. Ortayli (Istanbul n.d.), pp. 117–30; İslamoğlu and Keyder, 'The Ottoman Social Formation', p. 307ff.; and on peasant migration and movement, S. Faroqui, *Towns and Townsmen of Ottoman Anatolia: Trade, Crafts and Food Production in an Urban Setting, 1520–1650*, Cambridge 1984, ch. 11.

40. See H. İnalcık, 'The Emergence of Big Farms, *Çiftliks*: State, Landlords

and Tenants', in *Contributions à l'histoire économique et sociale de l'empire ottoman, Collection Turcica* III, Louvain 1984, 105–26 (repr. in *Studies in Ottoman Social and Economic History*, VIII).

41. See esp. Shaw, *History of the Ottoman Empire and Modern Turkey*, pp. 162–3; İnalcık, *Ottoman Empire*, pp. 142–50; *Shorter Encyclopaedia of Islam*, eds. H.A.R. Gibb and J.H. Kramers, Leiden and London 1953, pp. 624–8, esp. 627; and B. Lewis, *The Emergence of Modern Turkey*, Oxford 1961, pp. 91–2; also B. Yediyıldız, *Institution du Vaqf au XVIIIe siècle en Turquie*, Ankara 1985, esp. pp. 9–19 and 23–36; and note, for a good example, S. Faroqui, *Men of Modest Substance: House Owners and House Property in Seventeenth-Century Ankara and Kayseri*, Cambridge 1987, pp. 195–9.

42. The demographic contraction during and following the *celâli* wars appears to have reached its nadir in the middle of the seventeenth century, and is eloquently expressed in the records of a number of major urban centres, see R. Jennings, 'Urban Population in Anatolia in the Sixteenth Century: a Study of Kayseri, Karaman, Trabzon, and Erzurum', *International Journal of Middle East Studies* 7/1, 1976, pp. 21–57; Faroqui, *Men of Modest Substance*, pp. 43ff., and the warning against exaggerating the decline into a 'crisis' of M.N. Todorova, 'Was There a Demographic Crisis in the Ottoman Empire in the Seventeenth Century?', *Etudes Balkaniques* 2, 1988, pp. 55–63.

43. Kunt, *The Sultan's Servants*, presents a particularly clear analysis of (1) the decline of the *timâr* system in the face of the state's needs for cash for its central armies, on the one hand, and the consequent increasing irrelevance of the traditional provincial forces on the other; (2) the increased importance of the *avarız* taxes, which now became both regularized and standardized; and (3) the importance of households among the military-administrative elite of the empire. The latter played a key role in the undermining of central state authority: the armed mercenaries and servitors of provincial governors were crucial to the maintenance of their position and authority, and as long as their patron was in power, they carried out their policing and fiscal duties, paid and maintained, of course, by their patron himself, not by the state. If the patron lost his post, the retinues could no longer be paid, and extortion and organized brigandage were their only source of income.

44. See the detailed description of Shaw, *History of the Ottoman Empire and Modern Turkey*, pp. 132–9; and on the *Şeyh-ül-Islâm*, or chief *Mufti*, a position established under Suleiman the Great, ibid., pp. 137f.; Lewis, *The Emergence of Modern Turkey*, pp. 13–14; Findley, *Bureaucratic Reform in the Ottoman Empire*, pp. 61–3; and esp. S. Faroqui, 'Social Mobility and the Ottoman Ulema in the Later Sixteenth Century', *International Journal of Middle East Studies* 4, 1973, pp. 204–18, for a prosopographical analysis. It is worth noting that traditional assumptions of a clear demarcation between the *'Ulemâ* or 'religious institution' and the *devşirme* 'ruling institution' have been challenged and modified. Certainly until the middle of the sixteenth century it seems to have been possible for men to cross over from one 'career' to another with little or no hindrance. Only as a clearly delineated fiscal-bureaucratic administrative establishment entrenched itself – by the middle of the sixteenth century, roughly speaking – were men of *'Ulemâ* origins screened out of the secular running of the state. See in particular the remarks of N. Itzkowitz, 'Eighteenth Century Ottoman Realities', *Studia Islamica* 16, 1962, pp. 73–94. For the political theory of the Ottoman elite, together with a discussion

of Ottoman political treatises of the seventeenth century in particular, see H.G. Majer, 'Die Kritik an den Ulema in den osmanischen politischen Traktaten des 16.–18. Jahrhunderts', in H. İnalcık, O. Okyar and Ü. Nalbantoğlu, eds., *Social and Economic History of Turkey (1071–1920): Papers Presented to the First International Congress on the Social and Economic History of Turkey, 1977*, Ankara 1980, pp. 147–153. On the nature of the vested interest and identity of the various palatine factions in the ruling institution and the central establishment, see W.L. Wright, ed., *Ottoman Statecraft. The Book of Counsel for Vezirs and Governors (Nasâ'ih ül-vüzera ve'l ümera) of Sarı Mehmed Pasha, the Defterdâr*, Princeton 1935, pp. 53–60; and on the nature of the reforming elements within this elite, see Ş. Mardin, 'The Mind of the Ottoman Reformer', in S.A. Hanna and G.H. Gardner, eds., *Arab Socialism*, Salt Lake City 1969, pp. 24–48; N. Berkes, *The Development of Secularism in Turkey*, Montreal 1964. See in particular R. Murphey, ed. and trans., *Aziz Efendi's Book of Sultanic Laws*, for a contemporary understanding of the nature of the problems faced by the central authority.

45. See Y. Özkaya, *Osmanlı Imperatorluğunda Ayanlık* (The nobility in the Ottoman Empire), Ankara 1977; with the important discussion on the various meanings which this term can have (and which has misled a number of commentators) in M. Ursinus, *Regionale Reformen im osmanischen Reich am Vorabend der Tanzimat*, Berlin 1982. See also H. İnalcık, 'Military and Fiscal Transformation', pp. 307ff. and 315–16. Patronage and households played a key role: see especially C.V. Findley, 'Patrimonial Household Organisation and Factional Activity in the Ottoman Ruling Class', in İnalcık, Okyar and Nalbantoğlu, eds., *Social and Economic History of Turkey*, pp. 227–35.

46. Economic expansion and increased commercial activity added to the difficulties of the centre in maintaining control over the distribution of resources and the level of prices, see Goffman, *Izmir and the Levantine World*, pp. 50–76, esp. pp. 54ff.; the 'command economy' nature of Ottoman methods of supplying Istanbul and the imperial apparatus (fundamentally the same, in principle, as those of the late Roman and Byzantine states) were particularly problematic in this context – the difficulties faced in maintaining this system are discussed by Goffman, pp. 25–49; and S. Faroqui, 'Towns, Agriculture and the State in Seventeenth-Century Ottoman Anatolia', *Journal of the Economic and Social History of the Orient* 33, 1990, pp. 125–56, see pp. 134ff. In general, see Faroqui, *Towns and Townsmen of Ottoman Anatolia*, esp. pp. 268ff.

47. For the *derebeys* in the eighteenth and nineteenth centuries, for example, see A. Gould, 'Lords or Bandits? The Derebeys of Cilicia', *International Journal of Middle East Studies* 7, 1976, pp. 485–506.

48. See, for example, M.M. Van Bruinessen, *Aga, Scheich und Staat. Politik und Gesellschaft Kurdistans*, Berlin 1989; and on the crucial importance of these anti-Shi'ite policies in respect of Ottoman–Safavid relations and the securing of Anatolia, see H. Sohrweide, 'Der Sieg der Safawiden in Persien und seine Rückwirkungen auf die Schiiten Anatoliens im 16. Jahrhundert', *Der Islam* 41, 1965, pp. 95–123; A. Allouche, *The Origins and Development of the Ottoman–Safavid Conflict (906–962/1500–1555)*, Islamkundliche Untersuchungen, Bd. 91, Berlin 1983; and C. Imber, 'The Persecution of Ottoman Shi'ites According to the Mühimne Defterleri, 1565–1585', *Der Islam* 56/2, 1979, pp. 245–73.

49. The different aspects of this process, and especially the growth of an entrenched provincial landlord class, are described in *The Cambridge History of*

Islam, vol. 1, pp. 362–9; H. İnalcık, 'Centralisation and Decentralisation in Ottoman Administration', in T. Naff and R. Owen, eds., *Studies in Eighteenth Century Islamic History*, Carbondale 1977; A. Hourani, 'Ottoman Reform and the Politics of Notables', in Polk and Chambers, eds., *The Beginnings of Modernisation in the Middle East*, pp. 41–68; K.H. Karpat, 'Structural Change, Historical Stages of Modernisation and the Role of the Social Groups in Turkish Politics', in K.H. Karpat *et al.*, *Social Change and Politics in Turkey: a Structural–Historical Analysis*, Leiden 1973, pp. 11–92; Findley, *Bureaucratic Reform in the Ottoman Empire*, esp. chs 1–3; and Lewis, *The Emergence of Modern Turkey*, pp. 37–38.

50. For Izmir, see esp. Goffman, *Izmir and the Levantine World, 1550–1650*, pp. 77–137; for other examples, see, for example, T. Stoianovitch, 'The Conquering Balkan Orthodox Merchants', *Journal of Economic History* 20, 1960, pp. 234–313.

51. There is now a great deal of discussion over the origins and functioning of the *millet* system: traditionally, it was thought that each 'nation' (defined by religious creed) within the Ottoman lands continued to regulate its own internal affairs, so that the *millets* were seen as promoting a certain solidarity of interests across the empire's numerous subject populations. Each *millet* took responsibility for those of its affairs in which the state and the *Osmanlilar* ruling caste had no direct interest – education, religion, justice, provision for the poor, hospitals and welfare, and so on. Gibb and Bowen, *Islamic Society and the West*, vol. 1, pt. 2, pp. 179ff. present the traditional view; but contrast M.O.H. Ursinus, 'Zur Diskussion um "Millet" im osmanischen Reich', *Südost-Forschungen* 48, 1989, pp. 195–207; and especially B. Braude, 'Foundation Myths of the *Millet* System', in Braude and Lewis, eds., *Christians and Jews in the Ottoman Empire*, pp. 69–88, who suggests that the whole notion of a *millet* system is a much later projection onto the past.

52. See Findley, *Bureaucratic Reform in the Ottoman Empire*, pp. 43ff., who notes the evolution and progressive differentiation of the various elements which formed the ruling elite – see esp. pp. 67–8. For the effects of the French revolution, the rise of Napoleon and the attempted reforms, chiefly military, of Selim III, see Lewis, *The Emergence of Modern Turkey*, pp. 40–72; together with Findley, *Bureaucratic Reform in the Ottoman Empire*, pp. 114–20 on perceptions of the need for reform and the development of reformist and reactionary factions.

53. For the taming of the provincial nobility and the crushing of the Janissary corps, see Lewis, *The Emergence of Modern Turkey*, pp. 76–9; and for the course of Mahmud's reforms, ibid., pp. 79–104; and *The Cambridge History of Islam*, vol. 1, pp. 364–5. For a useful comment on the ways in which Mahmud and his supporters gained the upper hand and restored central absolutism by playing off one faction against another, see M.G.S. Hodgson, *The Venture of Islam: Conscience and History in a World Civilization*, Chicago 1961 and 1974, pt. 3: *The Gunpowder Empires and Modern Times*, pp. 228–9 (although the notion of 'gunpowder empires' has itself been substantively challenged as an explanation for the transformation of state power in the fifteenth century: see, for example, G. Parker, *The Military Revolution: Military Innovation and the Rise of the West 1500–1800*, Cambridge 1987; and İ. Metin Kunt, 'The Later Muslim Empires: Ottomans, Safavids, Mughals', in Marjorie Kelly, ed., *Islam: the Religious and Political Life of a World Community*, New York 1984, pp. 112–36).

54. The point is not new – see, for example, Anderson, *Lineages of the Absolutist State*, pp. 15–16. The problem of equilibrium and the nature of direct state intervention in the political relations of distribution is especially clear in the case

of the cyclical transformations which distinguish Chinese states and their evolution from the earliest times, for example. Both in the long period preceding the Sung dynasty (960–1279) and thereafter, political power depended upon a complex balance between the interests of the centre and those of the (potentially) independent provincial elites. With the development and extension of the power of the middling and lower gentry under the interested patronage of the Sung, in the form of the meritocratic bureaucracy for which China is well-known, the state was able to maintain its pre-eminence more easily. The system that evolved was designed to fragment any opposition to the state's economic and political/ideological control by integrating the middle and lower gentry into the state apparatus and by increasing their dependence on the emperors, in respect of both incomes and social status/titles and so on, while at the same time reducing the hold of the wealthier class of magnates on the machinery of state in the provinces. See W. Eberhard, *A History of China*, London 1977, pp. 205ff., for example. But, as has been pointed out, even here, and in spite of the ideological pre-eminence of the notion of the imperial state and the single emperor, these elements of the mandarinate in the provinces were still able to usurp state power and revenues at the local level, with only occasional interference from the central government. And this did not threaten the federal unity of the empire directly. See H.J. Beattie, *Land and Lineage in China: a Study of T'ung-Ch'eng County, Anhwei, in the Ming and Ch'ing Dynasties*, Cambridge 1979.

55. Mann, *The Sources of Social Power*, pp. 5–7.

56. The question of the specific forms of modes of distribution of power is particularly the concern of Runciman, *A Treatise on Social Theory*, vol. 2, especially as set out in his opening sections, pp. 1–86. N. Poulantzas' detailed morphological analysis of power (*Political Power and Social Classes*, London 1978, pp. 99–119) combines a useful critique of the numerous non-Marxist sociological attempts to define power in social theory; but it is constrained by a structuralist paradigm (structures–practices–overdetermination) which I do not find particularly helpful in generating a dynamic analysis of historical change; and by a class-centred method which tends to ignore the graded and emergent nature of the cline from constituted and constitutive social subjectivity to group and class ideologies and practices, and thus renders empirical analysis one-sided – structures become detached from human subjects (who remain their 'agents' or 'bearers') in a way which makes causal explanation in which human motivations play a role difficult.

57. This is precisely the point strongly argued by Plekhanov, 'On the Question of the Individual's Role in History' (1898) in Georgi Plekhanov, *Selected Philosophical Works*, vol. 2, Moscow 1976, pp. 283–315, esp. pp. 311ff.

58. A point made by Mann (among others) in his opening discussion: *The Sources of Social Power*, pp. 3–4.

59. On Bismarck, see in particular F. Engels, *The Role of Force in History: a Study of Bismarck's Policy of Blood and Iron*, Berlin 1964 and London 1968, esp. pp. 59ff.; and for more recent assessments, T.S. Hamerow, *Restoration, Revolution and Reaction: Economics and Politics in Germany, 1815–1871*, Princeton 1958; R. Pascal, *The Growth of Modern Germany*, London 1946. For Miliband's comments, see 'State Power and Class Interests', *New Left Review* 138, 1983, p. 66. See esp. G. McLennan, *Marxism, Pluralism and Beyond*, Cambridge 1989, pp. 233–6, for a fuller treatment of this point and a critique of the state-centred argumentation of, for example, Skocpol.

60. For 'developing' states as a general problem, see M.N. Cooper, 'State Capitalism, Class Structure and Social Transformation in the Third World: the Case of Egypt', *International Journal of Middle East Studies* 13, 1983, pp. 451–69; and see in particular the discussion of R. Fatton, jnr., 'The State of African Studies and Studies of the African State: the Theoretical Softness of the "Soft State"', *Journal of Asian and African Studies* 24/3–4, 1989, pp. 170–87. Fatton shows very clearly how post-colonial African states have become the medium through which the ruling elites, by means of both physical coercion and economic pressure, advance their own interests in both individual and factional terms, at the same time promoting the development of a corporative ruling class identity of political-economic interests. For some further discussion on the relationship between state and ruling class in the Third World, see, among others, B. Bozzoli, *The Political Nature of a Ruling Class*, London 1981; and D. Kaplan, 'Relations of Production, Class Struggle and the State in South Africa in the Inter-War Period', *Review of African Political Economy* 15–16, 1979.

61. On Turkish modernization and industrialization in particular, see N. Todorov, 'La révolution industrielle et l'Empire ottoman', in İnalcık, Okyar and Nalbantoğlu, *Social and Economic History of Turkey*, pp. 253–61; Ç. Keyder, 'Ottoman Economy and Finances (1881–1918)', in İnalcık, Okyar and Nalbantoğlu, *Social and Economic History of Turkey*, pp. 323–8. For the position of the Ottoman state as peripheral to the developed capitalist economies of Europe during the later nineteenth and twentieth centuries, see E. Wallerstein, 'The Ottoman Empire and the Capitalist World Economy', in İnalcık, Okyar and Nalbantoğlu, *Social and Economic History of Turkey*, pp. 117–22; H. İslamoğlu and Ç. Keyder, 'Agenda for Ottoman History', *Reviews* 1/1, 1977, pp. 31–55; and for the significance of state dirigist economic and fiscal policies and the creation of a 'state bourgeoisie' (in the process of the Young Turk movement) in respect of modernizing both fiscal and credit structures as well as production, see especially F. Ahmad, 'Vanguard of a Nascent Bourgeoisie: the Social and Economic Policy of the Young Turks, 1908–1918', in İnalcık, Okyar and Nalbantoğlu, *Social and Economic History of Turkey*, pp. 329–50; Ç. Keyder, 'Ottoman Economy and Finances'; and P.F. Sugar, 'Economic and Political Modernization: Turkey', in R.E. Ward and D.A. Rustow, eds., *Political Modernization in Japan and Turkey*, Princeton 1970, pp. 146–75. On the role of the army, see D.A. Rustow, 'The Military: Turkey', in Ward and Rustow, *Political Modernization in Japan and Turkey*, pp. 352–88. From a comparative standpoint, see also D.A. Rustow, 'The Military in Middle Eastern Society and Politics', in S.N. Fisher, ed., *The Military in the Middle East*, Columbus, Ohio 1963.

62. For a good analysis of the origins and rise of this class, see F. Winkelmann, *Quellenstudien zur herrschenden Klasse von Byzanz im 8. und 9. Jahrhundert*, Berlin 1987, pp. 143ff. For its structure in the tenth to twelfth centuries, see J.-C. Cheynet, *Pouvoir et contestations à Byzance (963–1210)*, Paris 1990, and chapter 3 above.

63. On Basil's policies regarding the magnates and the respective merits of war in East and West, see R. Morris, 'The Powerful and the Poor: Law and Reality in Tenth-Century Byzantium', *Past and Present* 73, 1976, pp. 3–27, esp. p. 13; A. Toynbee, *Constantine Porphyrogenitus and his World*, London 1975, pp. 167ff. For the eastern and western magnates, see Sp. Vryonis, 'Byzantium: the Social Basis of Decline in the Eleventh Century', *Greek, Roman and Byzantine Studies* 2, 1959, pp. 159–75 (repr. in S. Vryonis, *Byzantium: its Internal History and Relations with the Muslim*

World, London 1971, II), esp. pp. 161ff.; M.F. Hendy, *Studies in the Byzantine Monetary Economy c.300–1450*, Cambridge 1985, pp. 85ff. and 100ff. The internal differentiation within the dominant elite of magnates and state functionaries must be borne in mind, of course. Land, imperial titles, posts and sinecures, all provided incomes and sources of wealth, and reflected in turn the complex sets of interlocking vested interests which motivated the political actions of members of this elite, which formed thus a fluid and mobile set of factions. (See chapter 3 above.)

Basil's conquests may well have had something to do with the 'deep psychological reasons' assumed by traditional positivist historiography, but this is no reasons for also ignoring the elements under consideration here: see, for example, R.J.H. Jenkins, *Byzantium: the Imperial Centuries A.D. 610–1071*, London 1966, 312ff.

64. See J.F. Haldon: 'The Feudalism Debate Once More: the Case of Byzantium', *Journal of Peasant Studies* 17, 1989, pp.5–39, and *Byzantium in the Seventh Century: the Transformation of a Culture*, Cambridge 1990, esp. ch. 11. On the magnate clans of Anatolia and the political polarization of the conflicting interest groups within the ruling class see R. Morris, 'The Powerful and the Poor in Tenth-Century Byzantium'; M. Angold, *The Byzantine Empire 1025–1204: a Political History*, London 1984, esp. pp. 59–75; and most comprehensively for a detailed analysis of the internal structure of the social elite in the tenth and eleventh centuries, see A.P. Kazhdan, *Sotsial'nii sostav gospodstvuyushchego klassa v Vizantii XI–XII vv.*, Moscow 1974, pp. 226ff.; see especially Cheynet, *Pouvoir et contestations à Byzance*, who emphasizes the fluidity of the various competing power cliques and the constant re-ordering of their elements as individuals and family groups re-assessed their position and interests. Angold rightly notes the similarities in respect of the antagonisms between central authority and the elite which the former had initially promoted to serve its own interests, in both the late Roman state from the fourth century on, and the Byzantine state of the tenth–eleventh centuries (pp. 68ff.). For the conflict over resources, see J.F. Haldon, 'The Army and the Economy: the Allocation and Redistribution of Surplus Wealth', *Mediterranean Historical Review*, 1993.

65. See especially İnalcık, 'Military and Fiscal Transformation', pp. 283–4.

66. Clearly the non-servile bureaucratic elite of the Byzantine world was much more organically integrated into the normal pattern of social relations – it had not been natally deracinated, in Patterson's terms (see Patterson, 'On Slavery and Slave Formations', pp. 34–5); and with the exception of the numerically fairly limited number of eunuchs (in comparison with the *devşirme* elite of the Ottoman state) who served as soldiers and officials in the imperial palace and administration, it retained links of clientage and patronage, as well as of regional cultural and social identity, which could vary in degree both by period and by individual. For an analysis of this elite in the eleventh century, see also G. Weiss, *Oströmische Beamte im Spiegel der Schriften des Michael Psellos*, Miscellanea Byzantina Monacensia 16, Munich 1973.

67. See Haldon, 'The Feudalism Debate Once More'; and G. Ostrogorsky, *A History of the Byzantine State*, Oxford 1968, p. 306.

68. See the remarks of S. Faroqui, 'Civilian Society and Political Power in the Ottoman Empire: a Report on Research in Collective Biography (1480–1830)', *International Journal of Middle East Studies* 17, 1985, pp. 109–17. Yet again, this point was nicely elaborated by Plekhanov, 'On the Question of the Individual's Role

in History' (1898), in Georgi Plekhanov, *Selected Philosophical Works*, vol. 2, Moscow 1976, see pp. 294ff.

5. State Formation

1. On late Roman provincial administration and society, see C.J. Wickham, 'The Other Transition: from the Ancient World to Feudalism', *Past and Present* 103, 1984, pp. 3–36; J.-M. Wallace-Hadrill, *The Barbarian West 400–1000*, London 1967, pp. 9–42; P. Geary, *Before France and Germany*, Oxford 1988, pp. 96–103; R. Van Damm, *Leadership and Community in Late Antique Gaul*, Berkeley 1985; on the evolution and composition of the Merovingian nobility or magnate elite, see P. Donat, 'Gentiladel-Feudaladel. Forschungen in der BRD zur Adelsentstehung', *Jahrbuch für die Geschichte des Feudalismus* 11, 1988, pp. 9–27; and note the comments of H.K. Schulze, *Grundstrukturen der Verfassung im Mittelalter* I, Stuttgart 1985, at pp. 47ff. on retinues. See in particular H. Grahn-Hoek, *Die fränkische Oberschicht im 6. Jahrhundert*, Sigmaringen 1976.

2. See esp. H. Steuer, 'Archäologie und die Erforschung der germanischen Sozialgeschichte des 5. bis 8. Jahrhunderts', *Akten des 22. Deutschen Rechtshistorikertages. Studien zur Europäischen Rechtsgeschichte* Bd. 30, Frankfurt a. M. 1987, pp. 443ff.

3. See the valuable summary of H. Steuer, 'Archaeology and History: Proposals on the Social Structure of the Merovingian Kingdom', in *The Birth of Europe: Archaeology and Social Development in the First Millenium AD* (Analecta Romana Instituti Danici, Suppl. XVI), ed. K. Randsborg, Rome 1989, pp. 100–22.

4. H. Steuer: 'Die frühmittelalterliche Gesellschaftsstruktur im Spiegel der Grabfunde', in *Hessen im Frühmittelalter. Archäologie und Kunst*, eds. H. Roth, E. Wamers, Sigmaringen 1984, pp. 78–86; and *Frühgeschichtliche Sozialstrukturen in Mitteleuropa. Eine Analyse der Auswertungsmethoden des archäologischen Quellenmaterials*, Abhandlungen d. Akad. d. Wissenschaften in Göttingen, phil.-hist. Klasse, 3. Folge, Nr. 128, Göttingen 1982; and esp. R. Samson, 'Social Structures from Reihengräber: Mirror or Mirage?', *Scottish Archaeological Review* 4, 1987, pp. 116–26. For a good account of the nature of this evidence and the interpretational problems accompanying it, see E. James, 'Cemeteries and the Problem of Frankish Settlement in Gaul', in P.H. Sawyer, ed., *Names, Words and Graves: Early Medieval Settlement*, Leeds 1979, pp. 55–85.

5. Steuer, 'Archaeology and History' p. 107.

6. See H. Roth, 'Archäologische Beobachtungen zum Grabfrevel während der Merowingerzeit', in *Zum Grabfrevel in vor- und frühgeschichtliche Zeit. Untersuchungen zu Grabraub und 'haugbrot' in Mittel- und Nordeuropa*, eds. H. Jankuhn, H. Nehlsen and H. Roth, Abhandlungen d. Akad. d. Wissenschaften in Göttingen, phil.-hist. Kl., 3. Folge, Nr. 113, Göttingen 1978, pp. 53ff., and the interpretation offered by Steuer, 'Archaeology and History', pp. 116–17. See also E. James, *The Origins of France. From Clovis to the Capetians*, London 1982, pp. 131–2; and esp. C.J. Wickham, 'Problems of Comparing Rural Societies in Early Medieval Western Europe', *Transactions of the Royal Historical Society* 6th ser., 2, 1992, pp. 221–46, esp. pp. 238ff. for a good discussion of the nature of early medieval European 'ranked' peasant social structures and the effect upon them of aristocratic power.

7. On the structure of the Merovingian kingdom, see Wallace-Hadrill: *The Barbarian West*, pp. 64ff.; and *The Long-Haired Kings*, London 1962; Geary, *Before France and Germany*, pp. 88ff. and 120–139. For the role of bishops and dukes, see

esp. M. Heinzelmann, 'L'Aristocratie et les évêchés entre Loire et Rhin jusqu'à la fin du VIIe siècle', *Revue d'Histoire de l'église de France* 62, 1975, pp. 75–90; I. Wood, 'Kings, Kingdoms and Consent', in P.H. Sawyer and I.N. Wood, eds., *Early Medieval Kingship*, Leeds 1977/1979, pp. 6–29, esp. p. 24; James, *The Origins of France*; A.R. Lewis, 'The Dukes in the "Regnum Francorum" A.D. 550–751', *Speculum* 51, 1976, pp. 381–410. Bishops in particular represented a nexus of spiritual power and authority, backed by sometimes quite extensive ecclesiastical revenues, quite independent of the royal and lay establishment, even if closely connected with it. By the middle of the seventh century, and while the institutional differentiation of secular from ecclesiastical power continued to exist, the blending of Frankish and Gallo-Roman elites meant that the episcopate was more closely connected, through kinship, to the secular elites of the Merovingian kingdom. For the possible late Roman military survivals, see B.S. Bachrach, *Merovingian Military Organisation 481–751*, Minneapolis 1972, esp. pp. 77ff. and 124ff., although the author presents a somewhat over-optimistic view of the degree and coherence of such survivals.

8. There is some discussion as to the origins of this tradition of division, since it is not necessarily a simple reflection of the custom of dividing family property up equitably among male heirs, nor part of any pre-existing tradition of royal dynasties. See the discussion of Wood, 'Kings, Kingdoms and Consent', pp. 6–29.

9. See F. Irsigler, *Untersuchungen zur Geschichte des frühfränkischen Adels*, Bonn 1969; Lewis, 'The Dukes in the "Regnum Francorum" A.D. 550–750'; Grahn-Hoek, *Die fränkische Oberschicht*; and R. Sprandel, 'Struktur und Geschichte des Merowingischen Adels', *Historische Zeitschrift* 193, 1961, pp. 33–71.

10. For a discussion of the sources, see for example Irsigler, *Untersuchungen zur Geschichte des fränkischen Adels*, esp. ch. 3 (trans. as 'On the Aristocratic Character of Early Frankish Society', in *The Medieval Nobility: Studies on the Ruling Classes of France and Germany from the Sixth to the Twelfth Centuries*, T. Reuter, ed. and trans., *Europe in the Middle Ages*, Selected Studies 14, Amsterdam 1978, pp. 105–36). See the work of Steuer, cited above. For the traditional argument (aristocrats vs. non-aristocrats), see J. Werner, 'Zur Entstehung der Reihengräberzivilisation', *Siedlung, Sprache und Bevölkerungsstruktur im Frankenreich*, Wege der Forschung 49, Darmstadt 1973, pp. 285–325 (orig. in *Archaeologia Geographica* 1, 1959, pp. 23–32); followed in a modified form by, for example, James, *The Origins of France*, pp. 129ff.

11. See D. Claude, 'Untersuchungen zum frühfränkischen Comitat', *Zeitschrift der Savigny-Stiftung für Rechtsgeschichte*, germanistische Abteilung 81, 1964, pp. 1–79; and the valuable account of James, *The Origins of France*, pp. 132–3, 135–7. On the evolution of agnatic descent lines (and awareness) see K. Schmid, 'Religiöses und sippengebundenes Gemeinschaftsbewusstsein in frühmittelalterlichen Gedenkbucheinträgen', *Deutsches Archiv zur Erforschung des Mittelalters* 21, 1965, pp. 18–81; L. Genicot, 'Recent Research on the Medieval Nobility', in Reuter, ed. and trans., *The Medieval Nobility*, pp. 17–35, esp. p. 27 and notes 41, 42. I use the concept of a 'lineage' mode of production here to refer to what Marx called the 'primitive' or 'primitive communal' mode, a concept elaborated most recently by anthropologists such as Emmanuel Terray or Pierre-Philippe Rey, although criticized by Godelier. See, for example, E. Terray: *Marxism and Primitive Societies*, New York 1972; and 'Classes and Class-Consciousness in the Abron Kingdom of Guyana', in M. Bloch, ed., *Marxist Analyses and Social Anthropology*, London

1975/1984, pp. 85–135; and the comments of M. Godelier, *Perspectives in Marxist Anthropology*, London 1977, esp. pp. 76–87.

12. James, *The Origins of France*, p. 59 (Leudast). For the contradiction between royal power and noble independence, see especially the remarks of Irsigler, *Untersuchungen zur Geschichte des frühfränkischen Adels*; and also K. Schmid, 'The Structure of the Nobility in the Earlier Middle Ages', in Reuter, ed. and trans., *The Medieval Nobility*, pp. 37–59, esp. pp. 52–5.

13. James, *The Origins of France*, p. 125.

14. Geographical descriptions which bear little relation to the original subdivisions of the Frankish lands, connected much more directly with linguistic-cultural boundaries. Austrasia (the East land) comprised the regions of the Rhine, Meuse and Moselle; Neustria (the New land) in effect the lands of the West, also referred to simply as Francia. See F. Petri, *Siedlung, Sprache und Bevölkerungsstruktur im Frankenreich*, Darmstadt 1973.

15. See esp. L. Dupraz, *Le royaume des franques et l'ascension politique des maires du palais (656–680)*, Fribourg 1948; R. McKitterick, *The Frankish Kingdoms under the Carolingians, 751–987*, London 1983, esp. pp. 22ff.; P.J. Fouracre, 'Observations on the Outgrowth of Pippinid Influence in the "Regnum Francorum" after the Battle of Tertry (685–715)', *Medieval Prosopography* 5, 1984, pp. 1–31.

16. See in particular K.F. Werner, 'Les principautés périphériques dans le monde Franc du VIIIe siècle', in *I Problemi dell'Occidente nel secolo VIII*, Settimane di Studio del Centro Italiano di Studi sull'alto Medioevo 20, Spoleto 1973, pp. 483–582; and M. Rouche, *L'Aquitaine des Wisigoths aux Arabes 418–781: naissance d'une région*, Paris 1979; with P.J. Geary, *Provence: the Rhône Basin at the Dawn of the Carolingian Age*, Philadelphia 1985. For the trans-regional elements of elite politics and culture, and the importance of the court as a focus of political attention and arbitration (and the consequent residual power which accompanied these functions), see P. Fouracre, 'Merovingian History and Merovingian Hagiography', *Past and Present* 127, May 1990, pp. 3–38, esp. pp. 14, 18 and 31–5.

17. On the cycle of fragmentation and re-unification, see E. Ewig: 'Die fränkischen Teilungen und Teilreiche (511–613)', in Ewig, *Spätantikes und fränkisches Gallien*, vol. 1, Munich 1976, pp. 114–70; and 'Die fränkischen Teilreiche im 7. Jarhundert (613–714)', *Trierer Zeitschrift* 22, 1953, pp. 85–144 (repr. Ewig, *Spätantikes und fränkisches Gallien*, vol. 1, pp. 172–201); also 'Résidence et capitale pendant le haut moyen âge', *Revue Historique* 230, 1963, pp. 25–72; James, *The Origins of France*, pp. 127–55. On the growth of dependency and vassalage, see the survey of G. Duby, *The Early Growth of the European Economy: Warriors and Peasants from the Seventh to the Twelfth Century*, New York 1974, esp. pp. 36–47, and 76ff. on the expansion of Carolingian power; also R. Boutruche, *Seigneurie et féodalité*, vol. 1: *le premier âge des liens d'homme à homme*, Paris 1968. See K.F. Werner, 'Les principautés périphériques' on the growth in the power of the mayors of the palace and the nobility at the expense of the kings. For the power struggles between the Pippinid-Arnulfings and the magnates, see the account of McKitterick, *The Frankish Kingdoms under the Carolingians*, pp. 24ff. and 57.

18. See the summary of Wickham, 'The Other Transition: from the Ancient World to Feudalism', pp. 20–22; and J. Durliat, *Les finances publiques de Dioclétien aux Carolingiens*, Sigmaringen 1990, who argues that the basic elements of late Roman land tax remained in place throughout the Merovingian period into that of the Carolingians.

19. For a penetrating analysis of Merovingian kingship, see Wood, 'Kings, Kingdoms and Consent'. On the Carolongian system see in particular McKitterick, *The Frankish Kingdoms under the Carolingians*; and on the nature of Carolingian administrative structures – more extensive and sophisticated than is sometimes thought – see K.F. Werner, 'Missus – Marchio – Comes', in Paravicini, Werner, eds., *Histoire comparée de l'administration (IVᵉ–XVIIIᵉ siècles)*, Munich 1980, pp. 191–239

20. On Visigothic Spain, see R. Collins, *Early Medieval Spain: Unity in Diversity*, London 1983, esp. pp. 102ff.; E.A. Thompson, *The Goths in Spain*, Oxford 1969; F.X. Murphy, 'Julian of Toledo and the Fall of the Visigothic Kingdom in Spain', *Speculum* 27, 1952, pp. 1–21. It needs to be emphasized, of course, that the Catholic Frankish elite found a degree of social and political acceptance among the indigenous Gallo-Roman population more readily and more rapidly than their Arian counterparts in Spain, who remained both linguistically, culturally and ideologically isolated for longer.

21. For the idea of the segmentary state, see A. Southall: *Alur Society*, Cambridge 1956; and 'A Critique of the Typology of States and Political Systems', in *Political Systems and the Distribution of Power*, ed. M. Barton, New York 1965, pp. 113–40.

22. On Weber's characterization of the struggle between 'feudalism' and 'patrimonialism', see Max Weber, *Economy and Society*, vol. 3, Eng. edn., Berkeley 1968, pp. 1006ff. For comparative sociological analyses of pre-industrial states, see, for example, S. Eisenstadt, *The Political Systems of Empires*, Glencoe, Illinois 1963; J.H. Kautsky, *The Politics of Aristocratic Empires*, Chapel Hill 1982. This theme is also one of the main foci of Mann's analysis in M. Mann. *The Sources of Social Power*, vol. 1: *A History of Power from the Beginnings to AD 1760*, Cambridge 1986. For the Indian kin- and lineage-ties, see in particular R.G. Fox, *Kin, Clan, Raja and Rule: State–Hinterland Relations in Preindustrial India*, Berkeley, Los Angeles and London 1971, esp. pp. 164ff. It should not be necessary to apologize for deliberately avoiding any detailed exposition of the numerous kinship subsystems which co-existed in Indian social and cultural formations. The enormous variety of forms and expressions of what are fundamentally the same relations of production across a wide range of social-cultural formations can be seen by a simple glance at Appendices A, B and C in Marshall Sahlins, *Stone Age Economics*, London 1974, pp. 231–46 ('Notes on Reciprocity and Kinship Distance'), pp. 246–63 ('Notes on Reciprocity and Kinship Rank') and pp. 263–75 ('Notes on Reciprocity and Wealth), in which the structures of kinship and community through which wealth is exchanged and surplus distributed and redistributed in a wide range of lineage and sectional social formations throughout the world are catalogued for comparative anthropological purposes. For some approaches to the relationships between peasant economy, ideology and kinship, see the important discussion of Stephan Feuchtwang, 'Investigating Religion', in Bloch, ed., *Marxist Analyses and Social Anthropology*, pp. 61–82.

23. 'Caste' is a rather difficult term to use accurately. Technically, *varna* refers to broadly-defined status/occupation 'classes' or 'estates', brahmanic 'stages of life' (the four traditional 'castes' of *brahmans*, *kshatriyas* [warriors], *vaishyas* [peasants, merchants, etc.] and *shudras* [servants], and means, literally, colour (*brahmans* – white; *kshatriyas* – red; *vaishyas* – yellow; *shudras* – black). The 'untouchables' were a later addition to these archaic groupings. *Jati* refers to the natally

endogamous lineage groupings, which numbered several thousand across India, each of which observes its own particular rules with respect to its *varna*. Each *jati* was divided into a number of sub-castes, which were (are) normally exogamous. For convenient, if traditional, summaries, see *The Oxford History of India*, ed. P. Spear, Oxford 1964, pp. 61ff., and Fox, *Kin, Clan, Raja and Rule*, pp. 14ff.; and esp. J.H. Hutton, *Caste in India: its Nature, Function and Origins*, Cambridge 1946, pp. 42–61 (but see also the sharp critique of Hutton's assumption about the nature of caste in the article of Meillassoux, cited below). The value of much of the traditional literature is vitiated by its assumption (derived from British administrative demands and efforts at classification for purposes of economic and political control) of, or efforts to establish, a substantiveness and uniformity of caste structures at a supra-regional level. In practice, it is clear that elements of the same lineage group or caste might have different statuses in different regions; that different sub-castes might occupy apparently contradictory positions of authority and social power, according to local tradition and practice; and that an over-rigid 'basic form' has been ascribed to castes which merely conceals the nature of group and individual practice and social roles at the personal level of social being. Castes are thus to be seen less as substantive organizational social structures, more as context-bound sets of roles and practices which determine social responses fluidly according to different situations. See the useful comments of Rashmi Pant, 'The Cognitive Status of Caste in Colonial Ethnography: a Review of Some Literature on the North-West Provinces and Oudh', *The Indian Economic and Social History Review* 24, 1987, pp. 145–62; E.R. Leach, 'What Should We Mean by Caste?', in E.R. Leach, ed., *Aspects of Caste in South India, Ceylon and South-West Pakistan*, Cambridge 1960. This does not mean, of course, that caste is merely an 'ideological' phenomenon: caste identity is itself the structuring metaphor of production relations, and carries, therefore, also, a fundamental economic aspect. Note also the regional-historical study of R.B. Inden, *Marriage and Rank in Bengali Society: a History of Caste and Clan in Middle Period Bengal*, Berkeley, Los Angeles and London 1976, who discusses in great detail one regional variant of the complex relationship between lineage and clan structures, on the one hand, and 'class' (*varna*), on the other – see especially pp. 11–48. For an excellent survey of the ways in which the 'caste system' has served to mystify and conceal economic class relations in Indian society, and to mislead social and historical analysts in respect of the basic structure of Indian social relations and their underlying dynamic structures, see Cl. Meillassoux, 'Are there Castes in India?', *Economy and Society* 2, 1973, pp. 89–111. Meillassoux's analysis is particularly interesting, inasmuch as he notes the close structural similarities between forms of exclusivity, as represented through practices of endogamy and exogamy, for example, as well as by lineage identities and role attributions, as they occur in Indian society, and as they occur also in other social formations with 'caste' or 'caste-like' structures, in this case the Sahelo-Sudanian and Saharan cultures with which his own research has been concerned. It is an analysis which should demonstrate once and for all that the supposed uniqueness of the 'caste' system of the Indian subcontinent is an entirely ideological prejudice based on a failure to consider the structuring role of the relations of production.

24. This is not to suggest, of course, either that lineages as such are to be identified directly with identifiable economic strata (although this might be the case in some examples), or that there is a direct relationship between lineage identity and socio-economic position.

25. See Frank Perlin, 'State Formation Reconsidered: an Essay on Method and on the Generation of Authority and Popular Institutions', in Perlin, *'The Invisible City': Monetary, Administrative and Popular Infrastructures in Asia and Europe, 1500–1900*, London 1993, pp. 15–90, see esp. pp. 58ff.

26. On the nature of Indian society, see the remarks of D. Thorner, 'Marx on India and the Asiatic Mode of Production', *Contribution to Indian Sociology* 9, 1966. For recent brief accounts, see P.A. Anderson, *Lineages of the Absolutist State*, London 1974/1979, pp. 488ff. and 517ff. (although it will become clear that I would not accept many of Anderson's views in this area); and for an imaginative and more fruitful approach (in spite of some general reservations about Mann's deployment of the concept and functional effectiveness of 'ideological power', see the critique by C.J. Wickham, 'Historical Materialism, Historical Sociology', *New Left Review* 171, Sept.–Oct. 1988, pp. 63–78, esp. pp. 68ff.), see in particular Mann, *The Sources of Social Power*, pp. 348–63; and the discussion of T. Byres, 'Modes of Production and Non-European Pre-Colonial Societies: the Nature and Significance of the Debate', *Journal of Peasant Studies* 12, 1985, pp. 1–18. For the differences between North and South, see in particular Burton Stein's survey in *The Cambridge Economic History of India*, vol. 1: *c.1200–c.1750*, eds. T. Raychaudhuri and I. Habib, Cambridge 1982, pp. 23–36. For the left-hand/right-hand (*idangai/valangai*) division and its socio-economic significance, see V. Ramaswamy, 'Artisans in Vijayanagar Society', *The Indian Economic and Social History Review* 22, 1985, pp. 417–44. The notion of the 'ritual polity' and the 'transactional networks' which it generates and which in turn promote its reproduction has been central to recent discussions of South Indian states and society in particular. See especially S.J. Tambiah, *World Conqueror and World Renouncer*, Cambridge 1976, pp. 114ff.; and Burton Stein, *Peasant State and Society in Medieval South India*, Delhi 1980, esp. pp. 264ff. For transactional networks see in particular J.J. Preston, 'Sacred Centers and Symbolic Networks in South Asia', *The Mankind Quarterly* 20/3–4, Spring–Summer 1980, pp. 259–93; G. Spencer, 'Religious Networks and Royal Influence in Eleventh Century South India', *Journal of the Economic and Social History of the Orient* 12/1, 1969, pp. 42–56.

27. On attributional linkage (which is to say, the sharing of common practices, ideological motifs and narratives through which individuals and groups can interpret and situate themselves in the perceived social order) see M. Marriott, 'Attributional and Interactional Theories of Caste Ranking', *Man in India* 39, 1959, pp. 106–21. This system was constantly re-inforced in the North by the extensive exogamous marriage patterns within *jati* groups, which promoted a constant renewal of kin-solidarities. See M.N. Srinivas, *Caste in Modern India and Other Essays*, Bombay 1962, and the interpretation of Fox, *Kin, Clan, Raja and Rule*, pp. 169ff. On the resilience of these webs of genealogical connections, see also I. Karve, *Hindu Society: an Interpretation*, Poona 1968, esp. pp. 125ff. For a valuable discussion of the nature and underlying dynamic of these localized webs of lineage and caste relationships in the South, see in particular B. Stein, 'Politics, Peasants and the Deconstruction of Feudalism in Medieval India', *Journal of Peasant Studies* 12, 1985, pp. 54–86, esp. pp. 61ff. Stein tends to underestimate the functional role of these lineage systems as actually constituting specific sets of production relations, however. For a good analysis of the ways in which rank and lineage function also as economic relationships in a South-East Asian society, see J. Friedman, 'Tribes, States and Transformations', in Bloch, ed., *Marxist Analyses*

and Social Anthropology, pp. 161–202, who deals with the Kachin of Upper Burma. See also the discussion of Maurice Bloch in the same volume, pp. 203–22. For an illuminating analysis of the ways in which a lineage maintains and exerts its rights and status (in respect, for example, of revenue collection and surplus redistribution at the local level) across more than one state formation, see L.W. Preston, *The Devs of Cincvad: A Lineage and the State in Maharashtra*, Cambridge 1990.

28. On the locally-embedded nature of social-economic sub-systems, see *The Cambridge History of India*, vol. 4: *The Mughal Period*, ed. Sir R. Burn, Cambridge 1937, pp. 449ff; W.H. Moreland and A.C. Chatterjee, *A Short History of India*, London 1945, pp. 225–9. It is worth stressing the continued connections of 'state officials' in the provinces, nearly always local people, bound through kinship and lineage attribution, to the villages and revenues they administered and supervised. The state ratified the *de facto* authority of most persons of *zamindar/vatandar* status, for example, since these were themselves generally representatives of local dominant lineages, integrated into the social-economic fabric into which they were set. Certainly, they could be, and often were, oppressive (especially in the later Mughal period), and their lineage connections did not prevent their being set aside in peasant revolts against harsh treatment. But they still retained those connections, and in times of state weakness inevitably tended to favour the rural populace against the interests of the state. See I. Habib, *The Agrarian System of Mughal India (1556–1707)*, London 1963, pp. 119ff.; and esp. N.A. Siddiqi, *Land Revenue Administration under the Mughals 1700–1750*, Bombay 1970, which examines in detail the vast number of local complexes of power and authority which underlay the level of state-orientated politics, and which were centred on lineage control over resources, and their distribution. On the role of *zamindars* in popular uprisings against state fiscal oppression, see R.P. Rana: 'A Dominant Class in Upheaval: the Zamindars of a North Indian Region in the Late Seventeenth and Early Eighteenth Centuries', *The Indian Economic and Social History Review* 24, 1987, pp. 395–410, esp. pp. 401ff.; and 'Agrarian Revolts in North India during the Late Seventeenth and Early Eighteenth Century', *The Indian Economic and Social History Review* 18, 1981, pp. 294–302. Rana notes that, while *zamindar* and peasant revolts often coincided, they were not necessarily motivated by the same concerns; where they did combine, it appears to have been lineage connections which dictated co-operation, rather than any general awareness of shared political purpose. *Zamindars* fought in particular against the state's intervention in their traditional rights, rather than against fiscal oppression as such.

29. With regard to Indian trade in general, see K.N. Chaudhuri, *Trade and Civilisation in the Indian Ocean: an Economic History from the Rise of Islam to 1750*, Cambridge 1985; S. Digby, 'The Maritime Trade of India', in *The Cambridge Economic History of India*, vol. 1, pp. 125–59; Burton Stein, 'Coromandel Trade in Medieval India', in J. Parker, ed., *Merchants and Scholars: Essays in the History of Exploration and Trade*, Minneapolis 1965, pp. 47–62; and in particular the useful survey of Janet L. Abu-Lughod, *Before European Hegemony: the World System A.D. 1250–1350*, Oxford and New York 1989, pp. 261–90. For the extent of the involvement of nobles and members of elites in trade, see, for example, S. Subrahmanyam, 'Iranians Abroad: Intra-Asian Elite Migration and Early Modern State Formation', *The Journal of Asian Studies* 51/2, May 1992; for the possible extent of the integration of state fiscal structures with trade networks, see also the comments of I. Habib, 'Merchant Communities in Pre-Colonial India', in J.

Tracy, ed., *The Rise of Merchant Empires: Long-Distance Trade in the Early Modern World 1350–1750*, New York 1990, pp. 371ff.; and for the document, a *dastur-ul-amal* or order of appointment dating to the early eighteenth century, see J.F. Richards, *Document Form for Official Order of Appointment in the Mughal Empire: Translation, Notes and Text*, Cambridge 1986. For the ways in which late Roman commerce was facilitated by state shipping and transportation, see A.H.M. Jones, *The Later Roman Empire 284–602*, Oxford 1964, pp. 824ff., and especially J.W. Hayes, *Late Roman Pottery*, London 1972, pp. 414ff. for the distribution of African red slip wares throughout the Mediterranean on the back of the state's grain transportation system.

30. Note the comments of J.F. Richards, 'The Formulation of Imperial Authority under Akbar and Jahangir', in Richards, ed., *Kingship and Authority in South Asia*, Madison, Wisconsin 1978, pp. 252–85 (repr. in Richards, *Authority, Administration and Finance in the Mughal Empire*, London 1993, no. 3). For the general background, see the references in note 32 below; and J.F. Richards, 'The Islamic Frontier in the East: Expansion into South Asia', *South Asia* 4, 1974, pp. 91–109 (repr. in *Authority, Administration and Finance*, no. 1)

31. That the *mansab* system was evolved from earlier central Asian nomadic and pre-Mughal north Indian Muslim systems of numerical ranking, inherited from the Lodi rulers of Delhi (1451–1526) seems very likely: see W.H. Moreland, 'Rank (Mansab) in the Mughal State Service', *Journal of the Royal Asiatic Society*, 1936, pp. 641–65; *The Cambridge History of Islam*, vol. 1, p. 32; although it has been challenged by those who wish to attribute Akbar with major innovatory reforms: see, for example, S. Moosvi, 'Evolution of the Mansab System under Akbar until 1596–97', *Journal of the Royal Asiatic Society*, 1981, 2, pp. 178–85.

32. On Akbar's 'reform', see *The Oxford History of India*, pp. 344–5; Moreland and Chatterjee, *A Short History of India*, pp. 220–5; and S. Wolpert, *A New History of India*, New York 1977, pp. 164ff.; and for the structure of the state elite, see M. Athar Ali: *The Mughal Nobility under Aurangzeb*, Bombay 1970; and *The Apparatus of Empire: Awards of Ranks, Offices and Titles to the Mughal Nobility, 1574–1658*, Delhi 1985. The assumed pre-eminence of Akbar's reign, signalling a new departure in administrative structures and their effectiveness, has recently been stressed, or is implicitly taken for granted, in S.P. Blake, *Shahjahanabad: the Sovereign City in Mughal India 1639–1739*, Cambridge 1991; and D. E. Streusand, *The Formation of the Mughal Empire*, Delhi 1989. This interpretation of the evidence has been criticized for its acceptance, more or less at face value, of what is in effect Mughal imperial propaganda – the picture derived from treatises contemporary with Akbar in particular presents the latter's reforms in an especially rosy light, and glosses over the dynastic problems and the incompleteness of central power over outlying regions of Akbar's empire throughout his reign. For Mughal relations with the Uzbeks, see P.M. Holt, A.K.S. Lampton and B. Lewis, eds, *The Cambridge History of Islam*, vol. 1, *The Central Islamic Lands*, pp. 35ff. and 43–4; and for the incorporation of Bengal and Sind, as well as Mirza Hakim, ibid. pp. 43–4. On the conflict between Aurangzeb, Shah Jahan and Murad, Aurangzeb's brother, see ibid., pp. 48ff.; and for Aurangzeb's prior agreement to subdivide the empire with his brother – as well as for an excellent critique of the traditional perception of Akbar's reign – S. Subrahmanyam, 'The Mughal State – Structure or Process? Reflections on Recent Western Historiography', *The Indian Economic and Social History Review* 29/3, July–September 1992, pp. 291–321, esp. p. 300 (and pp.

296–301 on the example of Mirza Hakim). For a useful comparative discussion of the Mughal state in the context of similar empires, see H. Berktay, 'Three Empires and the Societies they Governed: Iran, India and the Ottoman Empire', *Journal of Peasant Studies* 18, 1991, pp. 242–63, which once again stresses the incompleteness of 'centralization' in such state systems.

33. See esp. P. Spear, *India: a Modern History*, Ann Arbor 1961, pp. 133ff. and 150ff. for a somewhat idealized picture of the administrative system and the *mansabdars* under Akbar. The same picture is presented in the more recent study by M. Athar Ali, mentioned above.

34. Although the claims of the *zamindars* to a portion of the produce were in turn limited by custom, this does not mean that the relationship cannot be readily subsumed within a particular form of the expression of tributary production relations, nor that the wealth or produce demanded by, and surrendered to, the *zamindars* cannot be understood as the political economy equivalent of 'rent', as Habib seems to suggest. See I. Habib, 'Classifying Pre-Colonial India', *Journal of Peasant Studies* 12, 1985, pp. 44–53.

35. See I. Habib, 'The Social Distribution of Landed Property in Pre-British India: a Historical Survey', in R.S. Sharma and V. Jha, eds., *Indian Society: Historical Probings in Honour of D.D. Kosambi*, New Delhi 1974, pp. 264–316, for a good discussion of the multi-layered, 'segmentary' nature of rights over and control of land and the revenues it produced.

36. Forced labour or corvée (*begar*) in the sense of compulsory labour and extraordinary services to both the state and local rulers or chiefs seems to have constituted a significant 'hidden' element of the surplus appropriated from the producers under the Mughal regime and before. See Habib, *The Agrarian System of Mughal India*, esp. pp. 150–67, 239ff. and 248; J.N. Sarkar, *Mughal Administration*, Delhi 1972, pp. 68ff. Habib (p. 248) has argued that, under Akbar at least, the imposition of corvées in respect of agricultural work and related tasks was stopped in some regions, but this has been challenged: see M.A. Kaw, 'Some Aspects of Begar in Kashmir in the Sixteenth to Eighteenth Centuries', *The Indian Economic and Social History Review* 27/4, 1990, pp. 465–75; and also V.S. Kadam, 'Forced Labour in Maharashtra in the Seventeenth and Eighteenth Centuries', *Journal of the Economic and Social History of the Orient* 34, 1991, pp. 55–87. On the whole, there is no reason to think that the Mughal state, like other large bureaucratic formations – such as the late Roman and Byzantine state and the Islamic Caliphate – did not make full use of such impositions in respect of state requirements such as road and bridge maintenance, construction and irrigation work, and so on.

37. These rights were enshrined in the concept of *vatan*, and included a wide range of what Perlin has called 'component sub-rights', such as headmanships of villages, for example. They were heritable and inalienable. But, again as Perlin stresses, the term shifts in its coverage and evolves over the period in which it has been studied. See F. Perlin, 'State Formation Reconsidered: an Essay on Method and on the Genesis of Authority and Popular Institutions', in Perlin, *'The Invisible City'. Monetary, Administrative and Popular Infrastructures in Asia and Europe*, pp. 15–90, esp. pp. 58–74.

38. On *zamindars* and local elites, see A.S.N. Hasan, 'Zamindars under the Mughals', in *Land Control and Social Structure in Indian History*, ed. E.C. Frykenberg, London 1969; and for the role of *zamindars* in the process of the state's surplus

appropriation, Habib, *Agrarian Systems of Mughal India*, esp. pp. 136ff. For *zamindars* as *mansabdars* and the increasing role of Hinduism in the Mughal state, see Spear, *India: a Modern History*, pp. 132ff.; and on local elites integrated into the state's regional administrative concerns, see the order of appointment issued in the early eighteenth century edited and translated by Richards, pp. 41–3. For some important sources on this theme, see the collection of D.C. Sircar, *Landlordism and Tenancy in Ancient and Medieval India as revealed by Epigraphical Records*, Lucknow 1969; and N.P. Ziegler, 'Some Notes on Rajput Loyalties during the Mughal Period', in J.F. Richards, ed., *Kingship and Authority in South Asia*, Madison 1978. The relationship between *zamindars* and lineage elites, on the one hand, and between dominant lineages or castes and lower ranking castes, on the other, points up the nature of social and economic stratification focused on the appropriation of surpluses within lineage societies, discussed by P.-Ph. Rey, 'Class Contradiction in Lineage Societies', *Critique of Anthropology* 13/14, Summer 1979, pp. 41–60, esp. pp. 51ff. It is well-described, particularly as concerns the power and economic dominance of *zamindars vis-à-vis* their tenants (generally belonging to *jati* or caste-groups lower in the hierarchy, locally) and the modes through which dominant lineages are able to reproduce their position, in a Muslim community, by. Z. Bhatty, 'Status and Power in a Muslim-Dominated Village of Uttar Pradesh', in I. Ahmad, ed., *Caste and Social Stratification among Muslims in India*, New Delhi 1978, pp. 207–24, esp. pp. 209–15. See also the survey in *The Cambridge Economic History of India*, vol. 1, pp. 198–9, 244–7 and 298ff.; A.S. Nurul Hasan, 'Further Light on the Zamindars under the Mughals – a Case Study of (Mirza) Raja Jai Singh under Shah Jahan', *Proceedings of the Indian Historical Congress, 29th session*, Hyderabad 1978.

39. The seventeenth-century French traveller François Bernier noted the point about 'maximization' of revenue incomes in his *Travels in the Mogul Empire A.D. 1656–1668*, trans. A. Constable, ed. V. Smith, Oxford 1916, see esp. pp. 226ff., with the comment of Anderson, *Lineages of the Absolutist State*, pp. 399ff., noting the hidden agenda in Bernier's description (to comment on the evils of autocracy, lack of private property and tax-farming). See also *The Cambridge Economic History of India*, vol. 1, p. 243 with literature. For the official limitations imposed on *jagirdars*, see ibid., pp. 176ff. and 241ff. For the establishment of this elite, and the frequency of transfers of assignments within families which did obtain in some regions, see Ali, *The Mughal Nobility under Aurangzeb*, esp. pp. 212ff. But for a very different picture, stressing the highly-localized nature of Mughal elite power and the semi-independent position of some elites, see C. Singh, *Region and Empire: Panjab in the Seventeenth Century*, Delhi 1991, esp. pp. 31ff.; note also J.F. Richards, 'Norms of Comportment among Imperial Mughal Officers', in B. Metcalf, ed., *Moral Conduct and Authority*, Berkeley, 1984, pp. 255–89 (repr. in Richards, *Authority, Administration and Finance in the Mughal Empire*, no. 4)

40. See Muzaffar Alam, *The Crisis of Empire in Mughal North India: Awadh and the Punjab, 1707–1748*, Oxford and New York 1986.

41. Contrary to the views of European commentators, of course – see the remark on Bernier's descriptions of the Ottoman and Mughal states in note 39 above.

42. See Richards, *Document Form for Official Order of Appointment in the Mughal Empire*, Cambridge 1986. Needless to say, such concerns tended to remain at a theoretical level.

43. Cf. the discussion in J.F. Richards, 'Mughal State Finance and the Pre-Modern World Economy', *Comparative Studies in Society and History* 23, 1981, pp. 285–308 (repr. in Richards, *Authority, Administration and Finance in the Mughal Empire*, no. 5).

44. See P. Vilar, *A History of Gold and Money 1450–1920*, London 1976, pp. 96, 101.

45. On the use of copper, which was stimulated by an international decline in the availability of gold and silver during the fifteenth century, see J. Day, 'The Great Bullion Famine of the Fifteenth Century', *Past and Present* 79, 1978, pp. 3–54; Vilar, *A History of Gold and Money*, pp. 36–7 and 96; W.H. Moreland, *From Akbar to Aurangzeb: a Study in Indian Economic History*, New Delhi 1923/1972, esp. pp. 183ff.

46. See for a good survey Abu-Lughod, *Before European Hegemony*, pp. 261ff.; the contributions in Tracy, ed., *The Rise of Merchant Empires*; the introductory chapters in H. Furber, *Rival Empires of Trade in the Orient (1600–1800)*, Minneapolis 1976; and F. Perlin, 'Financial Institutions and Business Practices across the Euro-Asian "Interface": Comparative and Structural Considerations', in Perlin, *'The Invisible City'*, pp. 283–338, esp. pp. 291ff.

47. See especially F. Perlin, 'Proto-Industrialization and Pre-Colonial South Asia', *Past and Present* 98, 1983, pp. 30–95, esp. pp. 60ff.; and note also J.F. Richards, 'Outflow of Precious Metals from Early Islamic India', in *Precious Metals in the Later Medieval and Early Modern World*, ed. J.F. Richards, Durham, North Carolina 1983, pp. 183–205 for some general comments on the background (repr. in Richards, *Authority, Administration and Finance in the Mughal Empire*, no. 2).

48. See Furber, *Rival Empires of Trade*, pp. 249ff. on cowries, for example.

49. On all of this see F. Perlin, 'Money-Use in Late Pre-Colonial South Asia and the World Trade in Currency Media', in Perlin, *'The Invisible City'*, pp. 131–281, esp. pp. 137–62.

50. On state revenues, see *The Cambridge History of India*, vol. 4, pp. 472ff.; *The Cambridge Economic History of India*, vol. 1, pp. 173 and 176ff. On tax-farming and entrepreneurial activities, see J.J. Brennig, 'Chief-Merchants and the European Enclaves of Seventeenth-Century Coromandel', *Modern Asian Studies* 11, 1977, pp. 321–40; and esp. the valuable discussion of Sanjay Subrahmanyam, 'Aspects of State Formation in South India and Southeast Asia, 1500–1650', *The Indian Economic and Social History Review* 23, 1986, pp. 357–77. Note also A. Wink, 'Maratha Revenue Farming', *Modern Asian Studies* 17, 1983, pp. 591–628; and esp. S. Subrahmanyam, *The Political Economy of Commerce: Southern India 1500–1650*, Cambridge and New York 1990. For the evolution and structure of the fiscal system, see the summary in *The Cambridge Economic History of India*, vol. 1, pp. 235–40; and W.H. Moreland, 'The Development of the Land Revenue System of the Mogul Empire', *Journal of the Royal Asiatic Society*, 1922; Siddiqi, *Land Revenue Administration under the Mughals*. For the currency, see esp. A. Hasan, 'The Silver Currency Output of the Mughal Empire and Prices in India during the Sixteenth and Seventeenth Centuries', *Indian Economic and Social History Review* 16, 1969, pp. 85–116; I. Habib, 'The Currency System of the Mughal Empire (1556–1707)', *Medieval India Quarterly* 4, 1960, nos. 1–2; and now the essays in J. F. Richards, ed., *The Imperial Monetary System of Mughal India*, Delhi 1987, but with the critical remarks of Perlin, 'Money-Use in Late Pre-Colonial India and the International Trade in Currency Media', pp. 232–373, a very detailed study. See also O.

Prakash, 'On Coinage in Mughal India', *The Indian Economic and Social History Review* 25, 1988, pp. 475–91. While opinion is divided on the degree to which the system of mint production was systematized, and on the degree to which the central authority was able to control the production and velocity of circulation of its currency, there seems little doubt that a remarkable degree of stability was achieved. Critical of applying the European model of a 'price revolution' to India, see O. Prakash, J. Krishnamurty, 'Mughal Silver Currency: a Critique', *Indian Economic and Social History Review* 7, 1970, pp. 139–50; M. Alam, 'Eastern India in the Early Eighteenth-Century "Crisis": Some Evidence from Bihar', *Indian Economic and Social History Review* 28, 1991, pp. 43–71, esp. pp. 63ff., and Sh. Moosvi, 'The Silver-Influx, Money Supply, Prices and Revenue-Extraction in Mughal India', *Journal of the Economic and Social History of the Orient* 30, 1987, pp. 47–94. For the background to the degree of monetization of both state fiscality and sub-state commercial and banking activities from the sixteenth century on, see the article, with literature, of F. Perlin, 'Growth of Money Economy and Some Questions of Transition in Late Pre-Colonial India', *Journal of Peasant Studies* 11, 1984, pp. 96–107. In general, see the survey of Shireen Moosvi, *The Economy of the Mughal Empire*, Oxford 1987.

51. For Ottoman structural parallels, note also Anderson, *Lineages of the Absolutist* State, p. 518. Already in the middle of the seventeenth century a small elite of *jagirdars* controlled over half the revenue and lands of the empire. And the fact that their assignments were transferable does not alter the fact that they thereby constituted a power elite which could, and eventually did, challenge the central authority for ultimate control of such resources. See I. Habib, 'The Social Distribution of Landed Wealth in Medieval India', *Mitteilungen des Instituts für Orientforschung* 13, 1967; *The Cambridge Economic History of India*, vol. 1, p. 242 with references; and S. Moosvi, 'Share of the Nobility in the Revenues of Akbar's Empire, 1595–96', *Indian Economic and Social History Review* 23, 1986, pp. 329–41. In addition, note the discussion of K.K. Trivedi, 'The Share of *Mansabdars* in State Revenue Resources: a Study of the Maintenance of Animals', *Indian Economic and Social History Review* 24, 1987, pp. 411–21.

52. See Spear, *India: a Modern History*, pp. 132ff. This policy of tolerance and co-operation was eventually abandoned, however, during the reign of Aurangzeb – after several years of muted persecution of Hindu traditions and customs, he re-imposed the *jizya* tax on all non-Muslims in 1679, thus further alienating the great majority of the empire's subjects and driving a wedge between Muslim and Hindu elites at court and in the administration in general. In view of the fact that many imperial territories were bound simply by ties of political loyalty enforced by occasional coercion, remaining otherwise more or less entirely autonomous and potentially hostile – Rajputana is a good example, but there are many others – co-existing rather uneasily with their Muslim overlords, Aurangzeb's policies were particularly short-sighted. For a discussion of Mughal policy in respect of the Rajputs, see A.R. Khan, *Chieftains in the Mughal Empire during the Reign of Akbar*, Simla 1977. For the Ottoman rulers' struggle against Shi'ism in Asia Minor in the early sixteenth century (a struggle determined largely by the danger posed to the state by the powerful Shi'a Safavid Persian state, which was encroaching on Ottoman interests in Anatolia by carefully exploiting the Shi'ite creed of much of the Turkic nomad and semi-nomad, as well as the settled, population of the region), see, amongst others, S. Labib, 'The Era of Suleyman the Magnificent:

Crisis of Orientation', *International Journal of Middle East Studies* 10, 1979, pp. 425–51, see 441–2; and see the literature cited in this connection in chapter 4, above.

53. On the *Din-i Ilahi* see Spear, *India: a Modern History*, pp. 134–5; and more particularly, *Encyclopaedia of Islam*, new edn., eds. B. Lewis, Ch. Pellat and J. Schacht, vol. 2, London and Leiden 1965, pp. 296–7; vol. 3, London and Leiden 1971, p. 439; vol. 7, London and Leiden 1991, p. 327. See also Sri Ram Sharma, *The Religious Policy of the Mughal Empire*, Oxford 1940, pp. 18–68. For the political context of Akbar's religious views and, more importantly, the image he and his court panegyrists wished to cultivate at different times, see the useful remarks of Subrahmanyam, 'The Mughal State – Structure or Process? Reflections on Recent Western Historiography', pp. 291–321, see pp. 303–7.

54. In emphasizing the difference between Muslim elite and the majority Hindu subject population, I do not wish to suggest, of course, that Muslim society and culture are in some way not an integral element of 'Indian' culture and history (a debate still ongoing in Indian historical and political writing: see M.L. Handa, 'Indian Historiography: Writing and Rewriting Indian History', *Journal of Asian and African Studies* 17/3–4, 1982, pp. 218–34; Gyan Prakash, 'Writing Post-Orientalist Histories of the Third World: Perspectives from Indian Historiography', *Comparative Studies in Society and History* 32, 1990, pp. 383–408; and M. Athar Ali, 'The Islamic Background to Indian History: an Interpretation', *Journal of the Economic and Social History of the Orient* 32, 1989, pp. 335–45); it is merely to assert that, in respect of its original determining structures, the Islamic Mughal state was inevitably fated to remain an imposition upon pre-existing social, cultural and political forms. The new conquerors were *de facto* excluded from the lineage/caste relationships which determined the fundamental patterns of surplus production and distribution. Only as indigenous Muslim and Hindu *zamindars* took on the duties and obligations (and political loyalties, up to a point) of appointments as *mansabdars* was the state apparatus drawn inside these structures, a process which at the same time, as I have already noted, qualitatively affected and changed the dynamics of the latter. In the North, of course, especially those provinces which had long been centres of Islamic culture, stretching in an arc across from Sind to Bengal, it seems on the basis of modern evidence that indigenous social and religious tradition did have a fairly important effect on the social structure and culture of the newcomers. Partly, this is explained through the simple fact that, after the initial phases of conquest, the great majority of Muslims in India were Indian, converts from Buddhism or Hinduism (for reasons of religious conviction, political or economic expediency, coerced conversion, and so forth). Thus it is clear that, in spite of the theoretical social egalitarianism of Islam, lineage-like structures continued to function within Islamic communities, particularly in respect of marriage-patterns, for example, but including also attitudes to purity and contagion; while social stratification and status in respect of occupation or genealogical origins also existed. Thus the Mughal state, which developed from its base around the old Islamized lands of the Sultanate of Delhi, had a territorial base in which the population of many areas was already heavily Islamized. Local administrators and leaders were, therefore, as likely to be Muslims as Hindus. Yet, even in these conditions, the acculturated lineage-structures continued to play a role in respect of economic sub-structures and access to control of means of production and surpluses. See, for the modern material, Ahmad, ed., introduction to *Caste and Social Stratification*

among Muslims in India, pp. 1–17; and 'Endogamy and Status Mobility among the Siddiqui Sheikhs of Allahabad, Uttar Pradesh', ibid., pp. 171–206; Bhatty, 'Status and Power in a Muslim-dominated Village of Uttar Pradesh', pp. 207–24. For the autonomous tribal cultures of Sind, see S. Zaidi, 'The Mughal State and Tribes in Seventeenth Century Sind', *Indian Economic and Social History Review* 26, 1989, pp. 343–62.

55. On the character of the ruling elite, see Spear, *India: a Modern History*, pp. 130–2, and the modern literature cited in the notes above.

56. See the discussions of J.F. Richards, for example: 'The Imperial Crisis in the Deccan', *Journal of Asian Studies* 35, 1976, pp. 236–56; and 'Mughal Retreat from Coastal Andhra', *Journal of the Royal Asiatic Society*, 1978, pp. 50–68 (both repr. in Richards, *Authority, Administration and Finance in the Mughal Empire*, nos. 12 and 8 respectively, in which a number of other essays on related topics are also reprinted).

57. *The Cambridge Economic History of India*, vol. 1, pp. 173ff. Up to three quarters of the total income extracted by the higher *mansabdars* in the mid seventeenth century went on the maintenance of the vast numbers of infantry and cavalry soldiers necessary to effectively secure those revenues from the lower officials and more particularly from the ordinary producing population. See in general A. Aziz, *The Mansabdari System and the Mughal Army*, Delhi 1972, and the older work of W. Irvine, *Army of the Indian Moghuls*, Delhi 1962.

58. See Siddiqi, *Land Revenue Administration under the Mughals*, pp. 15ff.; B.R. Grover, 'Nature of Land Rights in Mughal India', *Indian Economic and Social History Review* 1, 1963. For comment on Habib's thesis concerning peasant unrest, see Stein, 'Politics, Peasants and the Deconstruction of Feudalism in Medieval India', pp. 54–86, see pp. 59–60.

59. For the brutal nature of state revenue collections, see *The Cambridge Economic History of India*, vol. 1, pp. 173ff. and 240 with sources. For excellent accounts of the fluctuating nature of relations between centre and tributary periphery, and in particular the way in which local elites whose origins lay both in imperial service and in local patterns of lineage-based power were formed, see Richards, 'The Imperial Crisis in the Deccan', pp. 237ff.; and 'The Mughal Retreat from Coastal Andhra', pp. 39ff.; with B. Stein, *Vijayanagara*, Cambridge 1989, pp. 130–9 ('The Nayaka Kingdoms'). See also the discussion of Alam, 'Eastern India in the Early Eighteenth-Century "Crisis": Some Evidence from Bihar'.

60. On the general political and economic situation, see *The Cambridge Economic History of India*, vol. 1, pp. 174 and 192ff. For forms of tax-relief designed both to assist cultivators in times of economic stress and to promote the quantitative expansion of production, see Habib, *The Agrarian System of Mughal India*, esp. pp. 249ff.

61. *The Cambridge Economic History of India*, vol. 1, pp. 180, 266ff. and 468–71

62. See in particular the detailed work of Frank Perlin in this respect, cited in the notes above.

63. For succinct accounts of the decline of the empire, see Moreland and Chatterjee, *A Short History of India*, pp.265ff.; *Oxford History of India*, pp. 404ff. and 430ff.; a more detailed account in *The Cambridge History of India*, vol. 4, pp. 319–448. For the Mughal legacy, see *The Cambridge Economic History of India*, vol. 1, pp. 192–3.

64. See Stein, *Vijayanagara*, pp. 72–3 and 85ff.

65. For the origins of the Vijayanagara empire, see Stein, *Vijayanagara*, pp. 18ff.; and for the importance of ritual incorporation, ibid., pp. 102–5 with literature.

66. Stein, *Vijayanagara*, pp. 104ff.; *The Cambridge History of Islam*, vol. 1, pp. 102ff. (by Stein) with a discussion of sources and the modern literature. For a valuable discussion of the application of the idea of 'ritual polity' see J. Heitzman, 'Ritual Polity and Economy: the Transactional Network of an Imperial Temple in Medieval South India', *Journal of the Economic and Social History of the Orient* 34/1, February 1991, pp. 23–54. Heitzman stresses the fact that the patterns of ritual observance across the Chola state (c.849–1279 AD) can clearly be understood as modes of political legitimation, participation in the royal power structure by subordinate elites, and surplus distribution to the advantage of both the centre, in terms of its political control, and of local elites, in respect of their political legitimacy. For the ways in which participation in this network promoted the interests of local elites and lesser rulers, see Arjun Appadurai and Carol Breckenridge, 'The South Indian Temple: Authority, Honour and Redistribution', *Contributions to Indian Sociology* 10/2, July–Dec. 1976, pp. 187–211; P.S. Kanaka Durga and Y.A. Sudhakar Reddy, 'Kings, Temples and Legitimation of Autochthonous Communities: a Case Study of a South Indian Temple', *Journal of the Economic and Social History of the Orient* 35, 1992, pp. 145–66; and for the politically fragmented and highly localized structure of the South Indian geopolitical region, with special reference to the Tamil Nadu, see N.B. Dirks, *The Hollow Crown: Ethnohistory of an Indian Kingdom*, Cambridge 1987. On the ways in which surplus distribution can be mediated through the control of centres of religious devotion and the deities associated with them, see especially the discussion of J. Friedman, 'Tribes, States and Transformations', in Bloch, ed., *Marxist Analyses and Social Anthropology*, esp. pp. 170ff.

67. See Stein, 'Politics, Peasants and the Deconstruction of Feudalism in Medieval India', pp. 54–86, esp. pp. 78ff. Stein notes that this was a process begun before the Vijayanagara period, under the Chola kings. On economic divisions and differential relationships to the means of production and to the surpluses produced within lineages, see the article of Rey, 'Class Contradiction in Lineage Societies'; and G. Dupré, P.-Ph. Rey, 'Reflections on the Pertinence of a Theory of Exchange', *Economy and Society* 2/2, May 1973, pp. 131–63, esp. 147–53. (I take Rey's postulated 'lineage mode of production' to be the equivalent of the traditional 'primitive communal' mode – for a descriptive account of which, see S. Amin, *Unequal Development*, Hassocks 1976, pp. 14ff. See also note 11 above.) For the ways in which caste in both the senses discussed here has both misled many of those who have examined the nature of Indian societies, and has in turn been used to mystify and to conceal the nature of class relations in India, see the useful discussion of Meillassoux cited above, which provides an important corrective to the prejudices of much traditional social anthropology dealing with the subject. For the importance of revenue-farming and commercial outlets as both stimuli to and safeguards for local economies, see most recently Subrahmanyam, *The Political Economy of Commerce*; also Wink, 'Maratha Revenue Farming', pp. 591–628.

68. Stein, *Vijayanagara*, pp. 91–5 and 109ff.

69. Mann, *The Sources of Social Power*, p. 361. On the question of ritual

penetration, and against Mann's notion that it was only the major world – salvationist – religious systems which offered such possibilities, see Wickham, 'Historical Materialism, Historical Sociology', pp. 63–78, esp. pp. 68–72. For the function of ritual enclosure in pre-Columbian South American cultures, for example, see J. Marcus, *Emblem and State in the Classic Maya Lowlands*, Dumbarton Oaks, Washington DC 1976, and esp. 'Lowland Maya Archaeology at the Crossroads', *American Antiquity* 48, 1984, pp. 454–88.

70. See esp. B. Saraswati, *Brahmanic Ritual Tradition in the Crucible of Time*, Simla 1977, on the universality of the brahmanic dominance, in spite of the clear cultural differences between northern and southern Indian zones. Note also G.S. Ghurye, *Class, Caste and Occupation*, Bombay 1961, a good general survey. It is worth noting here that the dominance of the *brahmans* and the constitutive power of the religious-ideological system as a whole is, of course, itself the result of a long historical evolution and the struggle between the secular and non-secular traditions (from the fourth century BC to the third century AD), in particular during the period of the Mauryan empire (c.320–185 BC), which did attempt to establish a centralized and rooted bureaucratic apparatus. See P. Bannerjee, *Early Indian Religions*, Delhi 1973; R. Thapar, *A History of India*, vol. I, Harmondsworth 1966. The crucial importance of this complex of interlocking elements has been well described in Stein, 'Politics, Peasants and the Deconstruction of Feudalism in Medieval India', see pp. 74–5, who notes (a) their general relevance for an understanding of the relationship between state(s) and local society across the whole sub-continent, and (b) that the relationship is dynamic, insofar as it does not remain either static or unchanging. For a good account of the internal structuring of *jati* organization (and the wide degree of local variation across the sub-continent) see Hutton, *Caste in India*, esp. pp. 80–115. For the comment on the value of the 'ritual polity' concept, see Heitzman, 'Ritual Polity and Economy', p. 26; and for some critical responses to Stein's arguments (at least as originally expressed in *Peasant State and Society* and in 'The Segmentary State in South Indian History', in *Realm and Religion in Traditional India*, ed. R.G. Fox, Durham, North Carolina 1977, pp. 3–51), see R. Champakalakshmi, 'Peasant State and Society in Medieval South India: a Review Article', *The Indian Economic and Social History Review* 18/3–4, 1981, pp. 411–26; H. Kulke, 'Fragmentation and Segmentation Versus Integration? Reflections on the Concept of Indian Feudalism and the Segmentary State in Indian History', *Studies in History* 4/2, 1982, pp. 237–263.

71. Such a formulation, I would argue, bridges the gap between the observed historical phenomena (results of social action) and social praxis as perceived through the eyes of the agents, that is, ideology. It also obviates the need to contrast the notion of 'segmentary state' against that of 'bureaucratic empire' – both descriptive categories which are of only limited value in actually generating causal explanations for social change or structural transformation, and both typical of much recent debate on Indian and South-East Asian state formation. See the survey of aspects of this debate in Subrahmanyam, 'Aspects of State Formation in South India and Southeast Asia'. For the relationship between belief and social practice as perceived historically (together with the epistemological difficulties this presents) see my remarks in 'Ideology and Social Change in the Seventh Century: Military Discontent as a Barometer', *Klio* 68, 1986, pp. 139ff.; and on competitive selection, see W.G. Runciman, *A Treatise on Social Theory*, Cambridge 1989, pp. 37–48.

72. For the collapse of Vijayanagara power, see Stein, *Vijayanagar*, pp. 109ff., and esp. pp. 120–26.

73. See the valuable extended critique and analysis of F. Perlin, 'Concepts of Order and Comparison, with a Diversion on Counter Ideologies and Corporate Institutions in Late Pre-Colonial India', *Journal of Peasant Studies* 12, 1985, pp. 87–165.

74. Even the typically Indian 'caste system' was once a much more generalized Indo-Aryan phenomenon, it has been suggested. The origins of the tradition are much debated, of course, and some would argue for a pre-Indo-Aryan source, perhaps among the Dravidian cultures of the South (for example, Hutton, *Caste in India*, pp. 116–57 and 195ff.).

75. Harbans Mukhia's attempts to reject the notion of feudal (i.e. tributary) relations of production in India thus founder for two reasons: in the first place, he attempts to define feudalism in terms of the appearance of western European feudalism, partly misled by the fact that adherents of an Indian feudalism have for the most part done just this; in the second place, he regards feudalism as a social formation, perfectly exemplifying the conceptual confusions referred to in chapters 2 and 3 above. See H. Mukhia: 'Peasant Production and Medieval Indian Society', *Journal of Peasant Studies* 12, 1985, pp. 228–51; 'Was There Feudalism in Indian History?', *Journal of Peasant Studies* 8, 1981, pp. 273–310; and compare R.S. Sharma, 'How Feudal was Indian Feudalism?', *Journal of Peasant Studies* 12, 1985, pp. 19–43, for example, who seeks direct comparability between Indian and western European labour-processes and institutional arrangements.

76. Stein, *Vijayanagara*, p. 73.

77. The same points were made in chapter 3 above, and also by P.Q. Hirst in 'The Uniqueness of the West', *Economy and Society* 4/4, 1975, pp. 446–75.

78. The debate on the western European 'transition to capitalism' has been extremely complex. For the main contributions, see R.H. Hilton, ed., The *Transition from Feudalism to Capitalism*, London 1978, esp. Hilton's survey of the key features of the discussion and its outcome, pp. 9–30. Note that crucial to the break-up of feudal production relations in the medieval West were qualitative and quantitative changes in agricultural productivity and technology – again a unique feature of the ecology of western societies which must be seen to have influenced the particular ways in which feudal relations of production could evolve.

79. Amin, *Unequal Development*, pp. 17ff. On the role of merchant entrepreneurs and merchant capital, and a refutation of the notion that 'the money economy' acted as a solvent of feudal relationships in the West, see Hilton, ed, *The Transition from Feudalism to Capitalism*, pp. 22–6. For the exploitation of price-differentials by monopolistic groups of merchants and traders see E.R. Wolf, *Europe and the People Without History*, Berkeley 1982, esp. pp. 183ff., and for the ways in which technological advantages in transport and shipping can dramatically affect the power relations between competing groups of merchants (as, for example, between Indian and European traders), see S. Frankenstein, 'The Phoenicians in the Far West: a Function of Assyrian Imperialism', in M.T. Larsen, ed., *Power and Propaganda*, Copenhagen 1979.

80. See in particular the chapter by John Merrington, 'Town and Country in the Transition to Capitalism', in Hilton, ed., *The Transition from Feudalism to Capitalism*, pp. 170–95.

81. See in particular Perlin's analysis of the Vatan property-relationships and rights in Maharashtra, and comparable systems elsewhere in the North: 'Concepts of Order and Comparison', pp. 129–43, with further literature and examples.

82. For good accounts of the position of *zamindars*, albeit in a Muslim context, see Bhatty, 'Status and Power in a Muslim-Dominated Village of Uttar Pradesh', pp. 205–15.

6. Conclusion

1. A set of points which can be illustrated from the examples of South Indian states discussed in chapter 5 above. See also my 'Ideology and Social Change in the Seventh Century: Military Discontent as a Barometer', *Klio* 68, pp. 139–90, for an elaboration of a historical materialist theory of ideology which differs somewhat from that presented, for example, by M. Mann (*The Sources of Social Power*, vol. 1: *A History of Power from the Beginnings to AD 1760*, Cambridge 1986, pp. 22ff.); also J. Larrain: *The Concept of Ideology*, London 1979; and *Marxism and Ideology*, London 1983; Terry Lovell, *Pictures of Reality: Aesthetics, Pleasure, Politics*, London 1980, pp. 22ff. and 47ff.; and the article of J. Friedman, 'Tribes, States and Transformations', in *Marxist Analyses and Social Anthropology*, ed. M. Bloch, London 1984, pp. 161–202.

2. Marx, *Capital*, vol. 3, pp. 791–2.

3. There are, of course, a wide range of such factors which need to be considered in analysing the institutional forms, structuration and conjunctural history of any social formation – as we have seen, geography and climate were fundamental to the shape of Indian societies (as they are to all pre-capitalist social formations). For useful methodological discussion, see the symposium *Climate and History: Studies in Interdisciplinary History*, eds. R.I Rotberg and Th. K. Rabb, Princeton 1981, especially J. D. Post, 'The Impact of Climate on Political, Social and Economic Change: a Comment', pp. 139–43.

4. See H. Berktay, 'The Feudalism Debate: the Turkish End – is "Tax vs. Rent" Necessarily the Product and Sign of a Modal Difference?', *The Journal of Peasant Studies* 14, 1987, pp. 291–333, see pp. 310ff.

5. See G. McLennan, *Marxism, Pluralism and Beyond*, Cambridge 1989, pp. 224–57, esp. pp. 238ff.

Index

Printed in the United States
by Baker & Taylor Publisher Services